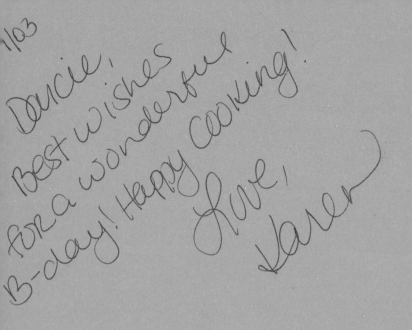

1/03

Darcie,
Best wishes
for a wonderful
B-day! Happy Cooking!
Love,
Karen

Favorite Recipes

Vegetarian

Favorite Recipes

Vegetarian

This is a Parragon Publishing Book
This edition published in 2003

Parragon Publishing
Queen Street House
4 Queen Street
Bath BA1 1HE, UK

ISBN: 1-40540-488-4

Printed in China

Produced by Haldane Mason, London

Notes

This book uses imperial, metric, or US cup measurements. Follow the same units of
measurement throughout; do not mix imperial and metric.
All spoon measurements are level: teaspoons are assumed to be 5 ml and tablespoons
are assumed to be 15 ml unless otherwise stated.
Milk is assumed to be whole, eggs and individual vegetables such as potatoes are
medium, and pepper is freshly ground black pepper.
The preparation times include chilling and marinating, where appropriate.
The times given for each recipe are an approximate guide only because the
preparation times may differ according to the techniques used by different people and
the cooking times may vary as a result of the type of oven used.
Ovens should be preheated to the specified temperature. If using a fan-assisted oven,
check the manufacturer's instructions for adjusting the time and temperature.
Recipes using raw or very lightly cooked eggs should be avoided by infants, the
elderly, pregnant women, convalescents, and anyone suffering from an illness.

Contents

Introduction   10

Soups

Bell Pepper & Chile Soup 36
Avocado & Mint Soup 37
Indian Bean Soup 38
Dhal Soup 39
Winter Soup .40
Plum Tomato Soup 41
Mixed Bean Soup 42
Pumpkin Soup 43
Minted Pea & Yogurt Soup 44
Thick Onion Soup 45
Vegetable & Corn Chowder 46
Gazpacho 47
Vichyssoise 48
Curried Parsnip Soup 49
Bean Soup 50
Beet Soup 51
Cauliflower & Broccoli Soup 52

Spanish Tomato Soup 53
Broccoli & Potato Soup 54
Spicy Dhal & Carrot Soup 55
Potato & Split Pea Soup 56
Avocado & Vegetable Soup 57
Indian Potato & Pea Soup 58
Cream Cheese & Herb Soup 59

Appetizers

Mushroom & Garlic Soufflés 62
Feta Cheese Tartlets 63
Mixed Bhajis 64
Dumplings in Yogurt Sauce 65
Spinach Phyllo Baskets 66
Vegetable Fritters 67
Walnut, Egg & Cheese Pâté 68
Samosas 69
Heavenly Garlic Dip 70
Mixed Bean Pâté 71
Spanish Tortilla 72
Hyderabad Pickles 73
Hummus & Garlic Toasts 74
Fiery Salsa 75
Spring Rolls 76
Toasted Nibbles 77
Cauliflower Roulade 78
Mini Vegetable Puffs 79
Vegetable & Nut Samosas 80

Onions à la Grecque 81
Garlicky Mushroom Pakoras 82
Cheese, Garlic & Herb Pâté 83
Tzatziki & Black Olive Dip 84
Soft Dumplings in Yogurt 85
Buttered Nut & Lentil Dip 86
Pakoras 87

Snacks & Light Meals

Roasted Vegetables 90
Falafel 91
Potato Fritters with Relish 92
Mixed Bean Pan-Fry 93
Spinach Crêpes 94
Broiled Potatoes 95
Paprika Chips 96
Cress & Cheese Tartlets 97
Lentils & Mixed Vegetables 98
Creamy Mushroom & Potato 99
Indian-Style Omelet 100
Vegetable Samosas 101
Garlic Mushrooms on Toast 102
Corn Patties 103
Buck Rarebit 104
Carrot & Potato Soufflé 105
Vegetable Kabobs 106
Lentil Croquettes .107
Potato Mushroom Cakes 108

Stuffed Vegetable Snacks 109
Spicy Potato Fries .110
Refried Beans with Tortillas 111
Crispy Potato Skins 112
Ciabatta Rolls 113
Brown Rice Gratin 114
Casseroled Potatoes 115
Cheese & Onion Rösti 116
Mini Kabobs 117
Stuffed Mushrooms 118
Potato Fritters 119
Potato & Mushroom Bake 120
Vegetable Enchiladas 121
Vegetable Burgers & Chips 122
Potato Omelet 123
Three-Cheese Fondue 124
Cheese & Potato Slices 125
Vegetable Jambalaya 126
Vegetable Hash 127

Pasta & Noodles

Vegetable Cannelloni 130
Vegetable Lasagna 131
Spinach & Nut Pasta 132
Macaroni Cheese & Tomato 133
Summertime Tagliatelle 134
Thai-Style Stir-Fried Noodles 135
Stir-Fried Japanese Noodles 136
Spicy Fried Noodles 137
Chow Mein 138
Spicy Japanese Noodles 139

Grains & Beans

Risotto Verde 142
Couscous Royale .143
Spiced Basmati Pilaf 144
Tabbouleh Salad .145
Deep South Rice & Beans 146
Kofta Kabobs 147
Vegetable Couscous 148
Risotto in Shells .149
Special Fried Rice 150
Spinach & Nut Pilaf 151
Pilaf Rice 152
Tomato Rice 153
Thai Jasmine Rice 154
Kitchouri 155
Creamy Vegetable Curry 156
Fried Spicy Rice 157
Green Herb Rice .158
Vegetable Pilaf 159
Spiced Rice & Lentils 160

Chana Dhal & Rice 161
Savory Flan 162
Red Bean Stew & Dumplings 163
Semolina Fritters .164
Fragrant Curry 165
Midweek Curry Special 166
Lentil & Vegetable Biryani 167
Dry Moong Dhal .168
Vegetable & Lentil Koftas 169
Spinach & Chana Dhal 170
Kabli Chana Sag 171
Spiced Spinach & Lentils 172
White Lentils 173
Onion Dhal 174
Chana Dhal 175
Oil-Dressed Dhal .176
Tarka Dhal 177

Stir-Fries & Sautés

Sauté of Summer Vegetables 180
Red Curry with Cashews 181
Potato Curry 182
Kidney Bean Kiev 183
Bubble & Squeak 184
Muttar Panir 185
Cheese Potato Cakes 186
Green Curry with Tempeh 187
Okra Curry 188
Cashew Nut Paella 189
Egg Curry 190
Spicy Mixed Vegetable Curry 191
Potato Hash 192

Spinach & Cheese Curry 193
Green Bean & Potato Curry 194
Feta Cheese Patties 195
Sweet & Sour Vegetables 196
Vegetable Pasta Stir-Fry 197

Casseroles & Bakes

Lentil & Rice Casserole 200
Vegetable Crispy Batter 201
Spinach Crêpe Layer 202
Winter Vegetable Casserole 203
Potato & Cheese Soufflé 204
Winter Vegetable Cobbler 205
Curry Pasties 206
Creamy Baked Fennel 207
Mushroom & Spinach Puffs 208
Vegetable Jalousie 209
Lentil & Vegetable Shells 210
Leek & Herb Soufflé 211
Potato & Vegetable Gratin 212
Italian Vegetable Tart 213
Potato-Topped Lentil Bake 214
Coconut Vegetable Curry 215
Artichoke & Cheese Tart 216
Chile Tofu 217
Spicy Potato Casserole 218
Mushroom & Pine Nut Tarts 219
Layered Pies 220
Green Vegetable Gougère 221
Baked Potatoes with Beans 222
Vegetable & Tofu Strudels 223

Cauliflower Bake 224
White Nut Phyllo Parcels 225
Baked Potatoes with Pesto 226
Spicy Potato & Nut Terrine 227
Mexican Chili Corn Pie 228
Nutty Harvest Loaf 229
Roast Bell Pepper Tart 230
Spinach Roulade 231
Cauliflower & Broccoli Flan 232
Cheese & Potato Braid 233
Garlic & Sage Bread 234
Sweet Potato Bread 235

Grills

Tasty Barbecue Sauce 238
Citrus & Herb Marinades 239
Three Favorite Dressings 240
Mixed Vegetables 241
Roasted Vegetables 242
Corn Cobs & Parsley Butter 243
Nutty Rice Burgers 244
Curried Kabobs 245
Spicy Sweet Potato Slices 246
Barbecue Bean Burgers 247
Turkish Kabobs 248

Roast Leeks 249
Cheese & Onion Baguettes 250
Vegetarian Sausages 251
Sidekick Vegetables 252
Garlic Potato Wedges 253
Marinated Brochettes 254
Chunky Italian Slices 255
Grape Leaf Pockets 256
Filled Pita Breads 257

Salads

Mexican Salad 260
Goat Cheese Salad 261
Green & White Salad 262
Moroccan Salad 263
Green Vegetable Salad 264
Middle Eastern Salad 265
Warm Goat Cheese Salad 266
Gado Gado 267
Three-Bean Salad 268
Potato & Radish Salad 269
Three-Way Potato Salad 270
Marinated Vegetable Salad 271
Melon & Strawberry Salad 272
Multicolored Salad 273
Carrot & Nut Coleslaw 274

Broiled Salad 275
Melon & Mango Salad 276
Alfalfa & Spinach Salad 277
Potato, Bean & Apple Salad 278
Garden Salad 279

Side Dishes

Spicy Potatoes & Onions 282
Seasonal Vegetables 283
Pommes Anna 284
Kashmiri Spinach 285
Sweet & Sour Vegetables 286
Zucchini Curry .287
Chili Roast Potatoes 288
Potatoes Dauphinois 289
Spicy Lentils & Spinach 290
Brindil Bhaji 291
Greek Green Beans 292
Gingered Potatoes 293
Potato Crumble 294
Curried Okra 295
Easy Cauliflower & Broccoli 296
Spanish Potatoes 297
Palak Panir 298
Carrot & Orange Bake 299
Cheese & Potato Layer Bake 300
Spinach & Cauliflower Bhaji 301
Long Beans with Tomatoes 302
Fried Cauliflower 303
Vegetable Galette 304
Candied Sweet Potatoes 305
Spicy Corn 306
Spiced Potatoes & Spinach 307
Tamarind Chutney 308
Curried Roast Potatoes 309
Colcannon 310
Saffron-Flavored Potatoes 311
Bombay Potatoes 312
Eggplant Bake 313
Potatoes Lyonnaise 314
Cauliflower & Spinach Curry 315
Fried Spiced Potatoes 316

Mango Chutney 317
Herby Potatoes & Onions 318
Naan Bread 319
Poori 320
Parathas 321
Peshwari Naan 322
Mixed Bell Pepper Pooris 323
Lightly Fried Bread 324
Spicy Oven Bread 325

Desserts

Chocolate Fudge Pudding 328
Raspberry Fool 329
Coconut Cream Molds 330
Almond Slices 331
Steamed Coffee Sponge 332
Chocolate Chip Ice Cream 333
Banana & Mango Tart 334
Rice & Banana Brûlée 335
Indian Bread Pudding 336
Almond Sherbet 337
Warm Currants in Cassis 338
Lime Cheesecakes 339
Chocolate Mousse 340
Quick Syrup Sponge 341
Mixed Fruit Crumble 342
Saffron-Spiced Rice Pudding 343
Christmas Shortbread 344
Passion Cake 345
Cherry Clafoutis 346
Bread & Butter Pudding 347
Fruit & Nut Loaf 348
Apricot Brûlée 349
Spiced Steamed Pudding 350
Pistachio Dessert 351
Upside-Down Cake 352
Baked Semolina Pudding 353
Traditional Apple Pie 354
Lemon & Lime Syllabub 355
Potato & Nutmeg Biscuits 356
Rice Pudding 357
Chocolate Cheesecake 358
Chocolate Bread Pudding 359
Ground Almonds in Milk 360
Summer Puddings 361
Fruit Brûlée 362
Toasted Tropical Fruit 363
Rhubarb & Orange Crumble 364
Potato Muffins 365
Butterscotch Melts 366
Traditional Tiramisu 367

Pink Syllabubs 368
Berry Cheesecake 369
Mango Ice Cream 370
Ginger & Apricot Alaskas 371
Apricot Slices 372
Boston Chocolate Pie 373
Coconut Candy 374
Fresh Fruit Compôte 375
Autumn Fruit Bread Pudding 376
Satsuma & Pecan Pavlova 377
Baked Cheesecake 378
Cherry Crêpes 379

Index   380

Introduction

Vegetarian food need not be boring—as this inspirational cookbook will demonstrate! Packed full of delicious recipes that are nutritious and substantial, even the most discerning palate is sure to be satisfied.

Healthy Eating

Variety, of course, is the keynote to healthy eating, whatever the diet. As long as the day's meals contain a good mixture of different food types—carbohydrates, proteins, and fats—a balanced diet and adequate supplies of essential vitamins and proteins are almost guaranteed. Typical dishes that are based on fresh vegetables—pulses, pasta, or rice, for example—also have the advantage of being low in fats, particularly saturated fats, and high in complex carbohydrates and fiber, resulting in a diet that is in tune with modern nutritional thinking.

Vegetables are an important source of vitamins, especially Vitamin C. Green vegetables and pulses contain many B-group vitamins. Both carrots and dark green vegetables contain high levels of carotene, which is used by the body to manufacture vitamin A. Carrots also contain useful quantities of vitamins B3, C, and E. Vegetable oils contain vitamin E and most are also high in polyunsaturated fats. Vegetables are also a particularly good source of many essential minerals, especially calcium, iron, magnesium, and potassium.

There is a long tradition of ascribing specific, health-giving properties to different vegetables, which dates back at least as far as the Middle Ages. Such beliefs, once dismissed as old wives' tales, are now being recognized and valued again. Onions and garlic, for

example, contain cycloallin, an anticoagulant that helps protect against heart disease. Garlic also contains a strong antibiotic, is thought to protect the body against some major diseases, and also increases the absorption of many vitamins.

There is no question that a sensible vegetarian diet is at least as healthy as a sensible meat-eating diet and some nutritionists maintain that it is better. However, there are

Healthy Eating

one or two particular points that are worth noting. Proteins are made up of "building blocks" called amino acids and, while all those essential to the human body are easily obtained from most animal products, they are not always present in many vegetarian foods. A good mixed diet will prevent this from being a problem. For example, beans are an excellent source of protein, but they do lack one essential amino acid called methionine. Grains, on the other hand, contain this amino acid, although they lack two others, tryptophan and lysine. A dish that contains both rice and beans, a plate of hummus and pita bread or a bowl of bean soup and a slice of whole-wheat toast, for example, will ensure that all the necessary first-class proteins are available to the body.

Dairy products are also a valuable source of protein, but they are high in fat. It is very easy for busy people to fall into the habit of basing rather a lot of meals around cheese, for example, resulting in an unhealthily high intake of cholesterol. Eaten in moderation, however, cheese is a very useful and versatile ingredient in the vegetarian diet. If you do use dairy products a lot, it may be worth considering buying low-fat types, such as skim or lowfat milk and soft and cream cheeses.

It is important to be aware that the body cannot absorb iron from vegetable sources unless vitamin C is ingested at the same meal. Although many vegetables also contain vitamin C, this is easily destroyed through

cooking. Some raw fruit, a glass of fruit juice or a side salad are simple and tasty solutions.

Vegans, who do not eat any dairy products, must be a little more scrupulous than straightforward vegetarians about ensuring that they obtain all the necessary nutrients. A lack of calcium, in particular, can be a problem, but this can be countered with a mineral supplement or by using calcium-enriched soy milk. A vegan diet may be just as healthy as a vegetarian or meat-eating one.

No foods can really be said to be bad for you, although some are best eaten in moderation. It is sensible to keep an eye on the quantities of butter, cream, high-fat cheeses, dried fruits, oils, and unsalted nuts that you eat each day. Other popular vegetarian ingredients, such as grains, vegetables, beans, fruit, bread, pasta, and noodles can be eaten more freely. All diets should include raw vegetables and fruit and these should comprise as much as 40 percent of a vegetarian diet.

Finally, a hidden advantage to changing to a vegetarian diet is that, usually, it initially entails thinking in a more detailed way about all the things you eat. This may extend across the whole spectrum of nutrition, including such things as your intake of salt, sugar, and refined foods. As a result, many long-term vegetarians have developed eating patterns that are among the healthiest in the world.

Vegetables

Vegetables are, of course, at the heart of a vegetarian diet, offering an almost endless choice of flavors and textures. Preparing and cooking them with care ensures that they may be enjoyed at their best and that they retain their full nutritional value.

Buying

The fresher vegetables are, the better. Nevertheless, some, such as root vegetables, can be stored for relatively long periods in a cool, dark place and most will keep for two or three days in the salad drawer of the refrigerator. While supermarkets are very convenient and carry a wide range of good-quality vegetables, time spent finding a really high-quality supplier—possibly of organically-grown vegetables—will be repaid many times over in terms of flavor and nutritional value.

Whatever type you are buying, always look for unblemished and undamaged vegetables with no discoloration. Greens should have a good color, with no wilting leaves; root vegetables should be firm; and crisp, vegetable fruits, such as tomatoes and bell peppers, should not have soggy patches or wrinkled skin. No vegetables should ever look or smell stale.

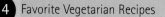

Preparing

Use vegetables as soon after buying them as possible, but try not to prepare them much in advance of cooking. If they are left exposed to air or soaking in water, many vitamins and other valuable nutrients are leached out or destroyed. The highest concentration of nutrients is in the layer directly under the skin, so if possible, avoid peeling them altogether. If they must be peeled, try to do it very thinly. A swivel vegetable peeler is a worthwhile investment. Also, consider cooking potatoes, for example, in their skins—first scrubbing off any soil or dirt —and peeling them afterward. The skin comes off in a much thinner layer than when they are peeled raw.

How thickly or thinly vegetables are sliced, or how large or small they are chopped, will depend, to some extent, on the method of cooking and the individual recipe instructions. However, remember that the smaller and finer the pieces, the greater the surface area from which nutrients can leach.

Green & Leafy Vegetables

Broccoli

Trim the stem. Leave whole or break into florets—small "flowers" with a little stem attached—according to the recipe. Wash thoroughly.

Brussels Sprouts

Trim the end of the stem and remove the outer leaves. Leave whole.

Cabbage

Remove the outer leaves, if necessary, then cut into fourths and cut out the stem. Slice or shred—follow the recipe.

Cauliflower

Cut off the thick stem level with the base of the head and cut out the core. Remove larger, coarse leaves, but smaller ones can be left.

Leave the head whole or break into florets.

Fava Beans

Trim and coarsely slice very young beans that are less than 3 inches/ 7.5 cm long. Shell older beans and, if wished, skin after cooking.

Green Beans

Trim young beans and leave whole. Snap off the ends of older beans and pull off any strings. Slice diagonally or shred before cooking.

Kale & Curly Kale

Break the leaves from the stem, then cut out thick stems and cook whole or shredded.

Napa Cabbage

Remove the outer leaves and slice the quantity required.

Peas

Pop the fat end of the pod, then split open and remove the peas.

Snow peas & Sugar Snap Peas

Trim, then leave whole.

Spinach

Rinse gently, but thoroughly, in two changes of cold water. Pull or cut off tough stems.

String Beans

Trim and string, then slice lengthwise, not diagonally.

Shoots & Stems

Asparagus

Trim the woody end of the stem. White asparagus stems usually require peeling.

Vegetables

Celery

Trim the base and separate the stalks. Wash thoroughly and slice thickly or thinly. If using raw in a salad, pull off any coarse strings.

Fennel

Remove the outer layer of skin, except from very young bulbs. Slice downward or horizontally according to the recipe. Use the fronds for a garnish.

Globe Artichokes

Twist off the stem and cut the base flat, removing any small, spiky leaves. Cut off the top ½ inch/1 cm and trim the points of the remaining leaves.

Root Vegetables

Carrots

Trim the ends and scrub young carrots, as they do not need peeling. They may be left whole, sliced, or diced. Thinly peel older carrots and, if necessary, cut out the woody core.

Celery Root

Peel off the thick skin immediately before cooking, as the flesh quickly discolors. Slice or chop according to the recipe. If necessary, put the pieces into a bowl of water acidulated with a little lemon juice.

Jerusalem Artichokes

Scrub in cold water and cook in their skins before peeling. Otherwise peel immediately before use, placing them in water acidulated with a little lemon juice to prevent discoloration.

Leeks

Trim the root and the dark leaves. Cut in half lengthwise or prepare according to the recipe and wash in plenty of cold water. Drain thoroughly.

Onions & Shallots

Peel off the papery skin, then trim and slice or chop according to the recipe.

Parsnips

Trim and thinly peel. Small parsnips may be left whole, but older parsnips may be halved, sliced, or diced according to the recipe.

Potatoes

Wash new potatoes in cold running water and cook in their skins. Scrub old potatoes and either cook in their skins, depending on the method, and peel afterward, or thinly peel before cooking.

Vegetables

Rutabaga

Trim and peel off the thick skin. Chop or dice according to the recipe.

Scallions

Trim the root and cut off any wilted green leaves. Slice or chop according to recipe.

Sweet Potatoes

Scrub and cook in their skins and peel afterward or peel thinly and put in water acidulated with lemon juice.

Turnips

Trim and thinly peel.

Salad Vegetables

Arugula

Discard any discolored leaves and wash the remainder.

Chicory

Using a sharp, pointed knife, remove the core from the base. Discard any wilted leaves, then wash and dry thoroughly.

Cucumbers

Wash and peel, if liked. Always peel glossy, waxed cucumbers. Slice thinly or dice for salads. If cooking cucumber, first cut into wedges and remove the seeds.

Daikon

Trim and wash, then slice, dice or grate, according to the recipe.

Escarole

Separate the leaves and discard any that are discolored. Wash thoroughly and pat dry.

Lettuce

Separate the leaves and wash in several changes of water. Adding vinegar to the first rinse will kill any insects in lettuces grown outdoors. Spin or wrap in a clean tea towel and shake dry. Tear loose-leafed lettuces into smaller pieces and slice or shred firm lettuce.

Radicchio

Separate the leaves and discard any that are discolored. Wash thoroughly and pat dry.

Radishes

Wash and leave whole or slice.

Watercress

Discard any wilted leaves and remove any thick stalks. Wash thoroughly. When unavailable, use arugula instead.

Squashes

Pumpkins

Peel and chop.

Summer Squashes

Wash, then peel if the skin is tough or if the vegetable is to be braised or sautéed.

Zucchini

Leave tiny, baby zucchini whole—with their flowers. Trim, then slice, dice, or stuff, according to the recipe.

Vegetable Fruits

Avocados

Halve and remove the pit, then sprinkle the flesh with lemon juice to prevent discoloration. Leave in halves for serving with a vinaigrette. For other dishes, slice and then peel, or dice in the shells and then scoop out the diced flesh. (Peeled avocados are slippery and difficult to handle.)

Bell Peppers

For stuffing, cut a slice from the top, then cut out the inner core and shake out any remaining seeds. For other dishes, halve and remove the core and seeds, then cut into fourths, slice, or dice. To peel bell peppers, cut into halves or fourths, then broil, skin side up, until charred and beginning to blister. Transfer the pieces of bell pepper to a plastic bag, then seal and set aside for 5–10 minutes. The skin will peel easily.

Eggplants

Newer varieties no longer require salting to remove the bitter taste; they are not so bitter as older varieties. However, salting still helps to draw out some of the moisture. Wash the eggplant and cut into slices or segments, according to the recipe, then place in a colander and sprinkle generously with salt. Leave for 30 minutes, then rinse well and pat dry with paper towels.

Tomatoes

Wash well. To peel, cut a cross in the skin at the base and briefly blanch in boiling water, then rinse in cold water. The skin should then peel off easily. Cut salad tomatoes and those for pizza toppings horizontally. Slice others according to the recipe.

Cooking Techniques

Vegetables can be cooked in a variety of ways and different cooking techniques are appropriate for different types of vegetable. See below for the best cooking methods for the vegetables you plan to use from the recipes in this book.

Different types of vegetables require particular cooking techniques in order to achieve their best potential. Robust root vegetables, such as rutabaga for example, require different treatment from delicate stems, such as asparagus. However, all vegetables benefit from the minimum cooking required to make them tender, as vitamins and other valuable nutrients may be destroyed by heat or water. Minimum cooking also helps to preserve the texture, flavor, and color of vegetables.

Boiling

This is the traditional way to cook many vegetables—from potatoes to cabbage. It is one of the best methods for vegetables, such as globe artichokes, that require a long cooking time. Use the minimum amount of water and cook until the vegetables are just tender, then drain immediately. Use a pan large enough to ensure the water circulates and cut vegetables, such as potatoes, into pieces of the same size, so that they are all ready at the same time. Use the cooking liquid to make gravy or a sauce.

Steaming

This is an increasingly popular method of cooking, often replacing traditional boiling. Less water comes into contact with the vegetables and they remain crisper. It is particularly suitable for vegetables that become limp when overcooked, such as snow peas, green beans, leeks, and zucchini. New potatoes are especially delicious when steamed. Use the cooking liquid to make a sauce or stock. Do not steam calabrese broccoli because it turns an unappetizing gray, but steaming is a good method for cooking purple sprouting broccoli.

Stir-Frying

This fast method of frying over a very high heat has long been established in China and Southeast Asia. It is particularly healthy, as it requires less oil than shallow frying. Typical Western vegetables also benefit from this technique in terms of flavor, texture, color, and nutritional content. Try thinly sliced cauliflower, Brussels sprouts, cucumber, carrots, or cabbage.

Cooking Techniques

Sautéing & Sweating

These are longer cooking processes at a lower temperature than stir-frying, but they are also ideal ways of preparing many vegetables, such as zucchini and onions.

Stewing & Braising

These methods involve much longer cooking times and are excellent with winter vegetables, such as turnips, rutabagas, celery, red cabbage, and carrots. As the cooking juices are an integral part of the dish, fewer nutrients are lost. Braised vegetables, such as fennel or carrots, also make excellent side dishes.

Roasting

This involves cooking at a fairly high heat, so an outer layer quickly forms to seal the vegetables. Roast potatoes are traditional in Britain and the United States, where sweet potatoes are also popular. It is fast becoming fashionable to serve other roast vegetables. Try asparagus roasted briefly in a little olive oil, for example. Roast bell peppers and zucchini may be served hot or cold.

Shallow Frying

This is not an ideal technique for most vegetables, although it works well with some, such as sliced eggplant. Deep-frying, during which vegetables absorb less oil than when they are shallow-fried, is traditional for potatoes—fries are known and enjoyed the world over. Coating vegetables in batter and then deep-frying is especially delicious and the coating forms a protective seal. Try Jerusalem artichokes, cauliflower, zucchini, fennel, and eggplants. Always ensure that the oil for deep-frying is hot before adding the vegetables, or they will absorb a lot of it and be soggy. Heat the oil to 350–375°F/180–190°C, or until a cube of day-old bread browns in 30 seconds.

Broiling, Grilling & Baking

While not suitable for delicate vegetables, as the heat is too intense, or for dense vegetables, as the process is too rapid to tenderize them, these are excellent ways of cooking bell peppers, corn cobs, onions, eggplants, and tomatoes.

Baking is a traditional way of cooking stuffed vegetables, and foil-wrapped pockets of mixed vegetables are quick, delicious, and nutritious. Baked potatoes lend themselves to a variety of toppings and fillings—from simple grated cheese to chili beans—to make a complete meal.

Finally, remember that vegetables cooked in the microwave require less liquid or oil and a shorter cooking time than those cooked by conventional methods.

Vegetarian Ingredients

Although vegetables are extremely versatile, they are only a part of the story and many other ingredients are necessary to provide vegetarians with a balanced diet and interesting meals.

Dried Beans

These include an immense variety of peas, beans, and lentils. Some of the commonest are adzuki beans, black kidney beans, black-eye peas, borlotti beans, brown beans, brown lentils, butter beans, cannellini beans, chickpeas (garbanzos), flageolets, green lentils, green split peas, gunga beans, navy beans, mung beans, pinto beans, Puy lentils, red kidney beans, soy beans, split red lentils, and yellow split peas. They are rich in proteins, carbohydrates, vitamins (especially B-group), and minerals (especially iron); have a high fiber content; and are inexpensive and versatile, so it is hardly surprising

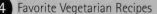

that they feature in so many dishes, from Indian curries and Mediterranean soups, to Mexican refried beans and the original baked beans of Boston.

They do not have a strong flavor, so they combine well with other ingredients, including herbs and spices, and as they are quite substantial, they satisfy the appetite. Most dried beans require soaking before they are cooked in order to rehydrate them and "plump" them up. The longer they have been stored, the greater the soaking time required. Wash them thoroughly under cold running water, then place in a bowl and cover with cold water and set aside to soak for as long as 8 hours, depending on the type.

Follow the soaking instructions on the package. Alternatively, cover them with boiling water and soak for half the time. Lentils do not require soaking before cooking.

Some beans, including kidney beans and soy beans, contain a toxic substance. This can be destroyed after soaking by vigorously boiling kidney beans in fresh water over a high heat for 15 minutes before simmering. Boil soy beans for 1 hour before simmering.

Soya Products

A vast range of substitutes for dairy products are produced from soy beans, including "milk," "cream," spreads, and "ice cream," as well as other useful ingredients, such as flour, oil, and soy sauce. Tofu or bean curd is one of the most versatile. It is widely available in a variety of forms and because it has little natural flavor, it combines well with other strong-tasting ingredients. It is high in protein and is a good source of B-group vitamins and iron. It is also high in fatty acids, essential for good nutrition, but contains no cholesterol.

Firm Tofu

This is sold in cakes and is the type best suited to cooking techniques such as stir-frying. It is easily cut into cubes with a sharp knife; do not use a blunt knife, as this will cause crumbling. It is also available smoked and marinated. Firm tofu can be roasted, broiled, stir-fried, or braised. Store, covered with water, in a sealed container in the refrigerator for up to 1 week. Change the water daily. Silken tofu may be used in place of cream or milk for sauces, soups, and sweet dishes.

Nuts & Seeds

Ideal for adding texture and flavor, as well as being an attractive garnish, nuts and seeds are small nutrition bombs. They are high in protein, carbohydrate, and fats, so they should be used in moderation. Most nuts and many seeds are best dry-roasted or dry-fried to release their full flavor and aroma before use. Almonds, cashews, hazelnuts, peanuts, pine nuts, pistachios, and walnuts are among the most useful and they can be used separately or in combination. Crushed nuts make a wonderful, crunchy coating. Useful seeds include fenugreek, melon, poppy, pumpkin, sesame, and sunflower. Both nuts and seeds will go rancid if stored for longer than six months, so buy in the quantities you use regularly and keep them in an airtight container.

Sprouting Beans, Peas & Seeds

Bean Sprouts

Well known from many popular Chinese dishes, these are usually grown from mung beans, but many other fresh sprouts can add flavor, texture, and color to salads and stir-fries. They are rich in protein, vitamins, minerals, complex carbohydrate, and fiber, and are inexpensive and easy to grow yourself.

Special layered sprouters are available, but most types will grow well in a jar covered with a piece of cheesecloth held in place with an elastic band. Place the seeds to be sprouted in the jar, then cover with

Vegetarian Ingredients

water and set aside for 15 minutes. Tip out the excess water and leave in a moderate, even temperature (50–70°F/13–21°C) for 24 hours. Tip out any water and repeat the rinsing process. Within a few days, depending on the variety, sprouts will appear. They can be used when they are about 1 inch/2.5 cm long. Always grow shoots from edible beans or seeds, rather than horticultural ones which may have been treated with preservatives. The following are suitable for sprouting: adzuki beans, alfalfa, chickpeas, fenugreek seeds, lentils, mung beans, poppy seeds, pumpkin seeds, sesame seeds, soy beans, and sunflower seeds. You can also sprout wheat grains.

Mushrooms & Other Fungi

Intensely flavored, mushrooms are an important and versatile addition to the vegetarian diet. They contain protein, B-group vitamins, and potassium, but have no cholesterol or fat. A huge variety of cultivated and wild mushrooms is available, each with its own individual qualities. Cultivated mushrooms are less strong-tasting than wild, although cultivated shiitake are very flavorsome. Cultivated mushrooms may be white, closed cup, open cup, or flat. Popular wild mushrooms, some of which are cultivated nowadays, include cèpes, also called porcini; chanterelles; chestnut, also called champignons de Paris; portobello mushrooms; morels; and oyster mushrooms. Chinese straw mushrooms, which are valued for their slippery texture rather than their flavor, are usually only available in cans in the West.

Dried mushrooms are a useful stand-by, as they will keep virtually indefinitely in an airtight container. Although expensive, a little goes a long way, as the flavor intensifies when they are dried. They must be soaked in hot water before use.

Fresh mushrooms cannot be stored for longer than three days and wild mushrooms should be used on the day of purchase or when they are gathered. Gathering wild mushrooms is a popular and practical pastime in many European countries, where pharmacies are willing to check the identification of edible species. This activity is less popular in Britain and the United States and it is vital that you never pick and eat any fungus that you cannot positively identify as edible.

Vegetarian Ingredients

Grains & Cereals

Once considered the ultimate evil in any diet, starchy ingredients have now been recognized as valuable foods which play an important role in ensuring good health and protection against disease. They release energy at a controlled rate over a period of time, which is much healthier than the sudden and short-lived "buzz" of sugar. Starchy foods also contain protein, B-group and other vitamins, iron, phosphorus, potassium, and zinc, and they are high in fiber. Bread and many breakfast cereals have added vitamins and minerals, such as calcium.

Rice

This is one of the world's staples and a "must" for the vegetarian pantry. High in fiber, it satisfies the appetite and goes well with both sweet and savory ingredients. It contains proteins, B-group, and other vitamins and minerals. Basmati, generally reckoned to be the "prince of rices" is a fragrant Indian variety that goes well with many savory dishes and makes excellent salads. Use it whenever light, fluffy, separate grains are required. Long-grain rice, also excellent in savory dishes, is less expensive and very easy to cook. Risotto rice is rounder than long grain and absorbs a lot of liquid, which is what gives this Italian dish its unique, creamy texture. Round-grain and glutinous, or sticky, rice are usually used for Asian dishes and desserts.

Brown rice is the whole grain with only the outer husk removed, whereas white rice has been polished and has lost the layers of bran. It has a chewy texture and a nutty flavor and is available in both long and round grain varieties. It contains more proteins, vitamins, and minerals than white rice and is a good source of vitamin B1, riboflavin, niacin, calcium and iron. It requires a longer cooking time than white rice, but this can be reduced by pre-soaking. Wild rice is an aquatic grass and not

a true rice. It contains plenty of protein and has a delicious flavor. It is often served mixed with long grain rice, but requires a longer cooking time.

A selection of different types of flour is a useful mainstay. Whole-wheat flour has nothing added or removed, so it retains all its nutrients. It may be used on its own or mixed with other flours, such as all-purpose white or buckwheat.

Other cereals that are useful and worth keeping in stock include cornmeal; bulgur or cracked wheat; couscous, which is made from semolina grains; and oats.

Pasta

This is another essential for the pantry. Arguably, the most versatile ingredient in the world, it goes well with almost all vegetables, cheeses, cream, herbs, and spices. Easy and quick to cook, pasta is available in hundreds of shapes and many colors, so why not experiment with different varieties?

Fats & Oils

Valuable sources of vitamins A, D, and E, fats and oils in moderate amounts are essential for a healthy diet. For general cooking, choose bland-flavored oils, such as corn, that are high in polyunsaturates. Extra virgin olive oil is best for salad dressings and virgin olive oil is a special treat when cooking Mediterranean dishes. Besides being high in monosaturates, which is thought to help reduce blood cholesterol levels, it has a truly delicious flavor. It may also be used to replace butter, margarine, or other spreads.

Basic Recipes

These recipes form the basis of several of the dishes contained throughout this book. Many of these basic recipes can be made in advance and stored in the refrigerator until required.

Fresh Vegetable Stock

8 oz/225 g shallots

1 large carrot, diced

1 celery stalk, chopped

½ fennel bulb

1 garlic clove

1 bay leaf

a few fresh parsley and tarragon sprigs

8 cups water

pepper

1 Put all of the ingredients in a large pan and bring to a boil. Skim off the surface scum with a flat spoon and reduce to a gentle simmer. Partially cover and cook for 45 minutes. Leave to cool.

2 Line a strainer with clean cheesecloth and put over a large pitcher or bowl. Pour the stock through the strainer. Discard the herbs and vegetables. Cover and store in small quantities in the refrigerator for up to 3 days.

Sesame Seed Cream

3 tbsp sesame seed paste (tahini)

6 tbsp water

2 tsp lemon juice

1 garlic clove, crushed

salt and pepper

1 Blend together the sesame seed paste and water.

2 Stir in the lemon juice and garlic. Season with salt and pepper to taste. The tahini cream is now ready to serve.

Sesame Dressing

2 tbsp sesame seed paste (tahini)

2 tbsp cider vinegar

2 tbsp medium sherry

2 tbsp sesame oil

1 tbsp soy sauce

1 garlic clove, crushed

1 Put the sesame seed paste in a bowl and gradually mix in the vinegar and sherry until smooth. Add the sesame oil, soy sauce, and garlic and mix together thoroughly.

Béchamel Sauce

2½ cups milk

4 cloves

1 bay leaf

pinch of freshly grated nutmeg

2 tbsp butter or margarine

2 tbsp all-purpose flour

salt and pepper

1 Put the milk in a saucepan and add the cloves, bay leaf, and nutmeg. Gradually bring to the boil. Remove from the heat and leave for 15 minutes.

2 Melt the butter in another pan and stir in the flour to make a roux. Cook, stirring, for 1 minute. Remove the pan from the heat.

3 Strain the milk and gradually blend into the roux. Return the pan to the heat and bring to a boil, stirring, until the sauce thickens. Season with salt and pepper to taste and add any flavorings.

Basic Recipes

Green Herb Dressing

¼ cup parsley

¼ cup mint

¼ cup chives

1 garlic clove, crushed

⅔ cup plain yogurt

salt and pepper

1 Remove the stems from the parsley and mint and put the leaves in a blender or food processor.

2 Add the chives, garlic, and yogurt and salt and pepper to taste. Blend until smooth, then store in the refrigerator until needed.

Sesame Dressing

2 tbsp sesame seed paste (tahini)

2 tbsp cider vinegar

2 tbsp medium sherry

2 tbsp sesame oil

1 tbsp soy sauce

1 garlic clove, crushed

1 Put the sesame seed paste in a bowl and gradually mix in the vinegar and sherry until smooth. Add the sesame oil, soy sauce, and garlic and mix together thoroughly.

Cucumber Dressing

1 cup plain yogurt

2-inch/5-cm piece of cucumber, peeled

1 tbsp chopped fresh mint leaves

½ tsp grated lemon rind

pinch of superfine sugar

salt and pepper

1 Put the yogurt, cucumber, mint, lemon rind, sugar, and salt and pepper to taste in a blender or food processor and work until smooth. Alternatively, finely chop the cucumber and combine with the other ingredients. Serve chilled.

Apple & Cider Vinegar Dressing

2 tbsp corn oil

2 tbsp concentrated apple juice

2 tbsp cider vinegar

1 tbsp Meaux mustard

1 garlic clove, crushed

salt and pepper

1 Put the oil, apple juice, cider vinegar, mustard, garlic, and salt and pepper to taste in a screw-top jar and shake vigorously until well-mixed.

Warm Walnut Dressing

6 tbsp walnut oil

3 tbsp white wine vinegar

1 tbsp clear honey

1 tsp whole-grain mustard

1 garlic clove, sliced

salt and pepper

1 Put the oil, vinegar, honey, mustard and salt and pepper to taste in a pan and whisk together.

2 Add the garlic and heat very gently for 3 minutes. Remove the garlic slices with a perforated spoon and discard. Pour the dressing over the salad and serve immediately.

Tomato Dressing

½ cup tomato juice

1 garlic clove, crushed

2 tbsp lemon juice

1 tbsp soy sauce

1 tsp clear honey

2 tbsp chopped chives

salt and pepper

1 Put the tomato juice, garlic, lemon juice, soy sauce, honey, chives, and salt and pepper to taste in a screw-top jar and shake vigorously until well-mixed.

How to Use This Book

Each recipe contains a wealth of useful information, including a breakdown of nutritional quantities, preparation and cooking times, and level of difficulty. All of this information is explained in detail below.

This amount of time represents the actual cooking time.

The nutritional information provided for each recipe is per serving or per portion. Optional ingredients, variations or serving suggestions have not been included in the calculations.

The number of chef's hats represents the difficulty of each recipe, ranging from easy (1 chef's hat) to difficult (5 chef's hats).

This amount of time represents the preparation of ingredients, including cooling, chilling, and soaking times.

The ingredients for each recipe are listed in the order that they are used.

The method is clearly explained with step-by-step instructions that are easy to follow.

The method is illustrated with step-by-step photographs, making the recipe easy to follow.

A full-color photograph of the finished dish.

Variations and cook's tips provide useful information regarding ingredients or cooking techniques.

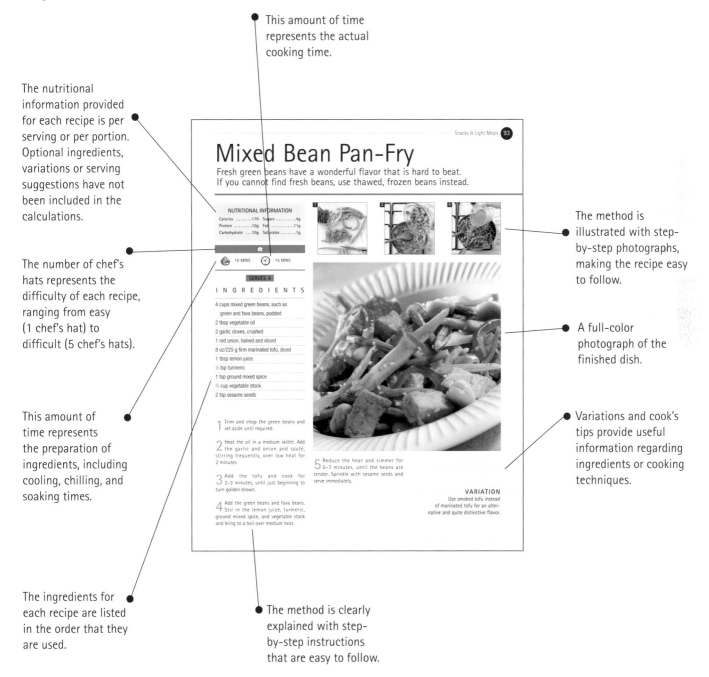

Snacks & Light Meals 93

Mixed Bean Pan-Fry

Fresh green beans have a wonderful flavor that is hard to beat. If you cannot find fresh beans, use thawed, frozen beans instead.

NUTRITIONAL INFORMATION

Calories 179   Sugars 4g
Protein ....10g   Fat 11g
Carbohydrate ...10g   Saturates 1g

10 MINS   15 MINS

SERVES 4

INGREDIENTS

4 cups mixed green beans, such as
  green and fava beans, podded
2 tbsp vegetable oil
2 garlic cloves, crushed
1 red onion, halved and sliced
8 oz/225 g firm marinated tofu, diced
1 tbsp lemon juice
½ tsp turmeric
1 tsp ground mixed spice
¼ cup vegetable stock
2 tsp sesame seeds

1 Trim and chop the green beans and set aside until required.

2 Heat the oil in a medium skillet. Add the garlic and onion and sauté, stirring frequently, over low heat for 2 minutes.

3 Add the tofu and cook for 2–3 minutes, until just beginning to turn golden brown.

4 Add the green beans and fava beans. Stir in the lemon juice, turmeric, ground mixed spice, and vegetable stock and bring to a boil over medium heat.

5 Reduce the heat and simmer for 5–7 minutes, until the beans are tender. Sprinkle with sesame seeds and serve immediately.

VARIATION
Use smoked tofu instead of marinated tofu for an alternative and quite distinctive flavor.

Soups

Soup is easy to make but always produces delicious results. There is an enormous variety of soups that you can make with vegetables. They can be rich and creamy, thick and chunky, light and delicate, and hot or chilled. The vegetables are often puréed to give a smooth consistency and thicken the soup, but you can also purée just some of

the mixture to give the soup more texture and interest. A wide range of ingredients can be used in addition to vegetables—beans, grains, noodles, cheese, and yogurt all work well. You can also experiment with different substitutions if you don't have certain ingredients to hand. Whatever your preference, you're sure to enjoy the variety of tasty soups contained in this chapter. Serve with plenty of fresh, crusty bread for a truly delicious meal.

Bell Pepper & Chile Soup

This soup has a real Mediterranean flavor, using red bell peppers, tomato, chile, and basil. It is great served with an olive bread.

NUTRITIONAL INFORMATION

Calories 55   Sugars 10g
Protein ....2g   Fat 0.5g
Carbohydrate ....11g   Saturates 0.1g

10 MINS   25 MINS

SERVES 4

INGREDIENTS

8 oz/225 g red bell peppers,
   seeded and sliced

1 onion, sliced

2 garlic cloves, crushed

1 green chile, chopped

1½ cups crushed tomatoes

2½ cups vegetable stock

2 tbsp chopped basil

basil sprigs, to garnish

1 Put the bell peppers in a large pan with the onion, garlic, and chile. Add the crushed tomatoes and vegetable stock and bring to a boil, stirring well.

2 Reduce the heat to a simmer and cook for 20 minutes, until the bell peppers have softened. Drain, reserving the liquid and vegetables separately.

3 Press the vegetables through a strainer with the back of a spoon. Alternatively, process in a food processor until smooth.

4 Return the vegetable purée to a clean pan with the reserved cooking liquid. Add the basil and heat through until hot. Garnish the soup with fresh basil sprigs and serve immediately.

VARIATION

This soup is also delicious served cold with ⅔ cup of plain yogurt swirled into it.

Avocado & Mint Soup

A rich and creamy pale green soup made with avocados and enhanced by a touch of chopped mint. Serve chilled in summer or hot in winter.

NUTRITIONAL INFORMATION

Calories 199   Sugars 3g
Protein . . . . .3g   Fat 18g
Carbohydrate . . . .7g   Saturates 6g

15 MINS   35 MINS

SERVES 6

I N G R E D I E N T S

3 tbsp butter or margarine

6 scallions, sliced

1 garlic clove, crushed

scant ¼ cup all-purpose flour

2½ cups vegetable stock

2 ripe avocados

2–3 tsp lemon juice

pinch of grated lemon rind

⅔ cup milk

⅔ cup light cream

1–1½ tbsp chopped mint

salt and pepper

mint sprigs, to garnish

MINTED GARLIC BREAD

generous ½ cup butter

1–2 tbsp chopped mint

1–2 garlic cloves, crushed

1 whole-wheat or white French bread stick

1 Melt the butter in a large, heavy-bottom pan. Add the scallions and garlic clove and cook over low heat, stirring occasionally, for 3 minutes, until soft and translucent.

2 Stir in the flour and cook, stirring, for 1–2 minutes. Gradually stir in the stock, then bring to a boil. Simmer gently while preparing the avocados.

3 Peel the avocados, discard the pits and chop coarsely. Add to the soup with the lemon juice and rind and seasoning. Cover and simmer for 10 minutes, until tender.

4 Cool the soup slightly, then press through a strainer with the back of a spoon or process in a food processor or blender until a smooth purée forms. Pour into a bowl.

5 Stir in the milk and cream, then adjust the seasoning and stir in the mint. Cover and chill thoroughly.

6 To make the minted garlic bread, soften the butter and beat in the mint and garlic. Cut the loaf into slanting slices, but not right through the bottom crust. Spread each slice with the butter and reassemble the loaf. Wrap in foil and place in a preheated oven, 350°F/180°C, for 15 minutes.

7 Serve the soup garnished with a sprig of mint and accompanied by the minted garlic bread.

Indian Bean Soup

A thick and hearty soup, nourishing and substantial enough to serve as an entrée with whole-wheat bread.

NUTRITIONAL INFORMATION

Calories	 237	Sugars	.... 9g
Protein	.... 9g	Fat	.... 9g
Carbohydrate	... 33g	Saturates	.... 1g

20 MINS   50 MINS

SERVES 6

INGREDIENTS

4 tbsp vegetable ghee or vegetable oil

2 onions, peeled and chopped

8 oz/225 g potato, cut into chunks

8 oz/225 g parsnip, cut into chunks

8 oz/225 g turnip or rutabaga,
    cut into chunks

2 celery stalks, sliced

2 zucchini, sliced

1 green bell pepper, seeded and cut into
    ½-inch/1-cm pieces

2 garlic cloves, crushed

2 tsp ground coriander

1 tbsp paprika

1 tbsp mild curry paste

5 cups vegetable stock

14 oz/400 g canned black-eye peas,
    drained and rinsed

salt

chopped cilantro, to garnish (optional)

1 Heat the ghee in a pan, add all the prepared vegetables, except the zucchini and green bell pepper, and cook over moderate heat, stirring frequently, for 5 minutes. Add the garlic, ground coriander, paprika, and curry paste and cook, stirring constantly, for 1 minute.

2 Stir in the stock and season with salt to taste. Bring to a boil, then cover and simmer over low heat, stirring occasionally, for 25 minutes.

3 Stir in the black-eye peas, sliced zucchini, and green bell pepper, cover and continue cooking for an additional 15 minutes, until all the vegetables are tender.

4 Process 1¼ cups of the soup mixture (about 2 ladlefuls) in a food processor or blender. Return the puréed mixture to the soup in the pan and reheat until piping hot. Sprinkle with chopped cilantro, if using, and serve hot.

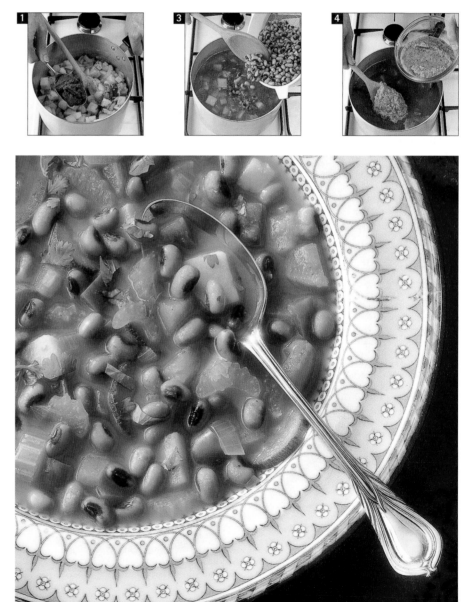

Dhal Soup

Dhal is the name given to a delicious Indian lentil dish. This soup is a variation of the theme—it is made with red lentils and curry powder.

NUTRITIONAL INFORMATION

Calories	284	Sugars	........13g
Protein	........16g	Fat	...........9g
Carbohydrate	...38g	Saturates	.......5g

5 MINS   40 MINS

SERVES 4

I N G R E D I E N T S

2 tbsp butter

2 garlic cloves, crushed

1 onion, chopped

½ tsp turmeric

1 tsp garam masala

¼ tsp chili powder

1 tsp ground cumin

2 lb 4 oz/1 kg canned, chopped
   tomatoes, drained

scant 1 cup red lentils

2 tsp lemon juice

2½ cups vegetable stock

1¼ cups coconut milk

salt and pepper

chopped cilantro and lemon slices,
   to garnish

naan bread, to serve

1 Melt the butter in a large pan. Add the garlic and onion and sauté, stirring, for 2–3 minutes. Add the turmeric, garam masala, chili powder, and cumin and cook for an additional 30 seconds.

2 Stir in the tomatoes, red lentils, lemon juice, vegetable stock, and coconut milk and bring to a boil.

3 Reduce the heat to low and simmer the soup, uncovered, for 25–30 minutes, until the lentils are tender and cooked.

4 Season to taste with salt and pepper and ladle the soup into a warm tureen. Garnish with chopped cilantro and lemon slices and serve immediately with warm naan bread.

COOK'S TIP

You can buy cans of coconut milk from supermarkets and delicatessens. It can also be made by grating creamed coconut, which comes in the form of a solid bar, and then mixing it with water.

Winter Soup

A thick vegetable soup that is a delicious meal in itself. Serve the soup with thin shavings of Parmesan and warm ciabatta bread.

NUTRITIONAL INFORMATION

Calories	285	Sugars	........11g
Protein	........16g	Fat	..........12g
Carbohydrate	...29g	Saturates	.......3g

10 MINS   20 MINS

SERVES 4

I N G R E D I E N T S

2 tbsp olive oil

2 leeks, thinly sliced

2 zucchini, chopped

2 garlic cloves, crushed

1 lb 12 oz/800 g canned chopped tomatoes

1 tbsp tomato paste

1 bay leaf

3½ cups vegetable stock

14 oz/400 g canned chickpeas, drained

8 oz/225 g spinach

1 oz/25 g Parmesan cheese,
    thinly shaved

salt and pepper

crusty bread, to serve

1 Heat the oil in a heavy-bottom pan. Add the sliced leeks and zucchini and cook over medium heat, stirring constantly, for 5 minutes.

2 Add the garlic, chopped tomatoes, tomato paste, bay leaf, vegetable stock, and chickpeas. Bring to a boil, lower the heat and simmer, stirring occasionally, for 5 minutes.

3 Shred the spinach finely, then add to the soup and boil for 2 minutes. Season to taste with salt and pepper.

4 Remove the bay leaf. Pour into a soup tureen and sprinkle over the Parmesan. Serve with crusty bread.

Plum Tomato Soup

Homemade tomato soup is easy to make and always tastes better than bought varieties. Try this version with its Mediterranean influences.

NUTRITIONAL INFORMATION

Calories	402	Sugars	........14g
Protein	.........7g	Fat	..........32g
Carbohydrate	...16g	Saturates	.......3g

20 MINS   30–35 MINS

SERVES 4

INGREDIENTS

2 tbsp olive oil

2 red onions, chopped

2 celery stalks, chopped

1 carrot, chopped

1 lb 2 oz/500 g plum tomatoes, halved

scant 3 cups vegetable stock

1 tbsp chopped oregano

1 tbsp chopped basil

⅔ cup dry white wine

2 tsp superfine sugar

scant 1 cup hazelnuts, toasted

scant 1 cup black or green olives

handful of basil leaves

1 tbsp olive oil

1 loaf ciabatta bread (Italian-style loaf)

salt and pepper

basil sprigs to garnish

1 Heat the oil in a large pan. Add the onions, celery, and carrot and fry over low heat, stirring frequently, until softened, but not colored.

2 Add the tomatoes, stock, chopped herbs, wine, and sugar. Bring to a boil, then cover and simmer for 20 minutes.

3 Place the toasted hazelnuts in a blender or food processor, together with the olives and basil leaves and process until thoroughly combined, but not too smooth. Alternatively, finely chop the nuts, olives, and basil leaves and pound them together in a mortar with a pestle, then turn into a small bowl. Add the olive oil and process or beat thoroughly for a few seconds. Turn the mixture into a serving bowl.

4 Warm the ciabatta bread in a preheated oven, 375°F/190°C, for 3–4 minutes.

5 Process the soup in a blender or a food processor, or press through a strainer, until smooth, Check the seasoning. Ladle into warmed soup bowls and garnish with sprigs of basil. Slice the warm bread and spread with the olive and hazelnut paste. Serve with the soup.

Mixed Bean Soup

This is a really hearty soup, filled with color, flavor, and goodness, which may be adapted to any vegetables that you have at hand.

NUTRITIONAL INFORMATION

Calories 190	Sugars 9g
Protein 10g	Fat 4g
Carbohydrate ...30g	Saturates 0.5g

10 MINS   40 MINS

SERVES 4

INGREDIENTS

1 tbsp vegetable oil

1 red onion, halved and sliced

scant ⅔ cup potato, diced

1 carrot, diced

1 leek, sliced

1 green chile, sliced

3 garlic cloves, crushed

1 tsp ground coriander

1 tsp chili powder

4 cups vegetable stock

1 lb/450 g mixed canned beans,
  such as red kidney, borlotti, black-eye,
  or flageolet, drained

salt and pepper

2 tbsp chopped cilantro, to garnish

1 Heat the vegetable oil in a large pan. Add the onion, potato, carrot, and leek and sauté, stirring constantly, for 2 minutes, until the vegetables are slightly softened.

2 Add the sliced chile and crushed garlic and cook for an additional 1 minute.

3 Stir in the ground coriander, chili powder, and the vegetable stock.

4 Bring the soup to a boil, then reduce the heat and cook for 20 minutes, until the vegetables are tender.

5 Stir in the beans and season well with salt and pepper, then cook, stirring occasionally, for an additional 10 minutes.

6 Transfer the soup to a warm tureen or individual bowls, then garnish with chopped cilantro and serve.

COOK'S TIP

Serve this soup with slices of warm corn bread or a cheese loaf.

Pumpkin Soup

This is an American classic that has now become popular worldwide. When pumpkin is out of season, use butternut squash in its place.

NUTRITIONAL INFORMATION

Calories 112   Sugars 7g
Protein . . . . .4g   Fat 7g
Carbohydrate . . . .8g   Saturates 2g

🍽 10 MINS   🕐 30 MINS

SERVES 6

I N G R E D I E N T S

about 2 lb 4 oz/1 kg pumpkin

3 tbsp butter or margarine

1 onion, sliced thinly

1 garlic clove, crushed

3½ cups vegetable stock

½ tsp ground ginger

1 tbsp lemon juice

3–4 thinly pared strips of orange
    rind (optional)

1–2 bay leaves or 1 bouquet garni

1¼ cups milk

salt and pepper

TO GARNISH

4–6 tablespoons light or heavy cream,
    plain yogurt, or mascarpone

snipped chives

1 Peel the pumpkin and remove the seeds, then cut the flesh into 1-inch/ 2.5-cm cubes.

2 Melt the butter in a large, heavy-bottom pan. Add the onion and garlic and fry over low heat until soft but not colored.

3 Add the pumpkin and toss with the onion for 2–3 minutes.

4 Add the stock and bring to a boil over medium heat. Season to taste with salt and pepper, then add the ginger, lemon juice, strips of orange rind, if using, and bay leaves. Cover and simmer over low heat for 20 minutes, until the pumpkin is tender.

5 Discard the orange rind, if using, and the bay leaves. Cool the soup slightly, then press through a strainer or process in a food processor until smooth. Pour into a clean pan.

6 Add the milk and reheat gently. Adjust the seasoning. Garnish with a swirl of cream and snipped chives, then serve.

Minted Pea & Yogurt Soup

A deliciously refreshing, summery soup that is full of goodness. It is also extremely tasty served chilled.

NUTRITIONAL INFORMATION

Calories	208	Sugars	.........9g
Protein	........10g	Fat	...........7g
Carbohydrate	...26g	Saturates	.......2g

15 MINS   25 MINS

SERVES 6

INGREDIENTS

2 tbsp vegetable ghee or corn oil

2 onions, coarsely chopped

8 oz/225 g potato, coarsely chopped

2 garlic cloves

1-inch/2.5-cm fresh gingerroot, chopped

1 tsp ground coriander

1 tsp ground cumin

1 tbsp all-purpose flour

3½ cups vegetable stock

1 lb/450 g frozen peas

2–3 tbsp chopped mint

⅔ cup strained Greek yogurt, plus extra
  to serve

½ tsp cornstarch

1¼ cups milk

salt and pepper

mint sprigs, to garnish

1 Heat the vegetable ghee in a pan, then add the onions and potato and cook over low heat, stirring occasionally, for 3 minutes, until the onion is soft and translucent.

2 Stir in the garlic, ginger, coriander, cumin, and flour and cook, stirring constantly, for 1 minute.

3 Add the vegetable stock, peas, and half the mint and bring to a boil, stirring. Reduce the heat, then cover and simmer gently for 15 minutes, until the vegetables are tender.

4 Process the soup, in batches, in a blender or food processor. Return the mixture to the pan and season with salt

and pepper to taste. Blend the yogurt with the cornstarch to a smooth paste and stir into the soup.

5 Add the milk and bring almost to a boil, stirring constantly. Cook very gently for 2 minutes. Serve hot, sprinkled with the remaining mint and a swirl of extra yogurt. Garnish with mint sprigs.

Thick Onion Soup

A delicious creamy soup with grated carrot and parsley for texture and color. Serve with crusty cheese biscuits for a hearty lunch.

NUTRITIONAL INFORMATION

Calories . . . . . . .277 Sugars 12g
Protein . . . . .6g Fat 20g
Carbohydrate . . .19g Saturates 8g

🐻 🐻

🍲 20 MINS   🕐 1HR 10 MINS

SERVES 6

I N G R E D I E N T S

5 tbsp butter

1 lb 2 oz/500 g onions, finely chopped

1 garlic clove, crushed

scant ⅓ cup all-purpose flour

2½ cups vegetable stock

2½ cups milk

2–3 tsp lemon or lime juice

good pinch of ground allspice

1 bay leaf

1 carrot, coarsely grated

4–6 tbsp heavy cream

salt and pepper

2 tbsp chopped parsley, to garnish

C H E E S E   B I S C U I T S

scant 1⅓ cups malted wheat or
    whole-wheat flour

2 tsp baking powder

¼ cup butter

4 tbsp grated Parmesan cheese

1 egg, beaten

scant ⅓ cup milk

1 Melt the butter in a pan and cook the onions and garlic over low heat, stirring frequently, for 10–15 minutes, until soft, but not colored. Stir in the flour and cook, stirring, for 1 minute, then gradually stir in the stock and bring to a boil, stirring frequently. Add the milk, then bring back to a boil.

2 Season to taste with salt and pepper and add 2 teaspoons of the lemon juice, the allspice, and bay leaf. Cover and simmer for 25 minutes, until the vegetables are tender. Discard the bay leaf.

3 Meanwhile, make the biscuits. Combine the flour, baking powder, and seasoning and rub in the butter until the mixture resembles fine bread crumbs. Stir in 3 tablespoons of the cheese, the egg, and enough milk to mix to a soft dough.

4 Shape into a bar about ¾ inch/2 cm thick. Place on a floured cookie sheet and mark into slices. Sprinkle with the remaining cheese and bake in a preheated oven, 425°F/220°C, for 20 minutes, until risen and golden brown.

5 Stir the carrot into the soup and simmer for 2–3 minutes. Add more lemon juice, if necessary. Stir in the cream and reheat. Garnish with chopped parsley and serve with the warm biscuits.

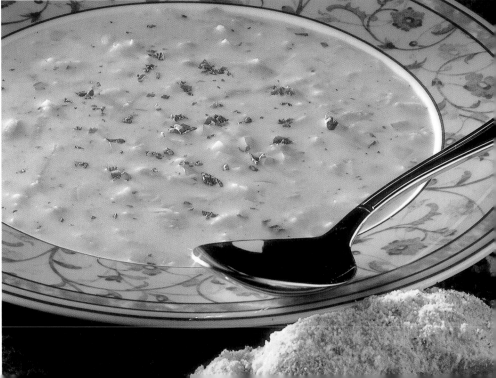

Vegetable & Corn Chowder

This is a really filling soup, which should be served before a light main course. It is easy to prepare and filled with flavor.

NUTRITIONAL INFORMATION

Calories	378	Sugars	........20g
Protein	........16g	Fat	..........13g
Carbohydrate	...52g	Saturates	.......6g

15 MINS   30 MINS

SERVES 4

INGREDIENTS

1 tbsp vegetable oil

1 red onion, diced

1 red bell pepper, seeded and diced

3 garlic cloves, crushed

1 large potato, diced

2 tbsp all-purpose flour

2½ cups milk

1¼ cups vegetable stock

½ cup broccoli florets

3 cups canned corn, drained

¾ cup grated Cheddar cheese

salt and pepper

1 tbsp chopped cilantro, to garnish

COOK'S TIP

Vegetarian cheeses are made with rennets of non-animal origin, using microbial or fungal enzymes.

1 Heat the oil in a large pan. Add the onion, bell pepper, garlic, and potato and sauté over low heat, stirring frequently, for 2–3 minutes.

2 Stir in the flour and cook, stirring for 30 seconds. Gradually stir in the milk and stock.

3 Add the broccoli and corn. Bring the mixture to a boil, stirring constantly, then reduce the heat and simmer for 20 minutes, until all the vegetables are tender.

4 Stir in ½ cup of the cheese until it melts.

5 Season and spoon the chowder into a warm soup tureen. Garnish with the remaining cheese and the cilantro and serve.

Gazpacho

This Spanish soup is full of chopped and grated vegetables with a puréed tomato base. It requires chilling, so prepare well in advance.

NUTRITIONAL INFORMATION

Calories 140   Sugars 12g
Protein ....3g   Fat 9g
Carbohydrate ...13g   Saturates 1g

6½ HOURS   0 MINS

SERVES 4

INGREDIENTS

½ small cucumber

½ small green bell pepper, seeded and
    very finely chopped

1 lb 2 oz/500 g ripe tomatoes, peeled or
    14 oz/400 g canned chopped tomatoes

½ onion, coarsely chopped

2–3 garlic cloves, crushed

3 tbsp olive oil

2 tbsp white wine vinegar

1–2 tbsp lemon or lime juice

2 tbsp tomato paste

scant 2 cups tomato juice

salt and pepper

TO SERVE

chopped green bell pepper

thinly sliced onion rings

garlic croûtons

1 Coarsely grate the cucumber into a large bowl and add the chopped green bell pepper.

2 Process the tomatoes, onion, and garlic in a food processor or blender, then add the oil, vinegar, lemon juice, and tomato paste and process until smooth. Alternatively, finely chop the tomatoes and finely grate the onion, then mix both with the garlic, oil, vinegar, lemon juice, and tomato paste.

3 Add the tomato mixture to the bowl and mix well, then add the tomato juice and mix again.

4 Season to taste, cover the bowl with plastic wrap and chill thoroughly—for at least 6 hours and preferably longer so that the flavors have time to meld together.

5 Prepare the side dishes of green bell pepper, onion rings, and garlic croûtons, and arrange in individual serving bowls.

6 Ladle the soup into bowls, preferably from a soup tureen set on the table with the side dishes placed around it. Hand the dishes around to let the guests help themselves.

Vichyssoise

This is a classic creamy soup made from potatoes and leeks. To achieve the delicate pale color, be sure to use only the white parts of the leeks.

NUTRITIONAL INFORMATION

Calories ....208 Sugars 5g
Protein ....5g Fat 12g
Carbohydrate ...20g Saturates 6g

10 MINS   40 MINS

SERVES 6

INGREDIENTS

3 large leeks

3 tbsp butter or margarine

1 onion, thinly sliced

1 lb 2 oz/500 g potatoes, chopped

3¾ cups vegetable stock

2 tsp lemon juice

pinch of ground nutmeg

¼ tsp ground coriander

1 bay leaf

1 egg yolk

⅔ cup light cream

salt and white pepper

TO GARNISH

freshly snipped chives

1 Trim the leeks and remove most of the green part. Slice the white part of the leeks very finely.

2 Melt the butter in a pan. Add the leeks and onion and sauté, stirring occasionally, for 5 minutes without browning.

3 Add the potatoes, vegetable stock, lemon juice, nutmeg, coriander, and bay leaf to the pan, then season to taste with salt and pepper and bring to a boil. Cover and simmer for 30 minutes, until all the vegetables are very soft.

4 Let the soup cool a little, then remove and discard the bay leaf. Press the soup through a strainer or process in a food processor or blender until smooth. Pour into a clean pan.

5 Blend the egg yolk into the cream and add a little of the soup to the mixture, then whisk it all back into the soup and reheat gently, without boiling. Adjust the seasoning to taste. Cool and then chill thoroughly in the refrigerator.

6 Serve the soup sprinkled with freshly snipped chives.

Curried Parsnip Soup

Parsnips make a delicious soup as they have a slightly sweet flavor.
In this recipe, spices are added to complement this sweetness.

NUTRITIONAL INFORMATION

Calories 152   Sugars 7g
Protein ....3g   Fat 8g
Carbohydrate ...18g   Saturates 3g

10 MINS   35 MINS

SERVES 4

I N G R E D I E N T S

1 tbsp vegetable oil

1 tbsp butter

1 red onion, chopped

3 parsnips, chopped

2 garlic cloves, crushed

2 tsp garam masala

½ tsp chili powder

1 tbsp all-purpose flour

3¾ cups vegetable stock

grated rind and juice of 1 lemon

salt and pepper

lemon rind, to garnish

1 Heat the oil and butter in a large pan until the butter has melted. Add the onion, parsnips, and garlic and sauté, stirring frequently, for 5–7 minutes, until the vegetables have softened, but not colored.

2 Add the garam masala and chili powder and cook, stirring constantly, for 30 seconds. Sprinkle in the flour, mixing well, and cook, stirring constantly, for an additional 30 seconds.

3 Stir in the stock and lemon rind and juice, then bring to a boil. Reduce the heat and simmer for 20 minutes.

4 Remove some of the vegetable pieces with a slotted spoon and reserve until required. Process the remaining soup and vegetables in a food processor or blender for 1 minute, or until a smooth purée. Alternatively, press the vegetables through a strainer with the back of a wooden spoon.

5 Return the soup to a clean pan and stir in the reserved vegetables. Heat the soup through for 2 minutes until piping hot.

6 Season to taste with salt and pepper, then transfer to soup bowls. Garnish with grated lemon rind and serve.

Bean Soup

Beans feature widely in Mexican cooking, and here pinto beans are used to give an interesting texture. Pinto beans require soaking overnight.

NUTRITIONAL INFORMATION

Calories 188   Sugars 9g
Protein ....13g   Fat 1g
Carbohydrate ...33g   Saturates 0.3g

20 MINS   3 HOURS

SERVES 4

INGREDIENTS

1 cup pinto beans

5 cups water

6–8 oz/175–225 g carrots, finely chopped

1 large onion, finely chopped

2–3 garlic cloves, crushed

½–1 chile, seeded and finely chopped

4 cups vegetable stock

2 tomatoes, peeled and finely chopped

2 celery stalks, very thinly sliced

salt and pepper

1 tbsp chopped cilantro (optional)

CROUTONS

3 slices white bread, crusts removed

oil, for deep-frying

1–2 garlic cloves, crushed

VARIATION

Pinto beans are widely available, but if you cannot find them or you wish to vary the recipe, you can use cannellini beans or black-eye peas as an alternative.

1 Soak the beans overnight in cold water; drain and place in a pan with the water. Bring to a boil and boil vigorously for 10 minutes. Lower the heat, cover and simmer for 2 hours, until the beans are tender.

2 Add the carrots, onion, garlic, chile, and stock and bring back to a boil. Cover and simmer for an additional 30 minutes, until very tender.

3 Remove half the beans and vegetables with the cooking juices and press through a strainer or process in a food processor or blender until smooth.

4 Return the bean purée to the pan and add the tomatoes and celery. Simmer for 10–15 minutes, until the celery is just tender, adding a little more stock or water if necessary.

5 Meanwhile, make the croûtons. Dice the bread. Heat the oil with the garlic in a small skillet and fry the croûtons until golden brown. Drain on paper towels.

6 Season the soup and stir in the chopped cilantro, if using. Transfer to a warm tureen and serve immediately with the croûtons.

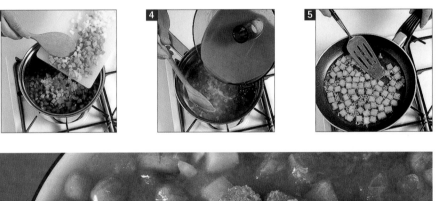

Beet Soup

Here are two variations using the same vegetable: a creamy soup made with puréed cooked beet and a traditional clear soup, Bortsch.

NUTRITIONAL INFORMATION

Calories . . . . .106 Sugars 11g
Protein . . . . .3g Fat 5g
Carbohydrate . . .13g Saturates 3g

25 MINS   35-55 MINS

SERVES 6

INGREDIENTS

BORTSCH

1 lb 2 oz/500 g raw beets, peeled
  and grated

2 carrots, finely chopped

1 large onion, finely chopped

1 garlic clove, crushed

1 bouquet garni

5 cups vegetable stock

2–3 tsp lemon juice

salt and pepper

⅔ cup sour cream, to serve

CREAMED BEET SOUP

¼ cup butter or margarine

2 large onions, finely chopped

1–2 carrots, chopped

2 celery stalks, chopped

1 lb 2 oz/500 g cooked beets, diced

1–2 tbsp lemon juice

3¾ cups vegetable stock

1¼ cups milk

salt and pepper

TO SERVE

grated cooked beet or 6 tbsp heavy cream,
  lightly whipped

1 To make bortsch, place the beets, carrots, onion, garlic, bouquet garni, stock, and lemon juice in a pan and season to taste with salt and pepper. Bring to a boil, then cover and simmer for 45 minutes.

2 Press the soup through a fine strainer or a strainer lined with cheesecloth, then pour into a clean pan. Taste and adjust the seasoning and add extra lemon juice, if necessary.

3 Bring to a boil and simmer for 1–2 minutes. Serve with a spoonful of sour cream swirled through.

4 To make creamed beet soup, melt the butter in a pan. Add the onions, carrots, and celery and sauté until just beginning to color.

5 Add the beet, 1 tablespoon of the lemon juice, the stock, and seasoning and bring to a boil. Cover and simmer for 30 minutes, until tender.

6 Cool slightly, then press through a strainer or process in a food processor or blender. Pour into a clean pan. Add the milk and bring to a boil. Adjust the seasoning and add extra lemon juice, if necessary. Top with grated beet or heavy cream.

Cauliflower & Broccoli Soup

Full of flavor, this creamy cauliflower and broccoli soup is simple to make and absolutely delicious to eat.

NUTRITIONAL INFORMATION

Calories	378	Sugars	........14g
Protein	........18g	Fat	..........26g
Carbohydrate	...20g	Saturates	.......7g

10 MINS　　35 MINS

SERVES 4

INGREDIENTS

3 tbsp vegetable oil

1 red onion, chopped

2 garlic cloves, crushed

2½ cups cauliflower florets

3 cups broccoli florets

1 tbsp all-purpose flour

2½ cups milk

1¼ cups vegetable stock

¾ cup grated Gruyère cheese

pinch of paprika

⅔ cup light cream

paprika and Gruyère cheese shavings,
　　to garnish

1 Heat the oil in a large, heavy-bottom pan. Add the onion, garlic, cauliflower florets, and broccoli florets and sauté over low heat, stirring constantly, for 3–4 minutes. Add the flour and cook, stirring constantly for an additional 1 minute.

2 Gradually stir in the milk and stock and bring to a boil, stirring constantly. Reduce the heat and simmer for 20 minutes.

3 Remove about one fourth of the vegetables with a slotted spoon and set aside. Put the remaining soup in a food processor or blender and process for 30 seconds, until smooth. Alternatively, press the vegetables through a strainer with the back of a wooden spoon. Transfer the soup to a clean pan.

4 Return the reserved vegetable pieces to the soup. Stir in the grated cheese, paprika, and light cream and heat through over low heat, without boiling, for 2–3 minutes, until the cheese starts to melt.

5 Transfer to warmed individual serving bowls, then garnish with shavings of Gruyère and dust with paprika and serve immediately.

COOK'S TIP

The soup must not start to boil after the cream has been added, otherwise it will curdle. Use plain yogurt instead of the cream if preferred, but again do not let it boil.

Spanish Tomato Soup

This Mediterranean tomato soup is thickened with bread, as is traditional in some parts of Spain, and served with garlic bread.

NUTRITIONAL INFORMATION

Calories	297	Sugars	.........7g
Protein	.........8g	Fat	...........13g
Carbohydrate	...39g	Saturates	.......2g

🥔 10 MINS   🕐 20 MINS

SERVES 4

INGREDIENTS

4 tbsp olive oil

1 onion, chopped

3 garlic cloves, crushed

1 green bell pepper, seeded and chopped

½ tsp chili powder

1 lb 2 oz/500 g tomatoes, chopped

8 oz/225 g French or Italian bread, cubed

4 cups vegetable stock

GARLIC BREAD

4 slices ciabatta or French bread

4 tbsp olive oil

2 garlic cloves, crushed

¼ cup grated Cheddar cheese

chili powder, to garnish

1 Heat the olive oil in a large skillet. Add the onion, garlic, and bell pepper and sauté over low heat, stirring frequently, for 2–3 minutes, until the onion has softened.

2 Add the chili powder and tomatoes and cook over medium heat until the mixture has thickened.

3 Stir in the bread cubes and stock and cook for 10–15 minutes, until the soup is thick and fairly smooth.

4 Meanwhile, make the garlic bread. Toast the bread slices under a medium broiler. Drizzle the oil over the top of the bread and rub with the garlic, then sprinkle with the cheese and return to the broiler for 2–3 minutes, until the cheese has melted. Sprinkle with chili powder and serve with the soup.

VARIATION

Replace the green bell pepper with red or orange bell pepper, if you prefer.

Broccoli & Potato Soup

This creamy soup has a delightful pale green coloring and rich flavor from the blend of tender broccoli and blue cheese.

NUTRITIONAL INFORMATION

Calories	.452	Sugars	.4g
Protein	.14g	Fat	.35g
Carbohydrate	.20g	Saturates	.19g

5–10 MINS   40 MINS

SERVES 4

INGREDIENTS

2 tbsp olive oil

2 potatoes, diced

1 onion, diced

8 oz/225 g broccoli florets

4½ oz/125 g blue cheese, crumbled

4 cups vegetable stock

⅔ cup heavy cream

pinch of paprika

salt and pepper

1 Heat the oil in a large pan. Add the potatoes and onion. Sauté, stirring constantly, for 5 minutes.

2 Reserve a few broccoli florets for the garnish and add the remaining broccoli to the pan. Add the cheese and vegetable stock.

COOK'S TIP

This soup freezes very successfully. Follow the method described here up to step 4, and freeze the soup after it has been puréed. Add the cream and paprika just before serving. Garnish and serve.

3 Bring to a boil, then reduce the heat and simmer, covered, for 25 minutes, until the potatoes are tender.

4 Transfer the soup to a food processor or blender in batches and process until the mixture is smooth. Alternatively, press the vegetables through a strainer with the back of a wooden spoon.

5 Return the purée to a clean pan and stir in the heavy cream and a pinch of paprika. Season to taste with salt and pepper.

6 Blanch the reserved broccoli florets in a little boiling water for 2 minutes, then lift them out of the pan with a slotted spoon.

7 Pour the soup into warmed individual bowls and garnish with the broccoli florets and a sprinkling of paprika. Serve immediately.

Spicy Dhal & Carrot Soup

This nutritious soup uses split red lentils and carrots as the two main ingredients and includes a selection of spices to give it a kick.

NUTRITIONAL INFORMATION

Calories	173	Sugars	........11g
Protein	.........9g	Fat	...........5g
Carbohydrate	...24g	Saturates	.......1g

🍳 15 MINS   🕐 45 MINS

SERVES 6

INGREDIENTS

½ cup split red lentils

5 cups vegetable stock

12 oz/350 g carrots, sliced

2 onions, chopped

8 oz/225 g can chopped tomatoes

2 garlic cloves, chopped

2 tbsp vegetable ghee or oil

1 tsp ground cumin

1 tsp ground coriander

1 fresh green chile, seeded and chopped,
    or 1 tsp minced chile

½ tsp ground turmeric

1 tbsp lemon juice

salt

1¼ cups milk

2 tbsp chopped cilantro

plain yogurt, to serve

1 Place the lentils in a strainer and rinse well under cold running water. Drain and place in a large pan, together with 3¾ cups of the stock, the carrots, onions, tomatoes, and garlic. Bring the mixture to a boil, then reduce the heat and simmer, covered, for 30 minutes, until the vegetables and lentils are tender.

2 Meanwhile, heat the ghee in a small pan. Add the cumin, ground coriander, chile, and turmeric and cook over low heat for 1 minute. Remove from the heat and stir in the lemon juice. Season with salt to taste.

3 Process the soup in batches in a blender or food processor. Return the soup to the pan, then add the spice mixture and the remaining 1¼ cups stock and simmer over low heat for 10 minutes.

4 Add the milk, then taste and adjust the seasoning, if necessary. Stir in the chopped cilantro and reheat gently. Serve hot with a swirl of yogurt.

Potato & Split Pea Soup

Split green peas are sweeter than other varieties of split pea and reduce down to a purée when cooked, which acts as a thickener in soups.

NUTRITIONAL INFORMATION

Calories	260	Sugars	.........5g
Protein	........11g	Fat	..........10g
Carbohydrate	...32g	Saturates	.......3g

5–10 MINS   45 MINS

SERVES 4

INGREDIENTS

2 tbsp vegetable oil

2 unpeeled mealy potatoes, diced

2 onions, diced

scant ⅓ cup split green peas

4 cups vegetable stock

5 tbsp grated Gruyère cheese

salt and pepper

CROUTONS

3 tbsp butter

1 garlic clove, crushed

1 tbsp chopped parsley

1 thick slice white bread, cubed

1 Heat the vegetable oil in a large pan. Add the potatoes and onions and sauté over low heat, stirring constantly, for 5 minutes.

VARIATION

For a richly colored soup, red lentils could be used instead of split green peas. Add a large pinch of brown sugar to the recipe for extra sweetness if red lentils are used.

2 Add the split green peas to the pan and stir to mix together well.

3 Pour the vegetable stock into the pan and bring to a boil. Reduce the heat to low and simmer for 35 minutes, until the potatoes are tender and the split peas cooked.

4 Meanwhile, make the croûtons. Melt the butter in a skillet. Add the garlic, parsley, and bread cubes and cook, turning

frequently, for 2 minutes, until the bread cubes are golden brown on all sides.

5 Stir the grated cheese into the soup and season to taste with salt and pepper. Heat gently until the cheese is starting to melt.

6 Pour the soup into warmed individual bowls and sprinkle the croûtons on top. Serve at once.

Avocado & Vegetable Soup

Avocado has a rich color and flavor, which makes a creamy flavored soup. It is best served chilled, but may be eaten warm as well.

NUTRITIONAL INFORMATION

Calories 167   Sugars 5g
Protein ....4g   Fat 13g
Carbohydrate ....8g   Saturates 3g

15 MINS   10 MINS

SERVES 4

INGREDIENTS

1 large, ripe avocado

2 tbsp lemon juice

1 tbsp vegetable oil

½ cup canned corn, drained

2 tomatoes, peeled and seeded

1 garlic clove, crushed

1 leek, chopped

1 red chile, chopped

scant 1¾ cups vegetable stock

⅔ cup milk

shredded leek, to garnish

1 Peel the avocado and mash the flesh with a fork, stir in the lemon juice and reserve until required.

2 Heat the oil in a large pan. Add the corn, tomatoes, garlic, leek, and chile and sauté over low heat for 2–3 minutes, until the vegetables have softened.

3 Put half the vegetable mixture in a food processor or blender, together with the mashed avocado and process until smooth. Transfer the mixture to a clean pan.

4 Add the vegetable stock, milk, and reserved vegetables and cook over low heat for 3–4 minutes, until hot. Transfer to a warmed individual serving bowls, then garnish with shredded leek and serve immediately.

COOK'S TIP

If serving chilled, transfer from the food processor to a bowl. Stir in the vegetable stock and milk, then cover and chill in the refrigerator for at least 4 hours.

Indian Potato & Pea Soup

A slightly hot and spicy Indian flavor is given to this soup with the use of garam masala, chile, cumin, and coriander.

NUTRITIONAL INFORMATION

Calories	153	Sugars	.........6g
Protein	.........6g	Fat	...........6g
Carbohydrate	...18g	Saturates	.......1g

10 MINS   35 MINS

SERVES 4

INGREDIENTS

2 tbsp vegetable oil

8 oz/225 g mealy potatoes, diced

1 large onion, chopped

2 garlic cloves, crushed

1 tsp garam masala

1 tsp ground coriander

1 tsp ground cumin

3¾ cups vegetable stock

1 red chile, chopped

scant 1 cup frozen peas

4 tbsp plain yogurt

salt and pepper

chopped cilantro, to garnish

warm bread, to serve

VARIATION

For slightly less heat, seed the chile before adding it to the soup. Always wash your hands after handling chiles as they contain volatile oils that can irritate the skin and make your eyes burn if you touch your face.

1 Heat the vegetable oil in a large pan. Add the potatoes, onion, and garlic and sauté over low heat, stirring constantly, for 5 minutes.

2 Add the garam masala, ground coriander, and cumin and cook, stirring constantly, for 1 minute.

3 Stir in the vegetable stock and chopped red chile and bring the mixture to a boil. Reduce the heat, then cover the pan and simmer for 20 minutes, until the potatoes begin to break down.

4 Add the peas and cook for an additional 5 minutes. Stir in the yogurt and season to taste with salt and pepper.

5 Pour into warmed soup bowls, then garnish with chopped fresh cilantro and serve hot with warm bread.

Cream Cheese & Herb Soup

Make the most of home-grown herbs to create this wonderfully creamy soup with its marvelous garden-fresh fragrance.

NUTRITIONAL INFORMATION

Calories ......275 Sugars 5g
Protein ....7g Fat 22g
Carbohydrate ...14g Saturates 11g

🍳 15 MINS   🕐 35 MINS

SERVES 4

INGREDIENTS

2 tbsp butter or margarine

2 onions, chopped

3¾ cups vegetable stock

1 oz/25 g coarsely chopped mixed
    herbs, such as parsley, chives, thyme,
    basil, and oregano

1 cup full-fat soft cheese

1 tbsp cornstarch

1 tbsp milk

chopped chives, to garnish

1 Melt the butter in a large, heavy-bottom pan. Add the onions and sauté over medium heat for 2 minutes, then cover and turn the heat to low. Continue to cook the onions for 5 minutes, then remove the lid.

2 Add the vegetable stock and herbs to the pan. Bring to a boil over a moderate heat. Lower the heat, then cover and simmer gently for 20 minutes.

3 Remove the pan from the heat. Transfer the soup to a food processor or blender and process for 15 seconds, until smooth. Alternatively, press it through a strainer with the back of a wooden spoon. Return the soup to the pan.

4 Reserve a little of the cheese for garnish. Spoon the remaining cheese into the soup and whisk until it has melted and is incorporated.

5 Mix the cornstarch with the milk to a paste, then stir the mixture into the soup. Heat, stirring constantly, until thickened and smooth.

6 Pour the soup into warmed individual bowls. Spoon some of the reserved cheese into each bowl and garnish with chives. Serve at once.

Appetizers

With so many fresh ingredients readily available, it is very easy to create some deliciously different appetizers to make the perfect introduction to a vegetarian meal. The ideas in this chapter are an inspiration to cook and a treat to eat, and they give an edge to the appetite that makes the main course even more enjoyable. When choosing a

appetizer, make sure that you provide a good balance of flavors, colors, and textures that offer variety and contrast. Balance the nature of the recipes too—a rich entrée is best preceded by a light appetizer, which is just enough to interest the palate and stimulate the taste buds.

Mushroom & Garlic Soufflés

These individual soufflés are very impressive appetizers, but must be cooked just before serving to prevent them from sinking.

NUTRITIONAL INFORMATION

Calories	179	Sugars	.........3g
Protein	.........6g	Fat	..........14g
Carbohydrate	....8g	Saturates	.......8g

10 MINS   20 MINS

SERVES 4

INGREDIENTS

4 tbsp butter

1⅓ cup chopped flat mushrooms,

2 tsp lime juice

2 garlic cloves, crushed

2 tbsp chopped marjoram

2 tbsp all-purpose flour

scant 1 cup milk

salt and pepper

2 eggs, separated

1 Lightly grease four ⅔-cup individual soufflé dishes with a little butter.

2 Melt 2 tablespoons of the butter in a skillet. Add the mushrooms, lime juice, and garlic and sauté for 2–3 minutes. Remove the mushroom mixture from the skillet with a slotted spoon and transfer to a mixing bowl. Stir in the marjoram.

COOK'S TIP

Insert a skewer into the center of the soufflés to test if they are cooked through—it should come out clean. If not, cook for a few minutes longer, but do not overcook otherwise they will become rubbery.

3 Melt the remaining butter in a pan. Add the flour and cook for 1 minute, then remove from the heat. Stir in the milk and return to the heat. Bring to a boil, stirring until thickened.

4 Mix the sauce into the mushroom mixture and beat in the egg yolks. Season to taste with salt and pepper.

5 Whisk the egg whites until they form peaks and fold into the mushroom mixture until fully incorporated.

6 Divide the mixture between the soufflé dishes. Place the dishes on a cookie sheet and cook in a preheated oven, 400°F/200°C, for about 8–10 minutes, or until the soufflés have risen and are cooked through (see Cook's Tip, lest). Serve immediately.

Feta Cheese Tartlets

These crisp-baked bread cases, filled with sliced tomatoes, feta cheese, black olives, and quail's eggs, are quick to make and taste delicious.

NUTRITIONAL INFORMATION

Calories 570	Sugars 3g
Protein 14g	Fat 42g
Carbohydrate . . .36g	Saturates 23g

30 MINS   10 MINS

SERVES 4

I N G R E D I E N T S

8 slices bread from a medium-cut large loaf

generous ½ cup butter, melted

1 cup feta cheese,
    cut into small cubes

4 cherry tomatoes, cut into wedges

8 pitted black or green olives, halved

8 quail's eggs, hard-cooked

2 tbsp olive oil

1 tbsp wine vinegar

1 tsp whole-grain mustard

pinch of superfine sugar

salt and pepper

parsley sprigs, to garnish

1 Remove the crusts from the bread. Trim the bread into squares and flatten each piece with a rolling pin.

2 Brush the bread with melted butter, and then arrange them in bun or muffin pans. Press a piece of crumpled foil into each bread case to secure in place. Bake in a preheated oven, 375°F/190°C, for 10 minutes, until crisp and browned.

3 Meanwhile, mix together the feta cheese, tomatoes, and olives. Shell the eggs and cut them into fourths. Mix together the olive oil, vinegar, mustard, and sugar. Season to taste with a little salt and pepper.

4 Remove the bread cases from the oven and discard the foil. Leave to cool.

5 Just before serving, fill the bread cases with the cheese and tomato mixture. Arrange the eggs on top and spoon over the dressing. Garnish with parsley sprigs.

Mixed Bhajis

These bhajis are often served as accompaniments to a main meal, but they are delicious as an appetizer with a small salad and yogurt sauce.

NUTRITIONAL INFORMATION

Calories 414   Sugars 7g
Protein . . . . .9g   Fat 26g
Carbohydrate . . .38g   Saturates 3g

25 MINS   30 MINS

SERVES 4

INGREDIENTS

BHAJIS

generous 1 cup gram (chickpea) flour

1 tsp baking soda

2 tsp ground coriander

1 tsp garam masala

1½ tsp turmeric

1½ tsp chili powder

2 tbsp chopped cilantro

1 small onion, halved and sliced

1 small leek, sliced

½ cup cooked cauliflower

generous ½–generous ¾ cup cold water

salt and pepper

vegetable oil, for deep-frying

SAUCE

⅔ cup plain yogurt

2 tbsp chopped mint

½ tsp turmeric

1 garlic clove, crushed

mint sprigs, to garnish

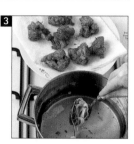

1 Sift the flour, baking soda, and salt to taste into a mixing bowl and add the spices and fresh cilantro. Mix thoroughly.

2 Divide the mixture into 3 and place in separate bowls. Stir the onion into one bowl, the leek into another and the cauliflower into the third bowl. Add 3–4 tablespoons of water to each bowl and mix each to form a smooth paste.

3 Heat the oil for deep-frying in a deep fryer to 350°F/180°C, until a cube of bread browns in 30 seconds. Using 2 dessert spoons, form the mixture into rounds and cook each in the oil for 3–4 minutes, until browned. Remove with a slotted spoon and drain well on absorbent paper towels. Keep the bhajis warm in the oven while cooking the remainder.

4 Mix all of the sauce ingredients together and pour into a small serving bowl. Garnish with mint sprigs and serve with the warm bhajis.

Dumplings in Yogurt Sauce

Adding a baghaar (seasoned oil dressing) just before serving makes this a mouth-watering accompaniment to any meal.

NUTRITIONAL INFORMATION

Calories 719   Sugars 9g
Protein . . . . .9g   Fat 60g
Carbohydrate . . .38g   Saturates 7g

35 MINS   35 MINS

SERVES 4

INGREDIENTS

DUMPLINGS

⅔ cup gram (chickpea) flour

1 tsp chili powder

½ tsp baking soda

1 medium onion, finely chopped

2 green chiles

cilantro leaves

⅔ cup water

1¼ cups vegetable oil

salt

YOGURT SAUCE

1¼ cups plain yogurt

3 tbsp gram flour

⅔ cup water

1 tsp chopped fresh gingerroot

1 tsp crushed garlic

1½ tsp chili powder

½ tsp turmeric

1 tsp ground coriander

1 tsp ground cumin

SEASONED DRESSING

⅔ cup vegetable oil

1 tsp white cumin seeds

6 dried red chiles

1 To make the dumplings, sift the gram flour into a large bowl. Add the chili powder, ½ teaspoon salt, baking soda, onion, green chiles, and cilantro and mix. Add the water and mix to form a thick paste. Heat the oil in a skillet. Place teaspoonfuls of the paste in the oil and cook over medium heat, turning once, until a crisp golden brown. Set aside.

2 To make the sauce, place the yogurt in a bowl and whisk with the gram flour and the water. Add all of the spices and 1½ teaspoons salt and mix well.

3 Press this mixture through a large strainer into a pan. Bring to a boil over low heat, stirring constantly. If the yogurt sauce becomes too thick, add a little extra water.

4 Pour the sauce into a deep serving dish and arrange all the dumplings on top. Set aside and keep warm.

5 To make the dressing, heat the oil in a skillet. Add the white cumin seeds and the dried red chiles and fry until darker in color and giving off their aroma. Pour the dressing over the dumplings and serve hot.

Spinach Phyllo Baskets

If you use frozen spinach, it only needs to be thawed and drained before being mixed with the cheeses and seasonings.

NUTRITIONAL INFORMATION

Calories 533	Sugars 3g	
Protein 24g	Fat 38g	
Carbohydrate ...26g	Saturates 22g	

55 MINS   30 MINS

MAKES 2

INGREDIENTS

4½ oz/125 g fresh leaf spinach,
   washed and chopped roughly, or
   scant ⅓ cup thawed frozen spinach

2–4 scallions, trimmed and chopped, or
   1 tbsp finely chopped onion

1 garlic clove, crushed

2 tbsp freshly grated Parmesan cheese

generous ¾ cup grated sharp
   Cheddar cheese

pinch of ground allspice

1 egg yolk

4 sheets phyllo pastry

2 tbsp butter, melted

salt and pepper

2 scallions, to garnish

1 If using fresh spinach, cook it in the minimum of boiling salted water for 3–4 minutes, until tender. Drain very thoroughly, using a potato masher to remove excess liquid, then chop and put into a bowl. If using frozen spinach, simply drain and chop.

2 Add the scallions, garlic, cheeses, allspice, egg yolk, and seasoning, and mix well.

3 Grease 2 individual muffin pans, or ovenproof dishes or pans, about 5 inches/12 cm in diameter, and 1½ inches/4 cm deep. Cut the phyllo pastry sheets in half to make 8 pieces and brush each lightly with melted butter.

4 Place one piece of phyllo pastry in a pan or dish and then cover with a second piece at right angles to the first. Add two more pieces at right angles, so that all the corners are in different places. Line the other pan in the same way.

5 Spoon the spinach mixture into the "baskets" and cook in a preheated oven, 350°F/180°C, for 20 minutes, until the pastry is golden brown. Garnish with a scallion tassel and serve hot or cold.

6 Make scallion tassels about 30 minutes before required. Trim off the root end and cut to a length of 2–3 inches/5–7 cm. Make a series of cuts from the green end to within ¾ inch/2 cm of the other end. Place in a bowl of iced water to open out. Drain well before use.

Vegetable Fritters

These mixed vegetable fritters are coated in a light batter and deep-fried until golden. They are ideal with the sweet-and-sour dipping sauce.

NUTRITIONAL INFORMATION

Calories	479	Sugars	........18g
Protein	.........8g	Fat	..........32g
Carbohydrate	...42g	Saturates	.......5g

20 MINS   20 MINS

SERVES 4

INGREDIENTS

scant ⅔ cup whole-wheat flour

pinch of cayenne pepper

4 tsp olive oil

12 tbsp cold water

1 cup broccoli florets

1 cup cauliflower florets

½ cup snow peas

1 large carrot, cut into batons

1 red bell pepper, seeded and sliced

2 egg whites, beaten

oil, for deep-frying

salt

SAUCE

⅔ cup pineapple juice

⅔ cup vegetable stock

2 tbsp white wine vinegar

2 tbsp light brown sugar

2 tsp cornstarch

2 scallions, chopped

1 Sift the flour and a pinch of salt into a mixing bowl and add the cayenne pepper. Make a well in the center and gradually beat in the oil and cold water to make a smooth batter.

2 Cook the vegetables in boiling water for 5 minutes and drain well.

3 Whisk the egg whites until they form peaks and gently fold them into the flour batter.

4 Dip the vegetables into the batter, turning to coat well. Drain off any excess batter. Heat the oil for deep-frying

in a deep-fryer to 350°F/180°C, until a cube of bread browns in 30 seconds. Fry the coated vegetables, in batches, for 1–2 minutes, until golden. Remove from the oil with a slotted spoon and drain on paper towels.

5 Place all of the sauce ingredients in a pan and bring to a boil, stirring, until thickened and clear. Serve with the fritters.

Walnut, Egg & Cheese Pâté

This unusual pâté, flavored with parsley and dill, can be served with crackers, crusty, bread or toast. The pâté requires chilling until set.

NUTRITIONAL INFORMATION

Calories	438	Sugars	.........2g
Protein	........21g	Fat	..........38g
Carbohydrate	....2g	Saturates	......18g

20 MINS   2 MINS

SERVES 2

INGREDIENTS

1 celery stalk

1–2 scallions, trimmed

¼ cup shelled walnuts

1 tbsp chopped fresh parsley

1 tsp chopped fresh dill or ½ tsp dried dill

1 garlic clove, crushed

dash of vegetarian Worcestershire sauce

½ cup cottage cheese

2 oz/55 g blue cheese, such as
    Stilton or Danish Blue

1 hard-cooked egg

2 tbsp butter

salt and pepper

herbs, to garnish

crackers, toast, or crusty bread and
    crudités, to serve

COOK'S TIP

You can also use this as a stuffing for vegetables. Cut the tops off extra-large tomatoes, then scoop out the seeds and fill with the pâté, piling it well up, or spoon into the hollows of celery stalks cut into 2-inch/5-cm pieces.

1 Finely chop the celery, slice the scallions very finely, and chop the walnuts evenly. Place in a bowl.

2 Add the chopped herbs and garlic and Worcestershire sauce to taste and mix well, then stir the cottage cheese evenly through the mixture.

3 Grate the blue cheese and hard-cooked egg finely into the pâté mixture, and season with salt and pepper.

4 Melt the butter and stir through the pâté, then spoon into one serving dish or two individual dishes, but do not press down firmly. Chill until set.

5 Garnish with fresh herbs and serve with crackers, toast, or fresh, crusty bread and a few crudités, if liked.

Samosas

Samosas, which are a sort of Indian pasty, make excellent appetizers. In India, they are popular snacks sold at roadside stalls.

NUTRITIONAL INFORMATION

Calories . . . . . . .261 Sugars 0.4g
Protein . . . . .2g Fat 23g
Carbohydrate . . .13g Saturates 4g

🄶 🄶 🄶

🥔 40 MINS   🕐 40 MINS

MAKES 12

I N G R E D I E N T S

PASTRY

⅔ cup self-rising flour

½ tsp salt

3 tbsp butter, cut into small pieces

4 tbsp water

FILLING

3 medium potatoes, boiled

1 tsp finely chopped fresh gingerroot

1 tsp crushed garlic

½ tsp white cumin seeds

½ tsp mixed onion and mustard seeds

1 tsp salt

½ tsp crushed red chiles

2 tbsp lemon juice

2 small green chiles, finely chopped

ghee or oil, for deep-frying

1 Sift the flour and salt into a bowl. Add the butter and rub into the flour until the mixture resembles fine bread crumbs.

2 Pour in the water and mix with a fork to form a dough. Pat it into a ball and knead for 5 minutes, until smooth. Cover and leave to rise.

3 To make the filling, mash the boiled potatoes gently and mix with the ginger, garlic, white cumin seeds, onion and mustard seeds, salt, crushed red chiles, lemon juice, and green chiles.

4 Break small balls off the dough and roll each out very thinly to form a round. Cut in half, then dampen the edges and shape into cones. Fill the cones with a little of the filling, then dampen the top and bottom edges of the cones and pinch together to seal. Set aside.

5 Fill a deep pan one-third full with oil and heat to 350°F/180°C, until a small cube of bread browns in 30 seconds. Carefully lower the samosas into the oil, a few at a time, and deep-fry for 2-3 minutes, until golden brown. Remove from the oil and drain thoroughly on paper towels. Serve hot or cold.

Heavenly Garlic Dip

Anyone who loves garlic will adore this dip—it is very potent! Serve it at a barbecue and dip raw vegetables or chunks of French bread into it.

NUTRITIONAL INFORMATION

Calories 344   Sugars 2g
Protein ....6g   Fat 34g
Carbohydrate ....3g   Saturates 5g

15 MINS   20 MINS

SERVES 4

INGREDIENTS

2 bulbs garlic

6 tbsp olive oil

1 small onion, finely chopped

2 tbsp lemon juice

3 tbsp sesame seed paste (tahini)

2 tbsp chopped parsley

salt and pepper

TO SERVE

fresh vegetable crudités

French bread or warmed pita breads

2 When they are cool enough to handle, peel the garlic cloves and then chop them finely.

3 Heat the olive oil in a pan or skillet and add the garlic and onion. Cook over low heat, stirring occasionally, for 8–10 minutes, until softened. Remove the pan from the heat.

4 Mix in the lemon juice, sesame seed paste, and parsley. Season to taste with salt and pepper. Transfer to a small heatproof bowl and keep warm at one side of the barbecue.

5 Serve with fresh vegetable crudités, chunks of French bread or warm pita breads.

1 Separate the bulbs of garlic into individual cloves. Place them on a cookie sheet and roast in a preheated oven, 400°F/200°C, for 8–10 minutes. Set aside to cool for a few minutes.

VARIATION

If you come across smoked garlic, use it in this recipe—it tastes wonderful. There is no need to roast the smoked garlic, so omit the first step. This dip can also be used to baste kabobs and vegetarian burgers.

Mixed Bean Pâté

This is a really quick appetizer to prepare if canned beans are used. Choose a wide variety of beans for color and flavor.

NUTRITIONAL INFORMATION

Calories	126	Sugars	.........3g
Protein	.........5g	Fat	...........6g
Carbohydrate	...13g	Saturates	.......1g

45 MINS   0 MINS

SERVES 4

INGREDIENTS

14 oz/400 g canned mixed beans, drained

2 tbsp olive oil

juice of 1 lemon

2 garlic cloves, crushed

1 tbsp chopped cilantro

2 scallions, chopped

salt and pepper

shredded scallions, to garnish

1 Rinse the beans thoroughly under cold running water and drain well.

2 Transfer the beans to a food processor or blender and process until smooth. Alternatively, place the beans in a bowl and mash thoroughly with a fork or potato masher.

3 Add the olive oil, lemon juice, garlic, cilantro and scallions and blend until fairly smooth. Season with salt and pepper to taste.

4 Transfer the pâté to a serving bowl and chill in the refrigerator for at least 30 minutes.

5 Garnish with shredded scallions and serve.

Spanish Tortilla

This classic Spanish dish is often served as part of a tapas (appetizer) selection. A variety of cooked vegetables can be added to this recipe.

NUTRITIONAL INFORMATION

Calories 430	Sugars 6g
Protein 16g	Fat 20g
Carbohydrate ...50g	Saturates 4g

10 MINS   35 MINS

SERVES 4

I N G R E D I E N T S

2 lb 4 oz/1 kg waxy potatoes, thinly sliced

4 tbsp vegetable oil

1 onion, sliced

2 garlic cloves, crushed

1 green bell pepper, seeded and diced

2 tomatoes, seeded and chopped

1 tbsp drained canned corn

6 large eggs, beaten

2 tbsp chopped parsley

salt and pepper

1 Parboil the potatoes in a pan of lightly salted boiling water for 5 minutes. Drain well.

2 Heat the oil in a large skillet, then add the potato and onions and sauté over a low heat, stirring constantly,

for 5 minutes, until the potatoes have browned.

3 Add the garlic, diced bell pepper, chopped tomatoes, and corn, and mix together well.

4 Pour in the eggs and add the chopped parsley. Season well with salt and pepper. Cook for 10-12 minutes, until the underside is cooked through.

5 Remove the skillet from the heat and continue to cook the tortilla under a preheated medium broiler for 5-7 minutes, until the tortilla is set and the top is golden brown.

6 Cut the tortilla into wedges or cubes, depending on your preference, and transfer to serving dishes. Serve with salad. In Spain tortillas are served hot, cold, or warm.

COOK'S TIP

Ensure that the handle of your pan is heatproof before placing it under the broiler and be sure to use an oven glove when removing it as it will be very hot.

Hyderabad Pickles

This is a very versatile dish that will go with almost anything and can be served warm or cold. It is perfect as an appetizer for a dinner party.

NUTRITIONAL INFORMATION

Calories ....732 Sugars 6g
Protein ....6g Fat 75g
Carbohydrate ....8g Saturates 10g

30 MINS   30 MINS

SERVES 6

INGREDIENTS

2 tsp ground coriander

2 tsp ground cumin

2 tsp dry unsweetened coconut

2 tsp sesame seeds

1 tsp mixed mustard and onion seeds

1¼ cups vegetable oil

3 medium onions, sliced

1 tsp finely chopped fresh gingerroot

1 tsp crushed garlic

½ tsp turmeric

1½ tsp chili powder

1½ tsp salt

3 medium eggplants, halved lengthwise

1 tbsp tamarind paste

1¼ cups water

3 hard-cooked eggs, halved, to garnish

BAGHAAR

1 tsp mixed onion and mustard seeds

1 tsp cumin seeds

4 dried red chiles

⅔ cup vegetable oil

cilantro leaves

1 green chile, finely chopped

1 Dry-fry the ground coriander, cumin, coconut, sesame seeds, and mustard and onion seeds in a pan. Grind in a pestle and mortar or food processor and set aside.

2 Heat the oil in a skillet and cook the onions until golden. Reduce the heat and add the ginger, garlic, turmeric, chili powder, and salt, stirring. Leave to cool, then grind this mixture to form a paste.

3 Make 4 cuts across each eggplant half. Blend the spices with the onion paste. Spoon this mixture into the slits in the eggplants.

4 In a bowl, mix the tamarind paste and 3 tablespoons water to make a fine paste and set aside.

5 For the baghaar, cook the onion and mustard seeds, cumin seed, and dried chiles in the oil. Reduce the heat, then place the eggplants in the baghaar and stir gently. Stir in the tamarind paste and remaining water and cook over medium heat for 15–20 minutes. Add the cilantro and green chile.

6 When cool, transfer to a serving dish and serve garnished with the hard-cooked eggs.

Hummus & Garlic Toasts

Home-made hummus, spread on these flavorsome garlic toasts, is a real favorite for a delicious appetizer or snack.

NUTRITIONAL INFORMATION

Calories	731	Sugars	.........2g
Protein	........22g	Fat	..........55g
Carbohydrate	...39g	Saturates	.......8g

20 MINS   3 MINS

SERVES 4

INGREDIENTS

HUMMUS

14 oz/400 g canned chickpeas

juice of 1 large lemon

6 tbsp sesame seed paste (tahini)

2 tbsp olive oil

2 garlic cloves, crushed

salt and pepper

chopped cilantro and black olives,
   to garnish

TOASTS

1 ciabatta loaf (Italian bread), sliced

2 garlic cloves, crushed

1 tbsp chopped cilantro

4 tbsp olive oil

COOK'S TIP

Make the hummus 1 day in advance, and chill, covered, in the refrigerator until required. Garnish and serve.

  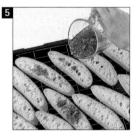

1 To make the hummus, firstly drain the chickpeas, reserving a little of the liquid. Put the chickpeas and a little of the liquid in a food processor and process, gradually adding the remaining liquid and the lemon juice. Blend well after each addition until smooth.

2 Stir in the sesame seed paste and all but 1 teaspoon of the olive oil. Add the garlic, then season to taste and blend again until smooth.

3 Spoon the hummus into a serving dish and smooth the top. Drizzle the

remaining olive oil over the top, then garnish with chopped cilantro and olives. Set aside in the refrigerator to chill while you are preparing the toasts.

4 Place the slices of ciabatta (Italian bread) on a broiler rack, spread out in a single layer.

5 Mix the garlic, cilantro, and olive oil together and drizzle over the bread slices. Cook under a hot broiler, turning once, for 2–3 minutes, until golden brown. Serve the toasts immediately, together with the hummus.

Fiery Salsa

Make this Mexican-style salsa to perk up jaded palates. Its lively flavors really get the taste buds going. Serve with hot tortilla chips.

NUTRITIONAL INFORMATION

Calories	328	Sugars	........2g
Protein	.........4g	Fat	..........26g
Carbohydrate	...21g	Saturates	.......5g

🕒 30 MINS   🕐 0 MINS

SERVES 4

I N G R E D I E N T S

2 small fresh red chiles

1 tbsp lime or lemon juice

2 large ripe avocados

2-inch/5-cm piece of cucumber

2 tomatoes, peeled

1 small garlic clove, crushed

few drops of Tabasco sauce

salt and pepper

lime or lemon slices, to garnish

tortilla chips, to serve

1 Remove and discard the stem and seeds from 1 fresh red chile. Chop the flesh very finely and place in a large mixing bowl.

2 To make a chile "flower" for garnish, using a small, sharp knife, slice the remaining chile from the stem to the tip several times without removing the stem. Place in a bowl of iced water, so that the "petals" open out.

3 Add the lime juice to the mixing bowl. Halve and pit, then peel the avocados. Add the flesh to the mixing bowl and mash thoroughly with a fork. The salsa should be slightly chunky. (The lime juice prevents the avocado from turning brown.)

4 Chop the cucumber and tomatoes finely and add to the avocado mixture with the crushed garlic.

5 Stir in the Tabasco sauce and season with salt and pepper. Transfer the dip to a serving bowl. Garnish with slices of lime and the chile flower.

6 Put the bowl on a large plate and surround with tortilla chips, then serve. Do not keep this dip standing for long, or it will discolor.

Spring Rolls

Thin slices of vegetables are wrapped in pastry and deep-fried until crisp. Spring roll skins are available fresh or frozen.

NUTRITIONAL INFORMATION

Calories	186	Sugars	.........2g
Protein	.........4g	Fat	...........11g
Carbohydrate	...18g	Saturates	.......1g

45 MINS   25-30 MINS

MAKES 12

INGREDIENTS

5 Chinese dried mushrooms (if unavailable,
    use open-cup mushrooms)

1 large carrot

½ cup canned bamboo shoots

2 scallions

2 oz/55 g Napa cabbage

2 tbsp vegetable oil

1½ cups bean sprouts

1 tbsp soy sauce

12 spring roll skins

1 egg, beaten

vegetable oil, for deep-frying

salt

1 Place the dried mushrooms in a small bowl and cover with warm water. Leave to soak for 20–25 minutes.

2 Drain the mushrooms and squeeze out the excess water. Remove the tough centers and slice the mushroom caps thinly. Cut the carrot and bamboo shoots into very thin julienne strips. Chop the scallions and shred the Napa cabbage.

3 Heat the 2 tablespoons of oil in a wok. Add the mushrooms, carrot, and bamboo shoots and stir-fry for 2 minutes. Add the scallions, Napa cabbage, bean sprouts, and soy sauce. Season with salt and stir-fry for 2 minutes. Leave to cool.

4 Divide the mixture into 12 equal portions and place one portion on the edge of each spring roll skin. Fold in the sides and roll each one up, brushing the join with a little beaten egg to seal.

5 Deep-fry the spring rolls in batches in hot oil in a wok or large pan for 4–5 minutes, until golden and crispy. Take care that the oil is not too hot, or the spring rolls will brown on the outside before cooking on the inside. Remove and drain on paper towels. Keep each batch warm while the others are being cooked. Serve at once.

COOK'S TIP

If spring roll skins are unavailable, use sheets of phyllo pastry instead.

Toasted Nibbles

These tiny cheese balls are rolled in fresh herbs, toasted nuts, or paprika to make tasty nibbles for parties, buffets, or predinner drinks.

NUTRITIONAL INFORMATION

Calories 310   Sugars 1g
Protein . . . . .15g   Fat 27g
Carbohydrate . . . .1g   Saturates 12g

40 MINS   5 MINS

SERVES 4

INGREDIENTS

½ cup ricotta cheese

1 cup finely grated brick cheese

2 tsp chopped parsley

½ cup chopped mixed nuts

3 tbsp chopped herbs, such as parsley,
    chives, marjoram, lovage, and chervil

2 tbsp mild paprika

pepper

herb sprigs, to garnish

1 Mix together the ricotta and brick cheeses. Add the parsley and pepper and work together until thoroughly combined.

2 Form the mixture into small balls and place on a plate. Cover and chill in the refrigerator for 20 minutes, until they are firm.

3 Scatter the chopped nuts onto a cookie sheet and place them under a preheated broiler until lightly browned. Take care as they can easily burn. Leave them to cool.

4 Sprinkle the nuts, herbs, and paprika into 3 separate small bowls. Remove the cheese balls from the refrigerator and

divide them into 3 equal piles. Roll 1 quantity of the cheese balls in the nuts, 1 quantity in the herbs, and 1 quantity in the paprika, turning them to make sure they are all well coated.

5 Arrange the coated cheese balls alternately on a large serving platter. Chill in the refrigerator until ready to serve and then garnish with sprigs of fresh herbs.

Cauliflower Roulade

A light-as-air mixture of eggs and vegetables produces a stylish vegetarian dish that can be enjoyed hot or cold.

NUTRITIONAL INFORMATION

Calories 271   Sugars 4g
Protein . . . . .15g   Fat 20g
Carbohydrate . . . .7g   Saturates 11g

30 MINS   40 MINS

SERVES 6

INGREDIENTS

1 small cauliflower, divided into florets

4 eggs, separated

generous ¾ cup grated Cheddar cheese

¼ cup cottage cheese

pinch of grated nutmeg

½ tsp mustard powder

salt and pepper

FILLING

1 bunch watercress or arugula, trimmed

¼ cup butter

scant ¼ cup flour

¾ cup plain yogurt

¼ cup grated Cheddar cheese

¼ cup cottage cheese

1 Line a jelly roll pan with baking parchment.

2 Steam the cauliflower until just tender, then drain under cold water. Process the cauliflower in a food processor or chop and press through a strainer.

3 Beat the egg yolks, then stir in the cauliflower, ½ cup of the Cheddar and the cottage cheese. Season with nutmeg, mustard, and salt and pepper. Whisk the egg whites until stiff but not dry, then fold them in.

4 Spread the mixture evenly in the pan. Bake in a preheated oven, 375°F/ 190°C, for 20-25 minutes, until risen and golden.

5 Chop the watercress, reserving a few sprigs for garnish. Melt the butter in a small pan. Cook the watercress, stirring, for 3 minutes, until wilted. Blend in the flour, then stir in the yogurt and simmer for 2 minutes. Stir in the cheeses.

6 Turn out the roulade on to a damp dish cloth covered with baking parchment. Peel off the paper and leave for a minute to let the steam escape. Roll up the roulade, including a new sheet of paper, starting from one narrow end.

7 Unroll the roulade, spread the filling to within 1 inch/2.5 cm of the edges, and roll up. Transfer to a cookie sheet, then sprinkle with the remaining Cheddar and return to the oven for 5 minutes. Serve immediately if serving hot, or leave to cool completely.

Mini Vegetable Puffs

These are ideal with a more formal meal, as they take a little time to prepare and look really impressive.

NUTRITIONAL INFORMATION

Calories 649   Sugars 3g
Protein ....9g   Fat 45g
Carbohydrate ...57g   Saturates 18g

15 MINS   35 MINS

SERVES 4

INGREDIENTS

1 lb/450 g puff pastry, thawed if frozen

1 egg, beaten

FILLING

8 oz/225 g sweet potato, cubed

3½ oz/100 g baby asparagus spears

2 tbsp butter or margarine

1 leek, sliced

2 small open-cup mushrooms, sliced

1 tsp lime juice

1 tsp chopped thyme

pinch of dried mustard

salt and pepper

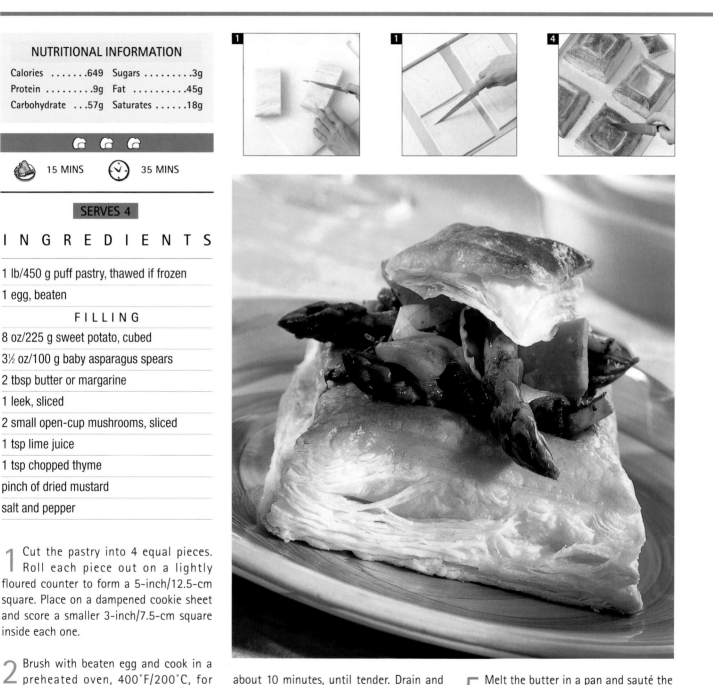

1 Cut the pastry into 4 equal pieces. Roll each piece out on a lightly floured counter to form a 5-inch/12.5-cm square. Place on a dampened cookie sheet and score a smaller 3-inch/7.5-cm square inside each one.

2 Brush with beaten egg and cook in a preheated oven, 400°F/200°C, for 20 minutes, until risen and golden brown.

3 Meanwhile, to make the filling, cook the sweet potato in a pan of boiling water for 15 minutes, until tender. Drain well and set aside. Meanwhile, blanch the asparagus in a pan of boiling water for about 10 minutes, until tender. Drain and reserve.

4 Remove the pastry squares from the oven, then carefully cut out the central square of pastry with a sharp knife. Lift out and reserve.

5 Melt the butter in a pan and sauté the leek and mushrooms for 2–3 minutes. Add the lime juice, thyme, and mustard, season well and stir in the sweet potatoes and asparagus. Spoon the mixture into the pastry cases, then top with the reserved pastry squares and serve.

Vegetable & Nut Samosas

These delicious little fried pastries are really quite simple to make. Serve them hot or cold as a appetizer to an Indian meal.

NUTRITIONAL INFORMATION

Calories	343	Sugars	.........2g
Protein	.........5g	Fat	..........26g
Carbohydrate	...24g	Saturates	.......5g

🥔 🥔 🥔

🥔 30 MINS　　🕒 40 MINS

MAKES 12

INGREDIENTS

12 oz/350 g potatoes, diced

salt

generous 1 cup frozen peas

3 tbsp vegetable oil

1 onion, chopped

1-inch/2.5-cm fresh gingerroot, chopped

1 garlic clove, crushed

1 tsp garam masala

2 tsp mild curry paste

½ tsp cumin seeds

2 tsp lemon juice

generous ⅓ cup unsalted cashews,
　coarsely chopped

vegetable oil, for shallow frying

cilantro sprigs, to garnish

mango chutney, to serve

PASTRY

1½ cups all-purpose flour

¼ cup butter

6 tbsp warm milk

1 Cook the potatoes in a pan of boiling, salted water for 5 minutes. Add the peas and cook for an additional 4 minutes, until the potatoes are tender. Drain well. Heat the oil in a skillet and cook the onion, potato and pea mixture, ginger, garlic, and spices for 2 minutes. Stir in the lemon juice and cook gently, uncovered, for 2 minutes. Remove from the heat and slightly mash the potato and peas. Add the cashews, then mix well and season with salt.

2 To make the pastry, put the flour in a bowl and rub in the butter. Mix in the milk to form a dough. Knead lightly and divide into 6 portions. Form each into a ball and roll out to an 7-inch/18-cm round. Cut each one in half.

3 Divide the filling equally between the semicircles of pastry, spreading it out to within ¼ inch/5 mm of the edges. Brush the edges of pastry all the way round with water and fold over to form triangular shapes, sealing the edges well together to enclose the filling completely.

4 Heat the vegetable oil in a skillet to 350°F/180°C, until a cube of bread browns in 30 seconds. Deep-fry the samosas, a few at a time, turning frequently until golden brown and heated through. Drain on paper towels and keep warm while cooking the remainder. Garnish with cilantro sprigs and serve hot with mango chutney.

Onions à la Grecque

This is a well-known method of cooking vegetables and is perfect with shallots or onions, served with a crisp salad.

NUTRITIONAL INFORMATION

Calories	 200	Sugars	.... 26g
Protein	.... 2g	Fat	.... 9g
Carbohydrate	... 28g	Saturates	.... 1g

10 MINS   15 MINS

SERVES 4

INGREDIENTS

1 lb/450 g shallots

3 tbsp olive oil

3 tbsp clear honey

2 tbsp garlic wine vinegar

3 tbsp dry white wine

1 tbsp tomato paste

2 celery stalks, sliced

2 tomatoes, seeded and chopped

salt and pepper

chopped celery leaves, to garnish

1 Peel the shallots. Heat the oil in a large pan, then add the shallots and cook, stirring, for 3–5 minutes, until they begin to brown.

2 Add the honey and cook over high heat for an additional 30 seconds, then add the garlic wine vinegar and dry white wine, stirring well.

3 Stir in the tomato paste, celery, and tomatoes and bring the mixture to a boil. Cook over high heat for 5–6 minutes. Season to taste and leave to cool slightly.

4 Garnish with chopped celery leaves and serve warm. Alternatively chill in the refrigerator before serving.

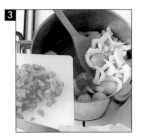

Garlicky Mushroom Pakoras

Whole mushrooms are dunked in a spiced garlicky batter and deep-fried until golden. They are at their most delicious served piping hot.

NUTRITIONAL INFORMATION

Calories 297	Sugars 3g	
Protein 5g	Fat 21g	
Carbohydrate . . .24g	Saturates 2g	

🍲 20 MINS   🕐 10–15 MINS

SERVES 6

I N G R E D I E N T S

generous 1 cup gram (chickpea) flour

½ tsp salt

¼ tsp baking powder

1 tsp cumin seeds

½–1 tsp chili powder

generous ¾ cup water

2 garlic cloves, crushed

1 small onion, finely chopped

vegetable oil, for deep-frying

1 lb 2 oz/500 g white mushrooms,
 trimmed and wiped

lemon wedges and cilantro
 sprigs, to garnish

COOK'S TIP

Gram flour, also known as besan flour, is a pale yellow flour made from chickpeas. It is now readily available from larger supermarkets, as well as Indian food shops and some ethnic delicatessens. Gram flour is also used to make onion bhajis.

1 Put the gram flour, salt, baking powder, cumin, and chili powder into a bowl and mix well together. Make a well in the center of the mixture and gradually stir in the water, mixing thoroughly to form a batter.

2 Stir the crushed garlic and the chopped onion into the batter and leave the mixture to infuse for 10 minutes. One-third fill a deep-fat fryer or pan with vegetable oil and heat to 350°F/180°C, or until a cube of bread browns in 30 seconds. Lower the basket into the hot oil.

3 Meanwhile, mix the mushrooms into the batter, stirring to coat. Remove a few at a time and place them into the hot oil. Fry for 2 minutes, until golden brown.

4 Remove the mushrooms from the pan with a slotted spoon and drain on paper towels while you are cooking the remainder in the same way.

5 Serve hot, sprinkled with coarse salt and garnished with lemon wedges and cilantro sprigs.

Cheese, Garlic & Herb Pâté

This wonderful soft cheese pâté is fragrant with the aroma of herbs and garlic. Serve with triangles of Melba toast for a perfect appetizer.

20 MINS   10 MINS

SERVES 4

INGREDIENTS

1 tbsp butter

1 garlic clove, crushed

3 scallions, finely chopped

generous ½ cup full-fat soft cheese

2 tbsp chopped mixed herbs,
    such as parsley, chives, marjoram,
    oregano, and basil

1½ cups finely grated sharp
    Cheddar cheese

pepper

4–6 slices of white bread from a
    medium-cut sliced loaf

mixed salad greens and cherry
    tomatoes, to serve

TO GARNISH

ground paprika

herb sprigs

1 Melt the butter in a small skillet and gently cook the garlic and scallions together for 3–4 minutes, until softened. Leave to cool.

2 Beat the soft cheese in a large mixing bowl until smooth, then add the garlic and scallions. Stir in the herbs and mix together well.

3 Add the Cheddar and work the mixture together to form a stiff paste. Cover and chill until ready to serve.

4 To make the Melba toast, toast the slices of bread on both sides, and then cut off the crusts. Using a sharp bread knife, cut through the slices horizontally to make very thin slices. Cut into triangles and then lightly broil the untoasted sides until golden.

5 Arrange the mixed salad greens on 4 serving plates with the cherry tomatoes. Pile the cheese pâté on top and sprinkle with a little paprika. Garnish with sprigs of fresh herbs and serve with the Melba toast.

Tzatziki & Black Olive Dip

Tzatziki is a Greek dish, made with yogurt, mint, and cucumber.
It tastes superb with warm pita bread.

NUTRITIONAL INFORMATION

Calories 381	Sugars 8g	
Protein 11g	Fat 15g	
Carbohydrate . . .52g	Saturates 2g	

1 HOUR   3 MINS

SERVES 4

I N G R E D I E N T S

½ cucumber

1 cup thick plain yogurt

1 tbsp chopped mint

salt and pepper

4 pita breads

D I P

2 garlic cloves, crushed

⅔ cup pitted black olives

4 tbsp olive oil

2 tbsp lemon juice

1 tbsp chopped parsley

T O   G A R N I S H

mint sprigs

parsley sprigs

COOK'S TIP

Sprinkling the cucumber
with salt draws out some of its
moisture, making it crisper. If
you are in a hurry, you can omit
this procedure. Use green olives
instead of black ones if you prefer.

1 To make the tzatziki, peel the cucumber and chop coarsely. Sprinkle it with salt and leave to stand for 15–20 minutes. Rinse with cold water and drain well.

2 Mix the cucumber, yogurt, and mint together. Season to taste with salt and pepper and transfer to a serving bowl. Cover and chill for 20–30 minutes.

3 To make the black olive dip, put the crushed garlic and olives into a blender or food processor and process for 15–20 seconds. Alternatively, chop them very finely.

4 Add the olive oil, lemon juice, and parsley to the blender or food processor and process for a few more seconds. Alternatively, mix with the chopped garlic and olives and mash together. Season with salt and pepper.

5 Wrap the pita breads in foil and place over a grill for 2–3 minutes, turning once to warm through. Alternatively, heat in the oven or under the broiler. Cut into pieces and serve with the tzatziki and black olive dip, garnished with sprigs of fresh mint and parsley.

Soft Dumplings in Yogurt

These are very light and make a good summer afternoon snack, as well as a good appetizer to any vegetarian meal.

NUTRITIONAL INFORMATION

Calories 476	Sugars 29g
Protein 11g	Fat 21g
Carbohydrate ...64g	Saturates 3g

15 MINS   20 MINS

SERVES 4

INGREDIENTS

1⅓ cups urid dhal powder

1 tsp baking powder

½ tsp ground ginger

1¼ cups water

oil, for deep-frying

scant 1¾ cups plain yogurt

5 tbsp sugar

MASALA

6 tbsp ground coriander

6 tbsp ground white cumin

1 oz/25 g crushed red chiles

½ cup citric acid

chopped fresh red chiles, to garnish

1 Place the powdered urid dhal in a large mixing bowl. Add the baking powder and ginger and stir to combine. Add the water and mix to form a paste.

2 Heat the oil in a deep pan. Pour in the batter, 1 teaspoon at a time, and deep-fry the dumplings until golden brown, lowering the heat when the oil gets too hot. Set the dumplings aside.

3 Place the yogurt in a separate bowl. Add scant 1¾ cups water and the

sugar and mix together with a whisk or fork. Set aside.

4 To make the masala, roast the ground coriander and the white cumin in a pan until a little darker in color and giving off their aroma. Grind coarsely in a food processor or in a mortar with a pestle. Add

the crushed red chiles and citric acid and blend well together.

5 Sprinkle about 1 tablespoon of the masala over the dumplings and store the remainder in an airtight jar for future use. Garnish with chopped red chiles. Serve with the reserved yogurt mixture.

Buttered Nut & Lentil Dip

This tasty dip is very easy to make. It is perfect to have at barbecues, as it gives your guests something to nibble while they are waiting.

NUTRITIONAL INFORMATION

Calories	395	Sugars	.........4g
Protein	........12g	Fat	..........31g
Carbohydrate	...18g	Saturates	......10g

5-10 MINS   40 MINS

SERVES 4

INGREDIENTS

¼ cup butter

1 small onion, chopped

generous ⅓ cup red lentils

1¼ cups vegetable stock

⅓ cup blanched almonds

⅓ cup pine nuts

½ tsp ground coriander

½ tsp ground cumin

½ tsp grated fresh gingerroot

1 tsp chopped fresh cilantro

salt and pepper

sprigs of fresh cilantro, to garnish

TO SERVE

fresh vegetable crudités

bread sticks

VARIATION

Green or brown lentils can be used, but they will take longer to cook than red lentils. If you wish, substitute peanuts for the almonds. Ground ginger can be used instead of fresh—substitute ½ teaspoon and add it with the other spices.

1 Melt half the butter in a pan and fry the onion over medium heat, stirring frequently, until golden brown.

2 Add the lentils and vegetable stock. Bring to a boil, then reduce the heat and simmer gently, uncovered, for 25–30 minutes, until the lentils are tender. Drain well.

3 Melt the remaining butter in a small skillet. Add the almonds and pine nuts and fry them over low heat, stirring frequently, until golden brown. Remove from the heat.

4 Put the lentils, almonds, and pine nuts, with any remaining butter, into a food processor blender. Add the ground coriander, cumin, ginger, and fresh cilantro. Process for 15–20 seconds, until the mixture is smooth. Alternatively, press the lentils through a strainer to purée them and then mix with the finely chopped nuts, spices, and herbs.

5 Season the dip with salt and pepper and garnish with sprigs of fresh cilantro. Serve with fresh vegetable crudités and bread sticks.

Pakoras

Pakoras are eaten all over India. They are made in many different ways and with a variety of fillings. Sometimes they are served in yogurt.

NUTRITIONAL INFORMATION

Calories 331   Sugars 5g
Protein . . . . .9g   Fat 22g
Carbohydrate . . .27g   Saturates 3g

15 MINS   15–20 MINS

SERVES 4

INGREDIENTS

6 tbsp gram (chickpea) flour

½ tsp salt

1 tsp chili powder

1 tsp baking powder

1½ tsp white cumin seeds

1 tsp pomegranate seeds

1¼ cups water

fresh cilantro leaves, finely chopped

vegetables of your choice: cauliflower, cut
    into small florets; onions, cut into rings;
    potatoes, sliced; eggplants,
    sliced; or fresh spinach leaves

oil, for deep-frying

1 Sift the gram flour into a large mixing bowl. Add the salt, chili powder, baking powder, cumin, and pomegranate seeds and blend together well. Pour in the water and beat thoroughly to form a smooth batter.

2 Add the cilantro and mix. Set the batter aside.

3 Dip the prepared vegetables of your choice into the batter, carefully shaking off any of the excess batter.

4 Heat the oil in a large heavy-bottom pan. Place the battered vegetables of your choice in the oil and deep-fry, in batches, turning once.

5 Repeat this process until all of the batter has been used up.

6 Transfer the battered vegetables to paper towels and drain thoroughly. Serve immediately.

COOK'S TIP

When deep-frying, it is important to use oil at the correct temperature. If the oil is too hot, the outside of the food will burn, as will the spices, before the inside is cooked. If the oil is too cool, the food will be sodden with oil before a crisp batter forms.

Snacks & Light Meals

The ability to rustle up a simple snack or a quickly prepared light meal can be very important in our busy lives. Sometimes we may not feel like eating a full-scale

meal but nevertheless want something appetizing and satisfying. Or if lunch or dinner is going to be served very late, then we may want something to tide us over and stave off those hunger pangs! Whether it is for a sustaining snack to break the day, hearty nibbles to serve with predinner drinks, or an informal lunch or supper party, you'll find a mouthwatering collection of recipes in this chapter.

Roasted Vegetables

Roasted vegetables are delicious and attractive. Served on warm muffins with a herb sauce, they are unbeatable.

NUTRITIONAL INFORMATION

Calories	509	Sugars	........12g
Protein	........15g	Fat	.........28g
Carbohydrate	...50g	Saturates	......12g

1¼ HOURS   30 MINS

SERVES 4

INGREDIENTS

1 red onion, cut into 8 pieces

1 eggplant, halved and sliced

1 yellow bell pepper, seeded and sliced

1 zucchini, sliced

4 tbsp olive oil

1 tbsp garlic vinegar

2 tbsp vermouth

2 garlic cloves, crushed

1 tbsp chopped thyme

2 tsp light brown sugar

4 English muffins, halved

salt and pepper

SAUCE

2 tbsp butter

1 tbsp flour

⅔ cup milk

scant ⅓ cup vegetable stock

¾ cup grated Cheddar cheese

1 tsp whole-grain mustard

3 tbsp chopped mixed herbs

1 Arrange the vegetables in a shallow ovenproof dish. Mix together the oil, vinegar, vermouth, garlic, thyme, and sugar and pour over the vegetables. Set aside to marinate for 1 hour.

2 Transfer the vegetables to a cookie sheet. Cook in a preheated oven, 400°F/200°C, for 20–25 minutes, until the vegetables have softened and become tender.

3 Meanwhile, make the sauce. Melt the butter in a small pan and add the flour. Cook for 1 minute, stirring constantly, and then remove from the heat. Gradually, stir in the milk and stock and return the pan to the heat. Bring to the boil, stirring constantly, until thickened. Stir in the cheese, mustard, and mixed herbs, then season to taste with salt and pepper.

4 Preheat the broiler to high. Cut the muffins in half and broil for 2–3 minutes, until golden brown, then remove and arrange on a serving plate.

5 Spoon the roasted vegetables onto the muffins and pour the sauce over the top. Serve immediately.

Falafel

These are a very tasty, well-known Middle Eastern dish of small chickpea-based balls, spiced and deep-fried.

NUTRITIONAL INFORMATION

Calories 491   Sugars 3g
Protein . . . . .15g   Fat 30g
Carbohydrate . . .43g   Saturates 3g

25 MINS   10–15 MINS

SERVES 4

I N G R E D I E N T S

1 lb 8 oz/675 g canned chickpeas, drained

1 red onion, chopped

3 garlic cloves, crushed

3½ oz/100 g whole-wheat bread

2 small fresh red chiles

1 tsp ground cumin

1 tsp ground coriander

½ tsp turmeric

1 tbsp chopped cilantro, plus
   extra to garnish

1 egg, beaten

2 cups whole-wheat bread crumbs

vegetable oil, for deep-frying

salt and pepper

tomato and cucumber salad
   and lemon wedges, to serve

1 Put the chickpea, onion, garlic, bread, chiles, spices, and cilantro in a food processor and process for 30 seconds. Stir and season to taste with salt and pepper.

2 Remove the falafel mixture from the food processor and shape into walnut-sized balls.

3 Place the beaten egg in a shallow bowl and place the whole-wheat bread crumbs on a plate. Dip the balls first into the egg to coat and then roll them in the bread crumbs, shaking off any excess.

4 Heat the oil for deep-frying to 350°F/180°C, or until a cube of bread browns in 30 seconds. Fry the falafel, in batches if necessary, for 2–3 minutes, until crisp and browned. Remove from the oil with a slotted spoon and dry on absorbent paper towels. Garnish with chopped cilantro and serve with a tomato and cucumber salad and lemon wedges.

Potato Fritters with Relish

These are incredibly simple to make and sure to be popular served as a tempting snack or as an accompaniment to almost any Indian meal.

NUTRITIONAL INFORMATION

Calories	294	Sugars	........4g
Protein	.........4g	Fat	..........24g
Carbohydrate	...18g	Saturates	.......3g

40 MINS   15 MINS

SERVES 8

INGREDIENTS

generous ⅓ cup whole-wheat flour

½ tsp ground coriander

½ tsp cumin seeds

¼ tsp chili powder

½ tsp ground turmeric

¼ tsp salt

1 egg

3 tbsp milk

12 oz/350 g potatoes, peeled

1–2 garlic cloves, crushed

4 scallions, chopped

½ cup corn kernels

vegetable oil, for shallow frying

ONION & TOMATO RELISH

1 onion, peeled

8 oz/225 g tomatoes

2 tbsp chopped cilantro

2 tbsp chopped mint

2 tbsp lemon juice

½ tsp roasted cumin seeds

¼ tsp salt

pinch of cayenne pepper

1 First make the relish. Cut the onion and tomatoes into small dice and place in a bowl with the remaining ingredients. Mix together well and let stand for at least 15 minutes before serving to leave time for the flavors to blend.

2 Place the flour in a bowl, then stir in the spices and salt and make a well in the center. Add the egg and milk and mix to form a fairly thick batter.

3 Coarsely grate the potatoes, then place in a strainer and rinse well under cold running water. Drain and squeeze dry, then stir into the batter with the garlic, scallions, and corn.

4 Heat about ¼ inch/5 mm vegetable oil in a large skillet and add a few tablespoonfuls of the mixture at a time, flattening each one to form a thin cake. Cook over low heat, turning frequently, for 2-3 minutes, until golden brown and cooked through.

5 Drain on paper towels and keep hot while cooking the remaining mixture in the same way. Serve hot with the onion and tomato relish.

Mixed Bean Pan-Fry

Fresh green beans have a wonderful flavor that is hard to beat.
If you cannot find fresh beans, use thawed, frozen beans instead.

NUTRITIONAL INFORMATION

Calories 179	Sugars 4g	
Protein 10g	Fat 11g	
Carbohydrate ...10g	Saturates 1g	

10 MINS   15 MINS

SERVES 4

INGREDIENTS

4 cups mixed green beans, such as
   green and fava beans, podded

2 tbsp vegetable oil

2 garlic cloves, crushed

1 red onion, halved and sliced

8 oz/225 g firm marinated tofu, diced

1 tbsp lemon juice

½ tsp turmeric

1 tsp ground mixed spice

⅔ cup vegetable stock

2 tsp sesame seeds

1 Trim and chop the green beans and set aside until required.

2 Heat the oil in a medium skillet. Add the garlic and onion and sauté, stirring frequently, over low heat for 2 minutes.

3 Add the tofu and cook for 2–3 minutes, until just beginning to turn golden brown.

4 Add the green beans and fava beans. Stir in the lemon juice, turmeric, ground mixed spice, and vegetable stock and bring to a boil over medium heat.

5 Reduce the heat and simmer for 5–7 minutes, until the beans are tender. Sprinkle with sesame seeds and serve immediately.

VARIATION

Use smoked tofu instead of
marinated tofu for an alternative
and quite distinctive flavor.

Spinach Crêpes

Serve these crêpes as a light lunch or supper dish, with a tomato and basil salad for a dramatic color contrast.

NUTRITIONAL INFORMATION

Calories 663	Sugars 9g	
Protein 32g	Fat 48g	
Carbohydrate ...28g	Saturates 18g	

🥘 25 MINS   🕐 1¼ HOURS

SERVES 4

INGREDIENTS

scant ⅔ cup whole-wheat flour

1 egg

⅔ cup plain yogurt

3 tbsp water

1 tbsp vegetable oil, plus extra for brushing

7 oz/200 g frozen leaf spinach, thawed
  and puréed

pinch of grated nutmeg

salt and pepper

lemon wedges and fresh cilantro sprigs,
  to garnish

FILLING

1 tbsp vegetable oil

3 scallions, thinly sliced

1 cup ricotta cheese

4 tbsp plain yogurt

¾ cup grated Gruyère cheese

1 egg, lightly beaten

scant 1 cup unsalted cashew nuts

2 tbsp chopped parsley

pinch of cayenne pepper

1 Sift the flour and salt into a bowl and tip in any bran in the strainer. Beat together the egg, yogurt, water, and oil. Gradually pour it on to the flour, beating constantly. Stir in the spinach and season with pepper and nutmeg.

2 To make the filling, heat the oil in a pan and sauté the scallions until translucent. Remove with a slotted spoon and drain on paper towels. Beat together the ricotta, yogurt, and half the Gruyère. Beat in the egg and stir in the cashew nuts and parsley. Season with salt and cayenne.

3 Lightly brush a small, heavy skillet with oil and heat. Pour in 3–4 tablespoons of the crêpe batter and tilt the skillet so that it covers the base.

Cook for about 3 minutes, until bubbles appear in the center. Turn and cook the other side for about 2 minutes, until lightly browned. Slide the crêpe onto a warmed plate, then cover with foil and keep warm while you cook the remainder. The batter should make 8–12 pancakes.

4 Spread a little filling over each crêpe and fold in half and then half again, envelope-style. Spoon the remaining filling into the opening.

5 Grease a shallow, ovenproof dish and arrange the crêpes in a single layer. Sprinkle on the remaining cheese and cook in a preheated oven. 350°F/180°C, for 15 minutes. Serve hot, garnished with lemon wedges and cilantro sprigs.

Broiled Potatoes

This dish is ideal with broiled or grilled foods, as the potatoes themselves may be cooked by either method.

NUTRITIONAL INFORMATION

Calories 417   Sugars 1g
Protein . . . . .3g   Fat 37g
Carbohydrate . . .20g   Saturates 10g

15 MINS   20 MINS

SERVES 4

INGREDIENTS

1 lb/450 g potatoes, unpeeled and scrubbed

3 tbsp butter, melted

2 tbsp chopped thyme

paprika, for dusting

LIME MAYONNAISE

⅔ cup mayonnaise

2 tsp lime juice

finely grated rind of 1 lime

1 garlic clove, crushed

pinch of paprika

salt and pepper

1 Cut the potatoes into ½-inch/1-cm thick slices.

2 Cook the potatoes in a pan of boiling water for 5–7 minutes—they should still be quite firm. Remove the potatoes with a slotted spoon and drain thoroughly.

3 Line a broiler pan with kitchen foil. Arrange the potato slices on top of the foil, without overlapping.

4 Brush the potatoes with the melted butter and sprinkle the chopped thyme on top. Season to taste with salt and pepper.

5 Cook the potatoes under a preheated broiler at medium heat for 10 minutes, turning once.

6 Meanwhile, make the lime mayonnaise. Thoroughly combine the mayonnaise, lime juice, lime rind, garlic, paprika, and salt and pepper to taste in a small bowl.

7 Dust the hot potato slices with a little paprika and serve immediately with the lime mayonnaise.

COOK'S TIP

The lime mayonnaise may be spooned over the broiled potatoes to coat them just before serving, if you prefer.

Paprika Chips

These wafer-thin potato chops are great cooked over a grill and served with spicy vegetable kabobs.

NUTRITIONAL INFORMATION

Calories 149	Sugars 0.6g
Protein 2g	Fat 8g
Carbohydrate ...17g	Saturates 1g

5 MINS   7 MINS

SERVES 4

INGREDIENTS

2 large potatoes

3 tbsp olive oil

½ tsp paprika

salt

1 Using a sharp knife, slice the potatoes very thinly so that they are almost transparent. Drain the potato slices thoroughly and pat dry with paper towels.

2 Heat the oil in a large skillet and add the paprika, stirring constantly to ensure that the paprika doesn't catch and burn.

3 Add the potato slices to the skillet and cook them in a single layer for about 5 minutes, until the potato slices just begin to curl slightly at the edges.

VARIATION

You could use curry powder or any other spice to flavor the chips instead of the paprika, if you prefer.

4 Remove the potato slices from the pan using a slotted spoon and transfer them to paper towels to drain thoroughly.

5 Thread the potato slices on to several wooden kabob skewers.

6 Sprinkle the potato slices with a little salt and cook over a medium hot grill or under a medium broiler, turning frequently, for 10 minutes, until the potato slices begin to crispen. Sprinkle with a little more salt, if preferred, and serve immediately.

Cress & Cheese Tartlets

These individual tartlets are great for lunchtime or for picnic food.
Watercress is a good source of folic acid, important in early pregnancy.

NUTRITIONAL INFORMATION

Calories 410	Sugars 4g
Protein 15g	Fat 29g
Carbohydrate ...24g	Saturates 19g

20 MINS   25 MINS

SERVES 4

INGREDIENTS

⅔ cup all-purpose flour

pinch of salt

⅓ cup butter or margarine

2–3 tbsp cold water

2 bunches watercress or arugula

2 garlic cloves, crushed

1 shallot, chopped

scant 1½ cups grated Cheddar cheese

4 tbsp plain yogurt

½ tsp paprika

1 Sift the flour into a mixing bowl and add the salt. Rub ¼ cup of the butter into the flour until the mixture resembles bread crumbs.

2 Stir in enough of the cold water to make a smooth dough.

3 Roll the dough out on a lightly floured counter and use to line four 4-inch/10-cm tartlet pans. Prick the bases with a fork and leave to chill.

4 Heat the remaining butter in a skillet. Discard the stems from the watercress and add to the skillet with the garlic and shallot, cooking for 1–2 minutes, until the watercress has wilted.

5 Remove the skillet from the heat and stir in the grated cheese, yogurt, and paprika.

6 Spoon the mixture into the pastry cases and cook in a preheated oven, 350°F/180°C, for 20 minutes, until the filling is firm. Turn out the tartlets and serve immediately.

VARIATION

Use spinach instead of the watercress or arugula, making sure it is well drained before mixing with the remaining filling ingredients.

Lentils & Mixed Vegetables

The green lentils used in this recipe require soaking, but are worth it for the flavor. If time is short, you could use red split peas instead.

NUTRITIONAL INFORMATION

Calories 386	Sugars 16g	
Protein 12g	Fat 23g	
Carbohydrate ...35g	Saturates 12g	

45 MINS   40-45 MINS

SERVES 4

I N G R E D I E N T S

scant 1 cups green lentils

4 tbsp butter or margarine

2 garlic cloves, crushed

2 tbsp olive oil

1 tbsp cider vinegar

1 red onion, cut into 8

6 baby corn cobs,
    halved lengthwise

1 yellow bell pepper, seeded and
    cut into strips

1 red bell pepper, seeded and
    cut into strips

½ cup green beans, halved

½ cup vegetable stock

2 tbsp clear honey

salt and pepper

crusty bread, to serve

VARIATION

This pan-fry is very versatile:
you can use a mixture of your
favourite vegetables, if you prefer.
Try zucchini, carrots, or snow peas.

1 Soak the lentils in a large pan of cold water for 25 minutes. Bring to a boil, then reduce the heat and simmer for 20 minutes. Drain thoroughly.

2 Add 1 tablespoon of the butter, one crushed garlic clove, 1 tablespoon of the olive oil, and the vinegar to the lentils and mix well.

3 Melt the remaining butter and oil in a skillet and stir-fry the second crushed

garlic clove with the onion, corn cobs, bell peppers, and beans for 3–4 minutes.

4 Add the vegetable stock and bring to a boil. Boil for 10 minutes, until the liquid has evaporated.

5 Add the honey and season with salt and pepper to taste. Stir in the lentil mixture and cook for 1 minute to heat through. Spoon onto warmed serving plates and serve with crusty bread.

Creamy Mushroom & Potato

These oven-baked mushrooms are covered with a creamy potato and mushroom filling topped with melted cheese.

NUTRITIONAL INFORMATION

Calories 214	Sugars 1g	
Protein 5g	Fat 17g	
Carbohydrate 11g	Saturates 11g	

40 MINS   40 MINS

SERVES 4

INGREDIENTS

1 oz/25 g dried cèpes

8 oz/225 g mealy potatoes, diced

2 tbsp butter, melted

4 tbsp heavy cream

2 tbsp chopped fresh chives

⅔ cup vegetable stock

¼ cup grated Emmental cheese

8 large open-cup mushrooms

salt and pepper

fresh chives, to garnish

1 Place the dried cèpes in a small bowl. Add sufficient boiling water to cover and set aside to soak for 20 minutes.

2 Meanwhile, cook the potatoes in a medium pan of lightly salted boiling water for 10 minutes, until cooked through and tender. Drain well and mash until smooth.

3 Drain the soaked cèpes and then chop them finely. Mix them into the mashed potato.

4 Thoroughly blend the butter, cream, and chives together and pour the mixture into the cèpes and potato mixture, mixing well. Season to taste with salt and pepper.

5 Remove the stems from the open-cup mushrooms. Chop the stems and stir them into the potato mixture. Spoon the mixture into the open-cup mushrooms and sprinkle the grated Emmantal cheese over the top.

6 Arrange the filled mushrooms in a shallow ovenproof dish and pour in the vegetable stock.

7 Cover the dish and cook in a preheated oven, 425°F/220°C, for 20 minutes. Remove the lid and cook for 5 minutes, until golden.

8 Garnish the mushrooms with fresh chives and serve at once.

VARIATION

Use fresh mushrooms instead of the dried cèpes, if preferred, and stir a mixture of chopped nuts into the mushroom stuffing mixture for extra crunch.

Indian-Style Omelet

Omelets are very versatile: they go with almost anything and you can also serve them at any time of the day.

NUTRITIONAL INFORMATION

Calories 132	Sugars 1g	
Protein 7g	Fat 11g	
Carbohydrate 2g	Saturates 2g	

10 MINS   20 MINS

SERVES 4

I N G R E D I E N T S

1 small onion, very finely chopped

2 green chiles, finely chopped

cilantro leaves, finely chopped

4 medium eggs

1 tsp salt

2 tbsp oil

toasted bread or crisp green salad, to serve

1 Place the onion, chiles, and cilantro in a large mixing bowl. Mix together until well combined.

2 Place the eggs in a separate bowl and whisk together.

3 Add the onion mixture to the eggs and mix together.

COOK'S TIP

Indian cooks use a variety of vegetable oils, and peanut or corn oils make good alternatives for most dishes, although sometimes more specialist ones, such as coconut oil, mustard oil, and sesame oil, are called for.

4 Add the salt to the egg and onion mixture and whisk together well.

5 Heat 1 tablespoon of the oil in a large skillet. Place a ladleful of the omelet batter into the skillet.

6 Fry the omelet, turning once and pressing down with a flat spoon to make sure that the egg is cooked right through, until the omelet is a golden brown color.

7 Repeat the same process for the remaining batter. Set the omelets aside and keep warm while you make the remaining batches of omelets.

8 Serve the omelets immediately with toasted bread. Alternatively, simply serve the omelets with a crisp green salad for a light lunch.

Vegetable Samosas

These Indian snacks are perfect for a quick or light meal. Served with a salad they can be made in advance and frozen for ease.

NUTRITIONAL INFORMATION

Calories 291	Sugars 2g	
Protein 4g	Fat 23g	
Carbohydrate . . .18g	Saturates 3g	

🥙 🥙 🥙

20 MINS   30 MINS

MAKES 12

INGREDIENTS

FILLING

2 tbsp vegetable oil

1 onion, chopped

½ tsp ground coriander

½ tsp ground cumin

pinch of turmeric

½ tsp ground ginger

½ tsp garam masala

1 garlic clove, crushed

8 oz/225 g potatoes, diced

1 cup frozen peas, thawed

5½ oz/150 g spinach, chopped

PASTRY

12 sheets phyllo pastry

oil, for deep-frying

1 To make the filling, heat the oil in a skillet. Add the onion and sauté, stirring frequently, for 1–2 minutes, until softened. Stir in all of the spices and garlic and cook for 1 minute.

2 Add the potatoes and cook over low heat, stirring frequently, for 5 minutes, until they begin to soften.

3 Stir in the peas and spinach and cook for an additional 3–4 minutes.

4 Lay the phyllo pastry sheets out on a clean counter and fold each sheet in half lengthwise.

5 Place 2 tablespoons of the vegetable filling at one end of each folded pastry sheet. Fold over one corner to make a triangle. Continue folding in this way to make a triangular package and seal the edges with water.

6 Repeat with the remaining pastry and the remaining filling.

7 Heat the oil for deep-frying to 350°F/180°C, or until a cube of bread browns in 30 seconds. Fry the samosas, in batches, for 1–2 minutes until golden. Drain on absorbent paper towels and keep warm while cooking the remainder. Serve immediately.

Garlic Mushrooms on Toast

This is so simple to prepare and looks great if you use a variety of mushrooms for shape and texture.

NUTRITIONAL INFORMATION

Calories 366	Sugars 2g
Protein 9g	Fat 18g
Carbohydrate . . .45g	Saturates 4g

10 MINS   10 MINS

SERVES 4

INGREDIENTS

6 tbsp margarine

2 garlic cloves, crushed

4 cups mixed mushrooms, such as
    open-cup, white, oyster, and
    shiitake, sliced

8 slices French bread

1 tbsp chopped parsley

salt and pepper

1 Melt the margarine in a skillet. Add the crushed garlic and cook, stirring constantly, for 30 seconds.

2 Add the mushrooms and cook, turning occasionally, for 5 minutes.

3 Toast the French bread slices under a preheated medium broiler for 2–3 minutes, turning once. Transfer the toasts to a serving plate.

COOK'S TIP

Always store mushrooms for a maximum of 24–36 hours in the refrigerator, in paper bags, as they sweat in plastic. Wild mushrooms should be washed, but other varieties can simply be wiped with paper towels.

4 Toss the parsley into the mushrooms, mixing well, and season well with salt and pepper to taste.

5 Spoon the mushroom mixture over the bread and serve immediately.

Corn Patties

These are a delicious addition to any party buffet, and very simple to prepare. Serve with a sweet chili sauce.

NUTRITIONAL INFORMATION

Calories 90   Sugars 3g
Protein ....2g   Fat 5g
Carbohydrate ....11g   Saturates 0.6g

10 MINS   10 MINS

SERVES 6

I N G R E D I E N T S

1½ cups drained canned corn

1 onion, finely chopped

1 tsp curry powder

1 garlic clove, crushed

1 tsp ground coriander

2 scallions, chopped

3 tbsp all-purpose flour

½ tsp baking powder

1 large egg

4 tbsp corn oil

salt

1 Mash the drained corn lightly in a medium-sized bowl. Add the onion, curry powder, garlic, ground coriander, scallions, flour, baking powder and egg, one at a time, stirring after each addition. Season to taste with salt.

2 Heat the corn oil in a skillet. Drop tablespoonfuls of the mixture carefully onto the hot oil, far enough apart for them not to run into each other as they cook.

3 Cook for 4–5 minutes, turning each patty once, until they are golden brown and firm to the touch. Take care not to turn them too soon, or they will break up in the skillet.

4 Remove the patties from the skillet with a slice and drain on paper towels. Serve immediately while still warm.

COOK'S TIP

To make this dish more attractive, you can serve the patties on large leaves, like those shown in the photograph. Be sure to cut the scallions on the diagonal, as shown, as this will give a more elegant appearance.

Buck Rarebit

This substantial version of cheese on toast—a creamy cheese sauce topped with a poached egg—makes a tasty, filling snack.

NUTRITIONAL INFORMATION

Calories	478	Sugars	.........2g
Protein	........29g	Fat	..........34g
Carbohydrate	...14g	Saturates	......20g

🌀

🥪 10 MINS   🕙 15-20 MINS

SERVES 4

I N G R E D I E N T S

12 oz/350 g sharp Cheddar

4½ oz/125 g Gouda (Dutch), Gruyère, or
  Emmental cheese

1 tsp mustard powder

1 tsp whole-grain mustard

2–4 tbsp brown ale, cider, or milk

½ tsp vegetarian Worcestershire sauce

4 thick slices white or brown bread

4 eggs

salt and pepper

T O G A R N I S H

tomato wedges

 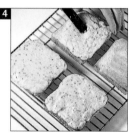 

1 Grate the cheeses and place in a non-stick pan.

2 Add the mustards, seasoning, brown ale, and vegetarian Worcestershire sauce and mix well.

3 Heat the cheese mixture gently, stirring until it has melted and is completely thick and creamy. Remove from the heat and leave to cool a little.

4 Toast the slices of bread on each side under a preheated broiler then spread the rarebit mixture evenly over each piece. Put under a moderate broiler until golden brown and bubbling.

5 Meanwhile, poach the eggs. If using a poacher, grease the cups, then heat the water in the pan and, when just boiling, break the eggs into the cups. Cover and simmer for 4-5 minutes, until just set. Alternatively, bring about 1½ inches/4 cm of water to a boil in a skillet or large pan and for each egg quickly swirl the water with a knife and drop the egg into the "hole" created. Cook for 4 minutes, until just set.

6 Top the rarebits with a poached egg and serve garnished with tomato wedges.

VARIATION

For a change, you can use part or all Stilton or other blue cheese; the appearance is not so attractive but the flavor is very good.

Carrot & Potato Soufflé

Hot soufflés have a reputation for being difficult to make, but this one is both simple and impressive. Make sure you serve it as soon as it is ready.

NUTRITIONAL INFORMATION

Calories	294	Sugars	.........6g
Protein	........10g	Fat	..........9g
Carbohydrate	...46g	Saturates	.......4g

1¼ HOURS   40 MINS

SERVES 4

I N G R E D I E N T S

2 tbsp butter, melted

4 tbsp fresh whole-wheat bread crumbs

1 lb 8 oz/675 g mealy potatoes, baked
in their skins

2 carrots, grated

2 eggs, separated

2 tbsp orange juice

¼ tsp grated nutmeg

salt and pepper

carrot curls, to garnish

1 Brush the inside of a 3¾-cup soufflé dish with butter. Sprinkle three-quarters of the bread crumbs over the base and sides.

2 Cut the baked potatoes in half and scoop the flesh into a mixing bowl.

3 Add the carrot, egg yolks, orange juice, and nutmeg to the potato flesh. Season to taste with salt and pepper.

4 In a separate bowl, whisk the egg whites until soft peaks form, then gently fold into the potato mixture with a metal spoon until well incorporated.

5 Gently spoon the potato and carrot mixture into the prepared soufflé dish. Sprinkle the remaining bread crumbs over the top of the mixture.

6 Cook in a preheated oven, 400°F/200°C, for 40 minutes, until risen and golden. Do not open the oven door during the cooking time, otherwise the soufflé will sink. Serve at once, garnished with carrot curls.

COOK'S TIP

To bake the potatoes, prick the skins and cook in a preheated oven, 375°F/190°C, for about 1 hour.

Vegetable Kabobs

These kabobs, made from a spicy vegetable mixture, are delightfully easy to make and taste delicious.

NUTRITIONAL INFORMATION

Calories 268	Sugars 1g	
Protein 2g	Fat 25g	
Carbohydrate 9g	Saturates 3g	

20 MINS 25–30 MINS

MAKES 12

INGREDIENTS

2 large potatoes, sliced

1 medium onion, sliced

½ medium cauliflower, cut into
   small florets

scant ½ cup peas

1 tbsp spinach purée

2–3 green chiles

fresh cilantro leaves

1 tsp finely chopped gingerroot

1 tsp crushed garlic

1 tsp ground coriander

1 pinch turmeric

1 tsp salt

1 cup fresh bread crumbs

1¼ cups vegetable oil

fresh chile strips, to garnish

1 Place the potatoes, onion, and cauliflower florets in a pan of water and bring to a boil. Reduce the heat and simmer until the potatoes are cooked through. Remove the vegetables from the pan with a slotted spoon and drain thoroughly. Set aside.

2 Add the peas and spinach to the vegetables and mix, mashing down thoroughly with a fork.

3 Using a sharp knife, finely chop the green chiles and fresh cilantro leaves.

4 Mix the chiles and cilantro with the ginger, garlic, ground coriander, turmeric, and salt.

5 Blend the spice mixture into the vegetables, mixing with a fork to make a paste.

6 Scatter the bread crumbs onto a large plate.

7 Break off 10-12 small balls from the spice paste. Flatten them with the palm of your hand to make flat, round shapes.

8 Dip each kabob in the bread crumbs, coating well.

9 Heat the oil in a heavy-bottom skillet and shallow-fry the kabobs, in batches, until golden brown, turning occasionally. Transfer to serving plates and garnish with fresh chile strips. Serve hot.

Lentil Croquettes

These croquettes are an ideal light lunch served with a crisp salad and a sesame seed paste (tahini) dip.

NUTRITIONAL INFORMATION

Calories 409	Sugars 5g	
Protein 19g	Fat 17g	
Carbohydrate ...48g	Saturates 2g	

10 MINS   55 MINS

SERVES 4

INGREDIENTS

1¼ cups split red lentils

1 green bell pepper, seeded and
    finely chopped

1 red onion, finely chopped

2 garlic cloves, crushed

1 tsp garam masala

1½ tsp chili powder

1 tsp ground cumin

2 tsp lemon juice

2 tbsp chopped unsalted peanuts

2½ cups water

1 egg, beaten

3 tbsp all-purpose flour

1 tsp turmeric

4 tbsp vegetable oil

salt and pepper

salad greens and herbs, to serve

1 Put the lentils in a large pan with the bell pepper, onion, garlic, garam masala, ½ tsp chili powder, ground cumin, lemon juice, and peanuts. Add the water and bring to a boil. Reduce the heat and simmer, stirring occasionally, for 30 minutes, until the liquid has been absorbed and the lentils are soft.

2 Remove the mixture from the heat and leave to cool slightly. Beat in the egg and season to taste with salt and pepper. Leave to cool completely.

3 With floured hands, form the mixture into 8 croquettes.

4 Mix the flour, turmeric, and 1 tsp chili powder together on a small plate.

Roll the croquettes in the spiced flour mixture to coat thoroughly.

5 Heat the oil in a large skillet. Add the croquettes, in batches, and cook, turning once, for 10 minutes, until crisp on both sides. Transfer to warm serving plates and serve the croquettes with crisp salad greens and fresh herbs.

Potato Mushroom Cakes

These cakes will be loved by vegetarians and meat-eaters alike. Packed with creamy potato and as wide a variety of mushrooms as possible.

NUTRITIONAL INFORMATION

Calories	298	Sugars	.......0.8g
Protein	.........5g	Fat	..........22g
Carbohydrate	...22g	Saturates	.......5g

🍴 🍴

🥔 20 MINS   🕐 25 MINS

SERVES 4

INGREDIENTS

1 lb 2 oz/500 g mealy potatoes, diced

2 tbsp butter

3 cups chopped mixed mushrooms

2 garlic cloves, crushed

1 small egg, beaten

1 tbsp chopped fresh chives, plus extra
   to garnish

flour, for dusting

oil, for frying

salt and pepper

1 Cook the potatoes in a pan of lightly salted boiling water for 10 minutes, until cooked through

2 Drain the potatoes well, then mash with a potato masher or fork and set aside.

3 Meanwhile, melt the butter in a skillet. Add the mushrooms and garlic and cook, stirring constantly, for 5 minutes. Drain well.

4 Stir the mushrooms and garlic into the potato, together with the beaten egg and chives.

5 Divide the mixture equally into 4 portions and shape them into round cakes. Toss them in the flour until the outsides of the cakes are completely coated.

6 Heat the oil in a skillet. Add the potato cakes and cook over medium heat for 10 minutes, until they are golden brown, turning them over halfway through. Serve the cakes at once, with a simple crisp salad.

COOK'S TIP

Prepare the cakes in advance, then cover and leave to chill in the refrigerator for up to 24 hours, if you wish.

Stuffed Vegetable Snacks

In this recipe, eggplants are filled with a spicy bulgur wheat and vegetable stuffing for a delicious light meal.

NUTRITIONAL INFORMATION

Calories	360	Sugars	........17g
Protein	.........9g	Fat	..........16g
Carbohydrate	...50g	Saturates	.......2g

40 MINS · 30 MINS

SERVES 4

INGREDIENTS

4 medium eggplants

salt

¾ cup bulgur wheat

1¼ cups boiling water

3 tbsp olive oil

2 garlic cloves, crushed

2 tbsp pine nuts

½ tsp turmeric

1 tsp chili powder

2 celery stalks, chopped

4 scallions, chopped

1 carrot, grated

1 cup chopped white mushrooms

2 tbsp raisins

2 tbsp chopped cilantro

green salad, to serve

1 Cut the eggplants in half lengthwise and scoop out the flesh with a teaspoon. Chop the flesh and set aside. Rub the insides of the eggplants with a little salt and leave to stand for 20 minutes.

2 Meanwhile, put the bulgur wheat in a mixing bowl and pour the boiling water over the top. Leave to stand for 20 minutes, until the water has been completely absorbed.

3 Heat the oil in a skillet. Add the garlic, pine nuts, turmeric, chili powder, celery, scallions, carrot, mushrooms, and raisins and cook for 2–3 minutes.

4 Stir in the reserved eggplant flesh and cook for an additional 2–3 minutes. Add the chopped cilantro, mixing well.

5 Remove the skillet from the heat and stir in the bulgur wheat. Rinse the eggplant shells under cold water and pat dry with paper towels.

6 Spoon the bulgur filling into the eggplants and place in a roasting pan. Pour in a little boiling water and cook in a preheated oven, 350°F/180°C, for 15–20 minutes, until piping hot. Remove from the oven and serve hot with a green salad.

Spicy Potato Fries

These home-made fries are flavored with spices and cooked in the oven.
Serve with Lime Mayonnaise (see page 95).

NUTRITIONAL INFORMATION

Calories	328	Sugars	.........2g
Protein	.........5g	Fat	...........11g
Carbohydrate	...56g	Saturates	.......7g

35 MINS   40 MINS

SERVES 4

INGREDIENTS

4 large waxy potatoes

2 sweet potatoes

4 tbsp butter, melted

½ tsp chili powder

1 tsp garam masala

salt

1 Cut the potatoes and sweet potatoes into slices about ½ inch/1 cm thick, then cut them into the shape of fries.

2 Place the potatoes in a large bowl of cold salted water. Set aside to soak for 20 minutes.

3 Remove the potato slices with a slotted spoon and drain thoroughly. Pat with paper towels until completely dry.

COOK'S TIP

Rinsing the potatoes in cold water before cooking removes the starch, thus preventing them from sticking together. Soaking the potatoes in a bowl of cold salted water actually makes the cooked fries crisper.

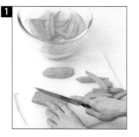

4 Pour the melted butter onto a cookie sheet. Transfer the potato slices to the cookie sheet.

5 Sprinkle with the chili powder and garam masala, turning the potato slices to coat them with the mixture.

6 Cook the chips in a preheated oven, 400°F/200°C, turning frequently, for 40 minutes, until browned and cooked through.

7 Drain the chips on paper towels to remove excess oil and serve at once.

Refried Beans with Tortillas

Refried beans are a classic Mexican dish and are usually served as an accompaniment. They are, however, delicious served with warm tortillas.

NUTRITIONAL INFORMATION

Calories 519	Sugars 14g
Protein 25g	Fat 28g
Carbohydrate . . .44g	Saturates 9g

15 MINS   15 MINS

SERVES 4

INGREDIENTS

BEANS

2 tbsp olive oil

1 onion, finely chopped

3 garlic cloves, crushed

1 green chile, chopped

14 oz/400 g canned red kidney beans, drained

14 oz/400 g canned pinto beans, drained

2 tbsp chopped cilantro

⅔ cup vegetable stock

8 wheat tortillas

¼ cup grated Cheddar cheese

salt and pepper

RELISH

4 scallions, chopped

1 red onion, chopped

1 green chile, chopped

1 tbsp garlic wine vinegar

1 tsp superfine sugar

1 tomato, chopped

1 Heat the oil for the beans in a large skillet over medium heat. Add the onion and sauté, stirring frequently, for 3–5 minutes. Add the garlic and chile and cook for 1 minute.

2 Mash the beans with a potato masher and stir into the skillet, together with the cilantro.

3 Stir in the vegetable stock and cook the beans, stirring constantly, for 5 minutes, until soft and pulpy.

4 Meanwhile, place the tortillas on a cookie sheet and heat through in a preheated oven, 350°F/180°C, for 1–2 minutes.

5 Mix the relish ingredients together. Spoon the beans into a serving dish and top with the cheese. Season to taste with salt and pepper. Roll the warm tortillas and serve with the onion relish and refried beans.

Crispy Potato Skins

Potato skins are always a favorite. Prepare the skins in advance and warm through before serving with the salad fillings.

NUTRITIONAL INFORMATION

Calories	332	Sugars	........18g
Protein	.........8g	Fat	..........14g
Carbohydrate	...47g	Saturates	.......5g

30 MINS   1HR 10 MINS

SERVES 4

INGREDIENTS

4 large baking potatoes

2 tbsp vegetable oil

4 tsp salt

snipped chives, to garnish

²⁄₃ cup sour cream and
   2 tbsp chopped chives, to serve

BEAN SPROUT SALAD

¹⁄₃ cup bean sprouts

1 celery stalk, sliced

1 orange, peeled and segmented

1 red eating apple, chopped

½ red bell pepper, seeded and chopped

1 tbsp chopped parsley

1 tbsp light soy sauce

1 tbsp clear honey

1 small garlic clove, crushed

BEAN FILLING

3½ oz/100 g canned, mixed beans, drained

1 onion, halved and sliced

1 tomato, chopped

2 scallions, chopped

2 tsp lemon juice

salt and pepper

1 Scrub the potatoes and put on a cookie sheet. Prick the potatoes all over with a fork and rub the oil and salt into the skins.

2 Cook in a preheated oven, 400°F/200°C, for 1 hour, until soft and cooked through.

3 Cut the potatoes in half lengthwise and scoop out the flesh, leaving a ½-inch/1-cm thick shell. Put the shells, skin side uppermost, in the oven for 10 minutes, until crisp.

4 Mix the ingredients for the bean sprout salad in a bowl, tossing in the soy sauce, honey, and garlic to coat.

5 Mix the ingredients for the bean filling in a separate bowl.

6 Mix the sour cream and chives in another bowl.

7 Serve the potato skins hot, with the two salad fillings, garnished with snipped chives, and the sour cream and chive sauce.

Ciabatta Rolls

Sandwiches are always a welcome snack, but can be mundane. These crisp rolls filled with roast bell peppers and cheese are irresistible.

NUTRITIONAL INFORMATION

Calories 328   Sugars 6g
Protein . . . . .8g   Fat 19g
Carbohydrate . . .34g   Saturates 9g

15 MINS   10 MINS

SERVES 4

I N G R E D I E N T S

4 ciabatta rolls

2 tbsp olive oil

1 garlic clove, crushed

FILLING

1 red bell pepper

1 green bell pepper

1 yellow bell pepper

4 radishes, sliced

1 bunch watercress or arugula

scant ½ cup cream cheese

1 Slice the ciabatta rolls in half. Heat the olive oil and crushed garlic in a pan. Pour the garlic and oil mixture over the cut surfaces of the rolls and leave to stand.

2 Halve the bell peppers and place, skin side uppermost, on a broiler rack. Cook under a hot broiler for 8–10 minutes, until just beginning to char. Remove the bell peppers from the broiler, then peel, seed, and slice thinly.

3 Arrange the radish slices on one half of each roll with a few watercress leaves. Spoon the cream cheese on top. Pile the bell peppers on top of the cream cheese and top with the other half of the roll. Serve immediately.

Brown Rice Gratin

This dish is extremely versatile and could be made with any vegetables that you have to hand.

NUTRITIONAL INFORMATION

Calories 321   Sugars 6g
Protein . . . . .10g   Fat 18g
Carbohydrate . . .32g   Saturates 9g

15 MINS   1 HOUR

SERVES 4

INGREDIENTS

½ cup brown rice

2 tbsp butter or margarine, plus extra
   for greasing

1 red onion, chopped

2 garlic cloves, crushed

1 carrot, cut into short thin sticks

1 zucchini, sliced

8 baby corn cobs,
   halved lengthwise

2 tbsp sunflower seeds

3 tbsp chopped mixed herbs

1 cup grated mozzarella cheese

2 tbsp whole-wheat bread crumbs

salt and pepper

1 Cook the rice in a pan of boiling lightly salted water for 20 minutes. Drain well.

2 Lightly grease a 3¾-cup ovenproof dish with butter.

3 Heat the butter in a skillet. Add the onion and cook, stirring constantly, for 2 minutes, until soft and translucent.

4 Add the garlic, carrot, zucchini, and corn cobs and cook, stirring constantly, for an additional 5 minutes.

5 Mix the rice with the sunflower seeds and mixed herbs and stir into the skillet.

6 Stir in half of the mozzarella cheese and season with salt and pepper to taste.

7 Spoon the mixture into the prepared dish and top with the bread crumbs and remaining cheese. Cook in a preheated oven, 350°F/180°C, for 25–30 minutes, until the cheese has begun to turn golden. Serve immediately.

VARIATION

Use an alternative rice, such as basmati, and flavor the dish with curry spices, if you prefer.

Casseroled Potatoes

This potato dish is cooked in the oven with leeks and white wine. It is very quick and simple to make and is delicious for lunch.

NUTRITIONAL INFORMATION

Calories 200   Sugars 3g
Protein . . . . .6g   Fat 4g
Carbohydrate . . .32g   Saturates 2g

15 MINS   45 MINS

SERVES 4

INGREDIENTS

1 lb 8 oz/675 g waxy potatoes, cut
   into chunks

1 tbsp butter

2 leeks, sliced

⅔ cup dry white wine

⅔ cup vegetable stock

1 tbsp lemon juice

2 tbsp chopped mixed herbs

salt and pepper

salad, to serve

TO GARNISH

grated lemon rind

mixed herbs (optional)

1 Cook the potato chunks in a pan of lightly salted boiling water for 5 minutes. Drain thoroughly.

2 Meanwhile, melt the butter in a skillet and sauté the leeks for 5 minutes, until they have softened.

3 Spoon the partly cooked potatoes and leeks into an ovenproof dish and spread out over the base.

4 Mix together the white wine, vegetable stock, lemon juice, and chopped mixed herbs. Season to taste with salt and pepper, then pour the mixture over the potatoes.

5 Cook in a preheated oven, 375°F/190°C, for 35 minutes, until the potatoes are tender.

6 Garnish the potato casserole with lemon rind and fresh herbs, if using, and serve immediately with salad.

COOK'S TIP

Cover the ovenproof dish halfway through cooking if the leeks start to brown on the top.

Cheese & Onion Rösti

These grated potato cakes are also known as straw cakes, as they resemble a straw mat. Serve them with a tomato sauce or salad.

NUTRITIONAL INFORMATION

Calories 307	Sugars 4g
Protein 8g	Fat 13g
Carbohydrate . . .42g	Saturates 6g

🍲 10 MINS   🕐 40 MINS

SERVES 4

INGREDIENTS

2 lb/900 g potatoes

1 onion, grated

½ cup grated Gruyère cheese

2 tbsp chopped parsley

1 tbsp olive oil

2 tbsp butter

salt and pepper

TO GARNISH

shredded scallion

1 small tomato, cut into fourths

1 Parboil the potatoes in a pan of lightly salted boiling water for 10 minutes and leave to cool. Peel the potatoes and grate with a coarse grater. Place the grated potatoes in a large mixing bowl.

COOK'S TIP

The potato cakes should be flattened as much as possible during cooking, otherwise the outside will be cooked before the center.

2 Stir in the onion, cheese, and parsley. Season well with salt and pepper. Divide the potato mixture into 4 portions of equal size and form them into cakes.

3 Heat half of the olive oil and butter in a skillet and cook 2 of the potato cakes over high heat for 1 minute, then reduce the heat and cook for 5 minutes,

until they are golden underneath. Turn them over and cook for an additional 5 minutes.

4 Repeat with the other half of the oil and the remaining butter to cook the remaining 2 cakes. Transfer to warm individual serving plates, then garnish and serve immediately.

Mini Kabobs

Cubes of smoked tofu are speared on bamboo satay sticks with crisp vegetables and marinated with lemon juice and olive oil.

NUTRITIONAL INFORMATION

Calories	322	Sugars 9g
Protein	........13g	Fat 24g
Carbohydrate	...13g	Saturates 7g

🦀 🦀

🥔 25 MINS   🕐 15–20 MINS

SERVES 6

I N G R E D I E N T S

10½ oz/300 g smoked tofu, cut into cubes

1 large red bell pepper, seeded and
cut into small squares

1 large yellow bell pepper, seeded and
cut into small squares

1½ cups white mushrooms

1 small zucchini, sliced

finely grated rind and juice of 1 lemon

3 tbsp olive oil

1 tbsp chopped parsley

1 tsp superfine sugar

salt and pepper

parsley sprigs, to garnish

S A U C E

scant 1 cup cashew nuts

1 tbsp butter

1 garlic clove, crushed

1 shallot, finely chopped

1 tsp ground coriander

1 tsp ground cumin

1 tbsp superfine sugar

1 tbsp dry unsweetened coconut

⅔ cup plain yogurt

1 Thread the tofu cubes, bell peppers, mushrooms, and zucchini onto bamboo satay sticks. Arrange them in a shallow dish.

2 Mix together the lemon rind and juice, olive oil, parsley, and sugar. Season to taste with salt and pepper. Pour over the kabobs, and brush them with the mixture. Leave for 10 minutes.

3 To make the sauce, scatter the cashew nuts onto a cookie sheet and toast them under a hot broiler until lightly browned.

4 Melt the butter in a pan and sauté the garlic and shallot gently until softened. Transfer to a blender or food processor and add the nuts, coriander, cumin, sugar, coconut, and yogurt. Process for about 15 seconds, until combined. Alternatively, chop the nuts very finely and mix with the remaining ingredients.

5 Place the kabobs under a preheated broiler and cook, turning and basting with the lemon juice mixture, until lightly browned. Garnish with sprigs of parsley, and serve with the cashew nut sauce.

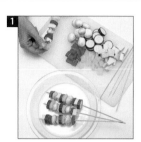

Stuffed Mushrooms

Use large open-cup mushrooms for this recipe for their flavor and suitability for filling.

NUTRITIONAL INFORMATION

Calories 273	Sugars 5g
Protein 13g	Fat 18g
Carbohydrate ...15g	Saturates 5g

15 MINS   25 MINS

SERVES 4

INGREDIENTS

8 open-cup mushrooms

1 tbsp olive oil

1 small leek, chopped

1 celery stalk, chopped

3½ oz/100 g firm tofu, diced

1 zucchini, chopped

1 carrot, chopped

scant 2 cups whole-wheat bread crumbs

2 tbsp chopped basil

1 tbsp tomato paste

2 tbsp pine nuts

¾ cup grated Cheddar cheese

⅔ cup vegetable stock

salt and pepper

salad, to serve

1 Remove the stems from the mushrooms and chop finely. Reserve the caps.

2 Heat the olive oil in a large, heavy-bottom skillet over medium heat. Add the chopped mushroom stems, leek, celery, tofu, zucchini, and carrot and cook, stirring constantly, for 3–4 minutes.

3 Stir in the bread crumbs, chopped basil, tomato paste, and pine nuts. Season with salt and pepper to taste and mix thoroughly.

4 Spoon the mixture into the mushroom caps and top with the grated cheese.

5 Place the mushrooms in a shallow ovenproof dish and pour the vegetable stock around them.

6 Cook in a preheated oven, 425°F/220°C, for 20 minutes, until cooked through and the cheese has melted. Remove the mushrooms from the dish and serve immediately with a salad.

Potato Fritters

Chunks of cooked potato are coated first in Parmesan cheese, then in a light batter before being fried until golden for a delicious hot snack.

NUTRITIONAL INFORMATION

Calories	599	Sugars	........9g
Protein	........22g	Fat	..........39g
Carbohydrate	...42g	Saturates	......13g

20 MINS   20-25 MINS

SERVES 4

I N G R E D I E N T S

1 lb 2 oz/500 g waxy potatoes, cut into
   large cubes

1¼ cups freshly grated Parmesan cheese

oil, for deep-frying

S A U C E

2 tbsp butter

1 onion, halved and sliced

2 garlic cloves, crushed

2 tbsp all-purpose flour

1¼ cups milk

1 tbsp chopped parsley

B A T T E R

⅓ cup all-purpose flour

1 small egg

⅔ cup milk

3 Meanwhile, cook the cubed potatoes in a pan of boiling water for 5–10 minutes, until just firm. Do not overcook, or they will fall apart.

6 In a large pan or deep-fryer, heat the oil to 350°F/180°C, until a cube of bread browns in 30 seconds. Add the fritters and cook for 3–4 minutes, until golden.

1 To make the sauce, melt the butter in a pan and cook the sliced onion and garlic over low heat, stirring frequently, for 2–3 minutes. Add the flour and cook, stirring constantly, for 1 minute.

4 Drain the potatoes and toss them in the Parmesan cheese. If the potatoes are still slightly wet, the cheese sticks to them and coats them well.

7 Remove the fritters with a slotted spoon and drain well. Transfer them to a warm serving bowl and serve immediately with the garlic sauce.

2 Remove from the heat and stir in the milk and parsley. Return to the heat and bring to a boil. Keep warm.

5 To make the batter, place the flour in a mixing bowl and gradually beat in the egg and milk until smooth. Dip the potato cubes into the batter to coat them.

Potato & Mushroom Bake

Use any mixture of mushrooms to hand for this creamy layered bake.
It can be served straight from the dish in which it is cooked.

NUTRITIONAL INFORMATION

Calories 304   Sugars 2g
Protein ....4g   Fat 24g
Carbohydrate ...20g   Saturates 15g

15 MINS   1 HOUR

SERVES 4

INGREDIENTS

2 tbsp butter

1 lb 2 oz/500 g waxy potatoes, thinly sliced

2³/₄ cups sliced mixed mushrooms

1 tbsp chopped rosemary

4 tbsp chopped chives

2 garlic cloves, crushed

²/₃ cup heavy cream

salt and pepper

snipped chives, to garnish

1 Grease a shallow round ovenproof dish with butter.

2 Parboil the sliced potatoes in a pan of boiling water for 10 minutes. Drain well. Layer one fourth of the potatoes in the base of the dish.

3 Arrange one fourth of the mushrooms on top of the potatoes and sprinkle with one fourth of the rosemary, chives, and garlic. Continue making layers in the same order, finishing with a layer of potatoes on top.

4 Pour the cream over the top of the potatoes. Season to taste with salt and pepper.

5 Cook in a preheated oven, 375°F/ 190°C, for 45 minutes, until the bake is golden brown and piping hot.

6 Garnish with snipped chives and serve at once straight from the dish.

COOK'S TIP

For a special occasion, the bake may be made in a lined cake pan and then turned out to serve.

Vegetable Enchiladas

This Mexican dish uses prepared tortillas, which are readily available in supermarkets, and these are then filled with a spicy vegetable mixture.

NUTRITIONAL INFORMATION

Calories 309	Sugars 14g	
Protein 12g	Fat 19g	
Carbohydrate ...23g	Saturates 8g	

20 MINS   55 MINS

SERVES 4

I N G R E D I E N T S

4 flour tortillas

¾ cup grated Cheddar cheese

F I L L I N G

2¾ oz/75 g spinach

2 tbsp olive oil

8 baby corn cobs, sliced

1 tbsp frozen peas, thawed

1 red bell pepper, seeded and diced

1 carrot, diced

1 leek, sliced

2 garlic cloves, crushed

1 red chile, chopped

salt and pepper

S A U C E

1¼ cups crushed tomatoes

2 shallots, chopped

1 garlic clove, crushed

1¼ cups vegetable stock

1 tsp superfine sugar

1 tsp chili powder

1 To make the filling, blanch the spinach in a pan of boiling water for 2 minutes. Drain well, pressing out as much excess moisture as possible, and chop.

2 Heat the oil in a skillet over medium heat. Add the baby corn cobs, peas, bell pepper, carrot, leek, garlic, and chile and sauté, stirring briskly, for 3–4 minutes. Stir in the spinach and season well with salt and pepper to taste.

3 Put all the sauce ingredients in a heavy-bottom pan and bring to a boil, stirring constantly. Cook over high heat, stirring constantly, for 20 minutes, until thickened and reduced by a third.

4 Spoon one fourth of the filling along the center of each tortilla. Roll the tortillas around the filling and place, seam side down, in a single layer in an ovenproof dish.

5 Pour the sauce over the tortillas and sprinkle the cheese on top. Cook in a preheated oven, 350°F/180°C, for 20 minutes, until the cheese has melted and browned. Serve immediately.

Vegetable Burgers & Chips

These spicy vegetable burgers are delicious, especially when served with the light oven fries and in a warm bun or roll.

NUTRITIONAL INFORMATION

Calories 461	Sugars 4g
Protein 18g	Fat 17g
Carbohydrate . . .64g	Saturates 2g

45 MINS   1 HOUR

SERVES 4

INGREDIENTS

VEGETABLE BURGERS

3½ oz/100 g spinach

1 tbsp olive oil

1 leek, chopped

2 garlic cloves, crushed

2 cups chopped mushrooms

10½ oz/300 g firm tofu, chopped

1 tsp chili powder

1 tsp curry powder

1 tbsp chopped cilantro

1½ cups fresh whole-wheat bread crumbs

1 tbsp olive oil

burger bap or roll and salad, to serve

FRIES

2 large potatoes

2 tbsp flour

1 tsp chile powder

2 tbsp olive oil

1 To make the burgers, cook the spinach in a little boiling water for 2 minutes. Drain thoroughly and pat dry with paper towels.

2 Heat the oil in a skillet and sauté the leek and garlic for 2–3 minutes. Add the remaining ingredients, except the bread crumbs, and cook for 5–7 minutes, until the vegetables have softened. Toss in the spinach and cook for 1 minute.

3 Transfer the mixture to a food processor and process for 30 seconds, until almost smooth. Transfer to a bowl, and stir in the bread crumbs, mixing well, then leave until cool enough to handle. Using floured hands, form the mixture into four equal-size burgers. Leave to chill for 30 minutes.

4 To make the fries, cut the potatoes into thin wedges and cook in a pan of boiling water for 10 minutes. Drain and toss in the flour and chili powder. Lay the chips on a cookie sheet and sprinkle with the oil. Cook in a preheated oven, 400°F/200°C, for 30 minutes, until golden.

5 Meanwhile, heat 1 tablespoon oil in a skillet and cook the burgers for 8–10 minutes, turning once. Serve with salad in a bap with the fries.

Potato Omelet

This quick chunky omelet has pieces of potato cooked into the egg mixture and is then filled with feta cheese and spinach.

NUTRITIONAL INFORMATION

Calories 564	Sugars 6g	
Protein 30g	Fat 39g	
Carbohydrate ...25g	Saturates 19g	

20 MINS   25–30 MINS

SERVES 4

I N G R E D I E N T S

6 tbsp butter

6 waxy potatoes, diced

3 garlic cloves, crushed

1 tsp paprika

2 tomatoes, peeled, seeded, and diced

12 eggs

pepper

F I L L I N G

8 oz/225 g baby spinach

1 tsp fennel seeds

1 cup diced feta cheese

4 tbsp plain yogurt

1 Heat 2 tablespoons of the butter in a skillet and cook the potatoes over low heat, stirring constantly, for 7–10 minutes until golden. Transfer to a bowl.

2 Add the garlic, paprika, and tomatoes to the skillet and cook for an additional 2 minutes.

3 Whisk the eggs together and season with pepper. Pour the eggs into the potatoes and mix well.

4 Cook the spinach in boiling water for 1 minute, until just wilted. Drain and refresh under cold running water. Pat dry with paper towels. Stir in the fennel seeds, feta cheese, and yogurt.

5 Heat one fourth of the remaining butter in a 6-inch/15-cm omelet pan. Ladle one fourth of the egg and potato mixture into the pan. Cook, turning once, for 2 minutes, until set.

6 Transfer the omelet to a serving plate. Spoon one fourth of the spinach mixture on to one half of the omelet, then fold the omelet in half over the filling. Repeat to make 4 omelets.

VARIATION

Use any other cheese, such as blue cheese, instead of the feta and blanched broccoli in place of the baby spinach, if you prefer.

Three-Cheese Fondue

A hot cheese dip made from three different cheeses can be prepared easily and with guaranteed success in the microwave oven.

NUTRITIONAL INFORMATION

Calories . . . . . . .565 Sugars 1g

Protein . . . . .29g Fat 38g

Carbohydrate . . .15g Saturates 24g

15 MINS   10 MINS

SERVES 4

I N G R E D I E N T S

1 garlic clove

1¼ cups dry white wine

2 cups grated mild Cheddar cheese

1 cup grated Gruyère cheese

1 cup grated mozzarella cheese

2 tbsp cornstarch

pepper

T O   S E R V E

French bread

vegetables, such as zucchini,
   mushrooms, baby corn cobs,
   and cauliflower

1 Bruise the garlic by placing the flat side of a knife on top and pressing down with the heel of your hand.

2 Rub the garlic around the inside of a large bowl. Discard the garlic.

3 Pour the wine into the bowl and heat, uncovered, on High power for 3–4 minutes, until hot but not boiling.

4 Gradually add the Cheddar and Gruyère cheeses, stirring well after each addition, then add the mozzarella. Stir until completely melted.

5 Mix the cornstarch with a little water to a smooth paste and stir into the cheese mixture. Season to taste with pepper.

6 Cover and cook on Medium power for 6 minutes, stirring twice during cooking, until the sauce is smooth.

7 Cut the French bread into cubes and the vegetables into batons, slices, or florets. To serve, keep the fondue warm over a spirit lamp or reheat as necessary in the microwave oven. Dip in cubes of French bread and batons, slices, or florets of vegetables.

COOK'S TIP

Make sure you add the cheese to the wine gradually, mixing well in between each addition, otherwise the mixture might curdle.

Cheese & Potato Slices

This recipe takes a while to prepare but it is well worth the effort. The golden potato slices coated in bread crumbs and cheese are delicious.

NUTRITIONAL INFORMATION

Calories	560	Sugars	.........3g
Protein	........19g	Fat	..........31g
Carbohydrate	...55g	Saturates	.......7g

10 MINS   40 MINS

SERVES 4

I N G R E D I E N T S

3 large waxy potatoes, unpeeled and
   thickly sliced

generous 1 cup fresh white bread crumbs

scant ½ cup freshly grated Parmesan
   cheese

1½ tsp chili powder

2 eggs, beaten

oil, for deep frying

chili powder, for dusting (optional)

1 Cook the sliced potatoes in a pan of boiling water for 10-15 minutes, until the potatoes are just tender. Drain thoroughly.

2 Mix the bread crumbs, cheese, and chili powder together in a bowl, then transfer to a shallow dish. Pour the beaten eggs into a separate shallow dish.

3 Dip the potato slices first in egg and then roll them in the bread crumbs to coat completely.

4 Heat the oil in a large pan or deep-fryer to 350°F/180°C, until a cube of bread browns in 30 seconds. Cook the cheese and potato slices, in several batches, for 4–5 minutes, until a golden brown color.

5 Remove the cheese and potato slices from the oil with a slotted spoon and drain thoroughly on paper towels. Keep the cheese and potato slices warm while you cook the remaining batches.

6 Transfer the cheese and potato slices to warm individual serving plates. Dust lightly with chili powder, if using, and serve immediately.

COOK'S TIP

The cheese and potato slices may be coated in the bread crumb mixture in advance and then stored in the refrigerator until ready to use.

Vegetable Jambalaya

This dish traditionally contains spicy sausage, but it is equally delicious filled with vegetables in this spicy vegetarian version.

NUTRITIONAL INFORMATION

Calories 181	Sugars 8g	
Protein 6g	Fat 7g	
Carbohydrate ...25g	Saturates 1g	

🍲 🍲

🥘 10 MINS   🕐 55 MINS

SERVES 4

INGREDIENTS

scant ½ cup brown rice

2 tbsp olive oil

2 garlic cloves, crushed

1 red onion, cut into eight

1 eggplant, diced

1 green bell pepper, diced

6 baby corn cobs,
    halved lengthwise

½ cup frozen peas

1 cup small broccoli florets

⅔ cup vegetable stock

8 oz/225 g canned chopped tomatoes

1 tbsp tomato paste

1 tsp creole seasoning

½ tsp chili flakes

salt and pepper

COOK'S TIP

Use a mixture of different kinds of rice, such as wild or red rice, for color and texture. Cook the rice in advance for a speedier recipe.

1 Cook the rice in a large pan of salted boiling water for 20 minutes, until cooked through. Drain. Rinse with boiling water, then drain again and set aside.

2 Heat the oil in a heavy-bottom skillet and cook the garlic and onion, stirring constantly, for 2–3 minutes.

3 Add the eggplant, bell pepper, corn, peas, and broccoli to the skillet and cook, stirring occasionally, for 2–3 minutes.

4 Stir in the vegetable stock and canned tomatoes, tomato paste, creole seasoning, and chili flakes.

5 Season to taste and cook over low heat for 15–20 minutes, until the vegetables are tender.

6 Stir the brown rice into the vegetable mixture and cook, mixing well, for 3–4 minutes, or until hot. Transfer the vegetable jambalaya to a warm serving dish and serve immediately.

Vegetable Hash

This is a quick one-pan dish that is ideal for a snack. Packed with color and flavor it is very versatile, as you can add other vegetables.

NUTRITIONAL INFORMATION

Calories ....182 Sugars 6g
Protein ....5g Fat 4g
Carbohydrate ...34g Saturates 0.5g

15 MINS   30 MINS

SERVES 4

INGREDIENTS

1 lb 8 oz/675 g potatoes, cubed

1 tbsp olive oil

2 garlic cloves, crushed

1 green bell pepper, seeded
    and cubed

1 yellow bell pepper, seeded
    and cubed

3 tomatoes, diced

¾ cup white mushrooms, halved

1 tbsp Worcestershire sauce

2 tbsp chopped basil

salt and pepper

basil sprigs, to garnish

warm, crusty bread, to serve

1 Cook the potatoes in a pan of boiling salted water for 7–8 minutes. Drain well and reserve.

2 Heat the olive oil in a large, heavy-bottom skillet. Add the potatoes and cook, stirring constantly, for 8–10 minutes, until browned.

3 Add the garlic and bell peppers and cook, stirring frequently, for 2–3 minutes.

4 Stir in the tomatoes and mushrooms and cook, stirring frequently, for 5–6 minutes.

5 Stir in the Worcestershire sauce and basil and season to taste with salt and pepper. Transfer to a warm serving dish, then garnish with basil sprigs and serve with warm crusty bread.

COOK'S TIP

Most brands of Worcestershire sauce contain anchovies, so check the label to make sure you choose a vegetarian variety.

Pasta & Noodles

Pasta is one of the most popular and versatile ingredients available, and it is both nourishing and satisfying. Fresh or dried, pasta is made in a variety of flavors and colors,

shapes, and sizes, all of which work well with a number of vegetarian sauces. Pasta combines well with vegetables, herbs, nuts, and cheeses to provide scores of interesting and tasty meals.

Noodles are also quick to cook and provide good basic food that can be dressed up in all kinds of different ways. Often flavored with Asian ingredients, the noodle recipes in this chapter are sure to liven up a vegetarian diet.

Vegetable Cannelloni

This dish is made with prepared cannelloni tubes, but may also be made by rolling ready-bought lasagna sheets.

NUTRITIONAL INFORMATION

Calories	594	Sugars	.......12g
Protein	........13g	Fat	..........38g
Carbohydrate	...52g	Saturates	.......7g

10 MINS   45 MINS

SERVES 4

I N G R E D I E N T S

1 eggplant

½ cup olive oil

8 oz/225 g spinach

2 garlic cloves, crushed

1 tsp ground cumin

1½ cups chopped mushrooms

12 cannelloni tubes

salt and pepper

T O M A T O   S A U C E

1 tbsp olive oil

1 onion, chopped

2 garlic cloves, crushed

1 lb 12 oz/800 g canned chopped tomatoes

1 tsp superfine sugar

2 tbsp chopped basil

1¾ oz//50 g sliced mozzarella

COOK'S TIP

You can prepare the tomato sauce in advance and store it in the refrigerator for up to 24 hours.

1 Cut the eggplant into small dice.

2 Heat the oil in a skillet. Add the eggplant and cook over moderate heat, stirring frequently, for 2–3 minutes.

3 Add the spinach, garlic, cumin, and mushrooms. Season and cook, stirring, for 2–3 minutes. Spoon the mixture into the cannelloni tubes and place in an ovenproof dish in a single layer.

4 To make the sauce, heat the olive oil in a pan and sauté the onion and garlic for 1 minute. Add the tomatoes, superfine sugar, and chopped basil and bring to a boil. Reduce the heat and simmer for 5 minutes. Pour the sauce over the cannelloni tubes.

5 Arrange the sliced mozzarella on top of the sauce and cook in a preheated oven, 375°F/190°C, for 30 minutes, until the cheese is bubbling and golden brown. Serve immediately.

Vegetable Lasagna

This colorful and tasty lasagna has layers of vegetables in tomato sauce and eggplants, all topped with a rich cheese sauce.

NUTRITIONAL INFORMATION

Calories 544	Sugars 18g
Protein 20g	Fat 26g
Carbohydrate . . .61g	Saturates 12g

35 MINS   55 MINS

SERVES 4

INGREDIENTS

1 eggplant, sliced

3 tbsp olive oil

2 garlic cloves, crushed

1 red onion, halved and sliced

3 mixed bell peppers, seeded and diced

4 cups sliced mixed mushrooms

2 celery stalks, sliced

1 zucchini, diced

½ tsp chili powder

½ tsp ground cumin

2 tomatoes, chopped

1¼ cups crushed tomatoes

2 tbsp chopped basil

8 no precook lasagna verdi sheets

salt and pepper

CHEESE SAUCE

2 tbsp butter or margarine

1 tbsp flour

⅔ cup vegetable stock

1¼ cups milk

¾ cup grated Cheddar cheese

1 tsp Dijon mustard

1 tbsp chopped basil

1 egg, beaten

1 Place the eggplant slices in a colander, then sprinkle with salt and leave for 20 minutes. Rinse under cold water, drain and reserve.

2 Heat the oil in a pan and sauté the garlic and onion for 1–2 minutes. Add the bell peppers, mushrooms, celery, and zucchini and cook, stirring constantly, for 3–4 minutes.

3 Stir in the spices and cook for 1 minute. Mix in the tomatoes, crushed tomatoes, and basil and season to taste with salt and pepper.

4 For the sauce, melt the butter in a pan, stir in the flour and cook for 1 minute. Remove from the heat and stir in the stock and milk, then return to the heat and add half the cheese and the mustard. Boil, stirring, until thickened. Stir in the basil. Remove from the heat and stir in the egg.

5 Place half the lasagna in an ovenproof dish. Top with half the vegetable mixture then half the eggplants. Repeat and spoon the cheese sauce on top. Sprinkle with the remaining cheese and cook in a preheated oven, 350°F/180°C, for 40 minutes. Serve immediately.

Spinach & Nut Pasta

Use any pasta shapes that you have for this recipe. Multicolored tricolore pasta is visually the most attractive to use.

NUTRITIONAL INFORMATION

Calories	603	Sugars	.........5g
Protein	........12g	Fat	..........41g
Carbohydrate	...46g	Saturates	.......6g

5 MINS   15 MINS

SERVES 4

INGREDIENTS

2 cups dried pasta shapes

½ cup olive oil

2 garlic cloves, crushed

1 onion, cut into fourths, then sliced

3 large flat mushrooms, sliced

8 oz/225 g spinach

2 tbsp pine nuts

scant ⅓ cup dry white wine

salt and pepper

Parmesan shavings, to garnish

1 Cook the pasta in a pan of boiling salted water for 8–10 minutes, until al dente. Drain well.

2 Meanwhile, heat the oil in a large pan and sauté the garlic and onion for 1 minute.

COOK'S TIP

Grate a little nutmeg over the dish for extra flavor, as this spice has a particular affinity with spinach.

3 Add the sliced mushrooms to the pan and cook over medium heat, stirring occasionally, for 2 minutes.

4 Lower the heat, then add the spinach to the pan and cook, stirring occasionally, for 4–5 minutes, until the spinach has wilted.

5 Stir in the pine nuts and wine, then season to taste with salt and pepper and cook for 1 minute.

6 Transfer the pasta to a warm serving bowl and toss the sauce into it, mixing well. Garnish with shavings of Parmesan cheese and serve.

Macaroni Cheese & Tomato

This is a really simple, family dish that is inexpensive and easy to prepare and cook. Serve with a salad or fresh green vegetables.

NUTRITIONAL INFORMATION

Calories	592	Sugars	........6g
Protein	........28g	Fat	..........29g
Carbohydrate	...57g	Saturates	......17g

15 MINS   35-40 MINS

SERVES 4

INGREDIENTS

2 cups dried elbow macaroni

1½ cups grated Cheddar cheese

1 cup freshly grated Parmesan cheese

4 tbsp fresh white bread crumbs

1 tbsp chopped basil

1 tbsp butter or margarine, plus extra
   for greasing

TOMATO SAUCE

1 tbsp olive oil

1 shallot, finely chopped

2 garlic cloves, crushed

1 lb 2 oz/500 g canned chopped tomatoes

1 tbsp chopped basil

salt and pepper

1 To make the tomato sauce, heat the oil in a heavy-bottom pan. Add the shallots and garlic and sauté for 1 minute. Add the tomatoes and basil and season with salt and pepper to taste. Cook over medium heat, stirring constantly, for 10 minutes.

2 Meanwhile, cook the macaroni in a large pan of boiling lightly salted water for 8 minutes, until al dente. Drain thoroughly and set aside.

3 Mix the Cheddar and Parmesan together in a bowl. Grease a deep, ovenproof dish. Spoon one-third of the tomato sauce into the base of the dish, then top with one-third of the macaroni and finally one-third of the cheeses. Season to taste with salt and pepper. Repeat these layers twice, ending with a layer of grated cheese.

4 Combine the bread crumbs and basil and sprinkle evenly over the top. Dot the topping with the butter or margarine and cook in a preheated oven, 375°F/190°C, for 25 minutes, until the topping is golden brown and bubbling. Serve immediately, straight from the dish.

Summertime Tagliatelle

This is a really fresh-tasting dish, made with zucchini and cream, which is ideal with a crisp white wine and some crusty bread.

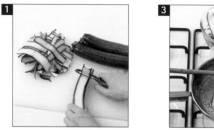

NUTRITIONAL INFORMATION

Calories 502	Sugars 5g	
Protein 16g	Fat 30g	
Carbohydrate ...44g	Saturates 9g	

10 MINS   20 MINS

SERVES 4

INGREDIENTS

1 lb 7 oz/650 g zucchini

6 tbsp olive oil

3 garlic cloves, crushed

3 tbsp chopped basil

2 red chiles, sliced

juice of 1 large lemon

5 tbsp light cream

4 tbsp freshly grated Parmesan cheese

8 oz/225 g dried tagliatelle

salt and pepper

crusty bread, to serve

1 Using a swivel vegetable peeler, slice the zucchini into thin ribbons.

2 Heat the oil in a skillet and sauté the garlic for 30 seconds.

COOK'S TIP

Lime juice could be used instead of the lemon. As limes are usually smaller, squeeze the juice from two.

3 Add the zucchini ribbons and cook over low heat, stirring constantly, for 5–7 minutes.

4 Stir in the basil, chiles, lemon juice, light cream, and grated Parmesan cheese and season with salt and pepper to taste. Keep warm over very low heat.

5 Meanwhile, cook the tagliatelle in a large pan of lightly salted boiling water for 10 minutes, until al dente. Drain the pasta thoroughly and put in a warm serving bowl.

6 Pile the zucchini mixture on top of the pasta. Serve immediately with crusty bread.

Thai-Style Stir-Fried Noodles

This dish is considered the Thai national dish, as it is made and eaten everywhere—a one-dish, fast food for eating on the move.

NUTRITIONAL INFORMATION

Calories 407   Sugars 11g
Protein . . . . .14g   Fat 16g
Carbohydrate . . .56g   Saturates 3g

15 MINS   5 MINS

SERVES 4

I N G R E D I E N T S

8 oz/225 g dried rice noodles

2 red chiles, seeded and finely chopped

2 shallots, finely chopped

2 tbsp sugar

2 tbsp tamarind water

1 tbsp lime juice

2 tbsp light soy sauce

1 tbsp corn oil

1 tsp sesame oil

6 oz/175 g diced smoked tofu

pepper

2 tbsp chopped roasted peanuts,
    to garnish

1 Cook the rice noodles as directed on the package, or soak them in boiling water for 5 minutes.

2 Grind together the chiles, shallots, sugar, tamarind water, lime juice, light soy sauce, and pepper to taste.

3 Heat both the oils together in a preheated wok or large, heavy skillet over high heat. Add the tofu and stir for 1 minute.

4 Add the chile mixture, then bring to a boil and cook, stirring constantly, for 2 minutes, until thickened.

5 Drain the rice noodles and add them to the chile mixture. Use 2 spoons to lift and stir them until they are no longer steaming. Serve immediately, garnished with the peanuts.

COOK'S TIP

This is a quick one-dish meal that is very useful if you are catering for a single vegetarian in the family.

Stir-Fried Japanese Noodles

This quick dish is an ideal lunchtime meal, packed with whatever mixture of mushrooms you like in a sweet sauce.

NUTRITIONAL INFORMATION

Calories 379   Sugars 8g
Protein . . . . .12g   Fat 13g
Carbohydrate . . .53g   Saturates 3g

15 MINS   15 MINS

SERVES 4

INGREDIENTS

8 oz/225 g Japanese egg noodles

2 tbsp corn oil

1 red onion, sliced

1 garlic clove, crushed

1 lb 2 oz/500 g mixed mushrooms, such as shiitake, oyster, brown cup

12 oz/350 g bok choy

2 tbsp sweet sherry

6 tbsp soy sauce

4 scallions, sliced

1 tbsp toasted sesame seeds

1 Place the egg noodles in a large bowl. Pour over enough boiling water to cover and leave to soak for 10 minutes.

2 Heat the corn oil in a large preheated wok.

3 Add the red onion and garlic to the wok and stir-fry for 2–3 minutes, until softened.

4 Add the mushrooms to the wok and stir-fry for 5 minutes, until the mushrooms have softened.

5 Drain the Japanese egg noodles thoroughly and set aside.

6 Add the the bok choy, noodles, sweet sherry, and soy sauce to the wok. Toss all of the ingredients together to mix well and stir-fry for 2–3 minutes, until the liquid is just bubbling.

7 Transfer the mushroom noodles to warm serving bowls and scatter with sliced scallions and toasted sesame seeds. Serve immediately.

COOK'S TIP

The variety of mushrooms in supermarkets has greatly improved and a good mixture should be easily obtainable. If not, use the more common white and flat mushrooms.

Spicy Fried Noodles

This is a simple idea to add an extra kick to noodles, which accompany many main course dishes in Thailand.

NUTRITIONAL INFORMATION

Calories	568	Sugars	.........3g
Protein	........16g	Fat	..........19g
Carbohydrate	...90g	Saturates	.......4g

15 MINS   3–5 MINS

SERVES 4

INGREDIENTS

1 lb 2 oz/500 g medium egg noodles

scant ½ cup bean sprouts

½ oz/15 g chives

3 tbsp corn oil

1 garlic clove, crushed

4 fresh green chiles, seeded, sliced, and
  soaked in 2 tbsp rice vinegar

salt

1 Place the noodles in a bowl, then cover with boiling water and soak for 10 minutes. Drain and set aside.

2 Pick over the bean sprouts and soak in cold water while you cut the chives into 1-inch/2.5-cm pieces. Set a few chives aside for the garnish. Drain the bean sprouts thoroughly.

3 Heat the oil in a preheated wok or large, heavy-bottom skillet. Add the crushed garlic and stir; then add the chiles and stir-fry for 1 minute, until fragrant.

4 Add the bean sprouts, then stir and add the noodles. Stir in salt to taste and add the chives. Using 2 spoons or a wok scoop, lift and toss the noodles for 1 minute.

5 Transfer the noodles to a warm serving dish, then garnish with the reserved chives and serve immediately.

COOK'S TIP

Soaking a chile in rice vinegar has the effect of distributing the hot chile flavor throughout the dish. To reduce the heat, you can slice the chile more thickly before soaking.

Chow Mein

Egg noodles are cooked and then fried with a colorful variety
of vegetables to make this well-known and ever-popular dish.

NUTRITIONAL INFORMATION

Calories	669	Sugars	.........9g
Protein	........19g	Fat	..........23g
Carbohydrate	..100g	Saturates	.......4g

15 MINS   10 MINS

SERVES 4

INGREDIENTS

1 lb 2 oz/500 g egg noodles

4 tbsp vegetable oil

1 onion, thinly sliced

2 carrots, cut into thin sticks

generous 1 cup white mushrooms,
 cut into fourths

4½ oz/125 g snow peas

½ cucumber, cut into sticks

4½ oz/125 g spinach, shredded

scant 1 cup bean sprouts

2 tbsp dark soy sauce

1 tbsp sherry

1 tsp salt

1 tsp sugar

1 tsp cornstarch

1 tsp sesame oil

COOK'S TIP

For a spicy hot chow mein,
add 1 tablespoon chili sauce
or substitute chili oil for the
sesame oil.

1 Cook the noodles according to the instructions on the package. Drain and rinse under cold running water until cool. Set aside.

2 Heat 3 tablespoons of the vegetable oil in a preheated wok or skillet. Add the onion and carrots, and stir-fry for 1 minute. Add the mushrooms, snow peas, and cucumber and stir-fry for 1 minute.

3 Stir in the remaining vegetable oil and add the drained noodles, together with the spinach and bean sprouts.

4 Blend together all the remaining ingredients and pour over the noodles and vegetables.

5 Stir-fry until the noodle mixture is thoroughly heated through, then transfer to a warm serving dish and serve.

Spicy Japanese Noodles

These noodles are highly spiced with chili and flavored with sesame seeds for a nutty taste that is a true delight.

NUTRITIONAL INFORMATION

Calories	381	Sugars	.........12g
Protein	.........11g	Fat	..........13g
Carbohydrate	...59g	Saturates	.......2g

5 MINS   15 MINS

SERVES 4

INGREDIENTS

1 lb 2 oz/500 g fresh Japanese noodles

1 tbsp sesame oil

1 tbsp sesame seeds

1 tbsp corn oil

1 red onion, sliced

1 cup snow peas

6 oz/175 g carrots, thinly sliced

12 oz/350 g white cabbage, shredded

3 tbsp sweet chili sauce

2 scallions, sliced, to garnish

1 Bring a large pan of water to a boil. Add the Japanese noodles to the pan and cook for 2–3 minutes. Drain the noodles thoroughly.

2 Toss the noodles with the sesame oil and sesame seeds.

3 Heat the corn oil in a large preheated wok.

4 Add the onion slices, snow peas, carrot slices, and shredded cabbage to the wok and stir-fry for 5 minutes.

5 Add the sweet chili sauce to the wok and cook, stirring occasionally, for an additional 2 minutes.

6 Add the sesame noodles to the wok, toss thoroughly to combine and heat through for an additional 2–3 minutes. (You may wish to serve the noodles separately, so transfer them to the serving bowls.)

7 Transfer the Japanese noodles and spicy vegetables to warm individual serving bowls. Scatter over the sliced scallions to garnish and serve immediately.

COOK'S TIP

If fresh Japanese noodles are difficult to get hold of, use dried rice noodles or thin egg noodles instead.

Grains & Beans

Grains and beans are universally important staple foods. They are highly nutritious as they are an excellent source of protein, iron, calcium, and B vitamins, and are also

virtually fat-free. Grains include wheat, corn, barley, rye, oats, buckwheat, and many different varieties of rice, as well as their associated flours. Beans include chickpeas, yellow and green split peas, a fascinating variety of beans, together with many types of lentil. Grains and beans form a substantial base to which other ingredients can be added. Each has its own flavor and texture, so it's worth experimenting with different combinations.

Risotto Verde

Risotto is an Italian dish that is easy to make and uses risotto rice, onion, and garlic as a base for a range of savory recipes.

NUTRITIONAL INFORMATION

Calories	374	Sugars	.........5g
Protein	........10g	Fat	..........9g
Carbohydrate	...55g	Saturates	.......2g

5 MINS   35 MINS

SERVES 4

INGREDIENTS

7½ cups vegetable stock

2 tbsp olive oil

2 garlic cloves, crushed

2 leeks, shredded

scant 1¼ cups risotto rice

1¼ cups dry white wine

4 tbsp chopped mixed herbs

8 oz/225 g baby spinach

3 tbsp plain yogurt

salt and pepper

shredded leek, to garnish

1 Pour the stock into a large pan and bring to a boil. Reduce the heat to a simmer.

2 Meanwhile, heat the oil in a separate pan. Add the garlic and leeks and sauté over low heat, stirring occasionally, for 2–3 minutes, until softened.

3 Stir in the rice and cook for 2 minutes, stirring until each grain is coated with oil.

4 Pour in half of the wine and a little of the hot stock. Cook over low heat until all of the liquid has been absorbed. Add the remaining stock and the wine, a little at a time, and cook over low heat for 25 minutes, until the rice is creamy.

5 Stir in the chopped mixed herbs and baby spinach, then season to taste with salt and pepper and cook for 2 minutes.

6 Stir in the plain yogurt. Transfer the risotto to a warm serving dish, then garnish with the shredded leek and serve immediately.

COOK'S TIP

Do not try to hurry the process of cooking the risotto as the rice must absorb the liquid slowly in order for it to reach the correct consistency.

Couscous Royale

Serve this stunning dish as a centerpiece for a North African-style feast; it will prove to be a truly memorable meal.

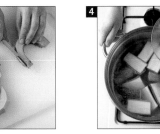

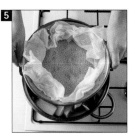

NUTRITIONAL INFORMATION

Calories 329	Sugars 31g	
Protein 6g	Fat 13g	
Carbohydrate ...50g	Saturates 6g	

25 MINS   45 MINS

SERVES 6

INGREDIENTS

3 carrots

3 zucchini

12 oz/350 g pumpkin or squash

5 cups vegetable stock

2 cinnamon sticks, broken in half

2 tsp ground cumin

1 tsp ground coriander

pinch of saffron strands

2 tbsp olive oil

pared rind and juice of 1 lemon

2 tbsp clear honey

1 lb 2 oz/500 g pre-cooked couscous

¼ cup butter, softened

scant 1 cup large seedless raisins

salt and pepper

cilantro, to garnish

1 Cut the carrots and zucchini into 3-inch/7-cm pieces and cut each in half lengthwise.

2 Trim the pumpkin and discard the seeds. Peel and cut into pieces the same size as the carrots and zucchini.

3 Put the stock, spices, saffron, and carrots in a large pan. Bring to a boil, then skim off any scum and add the olive oil. Simmer for 15 minutes.

4 Add the lemon rind and juice to the pan, together with the honey, zucchini, and pumpkin. Season well. Bring back to a boil and simmer for an additional 10 minutes.

5 Meanwhile, soak the couscous according to the packet instructions. Transfer to a steamer or large strainer lined with cheesecloth and place over the vegetable pan. Cover and steam as directed. Stir in the butter.

6 Pile the couscous onto a warmed serving plate. Drain the vegetables, reserving the stock, lemon rind, and cinnamon. Arrange the vegetables on top of the couscous. Put the raisins on top and spoon over 6 tablespoons of the reserved stock. Keep warm.

7 Return the remaining stock to the heat and boil for 5 minutes to reduce slightly. Discard the lemon rind and cinnamon. Garnish with sprigs of cilantro and serve immediately, handing the sauce separately.

Spiced Basmati Pilaf

The whole spices are not meant to be eaten and may be removed before serving. Omit the broccoli and mushrooms for a plain, spiced pilaf.

NUTRITIONAL INFORMATION

Calories 450   Sugars 3g
Protein . . . . .9g   Fat 15g
Carbohydrate . . .76g   Saturates 2g

20 MINS   25 MINS

SERVES 6

INGREDIENTS

2½ cups basmati rice

6 oz/175 g broccoli, trimmed

6 tbsp vegetable oil

2 large onions, chopped

4 cups sliced mushrooms

2 garlic cloves, crushed

6 cardamom pods, split

6 whole cloves

8 black peppercorns

1 cinnamon stick or piece of cassia bark

1 tsp ground turmeric

5 cups boiling vegetable stock or water

salt and pepper

generous ⅓ cup seedless raisins

scant ½ cup unsalted pistachios,
    coarsely chopped

VARIATION

For added richness, you could stir a spoonful of vegetable ghee through the rice mixture just before serving. A little diced red bell pepper and a few cooked peas forked through at step 4 add a colorful touch.

1 Place the rice in a strainer and wash well under cold running water. Drain. Trim off most of the broccoli stem and cut into small florets, then cut the stem into fourths lengthwise and cut these diagonally into ½-inch/1-cm pieces.

2 Heat the oil in a large pan. Add the onions and broccoli stems and cook over low heat, stirring frequently, for 3 minutes. Add the mushrooms, rice, garlic, and spices and cook for 1 minute, stirring, until the rice is coated in oil.

3 Add a boiling stock and season to taste with salt and pepper. Stir in the broccoli florets and return the mixture to a boil. Cover, then reduce the heat and cook over low heat for 15 minutes without uncovering the pan.

4 Remove from the heat and leave to stand for 5 minutes without uncovering. Add the raisins and pistachios and gently fork through to fluff up the grains. Serve hot.

Tabbouleh Salad

This kind of salad is eaten widely throughout the Middle East. The flavor improves as it is kept, so it tastes even better on the second day.

NUTRITIONAL INFORMATION

Calories	637	Sugars	.........8g
Protein	........20g	Fat	..........41g
Carbohydrate	...50g	Saturates	......11g

1½ HOURS   5–10 MINS

SERVES 2

INGREDIENTS

1 cup bulgur wheat

2½ cups boiling water

1 red bell pepper, seeded and halved

3 tbsp olive oil

1 garlic clove, crushed

grated rind of ½ lime

about 1 tbsp lime juice

1 tbsp chopped mint

1 tbsp chopped parsley

3–4 scallions, trimmed and thinly sliced

8 pitted black olives, halved

scant ⅓ cup large salted peanuts or
cashew nuts

1–2 tsp lemon juice

2–3 oz/55–85 g Gruyère cheese

salt and pepper

mint sprigs, to garnish

warm pita bread or crusty rolls, to serve

1 Put the bulgur wheat into a bowl and cover with a boiling water to reach about 1 inch/2.5 cm above the bulgur. Set aside to soak for up to 1 hour, until most of the water is absorbed and is cold.

2 Meanwhile, put the halved red bell pepper, skin side upward, on a broiler rack and cook under a preheated moderate broiler until the skin is thoroughly charred and blistered. Leave to cool slightly.

3 When cool enough to handle, peel off the skin and discard the seeds. Cut the bell pepper flesh into narrow strips.

4 Whisk together the oil, garlic, and lime rind and juice. Season to taste and whisk until thoroughly blended. Add 4½ teaspoons of the dressing to the bell peppers and mix lightly.

5 Drain the soaked bulgur wheat thoroughly, squeezing it in a dry cloth to make it even drier, then place in a bowl.

6 Add the chopped herbs, scallions, olives, and peanuts to the bulgur and toss. Add the lemon juice to the remaining dressing, and stir through the salad. Spoon the salad onto 2 serving plates.

7 Cut the cheese into narrow strips and mix with the bell pepper strips. Spoon alongside the bulgur salad. Garnish with mint sprigs and serve with warm pita bread or crusty rolls.

Deep South Rice & Beans

Cajun spices add a flavor of the American Deep South to this colorful rice and red kidney bean salad.

NUTRITIONAL INFORMATION

Calories 336	Sugars 8g
Protein 7g	Fat 13g
Carbohydrate ...51g	Saturates 2g

10 MINS   15 MINS

SERVES 4

INGREDIENTS

scant 1 cup long grain rice

4 tbsp olive oil

1 small green bell pepper, seeded
   and chopped

1 small red bell pepper, seeded
   and chopped

1 onion, finely chopped

1 small red or green chile, seeded and
   finely chopped

2 tomatoes, chopped

½ cup canned red kidney
   beans, rinsed and drained

1 tbsp chopped fresh basil

2 tsp chopped fresh thyme

1 tsp Cajun spice

salt and pepper

fresh basil leaves, to garnish

1 Cook the rice in plenty of boiling, lightly salted water for 12 minutes, until just tender. Rinse with cold water and drain well.

2 Meanwhile, heat the olive oil in a skillet and fry the green and red bell peppers and onion gently for 5 minutes, until softened.

3 Add the chile and tomatoes, and cook for an additional 2 minutes.

4 Add the vegetable mixture and red kidney beans to the rice. Stir well to combine thoroughly.

5 Stir the chopped herbs and Cajun spice into the rice mixture. Season to taste with salt and pepper, and serve, garnished with basil leaves.

Kofta Kabobs

Traditionally, koftas are made from a spicy meat mixture, but this bean and wheat version makes a tasty vegetarian alternative.

NUTRITIONAL INFORMATION

Calories	598	Sugars	.........7g
Protein	........26g	Fat	..........17g
Carbohydrate	...90g	Saturates	.......3g

1 HR 20 MINS   1½ HOURS

SERVES 4

I N G R E D I E N T S

6 oz/175 g adzuki beans

1⅓ cups bulgur wheat

scant 2 cups vegetable stock

3 tbsp olive oil, plus extra for brushing

1 onion, finely chopped

2 garlic cloves, crushed

1 tsp ground coriander

1 tsp ground cumin

2 tbsp chopped fresh cilantro

3 eggs, beaten

generous ¾ cup dried bread crumbs

salt and pepper

T A B B O U L E H

1⅓ cups bulgur wheat

2 tbsp lemon juice

1 tbsp olive oil

6 tbsp chopped parsley

4 scallions, finely chopped

2 oz/55 g cucumber, finely chopped

3 tbsp chopped mint

1 extra-large tomato, finely chopped

T O   S E R V E

black olives

pita bread

1 Cook the adzuki beans in boiling water for 40 minutes, until tender. Drain, then rinse and leave to cool. Cook the bulgur wheat in the stock for 10 minutes, until the stock is absorbed. Set aside.

2 Heat 1 tablespoon of the oil in a skillet and fry the onion, garlic, and spices for 4–5 minutes.

3 Transfer to a bowl, together with the beans, cilantro, seasoning, and eggs and mash with a potato masher or fork. Add the bread crumbs and bulgur wheat and stir well. Cover and chill for 1 hour, until firm.

4 To make the tabbouleh, soak the bulgur wheat in 1¾ cups of boiling water for 15 minutes. Combine with the remaining ingredients. Cover and chill.

5 With wet hands, mold the kofta mixture into 32 oval shapes.

6 Press onto skewers, then brush with oil and broil for 5–6 minutes until golden. Turn, then brush with oil again and cook for 5–6 minutes. Drain on paper towels. Serve with the tabbouleh, black olives, and pita bread.

Vegetable Couscous

Couscous is a semolina grain that is very quick and easy to cook, and it makes a pleasant change from rice or pasta.

NUTRITIONAL INFORMATION

Calories 280	Sugars 13g	
Protein 10g	Fat 7g	
Carbohydrate ...47g	Saturates 1g	

🍲 20 MINS   🕐 40 MINS

SERVES 4

INGREDIENTS

2 tbsp vegetable oil

1 large onion, coarsely chopped

1 carrot, chopped

1 turnip, chopped

2½ cups vegetable stock

scant 1½ cups couscous

2 tomatoes, peeled and cut into fourths

2 zucchini, chopped

1 red bell pepper, seeded and chopped

1 cup green beans, chopped

grated rind of 1 lemon

pinch of ground turmeric (optional)

1 tbsp finely chopped fresh cilantro
    or parsley

salt and pepper

fresh flat-leaf parsley sprigs,
    to garnish

1 Heat the oil in a large pan and sauté the onion, carrot, and turnip for 3–4 minutes. Add the stock and bring to a boil, then cover and simmer for 20 minutes.

2 Meanwhile, put the couscous in a bowl and moisten with a little boiling water, stirring, until the grains have swollen and separated.

3 Add the tomatoes, zucchini, bell pepper, and green beans to the pan.

4 Stir the lemon rind into the couscous and add the turmeric, if using, and mix thoroughly. Put the couscous in a steamer and position it over the pan of vegetables. Simmer the vegetables so that the couscous steams for 8–10 minutes.

5 Pile the couscous onto warmed serving plates. Ladle the vegetables and some of the liquid over the top. Scatter with the cilantro and serve at once, garnished with parsley sprigs.

Risotto in Shells

An eggplant is halved and filled with a risotto mixture, then topped with cheese and baked to make a snack or quick meal for two.

NUTRITIONAL INFORMATION

Calories	444	Sugars	........20g
Protein	........13g	Fat	..........23g
Carbohydrate	...50g	Saturates	.......8g

20 MINS   55 MINS

SERVES 2

INGREDIENTS

¼ cup mixed long grain and wild rice

1 eggplant, about 12 oz/350 g

1 tbsp olive oil

1 small onion, finely chopped

1 garlic clove, crushed

½ small red bell pepper, seeded
    and chopped

2 tbsp water

3 tbsp raisins

scant ¼ cup cashew nuts, coarsely chopped

½ tsp dried oregano

⅓ cup grated sharp Cheddar or
    Parmesan cheese

salt and pepper

oregano or parsley to garnish

1 Cook the rice in boiling salted water for 15 minutes, or until just tender. Drain, then rinse and drain again.

2 Bring a large pan of water to a boil. Cut the stem off the eggplant and cut in half lengthwise. Cut out the flesh from the center carefully, leaving about a ½-inch/1.5-cm shell. Blanch the shells in the boiling water for 3–4 minutes. Drain thoroughly. Chop the eggplant flesh finely.

3 Heat the oil in a pan or skillet. Add the onion and garlic and sauté over low heat until beginning to soften, then add the bell pepper and eggplant flesh and continue cooking for a 2–3 minutes before adding the water and cooking for an additional 2–3 minutes.

4 Stir the raisins, cashew nuts, dried oregano, and rice into the eggplant mixture and season to taste with salt and pepper.

5 Place the eggplant shells in an ovenproof dish and spoon in the rice mixture, piling it up well. Cover and cook in a preheated oven, 375°F/190°C, for 20 minutes.

6 Remove the lid and sprinkle the cheese over the rice. Place under a preheated moderate broiler and cook for 3–4 minutes, until golden brown and bubbling. Serve hot garnished with oregano.

Special Fried Rice

In this simple recipe, cooked rice is fried with vegetables and cashew nuts. It can either be eaten on its own or served as an accompaniment.

NUTRITIONAL INFORMATION

Calories	355	Sugars 6g
Protein	.........9g	Fat 15g
Carbohydrate	...48g	Saturates 3g

10 MINS   30 MINS

SERVES 4

INGREDIENTS

generous ¾ cup long grain rice

generous ⅓ cup cashew nuts

1 carrot

½ cucumber

1 yellow bell pepper

2 scallions

2 tbsp vegetable oil

1 garlic clove, crushed

1 cup frozen peas, thawed

1 tbsp soy sauce

1 tsp salt

cilantro leaves, to garnish

1 Bring a large pan of water to a boil. Add the rice and simmer for 15 minutes. Tip the rice into a strainer and rinse; drain thoroughly.

COOK'S TIP

You can replace any of the vegetables in this recipe with others suitable for a stir-fry, and using leftover rice makes this a perfect last-minute dish.

2 Heat a wok or large, heavy-bottom skillet, then add the cashew nuts and dry-fry until lightly browned. Remove and set aside.

3 Cut the carrot in half along the length, then slice thinly into semi-circles. Halve the cucumber and remove the seeds, using a teaspoon, then dice the flesh. Seed and slice the bell pepper and chop the scallions.

4 Heat the oil in a wok or large skillet. Add the prepared vegetables and the garlic. Stir-fry for 3 minutes. Add the rice, peas, soy sauce, and salt. Continue to stir-fry until well mixed and thoroughly heated.

5 Stir in the reserved cashew nuts. Transfer to a warmed serving dish, then garnish with cilantro leaves and serve immediately.

Spinach & Nut Pilaf

Fragrant basmati rice is cooked with cèpe mushrooms, spinach, and pistachio nuts in this easy microwave recipe.

NUTRITIONAL INFORMATION

Calories . . . . .403 Sugars 7g
Protein . . . . .10g Fat 15g
Carbohydrate . . .62g Saturates 2g

55 MINS   15-20 MINS

SERVES 4

I N G R E D I E N T S

¼ oz/10 g dried cèpe mushrooms

1¼ cups hot water

1 onion, chopped

1 garlic clove, crushed

1 tsp grated gingerroot

½ fresh green chile, seeded and chopped

2 tbsp oil

generous 1 cup basmati rice

1 large carrot, grated

¾ cup vegetable stock

½ tsp ground cinnamon

4 cloves

½ tsp saffron strands

8 oz/225 g fresh spinach, long stems
    removed

⅓ cup pistachio nuts

1 tbsp chopped cilantro

salt and pepper

cilantro leaves, to garnish

1 Place the cèpe mushrooms in a small bowl. Pour over the hot water and leave to soak for 30 minutes.

2 Place the onion, garlic, ginger, chile, and oil in a large bowl. Cover and cook on High power for 2 minutes. Rinse the rice, then stir it into the bowl, together with the carrot. Cover and cook on High power for 1 minute.

3 Strain and coarsely chop the mushrooms. Add the mushroom soaking liquid to the stock to make 1¾ cups. Pour on to the rice. Stir in the mushrooms, cinnamon, cloves, saffron, and ½ teaspoon salt. Cover and cook on High power for 10 minutes, stirring once. Leave to stand, covered, for 10 minutes.

4 Place the spinach in a large bowl. Cover and cook on High power for 3½ minutes, stirring once. Drain well and chop coarsely.

5 Stir the spinach, pistachio nuts, and chopped cilantro into the rice. Season to taste with salt and pepper and garnish with cilantro leaves. Serve immediately.

Pilaf Rice

Plain boiled rice is eaten by most people in India every day, but for entertaining, a more interesting rice dish, such as this, is served.

NUTRITIONAL INFORMATION

Calories 265	Sugars 0g
Protein 4g	Fat 10g
Carbohydrate ...43g	Saturates 6g

🔥

🍳 5 MINS   🕐 25 MINS

SERVES 4

INGREDIENTS

1 cup basmati rice

2 tbsp vegetable ghee

3 green cardamoms

2 cloves

3 peppercorns

½ tsp salt

½ tsp saffron

1¾ cups water

1 Rinse the rice twice under running water and set aside until required.

2 Heat the ghee in a pan. Add the cardamoms, cloves, and peppercorns to the pan and fry, stirring constantly, for 1 minute.

3 Add the rice and stir-fry over medium heat for an additional 2 minutes.

4 Add the salt, saffron, and water to the rice mixture and reduce the heat. Cover the pan and simmer over low heat until the water has been absorbed.

5 Transfer the pilaf rice to a serving dish and serve hot.

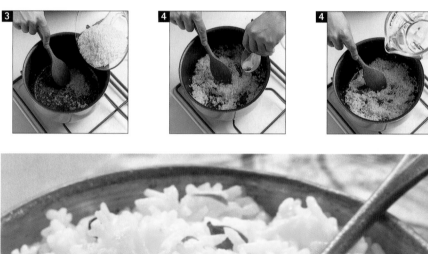

COOK'S TIP

The most expensive of all spices, saffron strands are the stamens of a type of crocus. They give dishes a rich, golden color, as well as adding a distinctive, slightly bitter taste. Saffron is sold as a powder or in the more expensive strands.

Tomato Rice

Rice cooked with tomatoes and onions will add color to your table, especially when garnished with green chiles and cilantro.

NUTRITIONAL INFORMATION

Calories ...... .866   Sugars 7g
Protein .... .15g   Fat .... .46g
Carbohydrate ..106g   Saturates 6g

10 MINS   35 MINS

SERVES 4

I N G R E D I E N T S

⅔ cup vegetable oil

2 medium onions, sliced

1 tsp onion seeds

1 tsp finely chopped gingerroot

1 tsp crushed garlic

½ tsp turmeric

1 tsp chili powder

1½ tsp salt

14 oz/400 g canned tomatoes

2½ cups basmati rice

2½ cups water

T O G A R N I S H

3 fresh green chiles, finely chopped

fresh cilantro leaves, chopped

3 hard-cooked eggs

1 Heat the oil in a pan. Add the onions and fry over moderate heat, stirring frequently, for 5 minutes, until golden brown.

2 Add the onion seeds, ginger, garlic, turmeric, chili powder, and salt, stirring to combine.

3 Reduce the heat, then add the tomatoes and stir-fry for 10 minutes, breaking them up.

4 Add the rice to the tomato mixture, stirring gently to coat the rice completely in the mixture. Stir in the water. Cover the pan and cook over low heat until the water has been absorbed and the rice is cooked.

5 Transfer the tomato rice to a warmed serving dish. Garnish with the finely chopped green chiles, cilantro leaves, and hard-cooked eggs. Serve the tomato rice immediately.

COOK'S TIP

Onion seeds are always used whole in Indian cooking. They are often used in pickles and often sprinkled over the top of naan breads. Onion seeds don't have anything to do with the vegetable, but they look similar to the plant's seed, hence the name.

Thai Jasmine Rice

Every Thai meal has as its centerpiece a big bowl of steaming, fluffy Thai jasmine rice, to which salt should not be added.

NUTRITIONAL INFORMATION

Calories 239	Sugars 0g	
Protein 5g	Fat 2g	
Carbohydrate ...54g	Saturates 0.6g	

5 MINS   10–15 MINS

SERVES 4

INGREDIENTS

OPEN PAN METHOD

generous 1 cup Thai jasmine rice

4 cups water

ABSORPTION METHOD

generous 1 cup Thai jasmine rice

1¾ cups water

COOK'S TIP

Thai jasmine rice can be frozen. Freeze in a plastic sealed container. Frozen rice is ideal for stir-fry dishes, as the process seems to separate the grains.

1 For the open pan method, rinse the rice in a strainer under cold running water and leave to drain.

2 Bring the water to a boil. Add the rice, then stir once and return to a medium boil. Cook, uncovered, for 8–10 minutes, until tender.

3 Drain thoroughly and fork through lightly before serving.

4 For the absorption method, rinse the rice under cold running water.

5 Put the rice and water into a pan and bring to a boil. Stir once and then cover the pan tightly. Lower the heat as much as possible. Cook for 10 minutes. Leave to rest for 5 minutes.

6 Fork through lightly and serve the rice immediately.

Kitchouri

The traditional breakfast plate of kedgeree reputedly has its roots in this Indian flavored rice dish, which English colonists adopted.

NUTRITIONAL INFORMATION

Calories 318   Sugars 5g
Protein . . . . .12g   Fat 10g
Carbohydrate . . .48g   Saturates 6g

10 MINS   30 MINS

SERVES 4

I N G R E D I E N T S

2 tbsp vegetable ghee or butter

1 red onion, finely chopped

1 garlic clove, crushed

½ celery stalk, finely chopped

1 tsp turmeric

½ tsp garam masala

1 green chile, seeded and finely chopped

½ tsp cumin seeds

1 tbsp chopped cilantro

generous ½ cup basmati rice,
    rinsed under cold water

½ cup green lentils

1¼ cups vegetable juice

2½ cups vegetable stock

1 Heat the ghee in a large heavy-bottom pan. Add the onion, garlic, and celery and cook for 5 minutes, until soft.

2 Add the turmeric, garam masala, green chile, cumin seeds, and cilantro. Cook over moderate heat, stirring constantly, for 1 minute, until fragrant.

3 Add the rice and lentils and cook for 1 minute, until the rice is translucent.

4 Pour the vegetable juice and stock into the pan and bring to a boil over medium heat. Cover and simmer over low heat, stirring occasionally, for 20 minutes, until the lentils are cooked. (They should be tender when pressed between two fingers.)

5 Transfer the kitchouri to a warmed serving dish and serve piping hot.

COOK'S TIP

This is a versatile dish, and can be served as a great-tasting and satisfying one-pot meal. It can also be served as a winter lunch dish with tomatoes and yogurt.

Creamy Vegetable Curry

Vegetables are cooked in a mildly spiced curry sauce with yogurt and fresh cilantro stirred in just before serving.

NUTRITIONAL INFORMATION

Calories	423	Sugars	........24g
Protein	........16g	Fat	..........19g
Carbohydrate	...50g	Saturates	.......7g

20 MINS   25 MINS

SERVES 4

INGREDIENTS

2 tbsp corn oil

1 onion, sliced

2 tsp cumin seeds

2 tbsp ground coriander

1 tsp ground turmeric

2 tsp ground ginger

1 tsp chopped fresh red chile

2 garlic cloves, chopped

14 oz/400 g canned chopped tomatoes

3 tbsp powdered coconut mixed with
    1¼ cups boiling water

1 small cauliflower, broken into florets

2 zucchini, sliced

2 carrots, sliced

1 potato, diced

14 oz/400 g canned chickpeas,
    drained and rinsed

¾ cup thick plain yogurt

2 tbsp mango chutney

3 tbsp chopped fresh cilantro

salt and pepper

fresh herbs, to garnish

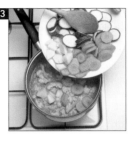

1 Heat the oil in a pan and sauté the onion until softened. Add the cumin, ground coriander, turmeric, ginger, chile, and garlic and cook for 1 minute.

2 Add the tomatoes and coconut mixture and mix well.

3 Add the cauliflower florets, zucchini, carrots, diced potato, and chickpeas and season to taste with salt and pepper. Cover and simmer for 20 minutes, until the vegetables are tender.

4 Stir in the yogurt, mango chutney, and fresh cilantro and heat through gently, but do not boil. Transfer to a warm serving dish, then garnish with fresh herbs and serve.

Fried Spicy Rice

Ginger and garlic give this beautifully aromatic rice dish its lovely flavor. If desired, you can add a few peas to it for extra color.

NUTRITIONAL INFORMATION

Calories 507   Sugars 2g
Protein . . . . .9g   Fat 11g
Carbohydrate . . .99g   Saturates 6g

10 MINS   35 MINS

SERVES 4

INGREDIENTS

2½ cups rice

1 medium onion

2 tbsp vegetable ghee

1 tsp finely chopped gingerroot

1 tsp crushed garlic

1 tsp salt

1 tsp black cumin seeds

3 whole cloves

3 whole green cardamoms

2 cinnamon sticks

4 peppercorns

3 cups water

1 Rinse the rice thoroughly under cold running water.

2 Using a sharp knife, cut the onion into thin slices.

3 Heat the ghee in a large pan. Add the onion and sauté over medium heat, stirring occasionally, until crisp and golden brown.

4 Add the ginger, garlic, and salt to the onions in the pan, stirring to combine.

5 Remove half of the spicy onions from the pan and set aside.

6 Add the rice, black cumin seeds, cloves, cardamoms, cinnamon sticks, and peppercorns to the pan and stir-fry for 3–5 minutes.

7 Add the water to the pan and bring to a boil over medium heat. Reduce the heat, then cover and simmer until steam comes out through the lid. Check to see whether the rice is cooked and the liquid has been absorbed.

8 Transfer the fried spicy rice to a warmed serving dish and serve immediately garnished with the reserved fried onions.

Green Herb Rice

This is a deliciously different way to serve plain rice for a special occasion or to liven up a simple meal.

NUTRITIONAL INFORMATION

Calories	652	Sugars	.........9g
Protein	........15g	Fat	..........17g
Carbohydrate	...116g	Saturates	.......6g

1HR 10 MINS   35 MINS

SERVES 4

INGREDIENTS

2 tbsp olive oil

2½ cups basmati or Thai jasmine rice,
    soaked for 1 hour, washed and drained

3 cups coconut milk

1 tsp salt

1 bay leaf

2 tbsp chopped cilantro

2 tbsp chopped mint

2 green chiles, seeded and finely
    chopped

1 Heat the oil in a pan, then add the rice and stir over medium heat until it becomes translucent.

2 Add the coconut milk, salt, and bay leaf. Bring to a boil and cook until all the liquid is absorbed.

COOK'S TIP

The contrasting colors of this dish make it particularly attractive, and it can be made to look even more interesting with a carefully chosen garnish. Two segments of fresh lime complement the cilantro perfectly.

3 Reduce the heat to very low, then cover the pan tightly and cook for 10 minutes. Take great care that the rice does not catch and burn on the bottom of the pan.

4 Remove the bay leaf and stir in the cilantro, mint, and green chiles. Fork through the rice gently to fluff up the grains. Transfer to a warm serving dish and serve immediately.

Vegetable Pilaf

This is a lovely way of cooking rice and vegetables together, and the saffron gives it a beautiful aroma. Serve this with any kabob.

NUTRITIONAL INFORMATION

Calories 557	Sugars 9g
Protein 11g	Fat 14g
Carbohydrate . .104g	Saturates 7g

20 MINS   55 MINS

SERVES 6

INGREDIENTS

2 medium potatoes, each cut into 6

1 medium eggplant, cut into 6

7 oz/200 g carrots, sliced

½ cup green beans, cut into pieces

4 tbsp vegetable ghee

2 medium onions, sliced

¾ cup plain yogurt

2 tsp finely chopped gingerroot

2 tsp crushed garlic

2 tsp garam masala

2 tsp black cumin seeds

½ tsp turmeric

3 black cardamoms

3 cinnamon sticks

2 tsp salt

1 tsp chili powder

½ tsp saffron strands

1¼ cups milk

3 cups basmati rice

5 tbsp lemon juice

TO GARNISH

4 green chiles, chopped

cilantro leaves, chopped

1 Prepare the vegetables. Heat the ghee in a skillet. Add the potatoes, eggplant, carrots, and beans and fry, turning frequently, until softened. Remove from the pan and set aside.

2 Add the onions and fry, stirring frequently, until soft. Add the yogurt, ginger, garlic, garam masala, 1 teaspoon black cumin seeds, the turmeric, 1 cardamom, 1 cinnamon stick, 1 teaspoon salt, and the chili powder and stir-fry for 3–5 minutes. Return the vegetables to the skillet and stir-fry for 4–5 minutes.

3 Put the saffron and milk in a pan and bring to a boil, stirring. Remove from the heat and set aside.

4 In a pan of boiling water, half-cook the rice with 1 teaspoon salt, 2 cinnamon sticks, 2 black cardamoms, and 1 teaspoon black cumin seeds. Drain the rice, leaving half in the pan, while transferring the other half to a bowl. Pour the vegetable mixture on top of the rice in the pan. Pour half of the lemon juice and half of the saffron milk over the vegetables and rice, then cover with the remaining rice and pour the remaining lemon juice and saffron milk over the top. Garnish with chiles and cilantro, then return to the heat and cover. Cook over low heat for 20 minutes. Serve hot.

Spiced Rice & Lentils

This is a lovely combination of rice and masoor dhal and is simple to cook. You can add a knob of unsalted butter before serving, if liked.

NUTRITIONAL INFORMATION

Calories 394	Sugars 3g
Protein 14g	Fat 8g
Carbohydrate . . .70g	Saturates 1g

5 MINS   30 MINS

SERVES 4

INGREDIENTS

1 cup basmati rice

¾ cup masoor dhal

2 tbsp vegetable ghee

1 small onion, sliced

1 tsp finely chopped gingerroot

1 tsp crushed garlic

½ tsp turmeric

2½ cups water

1 tsp salt

1 Combine the rice and dhal and rinse thoroughly in cold running water. Set aside until required.

2 Heat the ghee in a large pan. Add the onion and cook, stirring occasionally, for 2 minutes.

COOK'S TIP

Many Indian recipes specify using ghee as the cooking fat. This is because it is similar to clarified butter in that it can be heated to a very high temperature without burning. Ghee adds a nutty flavor to dishes and a glossy shine to sauces.

3 Reduce the heat, then add the ginger, garlic, and turmeric and stir-fry for 1 minute.

4 Add the rice and dhal to the mixture in the pan and blend together, mixing gently, but thoroughly.

5 Add the water to the mixture in the pan and bring to a boil over medium heat. Reduce the heat, then cover and cook for 20–25 minutes, until the rice is tender and the liquid is absorbed.

6 Just before serving, add the salt and mix to combine.

7 Transfer the spiced rice and lentils to a large warmed serving dish and serve immediately.

Chana Dhal & Rice

Saffron is used to flavor this dish, which makes it rather special.
It is absolutely delicious served with any curry.

NUTRITIONAL INFORMATION

Calories	479	Sugars	.........7g
Protein	........12g	Fat	..........14g
Carbohydrate	...80g	Saturates	.......8g

3¼ HOURS   1 HOUR

SERVES 6

INGREDIENTS

¾ cup chana dhal

4 tbsp ghee

2 medium onions, sliced

1 tsp finely chopped gingerroot

1 tsp crushed garlic

½ tsp turmeric

2 tsp salt

½ tsp chili powder

1 tsp garam masala

5 tbsp plain yogurt

5⅔ cups water

⅔ cup milk

1 tsp saffron

3 tbsp lemon juice

2 fresh green chiles

fresh cilantro leaves

3 black cardamoms

3 black cumin seeds

2½ cups basmati rice

1 Rinse and soak the chana dhal for 3 hours. Rinse the rice under running water and set aside.

2 Heat the ghee in a skillet. Add the onion and sauté until golden brown. Using a slotted spoon, remove half of the onion with a little of the ghee and set aside in a bowl.

3 Add the ginger, garlic, turmeric, 1 teaspoon of the salt, the chili powder, and garam masala to the mixture remaining in the skillet and stir-fry for 5 minutes. Stir in the yogurt and add the chana dhal and ⅔ cup water. Cook, covered, for 15 minutes. Set aside.

4 Meanwhile, boil the milk with the saffron and set aside with the reserved fried onion, lemon juice, green chiles, and cilantro leaves.

5 Boil the rest of the water and add the salt, black cardamoms, black cumin seeds, and the rice, and cook, stirring, until the rice is half-cooked. Drain, and place half of the fried onion, saffron, lemon juice, green chiles, and cilantro on top of the chana dhal mixture. Place the remaining rice on top of this and the rest of the fried onion, saffron, lemon juice, chiles, and cilantro on top of the rice. Cover tightly with a lid and cook for 20 minutes over very low heat. Mix with a slotted spoon before transferring to a warmed serving dish. Serve immediately.

Savory Flan

This tasty flan combines lentils and red bell peppers in a crisp whole-wheat pastry shell.

NUTRITIONAL INFORMATION

Calories	287	Sugars	.........5g
Protein	........10g	Fat	...........5g
Carbohydrate	...35g	Saturates	.......3g

45 MINS   50 MINS

SERVES 8

INGREDIENTS

PASTRY

scant 1⅔ cups whole-wheat flour

⅓ cup margarine, cut into small pieces

4 tbsp water

FILLING

⅔ cup red lentils, rinsed

1¼ cups vegetable stock

1 tbsp margarine

1 onion, chopped

2 red bell peppers, seeded and diced

1 tsp yeast extract

1 tbsp tomato paste

3 tbsp chopped parsley

pepper

1 To make the pastry, place the flour in a mixing bowl and rub in the margarine with your fingertips until the mixture resembles fine bread crumbs. Stir in the water and bring together to form a dough. Wrap and chill for 30 minutes.

2 Meanwhile, make the filling. Put the lentils in a pan with the stock, then bring to a boil and simmer for 10 minutes, until the lentils are tender and can be mashed to a purée.

3 Melt the margarine in a small pan, then add the chopped onion and diced red bell peppers and cook, stirring frequently, until just soft.

4 Add the lentil purée, yeast extract, tomato paste, and parsley. Season to taste with pepper. Mix until well combined.

5 On a lightly floured counter, roll out the dough and line a 9½-inch/24-cm loose-bottomed quiche pan. Prick the bottom of the pastry with a fork and spoon the lentil mixture into the pastry shell.

6 Bake in a preheated oven, 400°F/200°C, for 30 minutes, until the filling is firm.

VARIATION

Add corn to the flan in step 4 for a colorful and tasty change, if you prefer.

Red Bean Stew & Dumplings

There's nothing better on a cold day than a hearty dish topped with dumplings. This recipe is very quick and easy to prepare.

NUTRITIONAL INFORMATION

Calories 508	Sugars 15g	
Protein 22g	Fat 12g	
Carbohydrate ...83g	Saturates 4g	

20 MINS   40 MINS

SERVES 4

INGREDIENTS

1 tbsp vegetable oil

1 red onion, sliced

2 celery stalks, chopped

3¾ cups vegetable stock

8 oz/225 g carrots, diced

8 oz/225 g potatoes, diced

8 oz/225 g zucchini, diced

4 tomatoes, peeled and chopped

scant ½ cup split red lentils

14 oz/400 g canned kidney beans,
   rinsed and drained

1 tsp paprika

salt and pepper

DUMPLINGS

scant 1 cup all-purpose flour

½ tsp salt

2 tsp baking powder

1 tsp paprika

1 tsp dried mixed herbs

2 tbsp vegetable suet

scant ½ cup water

sprigs of flat-leaf parsley, to garnish

1 Heat the oil in a flameproof casserole or a large pan. Add the onion and celery and cook over low heat, stirring frequently, for 3–4 minutes, until just softened.

2 Pour in the stock and stir in the carrots and potatoes. Bring to a boil, then cover and cook for 5 minutes.

3 Stir in the zucchini, tomatoes, lentils, kidney beans, paprika, and seasoning. Bring to a boil, then cover and cook for 5 minutes.

4 Meanwhile, make the dumplings. Sift the flour, salt, baking powder, and paprika into a bowl. Stir in the herbs and suet. Bind together with the water to form a soft dough. Divide into 8 portions and roll gently to form balls.

5 Uncover the stew, stir, then add the dumplings, pushing them slightly into the stew. Cover, then reduce the heat so the stew simmers and cook for an additional 15 minutes, until the dumplings have risen and are cooked through. Garnish with flat-leaf parsley and serve immediately.

Semolina Fritters

Based on a gnocchi recipe, these delicious cheese-flavored fritters are accompanied by a fruity homemade apple relish.

NUTRITIONAL INFORMATION

Calories ....682 Sugars 40g
Protein ....19g Fat 32g
Carbohydrate ...85g Saturates 11g

30 MINS   40–45 MINS

SERVES 4

INGREDIENTS

2½ cups milk

1 small onion

1 celery stalk

1 bay leaf

2 cloves

⅔ cup semolina

1 cup grated sharp Cheddar cheese

½ tsp dried mustard powder

2 tbsp all-purpose flour

1 egg, beaten

scant ½ cup dried white bread crumbs

6 tbsp vegetable oil

salt and pepper

celery leaves, to garnish

coleslaw, to serve

RELISH

2 celery stalks, chopped

2 small eating apples, cored and diced

generous ½ cup golden raisins

½ cup ready-to-eat dried apricots, chopped

6 tbsp cider vinegar

pinch of ground cloves

½ tsp ground cinnamon

1 Pour the milk into a pan and add the onion, celery, bay leaf, and cloves. Bring to a boil, then remove from the heat and leave to stand for 15 minutes.

2 Strain into another pan, then bring to a boil and sprinkle in the semolina, stirring constantly. Reduce the heat and simmer for 5 minutes, until very thick, stirring occasionally to prevent it sticking.

3 Remove the pan from the heat. Beat in the cheese, mustard, and seasoning. Place in a greased bowl and leave to cool.

4 To make the relish, put all the ingredients in a pan and bring to a boil, then cover and simmer gently for 20 minutes, until tender. Leave to cool.

5 Put the flour, egg, and bread crumbs on separate plates. Divide the cooled semolina mixture into 8 and press into 2½-inch/6-cm rounds, flouring the hands if necessary.

6 Coat lightly in flour, then in egg and, finally, in bread crumbs. Heat the oil in a large skillet and gently cook the fritters for 3–4 minutes on each side, until golden. Drain on paper towels. Garnish with celery leaves and serve immediately with the apple relish and coleslaw.

Fragrant Curry

There are many different ways of cooking chickpeas, but this version is probably one of the most delicious and popular.

NUTRITIONAL INFORMATION

Calories	313	Sugars	.........5g
Protein	.........8g	Fat	..........19g
Carbohydrate	...29g	Saturates	.......2g

🐻 🐻

🍲 10 MINS   🕐 20 MINS

SERVES 4

I N G R E D I E N T S

6 tbsp vegetable oil

2 medium onions, sliced

1 tsp finely chopped gingerroot

1 tsp ground cumin

1 tsp ground coriander

1 tsp crushed garlic

1 tsp chili powder

2 fresh green chiles

cilantro leaves

⅔ cup water

1 large potato

14 oz/400 g canned chickpeas, drained

1 tbsp lemon juice

1 Heat the oil in a large pan. Add the onions and cook over medium heat, stirring occasionally, for 5–8 minutes, until golden brown.

2 Reduce the heat, then add the ginger, ground cumin, ground coriander, garlic, chili powder, fresh green chiles, and cilantro leaves to the pan and stir-fry for 2 minutes.

3 Add the water to the mixture in the pan and stir well to mix.

4 Using a sharp knife, cut the potato into small dice. Add the potato and the drained chickpeas to the mixture in the pan. Lower the heat, then cover and simmer, stirring occasionally, for 5-7 minutes.

5 Sprinkle the lemon juice over the curry and stir.

6 Transfer the chickpea curry to warmed individual serving dishes and serve immediately.

COOK'S TIP

Using canned chickpeas saves time, but you can use dried chickpeas if you prefer. Soak them overnight, then boil them for 15-20 minutes, until soft.

Midweek Curry Special

This easy curry is always enjoyed. Double the quantities for a great dish if you're cooking for a crowd.

NUTRITIONAL INFORMATION

Calories	403	Sugars	........19g
Protein	........19g	Fat	..........15g
Carbohydrate	...51g	Saturates	.......3g

20 MINS   40–45 MINS

SERVES 4

INGREDIENTS

2 tbsp vegetable oil

2 garlic cloves, crushed

1 large onion, chopped

1 large carrot, sliced

1 apple, cored and chopped

2 tbsp medium-hot curry powder

1 tsp finely grated fresh gingerroot

2 tsp paprika

3¾ cups vegetable stock

2 tbsp tomato paste

½ small cauliflower, broken into florets

15 oz/425 g canned chickpeas, rinsed
    and drained

2 tbsp golden raisins

2 tbsp cornstarch

2 tbsp water

4 hard-cooked eggs

salt and pepper

paprika, to garnish

CUCUMBER DIP

3-inch/7.5-cm piece of cucumber, chopped

1 tbsp chopped mint

¾ cup plain yogurt

mint sprigs, to garnish

1 Heat the oil in a large pan. Add the garlic, onion, carrot, and apple and cook, stirring frequently, for 4–5 minutes, until softened.

2 Add the curry powder, ginger, and paprika and cook for 1 minute. Stir in the vegetable stock and tomato paste.

3 Add the cauliflower, chickpeas, and golden raisins. Bring to a boil, then reduce the heat and simmer, covered, for 25–30 minutes, until the vegetables are tender.

4 Blend the cornstarch with the water to a smooth paste and add to the curry, stirring until thickened. Cook gently for 2 minutes. Season to taste with salt and pepper.

5 To make the dip, mix together the cucumber, mint, and yogurt in a small serving bowl.

6 Ladle the curry onto 4 warmed serving plates. Shell and cut the eggs into fourths, then arrange them on top of the curry. Sprinkle with a little paprika. Garnish the cucumber and mint dip with mint and serve with the curry.

Lentil & Vegetable Biryani

A delicious mix of vegetables, basmati rice, and French green lentils produces a wholesome and nutritious dish.

NUTRITIONAL INFORMATION

Calories 516   Sugars 9g
Protein . . . . .20g   Fat 19g
Carbohydrate . . .72g   Saturates 3g

20 MINS   45 MINS

SERVES 6

I N G R E D I E N T S

½ cup French green lentils

4 tbsp vegetable ghee or oil

2 onions, cut into fourths and sliced

2 garlic cloves, crushed

1-inch/2.5-cm piece of gingerroot, chopped

1 tsp ground turmeric

½ tsp chili powder

1 tsp ground coriander

2 tsp ground cumin

3 tomatoes, peeled and chopped

1 eggplant, trimmed and
    cut into ½-inch/1-cm pieces

6¼ cups boiling vegetable stock

1 red or green bell pepper, seeded
    and diced

1¾ cups basmati rice

1 cup green beans, halved

8 oz/225 g cauliflower florets

generous 1 cup mushrooms,
    sliced or cut into fourths

generous ⅓ cup unsalted cashews

3 hard-cooked eggs, shelled, and
    cilantro sprigs, to garnish

1 Rinse the lentils under cold running water and drain. Heat the ghee in a pan, then add the onions and cook gently for 2 minutes. Stir in the garlic, ginger, and spices and cook gently, stirring frequently, for 1 minute.

2 Add the lentils, tomatoes, eggplant, and 2½ cups of the stock and mix well, then cover and simmer gently for 20 minutes.

3 Add the red bell pepper and cook for an additional 10 minutes, until the lentils are tender and all the liquid has been absorbed.

4 Meanwhile, rinse the rice under cold running water. Drain and place in another pan with the remaining stock. Bring to a boil, add the green beans, cauliflower, and mushrooms, then cover and cook gently for 15 minutes, until rice and vegetables are tender. Remove from the heat and set aside, covered, for 10 minutes.

5 Add the lentil mixture and the cashews to the cooked rice and mix lightly together. Pile onto a warm serving platter and garnish with wedges of hard-cooked egg and cilantro sprigs. Serve hot.

Dry Moong Dhal

This dhal has a baghaar (seasoned oil dressing) of butter, dried red chiles, and white cumin seeds. It is simple to cook and tastes very good.

NUTRITIONAL INFORMATION

Calories 304	Sugars 1g
Protein 9g	Fat 21g
Carbohydrate ...21g	Saturates 14g

5 MINS   30-35 MINS

SERVES 4

INGREDIENTS

1 cup moong dhal

1 tsp finely chopped gingerroot

½ tsp ground cumin

½ tsp ground coriander

1 tsp fresh garlic, crushed

½ tsp chili powder

2½ cups water

1 tsp salt

BAGHAAR

scant ½ cup unsalted butter

5 dried red chiles

1 tsp white cumin seeds

TO SERVE

chapati

vegetable curry

1 Rinse the lentils under cold running water and place them in a large pan. Add the ginger, ground cumin, ground coriander, garlic, and chili powder, and stir to mix well.

2 Pour in enough of the water to cover the lentil mixture. Cook over medium heat, stirring frequently, until the lentils are soft but not mushy.

3 Stir in the salt, then transfer to a serving dish and keep warm.

4 Meanwhile, make the baghaar. Melt the butter in a heavy-bottom pan over fairly low heat. Add the dried red chiles and white cumin seeds and fry, stirring constantly, until they begin to pop.

5 Pour the baghaar over the lentils and serve immediately with chapati and a vegetable curry.

COOK'S TIP

Moong dhal are tear-drop-shaped yellow split lentils, more popular in northern India than in the south. Dried red chiles are the quickest way to add heat to a dish.

Vegetable & Lentil Koftas

A mixture of vegetables, nuts, and lentils is shaped into small balls and baked in the oven with a sprinkling of aromatic garam masala.

NUTRITIONAL INFORMATION

Calories	679	Sugars	.......20g
Protein	........29g	Fat	..........33g
Carbohydrate	...73g	Saturates	.......5g

30 MINS   50 MINS

SERVES 4

INGREDIENTS

6 tbsp vegetable ghee or oil

1 onion, finely chopped

2 carrots, finely chopped

2 celery stalks, finely chopped

2 garlic cloves, crushed

1 fresh green chile, seeded and
   finely chopped

4½ tsp curry powder or paste

scant 1 cup split red lentils

2½ cups vegetable stock

2 tbsp tomato paste

2 cups fresh whole-wheat bread crumbs

scant ⅔ cup unsalted cashews,
   finely chopped

2 tbsp chopped cilantro

1 egg, beaten

salt and pepper

garam masala, for sprinkling

YOGURT DRESSING

1 cup plain yogurt

1–2 tbsp chopped coriander

1–2 tbsp mango chutney,
   chopped if necessary

1 Heat 4 tablespoons of ghee in a large pan and gently cook the onion, carrots, celery, garlic, and chile, stirring frequently, for 5 minutes. Add the curry powder and the lentils and cook, stirring constantly, for 1 minute.

2 Add the stock and tomato paste and bring to a boil. Reduce the heat, then cover and simmer for 20 minutes, until the lentils are tender and all the liquid is absorbed.

3 Remove from the heat and cool slightly. Add the bread crumbs, nuts, cilantro, egg, and seasoning to taste. Mix well and leave to cool. Shape into rounds about the size of golf balls (use 2 spoons to help shape the rounds).

4 Place the balls on a greased cookie sheet, then drizzle with the remaining oil and sprinkle with a little garam masala, to taste. Cook in a preheated oven, at 350°F/180°C, for 15-20 minutes, until piping hot and lightly golden in color.

5 Meanwhile, make the yogurt dressing. Mix all the ingredients together in a bowl. Serve the koftas hot with the yogurt dressing.

Spinach & Chana Dhal

An attractive-looking dish, this makes a good accompaniment to almost any dish. For a contrast in color and taste, serve with a tomato curry.

NUTRITIONAL INFORMATION

Calories 175   Sugars 1g
Protein ....6g   Fat 12g
Carbohydrate ...12g   Saturates 1g

3 HRS 5 MINS   45 MINS

SERVES 6

INGREDIENTS

4 tbsp chana dhal

6 tbsp oil

1 tsp mixed onion and mustard seeds

4 dried red chiles

15 oz/425 g canned spinach, drained

1 tsp finely chopped gingerroot

1 tsp ground coriander

1 tsp ground cumin

1 tsp salt

1 tsp chili powder

2 tbsp lemon juice

1 green chile, to garnish

1 Soak the chana dhal in a bowl of warm water for at least 3 hours, preferably overnight.

COOK'S TIP

Very similar in appearance to moong dhal—the yellow split peas—chana dhal have slightly less shiny grains. It is used as a binding agent and may be bought from Indian and Pakistani grocers.

2 Place the lentils in a pan, then cover with water and bring to a boil. Simmer for 30 minutes.

3 Heat the oil in a pan. Add the mixed onion and mustard seeds and dried red chiles and fry, stirring constantly, until they turn a shade darker.

4 Add the drained spinach to the pan, mixing gently. Add the ginger, ground coriander, ground cumin, salt, and chili

powder to the mixture in the pan. Reduce the heat and gently stir-fry the mixture for 7–10 minutes.

5 Add the lentils to the pan and blend into the spinach mixture well, stirring gently so that it does not break up.

6 Transfer the mixture to a warm serving dish. Sprinkle over the lemon juice and garnish with the green chile. Serve immediately.

Kabli Chana Sag

Beans such as chickpeas are widely used in India. They need to be soaked overnight so prepare well in advance.

NUTRITIONAL INFORMATION

Calories 217	Sugars 5g
Protein 12g	Fat 9g
Carbohydrate . . .25g	Saturates 1g

10 MINS   1 HOUR

SERVES 6

INGREDIENTS

2 cups chickpeas, soaked overnight
   and drained

5 cloves

1-inch/2.5-cm piece of cinnamon stick

2 garlic cloves

3 tbsp corn oil

1 small onion, sliced

3 tbsp lemon juice

1 tsp coriander seeds

2 tomatoes, peeled, seeded and chopped

1 lb 2 oz/500 g spinach, rinsed and any
   tough stems removed

1 tbsp chopped cilantro

TO GARNISH

cilantro sprigs

lemon slices

1 Put the chickpeas into a pan with enough water to cover. Add the cloves, cinnamon, and 1 whole unpeeled garlic clove that has been lightly crushed with the back of a knife to release the juices. Bring to a boil, then reduce the heat and simmer for 40–50 minutes, until the chickpeas are tender when tested with a skewer. Skim off any surface foam.

2 Meanwhile, heat 1 tablespoon of the oil in a pan. Crush the remaining garlic clove. Put this into the pan with the oil and the onion, and cook over moderate heat for 5 minutes.

3 Remove the cloves, cinnamon, and garlic from the pan of chickpeas. Drain the chickpeas. Using a food processor or a fork, blend ¾ cup of the chickpeas with the onion and garlic, the lemon juice and 1 tablespoon of the oil until smooth. Stir this purée into the remaining chickpeas.

4 Heat the remaining oil in a large skillet, then add the coriander seeds and stir for 1 minute. Add the tomatoes and stir, then add the spinach. Cover and cook for 1 minute over moderate heat. The spinach should be wilted, but not soggy. Stir in the chopped cilantro and remove from the heat.

5 Transfer the chickpeas to a warm serving dish and spoon over the spinach. Garnish with the cilantro and slices of lemon and serve immediately.

Spiced Spinach & Lentils

This interesting combination of lentils and spiced vegetables is delicious served with parathas, chapatis, or naan bread and yogurt.

15 MINS   30 MINS

SERVES 4

INGREDIENTS

2 cups split red lentils

3 cups water

1 onion

1 eggplant

1 red bell pepper

2 zucchini

2 cups mushrooms

8 oz/225 g leaf spinach

4 tbsp vegetable ghee or oil

1 fresh green chile, seeded and chopped

1 tsp ground cumin

1 tsp ground coriander

1-inch/2.5-cm piece of fresh gingerroot, chopped

⅔ cup vegetable stock

salt

cilantro sprigs, to garnish

1 Wash the lentils and place in a pan with the water. Cover and simmer for 15 minutes, until the lentils are soft but still whole.

2 Meanwhile, slice the onion and cut into fourths. Trim the leaf end and cut the eggplant into ½-inch/1-cm pieces. Remove the stem end and seeds from the bell pepper and cut into ½-inch/1-cm pieces. Trim and cut the zucchini into ½-inch/1-cm thick slices. Thickly slice the mushrooms. Discard any coarse stems from the spinach leaves and wash the spinach well.

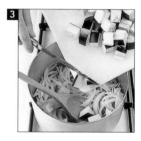

3 Heat the ghee in a large pan, then add the onion and red bell pepper and cook gently for 3 minutes, stirring frequently. Stir in the eggplant, mushrooms, chile, spices, and ginger and cook gently for 1 minute. Add the spinach and stock and season with salt to taste. Stir and turn until the spinach leaves wilt. Cover and simmer for 10 minutes, until the vegetables are just tender.

4 Make a border of the lentils on a warm serving plate and spoon the vegetable mixture into the center. (The lentils may be stirred into the vegetable mixture, instead of being used as a border, if wished.) Garnish with cilantro sprigs and serve immediately.

COOK'S TIP

Wash the spinach thoroughly in several changes of cold water as it can be gritty. Drain well and shake off excess water from the leaves before adding it to the pan.

White Lentils

This dhal is dry when cooked, so give it a baghaar (seasoned oil dressing). It makes an excellent accompaniment to any meal of kormas.

NUTRITIONAL INFORMATION

Calories	129	Sugars	.........1g
Protein	.........6g	Fat	...........6g
Carbohydrate	...14g	Saturates	.......1g

5 MINS   45 MINS

SERVES 4

INGREDIENTS

½ cup urid dhal

1 tsp finely chopped gingerroot

2½ cups water

1 tsp salt

1 tsp pepper

2 tbsp vegetable ghee

2 garlic cloves

2 fresh red chiles, finely chopped

mint leaves, to garnish

chapatis, to serve

1 Rinse the lentils thoroughly and put them in a large pan, together with the ginger.

2 Add the water and bring to a boil. Cover and simmer over medium heat for 30 minutes. Check to see whether the lentils are cooked by rubbing them between your finger and thumb. If they are still a little hard in the middle, cook for an additional 5–7 minutes. If necessary, remove the lid and cook until any remaining water has evaporated.

3 Add the salt and pepper to the lentils, mix well and set aside.

4 To make the baghaar, heat the ghee in a separate pan. Add the garlic cloves and chopped red chiles and stir well to mix thoroughly.

5 Pour the garlic and chile mixture over the lentils and then garnish with the fresh mint leaves.

6 Transfer the white lentils to warm individual serving dishes and serve hot with chapatis.

COOK'S TIP

Ghee was traditionally made from clarified butter, which can withstand higher temperatures than ordinary butter. Vegetable ghee has largely replaced it now because it is lower in saturated fats.

Onion Dhal

This dhal is semi-dry when cooked, so it is best to serve it with a curry that has a sauce. Ordinary onions can be used as a substitute.

NUTRITIONAL INFORMATION

Calories 232	Sugars 1g
Protein 6g	Fat 17g
Carbohydrate ...15g	Saturates 2g

5 MINS   30 MINS

SERVES 4

INGREDIENTS

½ cup masoor dhal (see Cook's Tip)

6 tbsp vegetable oil

1 small bunch scallions, chopped

1 tsp finely chopped gingerroot

1 tsp crushed garlic

½ tsp chile powder

½ tsp turmeric

1¼ cups water

1 tsp salt

TO GARNISH

1 fresh green chile, finely chopped

fresh cilantro leaves, roughly chopped

1 Rinse the lentils thoroughly and set aside until required.

2 Heat the oil in a heavy-bottom pan. Add the scallions to the pan and fry over medium heat, stirring frequently, until lightly browned.

3 Reduce the heat and add the ginger, garlic, chili powder, and turmeric. Briefly stir-fry the scallions with the spices. Add the lentils and mix to blend all the ingredients together.

4 Add the water to the lentil mixture, then reduce the heat to low and cook for 20–25 minutes.

5 When the lentils are cooked thoroughly, add the salt and stir gently to mix well.

6 Transfer the onion dhal to a serving dish. Garnish with the chopped green chile and fresh cilantro leaves and serve.

COOK'S TIP

Masoor dhal are small, round, pale orange split lentils. They turn a pale yellow color when cooked.

Chana Dhal

Dried beans and lentils can be cooked in similar ways, but the soaking and cooking times do vary, so check the package for instructions.

NUTRITIONAL INFORMATION

Calories	195	Sugars	.........4g
Protein	........11g	Fat	..........5g
Carbohydrate	...28g	Saturates	.......3g

1 HR 10 MINS   50 MINS

SERVES 6

INGREDIENTS

2 tbsp vegetable ghee

1 large onion, finely chopped

1 garlic clove, crushed

1 tbsp grated fresh gingerroot

1 tbsp cumin seeds, ground

2 tsp coriander seeds, ground

1 dried red chile

1-inch/2.5-cm piece of cinnamon stick

1 tsp salt

½ tsp ground turmeric

2 cups split yellow peas, soaked
   in cold water for 1 hour and drained

14 oz/400 g canned plum tomatoes

1¼ cups water

2 tsp garam masala

1 Heat the ghee in a large pan, then add the onion, garlic, and ginger and fry for 3–4 minutes, until the onion has softened slightly.

2 Add the cumin, coriander, chile, cinnamon, salt, and turmeric, then stir in the split peas until well mixed.

3 Add the tomatoes, together with their can juices, breaking the tomatoes up slightly with the back of a spoon.

4 Add the water and bring to a boil. Reduce the heat to very low and simmer, uncovered, stirring occasionally, for 40 minutes, until most of the liquid has been absorbed and the split peas are tender. Skim the surface occasionally with a slotted spoon to remove any scum.

5 Gradually stir in the garam masala, tasting after each addition, until it is of the required flavor. Serve hot.

COOK'S TIP

Use a non-stick pan if you have one, because the mixture is quite dense and does stick to the bottom of the pan occasionally. If the dhal is overstirred the split peas will break up and the dish will not have much texture or bite.

Oil-Dressed Dhal

This dhal is given a baghaar (seasoned oil dressing), just before serving, of ghee, onion, and a combination of spicy seeds.

NUTRITIONAL INFORMATION

Calories 173	Sugars 3g
Protein 8g	Fat 8g
Carbohydrate . . .20g	Saturates 5g

🖐 5 MINS   🕐 30 MINS

SERVES 4

INGREDIENTS

5 tbsp masoor dhal

4 tbsp moong dhal

1¾ cups water

1 tsp finely chopped fresh gingerroot

1 tsp crushed garlic

2 red chiles, chopped

1 tsp salt

BAGHAAR

2 tbsp ghee

1 medium onion, sliced

1 tsp mixed mustard and onion seeds

1 Rinse the lentils thoroughly and place in a large pan. Pour over the water, stirring. Add the ginger, garlic, and red chiles and bring to a boil over medium heat. Half cover with a lid and simmer for about 15–20 minutes, until they are soft enough to be mashed.

2 Mash the lentils and add more water if necessary to form a thick sauce.

3 Add the salt to the lentil mixture and stir well. Transfer the lentils to a heatproof serving dish.

4 Just before serving, melt the ghee in a small pan. Add the onion and cook over medium heat, stirring frequently, for 5–8 minutes, until golden brown. Add the mustard and onion seeds and stir to mix well.

5 Pour the onion mixture over the lentils while still hot. Stir to mix thoroughly and serve the oil-dressed dhal immediately.

COOK'S TIP

This dish makes a a very good accompaniment, especially for a dry curry. It also freezes well—simply reheat it in a pan or covered in the oven.

Tarka Dhal

This is just one version of many dhals that are served throughout India; as many people are vegetarian, dhals form a staple part of the diet.

NUTRITIONAL INFORMATION

Calories	183	Sugars	.........4g
Protein	.........8g	Fat	...........8g
Carbohydrate	...22g	Saturates	.......5g

10 MINS   25 MINS

SERVES 4

INGREDIENTS

2 tbsp ghee

2 shallots, sliced

1 tsp yellow mustard seeds

2 garlic cloves, crushed

8 fenugreek seeds

½-inch/1-cm piece of gingerroot, grated

½ tsp salt

½ cup red lentils

1 tbsp tomato paste

2½ cups water

2 tomatoes, peeled and chopped

1 tbsp lemon juice

4 tbsp chopped cilantro

½ tsp chili powder

½ tsp garam masala

1 Heat half of the ghee in a large pan and add the shallots. Cook for 2–3 minutes over high heat, then add the mustard seeds. Cover the pan until the seeds begin to pop.

2 Immediately remove the lid from the pan and add the garlic, fenugreek, ginger, and salt.

3 Stir once and add the lentils, tomato paste, and water. Bring to a boil, then lower the heat and simmer for 10 minutes.

4 Stir in the tomatoes, lemon juice, and cilantro and simmer for 4–5 minutes, until the lentils are tender.

5 Transfer to a serving dish. Heat the remaining ghee in a pan. Remove from the heat and stir in the garam masala and chili powder. Pour over the tarka dhal. Serve.

COOK'S TIP

The flavors in a dhal can be altered to suit your particular taste; for example, for extra heat, add more chili powder or chiles, or add fennel seeds for a pleasant anise flavor.

Stir-Fries & Sautés

Stir-frying is one of the most convenient and nutritious ways of cooking vegetarian food as ingredients are cooked quickly over a very high heat in very little oil. The high

heat seals in the natural juices and helps preserve nutrients. The short cooking time makes the vegetables more succulent and preserves texture as well as the natural flavor and color. A round-bottomed wok is ideal for stir-frying as it conducts and retains heat evenly and requires the use of less oil. You need a flat-bottomed pan for sautéing so that the food can be easily tossed and stirred. A brisk heat is essential so that the food turns golden brown and crisp.

Sauté of Summer Vegetables

The freshness of lightly cooked summer vegetables is enhanced by the aromatic flavor of a tarragon and white wine dressing.

NUTRITIONAL INFORMATION

Calories 217	Sugars 8g
Protein 2g	Fat 18g
Carbohydrate 9g	Saturates 9g

10 MINS   10-15 MINS

SERVES 4

INGREDIENTS

8 oz/225 g baby carrots, scrubbed

4½ oz/125 g string beans

2 zucchini, trimmed

1 bunch large scallions

1 bunch radishes

¼ cup butter

2 tbsp light olive oil

2 tbsp white wine vinegar

4 tbsp dry white wine

1 tsp superfine sugar

1 tbsp chopped tarragon

salt and pepper

tarragon sprigs, to garnish

1 Cut the carrots in half lengthwise, slice the beans and zucchini, and halve the scallions and radishes, so that all the vegetables are cut to even-size pieces.

2 Melt the butter in a large, heavy-bottom skillet or wok. Add all the vegetables and cook them over medium heat, stirring frequently, until they are tender, but still crisp and firm to the bite.

3 Heat the olive oil, vinegar, white wine, and sugar in a small pan over low

heat, stirring until the sugar has dissolved. Remove from the heat and add the chopped tarragon.

4 When the vegetables are just cooked, pour over the "dressing." Stir through,

tossing the vegetables well to coat, and then transfer to a warmed serving dish. Garnish with sprigs of fresh tarragon and serve at once.

Red Curry with Cashews

This is a wonderfully quick dish to prepare. If you don't have time to prepare the curry paste, it can be bought ready-made.

NUTRITIONAL INFORMATION

Calories ....274 Sugars 5g
Protein ....10g Fat 10g
Carbohydrate ...38g Saturates 3g

25 MINS   15 MINS

SERVES 4

INGREDIENTS

1 cup coconut milk

1 kaffir lime leaf

¼ tsp light soy sauce

4 baby corn cobs, halved lengthwise

1½ cups broccoli florets

¾ cup green beans, cut into
    2-inch/5-cm pieces

scant ¼ cup cashew nuts

15 fresh basil leaves

1 tbsp chopped cilantro

1 tbsp chopped roast peanuts, to garnish

RED CURRY PASTE

7 fresh red chiles, halved, seeded,
    and blanched

2 tsp cumin seeds

2 tsp coriander seeds

1-inch/2.5-cm piece galangal or fresh
    gingerroot, chopped

½ stalk lemon grass, chopped

1 tsp salt

grated rind of 1 lime

4 garlic cloves, chopped

3 shallots, chopped

2 kaffir lime leaves, shredded

1 tbsp vegetable oil

1 To make the curry paste, grind all the ingredients together in a large mortar with a pestle or a grinder. Alternatively, process briefly in a food processor. The quantity of red curry paste is more than required for this recipe. However, it will keep for up to 3 weeks in a sealed container in the refrigerator.

2 Put a wok or large, heavy-bottom skillet over high heat, add 3 tablespoons of the red curry paste and stir until it gives off its aroma. Reduce the heat to medium.

3 Add the coconut milk, kaffir lime leaf, light soy sauce, baby corn cobs, broccoli florets, green beans, and cashew nuts. Bring to a boil and simmer for 10 minutes, until the vegetables are cooked, but still firm and crunchy.

4 Remove and discard the lime leaf and stir in the basil leaves and cilantro. Transfer to a warmed serving dish, then garnish with peanuts and serve immediately.

Potato Curry

Very little meat is eaten in India, their diet being mainly vegetarian. This potato curry with added vegetables makes a very substantial main meal.

NUTRITIONAL INFORMATION

Calories 301   Sugars 10g
Protein . . . . .9g   Fat 12g
Carbohydrate . . .41g   Saturates 1g

15 MINS   45 MINS

SERVES 4

INGREDIENTS

4 tbsp vegetable oil

1 lb 8 oz/675 g waxy potatoes,
   cut into large chunks

2 onions, cut into fourths

3 garlic cloves, crushed

1 tsp garam masala

½ tsp turmeric

½ tsp ground cumin

½ tsp ground coriander

1-inch/2.5-cm fresh gingerroot, grated

1 fresh red chile, chopped

2 cups cauliflower florets

4 tomatoes, peeled and cut into fourths

¾ cup frozen peas

2 tbsp chopped cilantro

1¼ cups vegetable stock

shredded cilantro, to garnish

COOK'S TIP

Use a large heavy-bottom pan or skillet for this recipe to ensure that the potatoes are cooked thoroughly.

1 Heat the vegetable oil in a large heavy-bottom pan or skillet. Add the potato chunks, onion, and garlic and cook over low heat, stirring frequently, for 2–3 minutes.

2 Add the garam masala, turmeric, ground cumin, ground coriander, grated ginger, and chopped chile to the skillet, mixing the spices into the vegetables. Cook over low heat, stirring constantly, for 1 minute.

3 Add the cauliflower florets, tomatoes, peas, chopped cilantro, and vegetable stock to the curry mixture.

4 Cook the potato curry over low heat for 30–40 minutes, until the potatoes are tender and completely cooked through.

5 Garnish the potato curry with fresh cilantro and serve with plain boiled rice or warm Indian bread.

Kidney Bean Kiev

This is a vegetarian version of chicken Kiev—the bean patties are topped with garlic and herb butter and coated in bread crumbs.

NUTRITIONAL INFORMATION

Calories 688   Sugars 8g
Protein ....17g   Fat 49g
Carbohydrate ...49g   Saturates 20g

25 MINS   20 MINS

SERVES 4

INGREDIENTS

GARLIC BUTTER

scant ½ cup butter

3 garlic cloves, crushed

1 tbsp chopped parsley

BEAN PATTIES

1 lb 8 oz/675 g canned red kidney beans

scant 3 cups fresh white bread crumbs

2 tbsp butter

1 leek, chopped

1 celery stalk, chopped

1 tbsp chopped parsley

1 egg, beaten

salt and pepper

vegetable oil, for shallow frying

1 To make the garlic butter, put the butter, garlic, and parsley in a bowl and blend together with a wooden spoon. Place the garlic butter onto a sheet of baking parchment, then roll into a cigar shape and wrap in the baking parchment. Chill in the refrigerator until required.

2 Using a potato masher, mash the red kidney beans in a mixing bowl and stir in 1¼ cup of the bread crumbs until thoroughly blended.

3 Melt the butter in a heavy-bottom skillet. Add the leek and celery and sauté over low heat, stirring constantly, for 3–4 minutes.

4 Add the bean mixture to the pan, together with the parsley, then season with salt and pepper to taste and mix thoroughly. Remove the pan from the heat and set aside to cool slightly.

5 Divide the kidney bean mixture into 4 equal portions and shape them into ovals.

6 Slice the garlic butter into 4 pieces and place a slice in the center of each bean patty. With your hands, then mold the bean mixture around the garlic butter to encase it completely.

7 Dip each bean patty into the beaten egg to coat and then roll in the remaining bread crumbs.

8 Heat a little oil in a skillet and cook the patties, turning once, for 7–10 minutes, until golden brown. Serve immediately.

Bubble & Squeak

Bubble and squeak is best known as fried mashed potato and leftover greens served as an accompaniment.

NUTRITIONAL INFORMATION

Calories 301	Sugars 5g
Protein 11g	Fat 18g
Carbohydrate . . .24g	Saturates 2g

15 MINS   40 MINS

SERVES 4

I N G R E D I E N T S

1 lb/450 g mealy potatoes, diced

8 oz/225 g savoy cabbage, shredded

5 tbsp vegetable oil

2 leeks, chopped

1 garlic clove, crushed

8 oz/225 g smoked tofu, cubed

salt and pepper

shredded cooked leek, to garnish

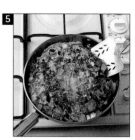

1 Cook the diced potatoes in a pan of lightly salted boiling water for 10 minutes, until tender. Drain and mash the potatoes.

2 Meanwhile, in a separate pan, blanch the cabbage in boiling water for 5 minutes. Drain well and add to the potato.

3 Heat the oil in a heavy-bottom skillet. Add the leeks and garlic and cook gently for 2–3 minutes. Stir into the potato and cabbage mixture.

4 Add the smoked tofu and season well with salt and pepper. Cook over moderate heat for 10 minutes.

5 Carefully turn the whole mixture over and continue to cook over moderate heat for an additional 5–7 minutes, until crispy underneath. Serve immediately, garnished with shredded leek.

COOK'S TIP

This vegetarian version is a perfect main meal, as the smoked tofu cubes added to the basic bubble and squeak mixture make it very substantial and nourishing.

Muttar Panir

Panir is a delicious fresh, soft cheese frequently used in Indian cooking. It is easily made at home, but must be made the day before it's required.

NUTRITIONAL INFORMATION

Calories 550	Sugars 25g	
Protein 19g	Fat 39g	
Carbohydrate . . .33g	Saturates 12g	

15 MINS   25 MINS

SERVES 6

INGREDIENTS

⅔ cup vegetable oil

2 onions, chopped

2 garlic cloves, crushed

1-inch/2.5-cm piece of gingerroot, chopped

1 tsp garam masala

1 tsp ground turmeric

1 tsp chili powder

4½ cups frozen peas

8 oz/225 g canned chopped tomatoes

½ cup vegetable stock

salt and pepper

2 tbsp chopped cilantro

PANIR

10 cups pasteurized whole milk

5 tbsp lemon juice

1 garlic clove, crushed (optional)

1 tbsp chopped cilantro (optional)

1 To make the panir, bring the milk to a rolling boil in a pan. Remove from the heat and stir in the lemon juice. Return to the heat for 1 minute, until the curds and whey separate. Remove from the heat. Line a colander with double-thickness cheesecloth and pour the mixture through the cheesecloth, adding the garlic and cilantro, if using. Squeeze all the liquid from the curds and leave to drain.

2 Transfer to a dish, then cover with a plate and a heavy weight and leave overnight in the refrigerator.

3 Cut the pressed panir into small cubes. Heat the oil in a large skillet. Add the panir and cook until golden on all sides. Remove from the skillet and drain on paper towels.

4 Pour off some of the oil, leaving about 4 tablespoons in the skillet. Add the onions, garlic, and ginger and cook gently, stirring frequently, for 5 minutes. Stir in the spices and cook gently for 2 minutes. Add the peas, tomatoes, and stock and season with salt and pepper. Cover and simmer, stirring occasionally, for 10 minutes, until the onion is tender. Add the fried panir cubes and cook for an additional 5 minutes. Taste and adjust the seasoning, if necessary. Sprinkle with the cilantro and serve at once.

Cheese Potato Cakes

Make these tasty potato cakes for a quick and simple supper dish. Serve them with scrambled eggs if you're very hungry.

NUTRITIONAL INFORMATION

Calories ....766 Sugars 7g
Protein ....22g Fat 50g
Carbohydrate ...60g Saturates 20g

25 MINS   35 MINS

SERVES 4

INGREDIENTS

2 lb 4 oz/1 kg potatoes

4 tbsp milk

¼ cup butter or margarine

2 leeks, finely chopped

1 onion, finely chopped

1½ cups grated sharp Cheddar cheese

1 tbsp chopped parsley or chives

1 egg, beaten

2 tbsp water

1½ cups fresh white or brown
   bread crumbs

vegetable oil, for shallow frying

salt and pepper

fresh flat-leaf parsley sprigs, to garnish

mixed salad greens, to serve

1 Cook the potatoes in lightly salted boiling water until tender. Drain and mash them with the milk and the butter.

2 Cook the leeks and onion in a small quantity of lightly salted boiling water for 10 minutes, until tender. Drain well.

3 In a large mixing bowl, combine the leeks and onion with the mashed potato, cheese, and parsley. Season to taste with salt and pepper.

4 Beat together the egg and water in a shallow bowl. Sprinkle the bread crumbs into a separate shallow bowl. Shape the potato mixture into 12 even-size cakes, brushing each with the egg mixture, then coating all over with the bread crumbs.

5 Heat the oil in a large skillet. Add the potato cakes, in batches if necessary, and cook over low heat for 2–3 minutes on each side, until light golden brown. Garnish with flat-leaf parsley and serve with mixed salad greens.

Green Curry with Tempeh

Green curry paste will keep for up to three weeks in the refrigerator. Serve the curry over rice or noodles.

20 MINS   15–20 MINS

SERVES 4

INGREDIENTS

1 tbsp corn oil

6 oz/175 g marinated or plain tempeh,
   cut into diamonds

6 scallions, cut into 1-inch/2.5-cm pieces

⅔ cup coconut milk

grated rind of 1 lime

¼ cup fresh basil leaves

¼ tsp liquid seasoning, such as Maggi

GREEN CURRY PASTE

2 tsp coriander seeds

1 tsp cumin seeds

1 tsp black peppercorns

4 large green chiles, seeded

2 shallots, cut into fourths

2 garlic cloves

2 tbsp chopped cilantro

grated rind of 1 lime

1 tbsp coarsely chopped galangal
   or fresh gingerroot

1 tsp ground turmeric

salt

2 tbsp oil

TO GARNISH

cilantro leaves

2 green chiles, thinly sliced

1 To make the green curry paste, grind together the coriander and cumin seeds and the peppercorns in a food processor or in a mortar with a pestle.

2 Blend the remaining ingredients together and add the ground spice mixture. Store in a clean, dry jar for up to 3 weeks in the refrigerator, or freeze in a suitable container.

3 Heat the oil in a wok or large, heavy skillet. Add the tempeh and stir over high heat for 2 minutes, until sealed on all sides. Add the scallions and stir-fry for 1 minute. Remove the tempeh and scallions and reserve.

4 Put half the coconut milk into the wok or skillet and bring to a boil. Add 6 tablespoons of the curry paste and the lime rind, and cook for 1 minute, until fragrant. Add the reserved tempeh and scallions.

5 Add the remaining coconut milk and simmer for 7–8 minutes. Stir in the basil leaves and liquid seasoning. Leave to simmer for 1 minute before serving, garnished with cilantro leaves and chiles.

Okra Curry

This is a delicious dry bhujia (vegetarian curry) which should be served hot with chapatis. As okra is such a tasty vegetable, it needs few spices.

NUTRITIONAL INFORMATION

Calories 371	Sugars 8g
Protein 4g	Fat 35g
Carbohydrate . . .10g	Saturates 4g

10 MINS   30 MINS

SERVES 4

INGREDIENTS

1 lb/450 g okra

⅔ cup oil

2 medium onions, sliced

3 green chiles, finely chopped

2 curry leaves

1 tsp salt

1 tomato, sliced

2 tbsp lemon juice

cilantro leaves

1 Rinse the okra and drain thoroughly. Using a sharp knife, chop and discard the ends of the okra. Cut the okra into 1-inch/2.5-cm long pieces.

2 Heat the oil in a large, heavy-bottomed skillet. Add the onions, green chiles, curry leaves, and salt and mix together. Stir-fry the vegetables for 5 minutes.

3 Gradually add the okra, mixing in gently with a slotted spoon. Stir-fry the vegetable mixture over medium heat for 12–15 minutes.

4 Add the sliced tomato to the pan and sprinkle over half the lemon juice. Taste and add more if required.

5 Garnish with cilantro leaves, then cover and simmer for an additional 3–5 minutes.

6 Transfer to warmed serving plates and serve hot.

COOK'S TIP

Okra have a remarkable glutinous quality which naturally thickens curries and casseroles.

Cashew Nut Paella

Paella traditionally contains chicken and fish, but this recipe is packed with vegetables and nuts for a truly delicious and simple vegetarian dish.

NUTRITIONAL INFORMATION

Calories 406	Sugars 8g
Protein 10g	Fat 22g
Carbohydrate ...44g	Saturates 6g

15 MINS   35 MINS

SERVES 4

INGREDIENTS

2 tbsp olive oil

1 tbsp butter

1 red onion, chopped

⅔ cup risotto rice

1 tsp ground turmeric

1 tsp ground cumin

½ tsp chili powder

3 garlic cloves, crushed

1 green chile, sliced

1 green bell pepper, seeded and diced

1 red bell pepper, seeded and diced

8 baby corn cobs,
    halved lengthwise

2 tbsp pitted black olives

1 large tomato, seeded and diced

2 cups vegetable stock

½ cup unsalted cashew nuts

½ cup frozen peas

2 tbsp chopped parsley

pinch of cayenne pepper

salt and pepper

herbs, to garnish

1 Heat the olive oil and butter in a large skillet or paella pan until the butter has melted.

2 Add the chopped onion to the skillet and sauté over medium heat, stirring constantly, for 2–3 minutes, until the onion has softened.

3 Stir in the rice, ground turmeric, ground cumin, chili powder, garlic, sliced chile, bell peppers, corn cobs, black olives, and diced tomato and cook over medium heat, stirring occasionally, for 1–2 minutes.

4 Pour in the stock and bring the mixture to a boil. Reduce the heat and cook, stirring constantly, for 20 minutes.

5 Add the cashew nuts and peas and cook, stirring occasionally, for 5 minutes. Season to taste with salt and pepper and sprinkle with parsley and cayenne pepper. Transfer the paella to warm serving plates, then garnish and serve immediately.

Egg Curry

This curry can be made very quickly. It can either be served as a side dish or, with parathas, as a light lunch.

NUTRITIONAL INFORMATION

Calories 189	Sugars 3g
Protein 7g	Fat 16g
Carbohydrate 4g	Saturates 3g

10 MINS   15 MINS

SERVES 4

INGREDIENTS

4 tbsp vegetable oil

1 medium onion, sliced

1 fresh red chile, finely chopped

½ tsp chili powder

½ tsp finely chopped fresh gingerroot

½ tsp fresh garlic, crushed

4 medium eggs

1 firm tomato, sliced

fresh cilantro leaves

parathas, to serve (optional)

1 Heat the oil in a large heavy-bottom pan. Add the sliced onion to the pan and cook over medium heat, stirring occasionally, for 5 minutes, until it is just softened and a light golden color.

2 Lower the heat. Add the red chile, chili powder, chopped ginger, and crushed garlic and cook over low heat, stirring constantly, for 1 minute.

3 Add the eggs and tomatoes to the pan and continue cooking, stirring to break up the eggs when they begin to cook, for 3–5 minutes.

4 Sprinkle over the fresh cilantro leaves.

5 Transfer the egg curry to warm serving plates and serve hot with parathas, if you wish.

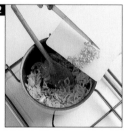

COOK'S TIP

Both the leaves and finely chopped stems of cilantro are used in Indian cooking, to flavor dishes and as edible garnishes. It has a very distinctive and pronounced taste.

Spicy Mixed Vegetable Curry

You can vary the vegetables used in this recipe according to personal preferences—experiment!

NUTRITIONAL INFORMATION

Calories	408	Sugars	20
Protein	........11g	Fat	..........24g
Carbohydrate	...39g	Saturates	.......3g

30 MINS   45 MINS

SERVES 4

INGREDIENTS

8 oz/225 g turnips or rutabaga, peeled

1 eggplant, leaf end trimmed

12 oz/350 g new potatoes, scrubbed

8 oz/225 g cauliflower

8 oz/225 g white mushrooms, wiped

1 large onion, peeled

8 oz/225 g carrots, peeled

6 tbsp vegetable ghee or oil

2 garlic cloves, peeled and crushed

2-inch/5-cm piece of fresh gingerroot, peeled and chopped

1–2 fresh green chiles, seeded and chopped

1 tbsp paprika

2 tsp ground coriander

1 tbsp mild or medium curry powder or paste

1¾ cups vegetable stock

14 oz/400 g canned chopped tomatoes

salt

1 green bell pepper, seeded and sliced

1 tbsp cornstarch

⅔ cup coconut milk

2–3 tbsp ground almonds

cilantro sprigs, to garnish

1 Using a sharp knife, cut the turnips, eggplant, and potatoes into ½-inch/1-cm cubes.

2 Divide the cauliflower into small florets. Leave the mushrooms whole, or slice thickly. Slice the onion and carrots.

3 Heat the ghee in a large pan, then add the onion, turnip, potato, and cauliflower and cook gently for 3 minutes, stirring frequently.

4 Add the garlic, ginger, chile, and spices and cook for 1 minute, stirring.

5 Add the stock, tomatoes, eggplant, and mushrooms and season with salt. Cover and simmer gently for 30 minutes, until tender, stirring occasionally. Add the green bell pepper, then cover and continue cooking for an additional 5 minutes.

6 Smoothly blend the cornstarch with the coconut milk and stir into the mixture. Add the ground almonds and simmer for 2 minutes, stirring all the time. Taste and adjust the seasoning, if necessary. Serve hot, garnished with cilantro sprigs.

Potato Hash

This is a variation of the traditional beef hash, which was made with salt beef and leftovers, and served to seagoing New Englanders.

NUTRITIONAL INFORMATION

Calories . . . . . . .302 Sugars 5g
Protein . . . . .15g Fat 10g
Carbohydrate . . .40g Saturates 4g

10 MINS   30 MINS

SERVES 4

INGREDIENTS

2 tbsp butter

1 red onion, halved and sliced

1 carrot, diced

⅓ cup green beans, halved

3 large waxy potatoes, diced

2 tbsp all-purpose flour

1¼ cups vegetable stock

8 oz/225 g tofu, diced

salt and pepper

chopped parsley, to garnish

1 Melt the butter in a large, heavy-bottom skillet. Add the onion, carrot, green beans, and potatoes and cook over fairly low heat, stirring constantly, for 5–7 minutes, until the vegetables begin to turn golden brown.

2 Add the flour to the skillet and cook, stirring constantly, for 1 minute. Gradually pour in the stock, stirring constantly.

3 Reduce the heat to low and simmer for 15 minutes, until the potatoes are tender.

4 Add the diced tofu to the skillet and cook for an additional 5 minutes. Season to taste with salt and pepper.

5 Sprinkle the chopped parsley over the top of the potato hash to garnish and then serve hot straight from the skillet.

COOK'S TIP

Hash is a term meaning to chop food into small pieces. Therefore a traditional hash dish is made from chopped fresh ingredients, such as bell peppers, onion, and celery.

Spinach & Cheese Curry

This vegetarian curry is full of protein and iron. Panir is a type of cheese that you can easily make at home the day before it is needed.

NUTRITIONAL INFORMATION

Calories	578	Sugars	........4g
Protein	........10g	Fat	..........58g
Carbohydrate	....4g	Saturates	.......7g

20–30 MINS   25 MINS

SERVES 4

INGREDIENTS

1¼ cups vegetable oil

7 oz/200 g panir, cubed (see page 185)

3 tomatoes, sliced

1 tsp ground cumin

1½ tsp ground chili powder

1 tsp salt

14 oz/400 g spinach

3 green chiles, roughly chopped

pooris or boiled rice, to serve

1 Heat the oil in a large, heavy-bottom skillet. Add the cubed panir and fry, stirring occasionally, until golden brown.

2 Remove the panir from the skillet with a slotted spoon and drain on paper towels.

3 Add the tomatoes to the remaining oil in the skillet and stir-fry, breaking them up with a spoon, for 5 minutes.

4 Add the ground cumin, chili powder, and salt to the skillet and mix well to combine.

5 Add the spinach to the skillet and stir-fry over low heat for 7–10 minutes, until wilted.

6 Add the green chiles and return the panir to the skillet. Cook, stirring constantly, for an additional 2 minutes.

7 Transfer to warmed serving plates and serve immediately with pooris or plain boiled rice.

VARIATION

You could used frozen spinach in this recipe. It should be completely thawed and squeezed as dry as possible before using.

Green Bean & Potato Curry

You can use fresh or canned green beans for this semi-dry vegetable curry. Serve an oil-dressed dhal for contrasting flavors and colors.

NUTRITIONAL INFORMATION

Calories 690   Sugars 4g
Protein . . . . .3g   Fat 69g
Carbohydrate . . .16g   Saturates 7g

🕒 15 MINS   🕐 30 MINS

SERVES 4

I N G R E D I E N T S

1¼ cups oil

1 tsp white cumin seeds

1 tsp mustard and onion seeds

4 dried red chiles

3 fresh tomatoes, sliced

1 tsp salt

1 tsp finely chopped fresh gingerroot

1 tsp crushed garlic

1 tsp chili powder

2 cups green beans, cut into pieces

2 medium potatoes, diced

1¼ cups water

cilantro leaves, chopped

2 green chiles, finely chopped

boiled rice, to serve

1 Heat the oil in a large, heavy-bottom pan. Lower the heat and add the white cumin seeds, mustard and onion seeds, and dried red chiles to the pan, stirring well.

2 Add the tomatoes to the pan and stir-fry the mixture for 3–5 minutes.

3 Mix together the salt, ginger, garlic, and chili powder and spoon into the pan. Blend the mixture together.

4 Add the green beans and potatoes to the pan and stir-fry for 5 minutes.

5 Add the water to the pan, then reduce the heat to low and simmer for 10–15 minutes, stirring occasionally.

6 Garnish the green bean and potato curry with chopped cilantro leaves and green chiles and serve hot with boiled rice.

COOK'S TIP

Mustard seeds are often fried in oil or ghee to bring out their flavor before being combined with other ingredients.

Feta Cheese Patties

Grated carrots, zucchini, and feta cheese are combined with cumin seeds, poppy seeds, curry powder, and chopped fresh parsley.

NUTRITIONAL INFORMATION

Calories 217   Sugars 6g
Protein . . . . .6g   Fat 16g
Carbohydrate . . .12g   Saturates 7g

15 MINS   20 MINS

SERVES 4

INGREDIENTS

2 large carrots

1 large zucchini

1 small onion

2 oz/55 g feta cheese

scant ¼ cup all-purpose flour

¼ tsp cumin seeds

½ tsp poppy seeds

1 tsp medium curry powder

1 tbsp chopped fresh parsley

1 egg, beaten

2 tbsp butter

2 tbsp vegetable oil

salt and pepper

herb sprigs, to garnish

1 Grate the carrots, zucchini, onion, and feta cheese coarsely, either by hand or process in a food processor.

2 Mix together the flour, cumin seeds, poppy seeds, curry powder, and parsley in a large bowl. Season to taste with salt and pepper.

3 Add the carrot mixture to the seasoned flour, tossing well to combine. Stir in the beaten egg.

4 Heat the butter and oil in a large, heavy-bottom skillet. Place heaped tablespoonfuls of the carrot mixture in the pan, flattening them slightly with the back of the spoon. Fry gently for 2 minutes on each side, until crisp and golden brown.

Drain on paper towels and keep warm until all the mixture is used.

5 Serve immediately, garnished with sprigs of fresh herbs.

Sweet & Sour Vegetables

Serve this dish with plain noodles or fluffy white rice for a filling, and flavorsome oriental meal.

NUTRITIONAL INFORMATION

Calories	401	Sugars	........16g
Protein	........14g	Fat	...........9g
Carbohydrate	...70g	Saturates	.......2g

10 MINS   15 MINS

SERVES 4

INGREDIENTS

1 tbsp peanut oil

2 garlic cloves, crushed

1 tsp grated fresh gingerroot

6 baby corn cobs

¾ cup snow peas

1 carrot, cut into short, thin sticks

1 green bell pepper, seeded and cut
   into short, thin sticks

8 scallions

1¾ oz/50 g canned bamboo shoots

8 oz/225 g marinated firm tofu, cubed

2 tbsp dry sherry or Chinese rice wine

2 tbsp rice vinegar

2 tbsp clear honey

1 tbsp light soy sauce

⅔ cup vegetable stock

1 tbsp cornstarch

noodles or boiled rice, to serve

1 Heat the oil in a preheated wok until almost smoking. Add the garlic and grated gingerroot and cook over medium heat, stirring frequently, for 30 seconds.

2 Add the baby corn cobs, snow peas, carrot, and bell pepper matchsticks and stir-fry for 5 minutes, until the vegetables are tender, but still crisp.

3 Add the scallions, bamboo shoots, and tofu and cook for 2 minutes.

4 Stir in the sherry, rice vinegar, honey, soy sauce, vegetable stock, and cornstarch and bring to a boil. Reduce the heat to low and simmer for 2 minutes, until heated through. Transfer to warmed serving dishes and serve immediately.

Vegetable Pasta Stir-Fry

East meets West in this delicious dish. Prepare all the vegetables and cook the pasta in advance, then the dish can be cooked in a few minutes.

NUTRITIONAL INFORMATION

Calories	383	Sugars	........18g
Protein	........14g	Fat	..........23g
Carbohydrate	...32g	Saturates	.......8g

20 MINS   30 MINS

SERVES 4

I N G R E D I E N T S

3½ cups dried whole-wheat pasta shells, or other short pasta shapes

1 tbsp olive oil

2 carrots, thinly sliced

12 baby corn cobs

3 tbsp peanut oil

1-inch/2.5-cm piece fresh gingerroot, thinly sliced

1 large onion, thinly sliced

1 garlic clove, thinly sliced

3 celery stalks, thinly sliced

1 small red bell pepper, seeded and sliced into short, thin sticks

1 small green bell pepper, seeded and sliced into short thin sticks

salt

steamed snow peas, to serve

S A U C E

1 tsp cornstarch

2 tbsp water

3 tbsp soy sauce

3 tbsp dry sherry

1 tsp clear honey

dash of hot pepper sauce (optional)

1 Cook the pasta in a large pan of boiling lightly salted water, adding the tablespoon of olive oil. When tender, but still firm to the bite, drain the pasta in a colander and return to the pan, then cover and keep warm.

2 Cook the carrots and baby corn cobs in boiling, salted water for 2 minutes. Drain in a colander, then plunge into cold water to prevent further cooking and drain again.

3 Heat the peanut oil in a large skillet over medium heat. Add the ginger and stir-fry for 1 minute, to flavor the oil. Remove with a slotted spoon and discard.

4 Add the onion, garlic, celery, and bell peppers to the oil and stir-fry over medium heat for 2 minutes. Add the carrots and baby corn cobs, and stir-fry for an additional 2 minutes, then stir in the reserved pasta.

5 Put the cornstarch in a small bowl and mix to a smooth paste with the water. Stir in the soy sauce, sherry, and honey.

6 Pour the sauce into the skillet, stir well and cook for 2 minutes, stirring once or twice. Taste the sauce and season with hot pepper sauce if wished. Serve with a steamed green vegetable, such as snow peas.

Casseroles & Bakes

Anyone who ever thought that vegetarian meals were dull will be proved wrong by the rich variety of dishes in this chapter. You'll recognize influences from Mexican and

Chinese cooking, but there are also traditional stews and casseroles, as well as hearty bakes and roasts. They all make exciting meals, at any time of year, and for virtually any occasion.

Don't be afraid to substitute your own personal favorite ingredients where appropriate. There is no reason why you cannot enjoy experimenting and adding your own touch to these imaginative ideas.

Lentil & Rice Casserole

This is a really hearty dish, perfect for cold days when a filling hot dish is just what you need.

NUTRITIONAL INFORMATION

Calories 312	Sugars 9g
Protein 20g	Fat 2g
Carbohydrate . . .51g	Saturates 0.4g

15 MINS　　40 MINS

SERVES 4

INGREDIENTS

scant 1 cup split red lentils

¼ cup long grain white rice

5 cups vegetable stock

1 leek, cut into chunks

3 garlic cloves, crushed

14 oz/400 g canned chopped tomatoes

1 tsp ground cumin

1 tsp chili powder

1 tsp garam masala

1 red bell pepper, seeded and sliced

1 cup small broccoli florets

8 baby corn cobs, halved lengthwise

½ cup green beans, halved

1 tbsp shredded basil

salt and pepper

fresh basil sprigs, to garnish

VARIATION

You can vary the rice in this recipe—use brown or wild rice, if you prefer.

1 Place the lentils, rice, and vegetable stock in a large flameproof casserole and cook over low heat, stirring occasionally, for 20 minutes.

2 Add the leek, garlic, tomatoes and their can juice, ground cumin, chili powder, garam masala, sliced bell pepper, broccoli, corn cobs, and green beans to the pan.

3 Bring the mixture to the boil, then reduce the heat and simmer, covered, for an additional 10–15 minutes, until the vegetables are tender.

4 Add the shredded basil and season with salt and pepper to taste.

5 Garnish with fresh basil sprigs and serve immediately.

Vegetable Crispy Batter

This dish can be cooked in a single large dish or in four individual large shallow muffin pans.

NUTRITIONAL INFORMATION

Calories 313	Sugars 9g
Protein 9g	Fat 18g
Carbohydrate . . .31g	Saturates 7g

15 MINS · 55 MINS

SERVES 4

INGREDIENTS

BATTER

⅔ cup all-purpose flour

2 eggs, beaten

generous ¾ cup milk

2 tbsp whole-grain mustard

2 tbsp vegetable oil

FILLING

2 tbsp butter

2 garlic cloves, crushed

1 onion, cut into eight

8 baby carrots, halved lengthwise

½ cup green beans, cut into pieces

¼ cup canned corn, drained

2 tomatoes, seeded and cut into chunks

1 tsp whole-grain mustard

1 tbsp chopped mixed herbs

salt and pepper

1 To make the batter, sift the flour and a pinch of salt into a bowl. Beat in the eggs and milk to make a batter. Stir in the mustard and leave to stand.

2 Pour the oil into a shallow ovenproof dish and heat in a preheated oven, 400°F/200°C, for 10 minutes.

3 To make the filling, melt the butter in a skillet and sauté the garlic and onion, stirring constantly, for 2 minutes. Cook the carrots and beans in a pan of boiling water for 7 minutes, until tender. Drain well.

4 Add the corn and tomatoes to the skillet with the mustard and herbs.

Season well and add the carrots and beans.

5 Remove the dish from the oven and pour in the batter. Spoon the vegetables into the center, then return to the oven and cook for 30–35 minutes, until the batter has risen and set. Serve the vegetable toad-in-the-hole immediately.

Spinach Crêpe Layer

Nutty-tasting buckwheat crêpes are combined with a cheese and spinach mixture and baked with a crispy topping.

NUTRITIONAL INFORMATION

Calories	467	Sugars	........10g
Protein	........29g	Fat	..........26g
Carbohydrate	...31g	Saturates	.......7g

45 MINS   1 HR 5 MINS

SERVES 4

INGREDIENTS

scant 1 cup buckwheat flour

1 egg, beaten

1 tbsp walnut oil

1¼ cups milk

2 tsp vegetable oil

FILLING

2 lb 4 oz/1 kg young spinach leaves

2 tbsp water

1 bunch scallions, white and green parts, chopped

2 tsp walnut oil

1 egg, beaten

1 egg yolk

1 cup cottage cheese

½ tsp grated nutmeg

¼ cup grated sharp Cheddar cheese

scant ¼ cup walnut pieces

salt and pepper

1 Sift the flour into a bowl and add any husks that remain in the strainer.

2 Make a well in the center and add the egg and walnut oil. Gradually whisk in the milk to make a smooth batter. Leave to stand for 30 minutes.

3 To make the filling, wash the spinach and pack into a pan with the water. Cover tightly and cook on high heat for 5–6 minutes, until soft.

4 Drain well and leave to cool. Gently fry the scallions in the walnut oil for 2–3 minutes, until just soft. Drain on paper towels and set aside.

5 Whisk the batter. Brush a small crêpe pan with oil, then heat until hot and pour in enough batter just to cover the base. Cook for 1–2 minutes, until set, then flip over and cook for 1 minute, until golden on the underside. Turn onto a warmed plate. Repeat to make 8–10 crêpes, layering them with baking parchment.

6 Chop the spinach and dry with paper towels. Mix with the scallions, beaten egg, egg yolk, cottage cheese, and nutmeg and season to taste with salt and pepper.

7 Layer the crêpes and spinach mixture on a cookie sheet lined with baking parchment, finishing with a crêpe. Sprinkle with Cheddar cheese and bake in a preheated oven, 375°F/190°C, for 20–25 minutes, until firm and golden. Sprinkle with the walnuts and serve immediately.

Winter Vegetable Casserole

This hearty supper dish is best served with plenty of warm crusty bread to mop up the delicious juices.

NUTRITIONAL INFORMATION

Calories 211   Sugars 6g
Protein . . . . .11g   Fat 6g
Carbohydrate . . .26g   Saturates 0.8g

10 MINS   40 MINS

SERVES 4

I N G R E D I E N T S

1 tbsp olive oil

1 red onion, halved and sliced

3 garlic cloves, crushed

8 oz/225 g spinach

1 fennel bulb, cut into eight

1 red bell pepper, seeded and cubed

1 tbsp all-purpose flour

1¾ cups vegetable stock

6 tbsp dry white wine

14 oz/400 g canned chickpeas, drained

1 bay leaf

1 tsp ground coriander

½ tsp paprika

salt and pepper

fennel fronds, to garnish

1 Heat the olive oil in a large flameproof casserole. Add the onion and garlic and sauté over low heat, stirring frequently, for 1 minute. Add the spinach and cook, stirring occasionally, for 4 minutes, until wilted.

2 Add the fennel pieces and red bell pepper and cook, stirring constantly, for 2 minutes.

3 Stir in the flour and cook, stirring constantly, for 1 minute.

4 Add the vegetable stock, white wine, chickpeas, bay leaf, ground coriander, and paprika, cover and simmer for 30 minutes. Season to taste with salt and pepper, then garnish with fennel fronds and serve immediately straight from the casserole.

COOK'S TIP

Use other canned mixed beans instead of the chickpeas, if you prefer.

Potato & Cheese Soufflé

This soufflé is very simple to make, yet it has a delicious flavor and melts in the mouth. Choose three alternative cheeses, if preferred.

NUTRITIONAL INFORMATION

Calories	447	Sugars	.........1g
Protein	........22g	Fat	..........23g
Carbohydrate	...41g	Saturates	......11g

10 MINS   55 MINS

SERVES 4

INGREDIENTS

2 tbsp butter

2 tsp all-purpose flour

2 lb/900 g mealy potatoes

8 eggs, separated

¼ cup grated Gruyère cheese

¼ cup crumbled blue cheese

¼ cup grated sharp Cheddar cheese

salt and pepper

1 Butter a 10-cup soufflé dish and dust with the flour. Set aside.

2 Cook the potatoes in a pan of boiling water until tender. Mash until very smooth and then transfer to a mixing bowl to cool.

3 Beat the egg yolks into the potato and stir in the Gruyère cheese, blue cheese, and Cheddar, mixing well. Season to taste with salt and pepper.

4 Whisk the egg whites until standing in peaks, then gently fold them into the potato mixture with a metal spoon until fully incorporated.

5 Spoon the potato mixture into the prepared soufflé dish.

6 Cook in a preheated oven, 425°F/220°C, for 35–40 minutes, until risen and set. Serve immediately.

COOK'S TIP

Insert a fine skewer into the center of the soufflé; it should come out clean when the soufflé is fully cooked through.

Winter Vegetable Cobbler

Seasonal fresh vegetables are casseroled with lentils, then topped with a ring of fresh cheese biscuits to make this tasty cobbler.

20 MINS   40 MINS

SERVES 4

I N G R E D I E N T S

1 tbsp olive oil

1 garlic clove, crushed

8 small onions, halved

2 celery stalks, sliced

2 cups rutabaga, chopped

2 carrots, sliced

½ small cauliflower, broken into florets

8 oz/225 g mushrooms, sliced

14 oz/400 g canned chopped tomatoes

¼ cup red lentils

2 tbsp cornstarch

3–4 tbsp water

1¼ cups vegetable stock

2 tsp Tabasco sauce

2 tsp chopped oregano

oregano sprigs, to garnish

COBBLER TOPPING

1½ cups self-rising flour

¼ cup butter

generous 1 cup grated sharp
   Cheddar cheese

2 tsp chopped oregano

1 egg, beaten

⅔ cup milk

salt

1 Heat the oil in a large pan. Fry the garlic and onions for 5 minutes. Add the celery, rutabaga, carrots, and cauliflower and fry for 2–3 minutes. Add the mushrooms, tomatoes, and lentils.

2 Mix the cornstarch and water and add to the pan with the stock, Tabasco, and oregano. Bring to a boil, stirring. Transfer to an ovenproof dish, cover and bake in a preheated oven, 350°F/180°C, for 20 minutes.

3 To make the topping, sift the flour and salt into a bowl. Rub in the butter,

then stir in most of the cheese and the chopped herbs. Beat together the egg and milk and add enough to the dry ingredients to make a soft dough. Knead lightly, roll out to ½-inch/1-cm thick and cut into 2-inch/5-cm rounds.

4 Remove the dish from the oven and increase the temperature to 400°F/ 200°C. Arrange the rounds around the edge of the dish, then brush with the remaining egg and milk and sprinkle with the reserved cheese. Cook for an additional 10–12 minutes, until the topping is risen and golden. Garnish and serve.

Curry Pasties

These pasties, which are suitable for vegans, are a delicious combination of vegetables and spices. They can be eaten either hot or cold.

NUTRITIONAL INFORMATION

Calories 455	Sugars 5g
Protein 8g	Fat 27g
Carbohydrate . . .48g	Saturates 5g

1 HOUR   1 HOUR

SERVES 4

INGREDIENTS

scant 1½ cups whole-wheat flour

generous ⅓ cup margarine,
    cut into small pieces

4 tbsp water

2 tbsp oil

8 oz/225 g diced root vegetables, such as
    potatoes, carrots, and parsnips

1 small onion, chopped

2 garlic cloves, finely chopped

½ tsp curry powder

½ tsp ground turmeric

½ tsp ground cumin

½ tsp whole-grain mustard

5 tbsp vegetable stock

soy milk, to glaze

1 Place the flour in a mixing bowl and rub in the margarine with your fingertips until the mixture resembles bread crumbs. Stir in the water and bring together to form a soft dough. Wrap and set aside to chill in the refrigerator for 30 minutes.

2 To make the filling, heat the oil in a large pan. Add the diced root vegetables, chopped onion, and garlic and cook, stirring occasionally, for 2 minutes. Stir in all of the spices, turning the vegetables to coat them thoroughly. Cook the vegetables, stirring constantly, for an additional 1 minute.

3 Add the stock to the pan and bring to a boil. Cover and simmer, stirring occasionally, for 20 minutes, until the vegetables are tender and the liquid has been absorbed. Leave to cool.

4 Divide the pastry into 4 portions. Roll each portion into a 6-inch/15-cm round. Place the filling on one half of each round.

5 Brush the edges of each round with soy milk, then fold over and press the edges together to seal. Place on a cookie sheet. Bake in a preheated oven, 400°F/200°C, for 25–30 minutes, until golden brown.

Creamy Baked Fennel

Fennel tastes fabulous in this creamy sauce, flavored with caraway seeds. A crunchy bread crumb topping gives an interesting texture.

NUTRITIONAL INFORMATION

Calories 292   Sugars 5g
Protein . . . . .10g   Fat 23g
Carbohydrate . . .12g   Saturates 14g

10 MINS   45 MINS

SERVES 4

INGREDIENTS

2 tbsp lemon juice

2 fennel bulbs, thinly sliced

¼ cup butter, plus extra for greasing

½ cup lowfat soft cheese

⅔ cup light cream

⅔ cup milk

1 egg, beaten

2 tsp caraway seeds

1 cup fresh white bread crumbs

salt and pepper

parsley sprigs, to garnish

1 Bring a pan of water to a boil and add the lemon juice and fennel. Cook for 2–3 minutes to blanch, then drain and place in a greased ovenproof dish.

2 Beat the soft cheese in a bowl until smooth. Add the cream, milk, and beaten egg, and whisk together until combined. Season with salt and pepper and pour the mixture over the fennel.

3 Melt 1 tablespoon of the butter in a small skillet and fry the caraway seeds gently for 1–2 minutes, until they release their aroma. Sprinkle them over the fennel.

4 Melt the remaining butter in a skillet. Add the bread crumbs and fry over low heat, stirring frequently, until lightly browned. Sprinkle them evenly over the surface of the fennel.

5 Place in a preheated oven, 350°F/ 180°C, and bake for 25–30 minutes, until the fennel is tender. Serve immediately, garnished with sprigs of parsley.

Mushroom & Spinach Puffs

These puff pastry parcels, filled with garlic, mushrooms, and spinach, are easy to make and simply melt in the mouth.

NUTRITIONAL INFORMATION

Calories ....467 Sugars 4g
Protein ....8g Fat 38g
Carbohydrate ...24g Saturates 18g

20 MINS   30 MINS

SERVES 4

INGREDIENTS

2 tbsp butter

1 red onion, halved and sliced

2 garlic cloves, crushed

4 cups sliced open-cup mushrooms

6 oz/175 g baby spinach

pinch of nutmeg

4 tbsp heavy cream

8 oz/225 g puff pastry

1 egg, beaten

salt and pepper

2 tsp poppy seeds

1 Melt the butter in a skillet. Add the onion and garlic and sauté over low heat, stirring, for 3–4 minutes, until the onion has softened.

2 Add the mushrooms, spinach, and nutmeg and cook over medium heat, stirring occasionally, for 2–3 minutes.

3 Stir in the heavy cream, mixing thoroughly. Season with salt and pepper to taste and remove the skillet from the heat.

4 Roll the pastry out on a lightly floured surface and cut into four 6-inch/ 15-cm rounds.

5 Put one fourth of the filling onto one half of each round and fold the pastry over to encase it. Press down to seal the edges and brush with the beaten egg. Sprinkle with the poppy seeds.

6 Place the parcels on a dampened cookie sheet and cook in a preheated oven, 400°F/200°C, for 20 minutes, until risen and golden brown in color.

7 Transfer the mushroom and spinach puffs to warmed serving plates and serve immediately.

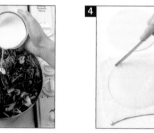

COOK'S TIP

The cookie sheet is dampened so that steam forms with the heat of the oven, which helps the pastry to rise and set.

Vegetable Jalousie

This is a really easy dish to make, but looks impressive. The mixture of vegetables gives the dish a wonderful color and flavor.

NUTRITIONAL INFORMATION

Calories	660	Sugars	.........7g
Protein	........11g	Fat	..........45g
Carbohydrate	...53g	Saturates	......15g

🍱 🍱 🍱

🍰 25 MINS   🕐 45 MINS

SERVES 4

I N G R E D I E N T S

1 lb 2 oz/500 g puff pastry

1 egg, beaten

FILLING

2 tbsp butter or margarine

1 leek, shredded

2 garlic cloves, crushed

1 red bell pepper, seeded and sliced

1 yellow bell pepper, seeded and sliced

1 cup sliced mushrooms

2¾ oz/75 g small asparagus spears

2 tbsp all-purpose flour

6 tbsp vegetable stock

6 tbsp milk

4 tbsp dry white wine

1 tbsp chopped oregano

salt and pepper

1 Melt the butter in a skillet and sauté the leek and garlic, stirring frequently, for 2 minutes. Add the remaining vegetables and cook, stirring, for 3–4 minutes.

2 Add the flour and cook for 1 minute. Remove the skillet from the heat and stir in the vegetable stock, milk, and white wine. Return the skillet to the heat and bring to a boil, stirring, until thickened.

Stir in the oregano and season with salt and pepper to taste.

3 Roll out half of the pastry on a lightly floured counter to form a rectangle 15 x 6 inches/38 x 15 cm.

4 Roll out the other half of the pastry to the same shape, but a little larger all round. Put the smaller rectangle on a cookie sheet lined with dampened baking parchment.

5 Spoon the filling evenly on top of the smaller rectangle, leaving a ½-inch/1-cm clear margin around the edges.

6 Using a sharp knife, cut parallel diagonal slits across the larger rectangle to within 1 inch/2.5 cm of each of the long edges.

7 Brush the edges of the smaller rectangle with beaten egg and place the larger rectangle on top, pressing the edges firmly together to seal.

8 Brush the whole jalousie with egg to glaze and bake in a preheated oven, 400°F/200°C, for 30–35 minutes, until risen and golden. Transfer to a warmed serving dish and serve immediately.

Lentil & Vegetable Shells

These stuffed eggplants are delicious served hot or cold, topped with plain yogurt or cucumber raita.

NUTRITIONAL INFORMATION

Calories 386   Sugars 9g
Protein . . . . .14g   Fat 24g
Carbohydrate . . .30g   Saturates 3g

🥗 25 MINS   🕐 1 HOUR

SERVES 6

INGREDIENTS

1 cup continental lentils

3¾ cups water

2 garlic cloves, crushed

3 well-shaped eggplants

⅔ cup vegetable oil, plus extra for brushing

2 onions, chopped

4 tomatoes, chopped

2 tsp cumin seeds

1 tsp ground cinnamon

2 tbsp mild curry paste

1 tsp minced chile

2 tbsp chopped mint

salt and pepper

plain yogurt and mint sprigs, to serve

1 Rinse the lentils under cold running water. Drain and place in a pan with the water and garlic. Cover and simmer for 30 minutes.

2 Cook the eggplants in a pan of boiling water for 5 minutes. Drain, then plunge into cold water for 5 minutes. Drain again, then cut the eggplants in half lengthwise and scoop out most of the flesh and reserve, leaving a ½-inch/1-cm thick border to form a shell.

3 Place the eggplant shells in a shallow greased ovenproof dish, brush with a little oil and sprinkle with salt and pepper. Cook in a preheated oven, 375°F/190°C, for 10 minutes. Meanwhile, heat half the remaining oil in a skillet, then add the onions and tomatoes and cook gently for 5 minutes. Chop the reserved eggplant flesh, then add to the skillet with the spices and cook gently for 5 minutes. Season with salt.

4 Stir in the lentils, most of the remaining oil, reserving a little for later, and the mint. Spoon the mixture into the shells. Drizzle with remaining oil and bake for 15 minutes. Serve hot or cold, topped with a spoonful of plain yogurt and mint sprigs.

COOK'S TIP

Choose nice plump eggplants, rather than thin tapering ones, as they retain their shape better when filled and baked with a stuffing.

Leek & Herb Soufflé

Hot soufflés look very impressive if served as soon as they come out of the oven, otherwise they will sink quite quickly.

NUTRITIONAL INFORMATION

Calories	182	Sugars	.........4g
Protein	.........8g	Fat	..........15g
Carbohydrate	....5g	Saturates	.......2g

15 MINS   50 MINS

SERVES 4

INGREDIENTS

12 oz/350 g baby leeks

1 tbsp olive oil

½ cup vegetable stock

⅓ cup walnuts

2 eggs, separated

2 tbsp chopped mixed herbs

2 tbsp plain yogurt

salt and pepper

1 Using a sharp knife, chop the leeks finely. Heat the oil in a skillet. Add the leeks and sauté over medium heat, stirring occasionally, for 2–3 minutes.

2 Add the vegetable stock to the skillet, then lower the heat and simmer gently for an additional 5 minutes.

3 Place the walnuts in a food processor and process until finely chopped. Add the leek mixture to the nuts and process briefly to form a purée. Transfer to a mixing bowl.

4 Mix together the egg yolks, herbs, and yogurt until thoroughly combined. Pour the egg mixture into the leek purée. Season with salt and pepper to taste and mix well.

5 In a separate mixing bowl, whisk the egg whites until firm peaks form.

6 Fold the egg whites into the leek mixture. Spoon the mixture into a lightly greased 3¾-cup soufflé dish and place on a warmed cookie sheet.

7 Cook in a preheated oven, 350°F/180°C, for 35–40 minutes, until risen and set. Serve the soufflé immediately.

COOK'S TIP

Placing the soufflé dish on a warm cookie sheet helps to cook the soufflé from the bottom, thus aiding its cooking and lightness.

Potato & Vegetable Gratin

Similar to a simple moussaka, this recipe is made up of layers of eggplant, tomato, and potato baked with a yogurt topping.

NUTRITIONAL INFORMATION

Calories 409   Sugars 17g
Protein . . . . .28g   Fat 14g
Carbohydrate . . .45g   Saturates 3g

🥪 25 MINS   🕐 1¼ HOURS

SERVES 4

I N G R E D I E N T S

1 lb 2 oz/500 g waxy potatoes, sliced

1 tbsp vegetable oil

1 onion, chopped

2 garlic cloves, crushed

1 lb 2 oz/500 g tofu, diced

2 tbsp tomato paste

2 tbsp all-purpose flour

1¼ cups vegetable stock

2 large tomatoes, sliced

1 eggplant, sliced

2 tbsp chopped fresh thyme

scant 2 cups plain yogurt

2 eggs, beaten

salt and pepper

salad, to serve

VARIATION

You can use marinated or smoked tofu for extra flavor, if you wish.

1 Cook the sliced potatoes in a pan of boiling water for 10 minutes, until tender, but not breaking up. Drain and set aside.

2 Heat the oil in a skillet. Add the onion and garlic and cook, stirring occasionally, for 2–3 minutes.

3 Add the tofu, tomato paste, and flour and cook for 1 minute. Gradually stir in the stock and bring to a boil, stirring. Reduce the heat and simmer for 10 minutes.

4 Arrange a layer of the potato slices in the base of a deep ovenproof dish.

Spoon the tofu mixture evenly on top. Layer the sliced tomatoes, then the eggplant, and, finally, the remaining potato slices on top of the tofu mixture, making sure that it is completely covered. Sprinkle with thyme.

5 Mix the yogurt and beaten eggs together in a bowl and season to taste with salt and pepper. Spoon the yogurt topping over the sliced potatoes to cover them completely.

6 Bake in a preheated oven, 375°F/190°C, for 35–45 minutes, until the topping is browned. Serve with a crisp salad.

Italian Vegetable Tart

This mouthwateringly attractive tart is full of Mediterranean flavors—spinach, red bell peppers, ricotta cheese, and pine nuts.

NUTRITIONAL INFORMATION

Calories	488	Sugars	.........7g
Protein	........13g	Fat	..........40g
Carbohydrate	...21g	Saturates	......19g

30 MINS   30 MINS

SERVES 6

INGREDIENTS

8 oz/225 g frozen phyllo pastry, thawed

generous ½ cup butter, melted

12 oz/350 g frozen spinach, thawed

2 eggs

⅔ cup single thin cream

1 cup ricotta cheese

1 red bell pepper, seeded and
    sliced into strips

⅓ cup pine nuts

salt and pepper

1 Use the sheets of phyllo pastry to line an 8-inch/20-cm flan pan, brushing each layer with melted butter.

2 Put the spinach into a strainer or colander and squeeze out the excess moisture with the back of a spoon or your hand. Form the spinach into 8–9 small balls and arrange them in the prepared flan pan.

3 Beat the eggs, cream, and ricotta cheese together until thoroughly blended. Season to taste with salt and pepper and pour over the spinach.

4 Put the remaining butter into a pan. Add the red bell pepper strips and sauté over low heat, stirring frequently, for

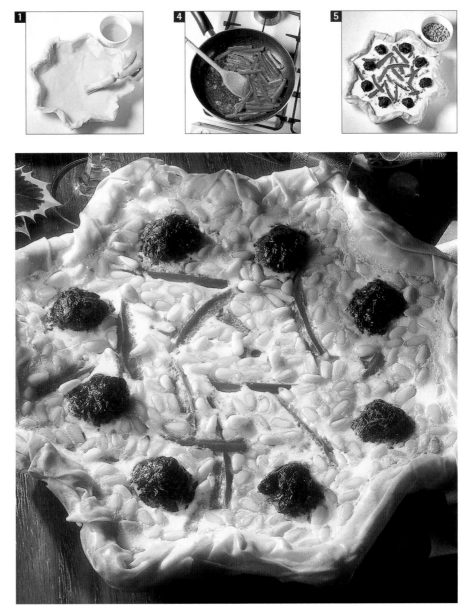

4–5 minutes, until softened. Arrange the strips on the flan.

5 Scatter the pine nuts over the surface and bake in a preheated oven at 375°F/190°C for 20–25 minutes, until the filling has set and the pastry is golden brown. Serve immediately or leave to cool completely and serve at room temperature.

VARIATION

If you are not fond of bell peppers, you could use mushrooms instead. Wild mushrooms would be especially delicious. Add a few sliced sun-dried tomatoes for extra color and flavor.

Potato-Topped Lentil Bake

A wonderful mixture of red lentils, tofu, and vegetables is cooked beneath a crunchy potato topping for a really hearty meal.

NUTRITIONAL INFORMATION

Calories	627	Sugars	........7g
Protein	........26g	Fat	..........30g
Carbohydrate	...66g	Saturates	......13g

10 MINS   1½ HOURS

SERVES 4

INGREDIENTS

TOPPING

1 lb 8 oz/675 g mealy potatoes, diced

2 tbsp butter

1 tbsp milk

⅓ cup chopped pecan nuts

2 tbsp chopped thyme

thyme sprigs, to garnish

FILLING

scant 1 cup red lentils

½ cup butter

1 leek, sliced

2 garlic cloves, crushed

1 celery stalk, chopped

generous 1 cup broccoli florets

6 oz/175 g smoked tofu, cubed

2 tsp tomato paste

salt and pepper

1 To make the topping, cook the potatoes in a pan of boiling water for 10–15 minutes, until cooked through. Drain well, then add the butter and milk and mash thoroughly. Stir in the pecan nuts and chopped thyme and set aside.

2 Cook the lentils in boiling water for 20–30 minutes, until tender. Drain and set aside.

3 Melt the butter in a skillet. Add the leek, garlic, celery, and broccoli. Fry over medium heat, stirring frequently, for 5 minutes, until softened. Add the tofu cubes. Stir in the lentils, together with the tomato paste. Season with salt and pepper to taste, then turn the mixture into the base of a shallow ovenproof dish.

4 Spoon the mashed potato on top of the lentil mixture, spreading to cover it completely.

5 Cook in a preheated oven, 400°F/ 200°C, for 30–35 minutes, until the topping is golden. Garnish with sprigs of fresh thyme and serve hot.

VARIATION

You can use almost any combination of your favorite vegetables in this dish.

Coconut Vegetable Curry

A mildly spiced, but richly flavored Indian-style dish full of different textures and flavors. Serve with naan bread to soak up the tasty sauce.

NUTRITIONAL INFORMATION

Calories	159	Sugars	.........8g
Protein	.........8g	Fat	...........6g
Carbohydrate	...19g	Saturates	.......1g

🥄 45 MINS   🕐 35 MINS

SERVES 6

I N G R E D I E N T S

1 large eggplant,
    cut into 1-inch/2.5-cm cubes

2 tbsp salt

2 tbsp vegetable oil

2 garlic cloves, crushed

1 fresh green chile,
    seeded and finely chopped

1 tsp grated fresh gingerroot

1 onion, finely chopped

2 tsp garam masala

8 cardamom pods

1 tsp ground turmeric

1 tbsp tomato paste

3 cups vegetable stock

1 tbsp lemon juice

1½ cups diced potatoes

2 cups small cauliflower florets

1 cup okra, trimmed

2 cups frozen peas

⅔ cup coconut milk

salt and pepper

flaked coconut, to garnish

naan bread, to serve

1 Layer the eggplant in a bowl, sprinkling with salt as you go. Set aside for 30 minutes.

2 Rinse well under cold running water to remove all the salt. Drain and pat dry with paper towels. Set aside.

3 Heat the oil in a large pan. Add the garlic, chile, ginger, onion, and spices and cook over medium heat, stirring occasionally, for 4–5 minutes, until lightly browned.

4 Stir in the tomato paste, stock, lemon juice, potatoes, and cauliflower and mix well. Bring to a boil, then lower the heat, and simmer, covered, for 15 minutes.

5 Stir in the eggplant, okra, peas, and coconut milk and season to taste with salt and pepper. Return to a boil and continue to simmer, uncovered, for an additional 10 minutes, until tender. Remove and discard the cardamom pods.

6 Pile onto a warmed serving platter, then garnish with flaked coconut and serve immediately with naan bread.

Artichoke & Cheese Tart

Artichoke hearts are delicious to eat, as they are delicate in flavor and appearance. They are ideal for cooking in a cheese-flavored pastry case.

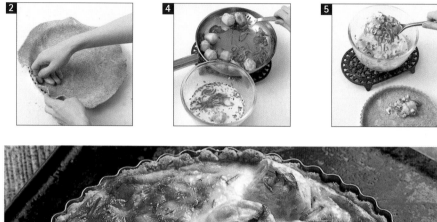

NUTRITIONAL INFORMATION

Calories	276	Sugars	........3g
Protein	........10g	Fat	..........19g
Carbohydrate	...18g	Saturates	......10g

15 MINS   30 MINS

SERVES 8

I N G R E D I E N T S

scant 1¼ cups whole-wheat flour

2 garlic cloves, crushed

6 tbsp butter or margarine

3 tbsp water

salt and pepper

F I L L I N G

2 tbsp olive oil

1 red onion, halved and sliced

10 canned or fresh artichoke hearts

1 cup grated Cheddar cheese

½ cup crumbled Gorgonzola cheese

2 eggs, beaten

1 tbsp chopped rosemary

⅔ cup milk

COOK'S TIP

Always roll pastry in one direction only to ensure an even thickness with no ridges. Do not press down on the dough; let the weight of a heavy rolling pin do the work for you.

1 To make the pastry, sift the flour into a mixing bowl, then add a pinch of salt and the garlic. Rub in the butter until the mixture resembles bread crumbs. Stir in the water and bring the mixture together to form a dough.

2 Roll the pastry out on a lightly floured counter to fit an 8-inch/20-cm flan pan. Prick the pastry with a fork.

3 Heat the oil in a skillet. Add the onion and sauté over medium heat for 3 minutes. Add the artichoke hearts and cook, stirring frequently, for an additional 2 minutes.

4 Mix the cheeses with the beaten eggs, rosemary, and milk. Stir in the drained artichoke mixture and season to taste.

5 Spoon the artichoke and cheese mixture into the pastry case and cook in a preheated oven, 400°F/200°C, for 25 minutes, until cooked and set. Serve the flan hot or cold.

Chile Tofu

A tasty Mexican-style dish with a melt-in-the-mouth combination of tofu and avocado served with a tangy tomato sauce.

NUTRITIONAL INFORMATION

Calories ....806 Sugars 20g
Protein ....37g Fat 54g
Carbohydrate ...45g Saturates 19g

30 MINS   35 MINS

SERVES 4

INGREDIENTS

½ tsp chili powder

1 tsp paprika

2 tbsp all-purpose flour

8 oz/225 g tofu,
    cut into ½-inch/1-cm pieces

2 tbsp vegetable oil

1 onion, finely chopped

1 garlic clove, crushed

1 large red bell pepper, seeded and
    finely chopped

1 large ripe avocado

1 tbsp lime juice

4 tomatoes, peeled, seeded and chopped

generous 1 cup grated Cheddar cheese

8 soft flour tortillas

⅔ cup sour cream

salt and pepper

cilantro sprigs to garnish

pickled green jalapeño chiles, to serve

SAUCE

3¾ cups homemade tomato sauce

3 tbsp chopped parsley

3 tbsp chopped cilantro

1 Mix the chili powder, paprika, flour, and salt and pepper on a plate and coat the tofu pieces.

2 Heat the oil in a skillet and gently cook the tofu for 3–4 minutes, until golden. Remove with a slotted spoon, then drain on paper towels and set aside.

3 Add the onion, garlic, and bell pepper to the oil and cook for 2–3 minutes, until just softened. Drain and set aside.

4 Halve the avocado, then peel and remove the pit. Slice lengthwise, then put in a bowl with the lime juice and toss to coat.

5 Add the tofu and onion mixture and gently stir in the tomatoes and half the cheese. Spoon one-eighth of the filling down the center of each tortilla, then top with sour cream and roll up. Arrange the tortillas in a shallow ovenproof dish in a single layer.

6 To make the sauce, mix together all the ingredients. Spoon the sauce over the tortillas, then sprinkle with the remaining grated cheese and bake in a preheated oven, 375°F/190°C, for 25 minutes, until golden and bubbling. Garnish with cilantro sprigs and serve immediately with pickled jalapeño chiles.

Spicy Potato Casserole

This is based on a Moroccan dish in which potatoes are spiced with cilantro and cumin and cooked in a lemon sauce.

NUTRITIONAL INFORMATION

Calories	338	Sugars	.........8g
Protein	.........5g	Fat	..........23g
Carbohydrate	...29g	Saturates	.......2g

15 MINS　　35 MINS

SERVES 4

I N G R E D I E N T S

scant ½ cup olive oil

2 red onions, cut into eight

3 garlic cloves, crushed

2 tsp ground cumin

2 tsp ground coriander

pinch of cayenne pepper

1 carrot, thickly sliced

2 small turnips, cut into fourths

1 zucchini, sliced

1 lb 2 oz/500 g potatoes, thickly sliced

juice and rind of 2 large lemons

1¼ cups vegetable stock

2 tbsp chopped cilantro

salt and pepper

COOK'S TIP

Check the vegetables while they are cooking, as they may begin to stick to the pan. Add a little more boiling water or stock if necessary.

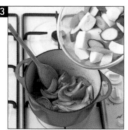  

1 Heat the olive oil in a flameproof casserole. Add the onion and sauté over medium heat, stirring frequently, for 3 minutes.

2 Add the garlic and cook for 30 seconds. Stir in the spices and cook, stirring constantly, for 1 minute.

3 Add the carrot, turnips, zucchini, and potatoes and stir to coat in the oil.

4 Add the lemon juice and rind and the vegetable stock. Season to taste with salt and pepper. Cover and cook over medium heat, stirring occasionally, for 20–30 minutes, until tender.

5 Remove the lid, then sprinkle in the cilantro and stir well. Serve immediately.

Mushroom & Pine Nut Tarts

Different varieties of mushroom are becoming more widely available in supermarkets, so use this recipe to make the most of them.

NUTRITIONAL INFORMATION

Calories 494   Sugars 2g
Protein . . . . .9g   Fat 35g
Carbohydrate . . .38g   Saturates 18g

15 MINS   20 MINS

SERVES 4

I N G R E D I E N T S

1 lb 2 oz/500 g phyllo pastry

generous ½ cup butter, melted

1 tbsp hazelnut oil

scant ¼ cup pine nuts

3 cups mixed mushrooms, such as
    white, chestnut (crimini), oyster,
    and shiitake

2 tsp chopped parsley

8 oz/225 g soft goat cheese

salt and pepper

parsley sprigs to garnish

lettuce, tomatoes, cucumber, and
    scallions, to serve

1 Cut the sheets of phyllo pastry into pieces about 4-inches/10-cm square and use them to line 4 individual tart pans, brushing each layer of pastry with melted butter. Line the pans with foil or baking parchment and baking beans. Bake in a preheated oven at 400°F/200°C for 6–8 minutes, until light golden brown.

2 Remove the tarts from the oven and carefully take out the foil or parchment and baking beans. Reduce the oven temperature to 350°F/180°C.

3 Put any remaining butter into a large pan with the hazelnut oil and cook the pine nuts gently until golden brown. Lift them out with a slotted spoon and drain on paper towels.

4 Add the mushrooms to the pan and cook them gently, stirring frequently, for about 4–5 minutes. Add the chopped parsley and season to taste with salt and pepper.

5 Spoon one fourth of the goat cheese into the base of each cooked phyllo tart. Divide the mushrooms equally between them and scatter the pine nuts over the top.

6 Return the tarts to the oven for 5 minutes to heat through, and then serve them, garnished with sprigs of parsley. Serve with lettuce, tomatoes, cucumber, and scallions.

Layered Pies

These individual pies of layered potato, eggplant, and zucchini baked in a tomato sauce can be made in advance.

NUTRITIONAL INFORMATION

Calories	427	Sugars	.........8g
Protein	........22g	Fat	..........21g
Carbohydrate	...41g	Saturates	.......8g

40 MINS   1 HR 20 MINS

SERVES 4

INGREDIENTS

3 large waxy potatoes, thinly sliced

1 small eggplant, thinly sliced

1 zucchini, sliced

3 tbsp vegetable oil

1 onion, diced

1 green bell pepper, seeded and diced

1 tsp cumin seeds

2 tbsp chopped basil

7 oz/200 g canned chopped tomatoes

6 oz/175 g sliced mozzarella cheese

8 oz/225 g tofu, sliced

1 cup fresh white bread crumbs

2 tbsp grated Parmesan cheese

salt and pepper

basil leaves, to garnish

1 Cook the sliced potatoes in a pan of boiling water for 5 minutes. Drain and set aside.

2 Put the eggplant slices on a plate, then sprinkle with salt and leave for 20 minutes. Meanwhile, blanch the zucchini in a pan of boiling water for 2–3 minutes. Drain and set aside.

3 Meanwhile, heat 2 tablespoon of the oil in a skillet. Add the onion and cook over low heat, stirring occasionally, for 2–3 minutes, until softened. Add the bell pepper, cumin seeds, basil, and canned tomatoes. Season to taste with salt and pepper and simmer for 30 minutes.

4 Rinse the eggplant slices and pat dry. Heat the remaining oil in a large skillet and fry the eggplant slices for 3–5 minutes, turning to brown both sides. Drain and set aside.

5 Arrange half of the potato slices in the base of 4 small loose-based flan pans. Cover with half of the zucchini slices, half of the eggplant slices, and half of the mozzarella slices. Lay the tofu on top and spoon over the tomato sauce. Repeat the layers of vegetables and cheese in the same order.

6 Mix the bread crumbs and Parmesan together and sprinkle over the top. Cook in a preheated oven, 375°F/190°C, for 25–30 minutes, until golden. Garnish with basil leaves.

Green Vegetable Gougère

A tasty, simple supper dish of choux pastry and crisp green vegetables. The choux pastry ring can be filled with all kinds of vegetables.

30 MINS   40 MINS

SERVES 4

INGREDIENTS

1 cup all-purpose flour

generous ½ cup butter

1¼ cups water

4 eggs, beaten

¾ cup grated Gruyère cheese

1 tbsp milk

salt and pepper

FILLING

2 tbsp garlic and herb butter

2 tsp olive oil

2 leeks, shredded

2 cups green cabbage, finely shredded

scant 1 cup bean sprouts

½ tsp grated lime rind

1 tbsp lime juice

celery salt and pepper

lime slices, to garnish

1 Sift the flour onto a piece of baking parchment. Cut the butter into dice and put in a pan with the water. Heat until the butter has melted.

2 Bring the butter and water to a boil, then tip in the flour all at once. Beat until the mixture becomes thick. Remove from the heat and beat until the mixture is glossy and comes away from the sides of the pan.

3 Transfer to a mixing bowl and cool for 10 minutes. Gradually beat in the eggs, a little at a time, making sure they are thoroughly incorporated after each addition. Stir in ½ cup of the cheese and season with salt and pepper.

4 Place spoonfuls of the mixture in a 9-inch/23-cm round on a dampened cookie sheet. Brush with milk and sprinkle with the remaining cheese. Bake in a preheated oven, 425°F/220°C, for 30–35 minutes, until golden and crisp. Transfer to a warmed serving plate.

5 Meanwhile, make the filling. Heat the butter and the oil in a large skillet and stir-fry the leeks and cabbage for 2 minutes. Add the bean sprouts, lime rind, and juice and stir-fry for 1 minute. Season to taste.

6 Pile into the center of the pastry ring. Garnish with lime slices and serve.

Baked Potatoes with Beans

Baked potatoes in their skins, topped with a tasty mixture of beans in a spicy sauce, provide a deliciously filling, high-fiber dish.

NUTRITIONAL INFORMATION

Calories 378	Sugars 9g
Protein 15g	Fat 9g
Carbohydrate ...64g	Saturates 1g

15 MINS   1¼ HOURS

SERVES 6

I N G R E D I E N T S

6 large potatoes

4 tbsp vegetable ghee or oil

1 large onion, chopped

2 garlic cloves, crushed

1 tsp ground turmeric

1 tbsp cumin seeds

2 tbsp mild or medium curry paste

24 cherry tomatoes

14 oz/400 g canned black-eye peas,
   drained and rinsed

14 oz/400 g canned red kidney beans,
   drained and rinsed

1 tbsp lemon juice

2 tbsp tomato paste

⅔ cup water

2 tbsp chopped fresh mint or cilantro

salt and pepper

VARIATION

Instead of cutting the potatoes in half, cut a cross in each and squeeze gently to open out. Spoon some of the prepared filling into the cross and place any remaining filling to the side.

1 Scrub the potatoes and prick several times with a fork. Place in a preheated oven, 350°F/180°C, and cook for 1–1¼ hours, until the potatoes feel soft when gently squeezed.

2 About 20 minutes before the end of cooking time, prepare the topping. Heat the ghee or oil in a pan, then add the onion and cook over low heat, stirring frequently, for 5 minutes. Add the garlic, turmeric, cumin seeds, and curry paste and cook gently for 1 minute.

3 Stir in the tomatoes, black-eye peas, and red kidney beans, lemon juice, tomato paste, water, and chopped mint. Season to taste with salt and pepper, then cover and simmer over low heat, stirring frequently, for 10 minutes.

4 When the potatoes are cooked, cut them in half and mash the flesh lightly with a fork. Spoon the prepared bean mixture on top, then place on warm serving plates and serve immediately.

Vegetable & Tofu Strudels

These strudels look really impressive and are perfect if friends are coming round or for a more formal dinner party dish.

NUTRITIONAL INFORMATION

Calories ....485 Sugars 5g
Protein ....16g Fat 27g
Carbohydrate ...47g Saturates 5g

25 MINS   30 MINS

SERVES 4

INGREDIENTS

FILLING

2 tbsp vegetable oil

2 tbsp butter

1 cup finely diced potatoes

1 leek, shredded

2 garlic cloves, crushed

1 tsp garam masala

½ tsp chili powder

½ tsp turmeric

¼ cup okra, sliced

scant 2 cups sliced white mushrooms

2 tomatoes, diced

8 oz/225 g firm tofu, diced

12 sheets phyllo pastry

2 tbsp butter, melted

salt and pepper

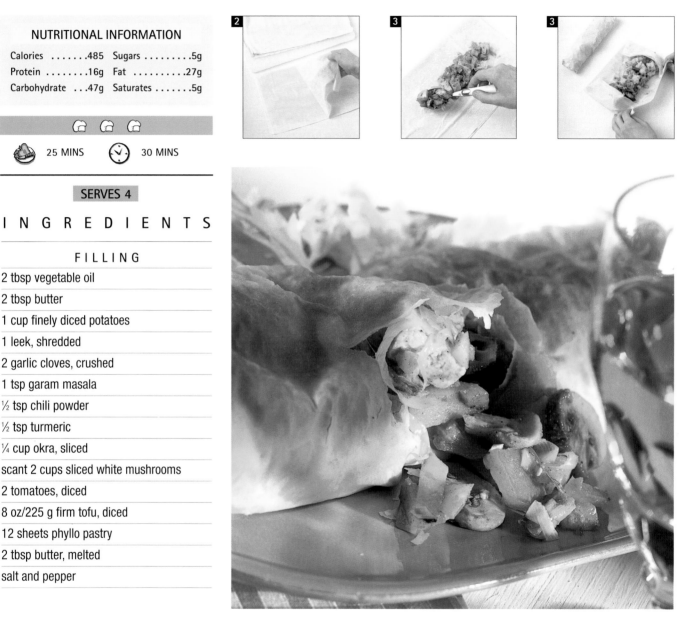

1 To make the filling, heat the oil and butter in a skillet. Add the potatoes and leek and cook, stirring constantly, for 2–3 minutes. Add the garlic and spices, okra, mushrooms, tomatoes, and tofu and season to taste with salt and pepper. Cook, stirring, for 5–7 minutes, until tender.

2 Lay the pastry out on a cutting board and brush each individual sheet with melted butter. Place 3 sheets on top of one another; repeat to make 4 stacks.

3 Spoon one fourth of the filling along the center of each stack and brush the edges with melted butter. Fold the short edges in and roll up lengthwise to form a cigar shape. Brush the outside with melted butter. Place the strudels on a greased cookie sheet.

4 Cook in a preheated oven, 375°F/ 190°C, for 20 minutes, until golden brown and crisp. Transfer to a warm serving dish and serve immediately.

Cauliflower Bake

The red of the tomatoes is a great contrast to the cauliflower and herbs, making this dish appealing to both the eye and the palate.

NUTRITIONAL INFORMATION

Calories 305   Sugars 9g
Protein . . . . .15g   Fat 14g
Carbohydrate . . .31g   Saturates 6g

🍲 🍲

🥄 10 MINS   🕐 40 MINS

SERVES 4

INGREDIENTS

1 lb 2 oz/500 g cauliflower, broken
  into florets

2 large potatoes, cubed

8 cherry tomatoes

SAUCE

2 tbsp butter or margarine

1 leek, sliced

1 garlic clove, crushed

2 tbsp all-purpose flour

1¼ cups milk

¾ cup mixed grated cheese, such as
  Cheddar, Parmesan, and Gruyère

½ tsp paprika

2 tbsp chopped flat-leaf parsley

salt and pepper

chopped parsley, to garnish

VARIATION

This dish could be made
with broccoli instead of the
cauliflower as an alternative.

1 Cook the cauliflower in a pan of boiling water for 10 minutes. Drain well and reserve. Meanwhile, cook the potatoes in a pan of boiling water for 10 minutes, then drain and reserve.

2 To make the sauce, melt the butter in a pan and sauté the leek and garlic for 1 minute. Stir in the flour and cook, stirring constantly, for 1 minute. Remove the pan from the heat and gradually stir in the milk, ½ cup of the mixed grated cheese, the paprika, and parsley. Return the pan to the heat and bring to a boil, stirring constantly. Season with salt and pepper to taste.

3 Spoon the cauliflower into a deep ovenproof dish. Add the cherry tomatoes and top with the potatoes. Pour the sauce over the potatoes and sprinkle on the remaining cheese.

4 Cook in a preheated oven, 350°F/ 180°C, for 20 minutes, until the vegetables are cooked through and the cheese is golden brown and bubbling. Garnish and serve immediately.

White Nut Phyllo Pockets

These crisp, buttery parcels, filled with nuts and pesto, would make an interesting break with tradition for Sunday lunch.

15 MINS   25 MINS

SERVES 4

INGREDIENTS

3 tbsp butter or margarine

1 large onion, finely chopped

scant 2 cups mixed white nuts,
    such as pine nuts, unsalted cashew nuts,
    blanched almonds, unsalted peanuts,
    finely chopped

1½ cups fresh white bread crumbs

½ tsp ground mace

1 egg, beaten

1 egg yolk

3 tbsp pesto sauce

2 tbsp chopped basil

generous ½ cup butter or
    margarine, melted

16 sheets phyllo pastry

salt and pepper

basil sprigs to garnish

TO SERVE

cranberry sauce

steamed vegetables

1 Melt the butter in a skillet and gently cook the onion for 2–3 minutes, until just softened but not browned.

2 Remove from the heat and stir in the nuts, two-thirds of the bread crumbs, the mace, and beaten egg. Season to taste with salt and pepper. Set aside.

3 Place the remaining bread crumbs in a bowl and stir in the egg yolk, pesto sauce, basil, and 1 tablespoon of the melted butter. Mix well.

4 Brush 1 sheet of phyllo with melted butter. Fold in half and brush again. Repeat with a second sheet and lay it on top of the first one so that it forms a cross.

5 Put one-eighth of the nut mixture in the center of the pastry. Top with one-eighth of the pesto mixture. Fold over the edges, brushing with more butter, to form a parcel. Brush the top with butter and transfer to a cookie sheet. Make eight pockets in the same way and brush with the remaining butter.

6 Bake in a preheated oven at 425°F/ 220°C for 15–20 minutes, until golden. Transfer to serving plates, then garnish with basil sprigs and serve with cranberry sauce and steamed vegetables.

Baked Potatoes with Pesto

This is an easy, but very filling meal. The potatoes are baked until fluffy, then they are mixed with a tasty pesto filling and baked again.

NUTRITIONAL INFORMATION

Calories	444	Sugars	.........3g
Protein	........10g	Fat	..........28g
Carbohydrate	...40g	Saturates	......13g

🥔 10 MINS   🕐 1½ HOURS

SERVES 4

INGREDIENTS

4 baking potatoes, about 8 oz/225 g each

⅔ cup heavy cream

scant ⅓ cup vegetable stock

1 tbsp lemon juice

2 garlic cloves, crushed

3 tbsp chopped basil

2 tbsp pine nuts

2 tbsp grated Parmesan cheese

salt and pepper

1 Scrub the potatoes well and prick the skins with a fork. Rub a little salt into the skins and place on a cookie sheet.

2 Cook the potatoes in a preheated oven, 375°F/190°C, for 1 hour, until they are cooked through and the skins are crisp.

3 Remove the potatoes from the oven and cut them in half lengthwise. Using a spoon, scoop the potato flesh into a mixing bowl, leaving a thin shell of potato inside the skins. Mash the potato flesh with a fork.

4 Meanwhile, mix the cream and stock in a pan and simmer over low heat for 8-10 minutes, until reduced by half.

5 Stir in the lemon juice, garlic, and basil and season to taste with salt and pepper. Stir the mixture into the mashed potato flesh, together with the pine nuts.

6 Spoon the mixture back into the potato shells and sprinkle the Parmesan cheese on top. Return the potatoes to the oven for 10 minutes, until the cheese has browned. Serve.

VARIATION

Add full-fat soft cheese or thinly sliced mushrooms to the mashed potato flesh in step 5, if you prefer.

Spicy Potato & Nut Terrine

This delicious baked terrine has a base of mashed potato, which is flavored with nuts, cheese, herbs, and spices.

NUTRITIONAL INFORMATION

Calories 1100   Sugars 13g
Protein . . . . .34g   Fat 93g
Carbohydrate . . .31g   Saturates 22g

15 MINS   1½ HOURS

SERVES 4

I N G R E D I E N T S

1½ cups diced mealy potatoes

1½ cups pecan nuts

1½ cups unsalted cashew nuts

1 onion, finely chopped

2 garlic cloves, crushed

2¼ cups diced open-cup mushrooms

2 tbsp butter

2 tbsp chopped mixed herbs

1 tsp paprika

1 tsp ground cumin

1 tsp ground coriander

4 eggs, beaten

½ cup full-fat soft cheese

½ cup grated Parmesan cheese

salt and pepper

S A U C E

3 large tomatoes, peeled,
    seeded and chopped

2 tbsp tomato paste

scant ⅓ cup red wine

1 tbsp red wine vinegar

pinch of superfine sugar

1 Lightly grease a 2 lb 4 oz/1 kg loaf pan and line with baking parchment.

2 Cook the potatoes in a large pan of lightly salted boiling water for 10 minutes, until cooked through. Drain and mash thoroughly.

3 Finely chop the pecan and cashew nuts or process in a food processor. Mix the nuts with the onion, garlic, and mushrooms. Melt the butter in a skillet and cook the nut mixture for 5–7 minutes. Add the herbs and spices. Stir in the eggs, cheeses, and potatoes and season to taste with salt and pepper.

4 Spoon the mixture into the prepared loaf pan, pressing down firmly. Cook in a preheated oven, 375°F/190°C, for 1 hour, until set.

5 To make the sauce, mix the tomatoes, tomato paste, wine, wine vinegar, and sugar in a pan and bring to a boil, stirring. Cook for 10 minutes, until the tomatoes have reduced. Press the sauce through a strainer or process in a food processor for 30 seconds. Turn the terrine out of the pan onto a serving plate and cut into slices. Serve with the tomato sauce.

Mexican Chili Corn Pie

This bake of corn and kidney beans, flavored with chile and fresh cilantro, is topped with crispy cheese cornbread.

NUTRITIONAL INFORMATION

Calories 519	Sugars 17g
Protein 22g	Fat 22g
Carbohydrate . . .61g	Saturates 9g

🥗 🥗 🥗

🥗 25 MINS   🕐 20 MINS

SERVES 4

INGREDIENTS

1 tbsp corn oil

2 garlic cloves, crushed

1 red bell pepper, seeded and diced

1 green bell pepper, seeded and diced

1 celery stalk, diced

1 tsp hot chili powder

14 oz/400 g canned chopped tomatoes

1½ cups canned corn, drained

¾ cup canned kidney beans,
    drained and rinsed

2 tbsp chopped cilantro

salt and pepper

cilantro sprigs, to garnish

tomato and avocado salad, to serve

TOPPING

⅔ cup cornmeal

1 tbsp all-purpose flour

½ tsp salt

2 tsp baking powder

1 egg, beaten

6 tbsp milk

1 tbsp corn oil

generous 1 cup grated sharp Cheddar
    cheese

1 Heat the oil in a large skillet and gently cook the garlic, bell peppers, and celery for 5–6 minutes, until just softened.

2 Stir in the chili powder, tomatoes, corn, beans, and seasoning. Bring to a boil and simmer for 10 minutes. Stir in the cilantro and spoon into an ovenproof dish.

3 To make the topping, mix together the cornmeal, flour, salt, and baking powder. Make a well in the center, then add the egg, milk, and oil and beat until a smooth batter is formed.

4 Spoon over the bell pepper and corn mixture and sprinkle with the cheese. Bake in a preheated oven, at 425°F/220°C, for 25–30 minutes, until golden and firm.

5 Garnish with cilantro sprigs and serve immediately with a tomato and avocado salad.

Nutty Harvest Loaf

This attractive and nutritious loaf is also utterly delicious. Served with a fresh tomato sauce, it can be eaten hot or cold with salad.

NUTRITIONAL INFORMATION

Calories	554	Sugars	........12g
Protein	........16g	Fat	..........37g
Carbohydrate	...43g	Saturates	......16g

20 MINS   1HR 20 MINS

SERVES 4

INGREDIENTS

2 tbsp butter, plus extra for greasing

1 lb/450 g mealy potatoes, diced

1 onion, chopped

2 garlic cloves, crushed

scant 1 cup unsalted peanuts

1½ cups fresh white bread crumbs

1 egg, beaten

2 tbsp chopped cilantro

⅔ cup vegetable stock

1½ cups sliced mushrooms

scant 1 cup sun-dried tomatoes, sliced

salt and pepper

SAUCE

⅔ cup sour cream or yogurt

2 tsp tomato paste

2 tsp clear honey

2 tbsp chopped cilantro

1 Grease a 1 lb/450 g loaf pan. Cook the potatoes in a pan of boiling water for 10 minutes, until cooked through. Drain well, then mash and set aside.

2 Melt half of the butter in a skillet. Add the onion and garlic and cook gently for 2–3 minutes, until soft. Finely chop the nuts or process them in a food processor for 30 seconds with the bread crumbs.

3 Mix the chopped nuts and bread crumbs into the potatoes with the egg, cilantro, and vegetable stock. Stir in the onion and garlic and mix well.

4 Melt the remaining butter in the skillet, then add the sliced mushrooms and cook for 2–3 minutes.

5 Press half of the potato mixture into the base of the loaf pan. Spoon the mushrooms on top and sprinkle with the sun-dried tomatoes. Spoon the remaining potato mixture on top and smooth the surface. Cover with foil and bake in a preheated oven, 350°F/190°C, for 1 hour, until firm to the touch.

6 Meanwhile, mix the sauce ingredients together. Cut the nutty harvest loaf into slices and serve with the sauce.

Roast Bell Pepper Tart

This tastes truly delicious, the flavor of roasted vegetables being entirely different from that of boiled or fried.

NUTRITIONAL INFORMATION

Calories 237   Sugars 3g
Protein . . . . .6g   Fat 15g
Carbohydrate . . .20g   Saturates 4g

🕑 25 MINS   🕐 40 MINS

SERVES 8

INGREDIENTS

PASTRY

generous 1 cup all-purpose flour

pinch of salt

6 tbsp butter or margarine

2 tbsp green pitted olives,
    finely chopped

3 tbsp cold water

FILLING

1 red bell pepper

1 green bell pepper

1 yellow bell pepper

2 garlic cloves, crushed

2 tbsp olive oil

1 cup grated mozzarella cheese

2 eggs

⅔ cup milk

1 tbsp chopped basil

salt and pepper

1 To make the pastry, sift the flour and salt into a bowl. Rub in the butter until the mixture resembles bread crumbs. Add the olives and cold water, bringing the mixture together to form a dough.

2 Roll the dough out on a floured surface and use to line an 8-inch/ 20-cm loose-based flan pan. Prick the base with a fork and leave to chill.

3 Cut all the bell peppers in half lengthwise and remove the seeds, then place them, skin side uppermost, on a cookie sheet. Mix the garlic and oil and brush over the bell peppers. Cook in a preheated oven, 400°F/200°C, for 20 minutes, until beginning to char slightly. Let the bell peppers cool slightly and thinly slice. Arrange in the base of the pastry case, layering with the mozzarella.

4 Beat the egg and milk and add the basil. Season and pour over the bell peppers. Put the tart on a cookie sheet and return to the oven for 20 minutes, or until set. Serve hot or cold.

Spinach Roulade

A delicious savory roll, stuffed with mozzarella and broccoli. Serve as a main course or as an appetizer, in which case it would easily serve six.

NUTRITIONAL INFORMATION

Calories 287	Sugars 8g	
Protein 23g	Fat 12g	
Carbohydrate 8g	Saturates 6g	

15 MINS   25 MINS

SERVES 4

I N G R E D I E N T S

1 lb 2 oz/500 g small spinach leaves

2 tbsp water

4 eggs, separated

½ tsp ground nutmeg

salt and pepper

1¼ cups homemade tomato sauce, to serve

F I L L I N G

1½ cups small broccoli florets

¼ cup freshly grated Parmesan cheese

1½ cups grated mozzarella cheese

1 Wash the spinach and pack, still wet, into a large pan. Add the water. Cover with a tight-fitting lid and cook over high heat for 4–5 minutes, until reduced and soft. Drain thoroughly, squeezing out excess water. Chop finely and pat dry.

2 Mix the spinach with the egg yolks, seasoning, and nutmeg. Whisk the egg whites until very frothy but not too stiff, and fold into the spinach mixture.

3 Grease and line a 13 x 9 inch/ 32 x 23 cm jelly roll pan. Spread the mixture in the pan and smooth the surface. Bake in a preheated oven, 425°F/ 220°C, for 12–15 minutes, until firm to the touch and golden.

4 Meanwhile, cook the broccoli florets in lightly salted boiling water for 4–5 minutes, until just tender. Drain and keep warm.

5 Sprinkle Parmesan on a sheet of baking parchment. Turn the base on to it and peel away the lining paper. Sprinkle with mozzarella and top with broccoli.

6 Hold one end of the paper and roll up the spinach base like a jelly roll. Heat the tomato sauce and spoon onto warmed serving plates. Slice the roulade and place on top of the tomato sauce.

Cauliflower & Broccoli Flan

This really is a tasty flan, the pastry shell for which may be made in advance and frozen until required.

NUTRITIONAL INFORMATION

Calories	 252	Sugars	.... 3g
Protein	.... 7g	Fat	.... 16g
Carbohydrate	... 22g	Saturates	.... 5g

15 MINS   50 MINS

SERVES 8

INGREDIENTS

PASTRY

generous 1 cup all-purpose flour

pinch of salt

½ tsp paprika

1 tsp dried thyme

6 tbsp margarine

3 tbsp water

FILLING

1 cup cauliflower florets

1 cup broccoli florets

1 onion, cut into eight

2 tbsp butter or margarine

1 tbsp all-purpose flour

6 tbsp vegetable stock

½ cup milk

¾ cup grated Cheddar cheese,

salt and pepper

paprika, to garnish

1 To make the pastry, sift the flour and salt into a bowl. Add the paprika and thyme and rub in the margarine. Stir in the water and bind to form a dough.

2 Roll out the pastry on a floured surface and use to line an 7-inch/18-cm loose-based flan pan. Prick the base with a fork and line with baking parchment. Fill with baking beans and bake in a preheated oven, 375°F/190°C, for 15 minutes. Remove the parchment and beans and return the pastry case to the oven for 5 minutes.

3 To make the filling, cook the vegetables in a pan of lightly salted boiling water for 10–12 minutes, until tender. Drain and reserve.

4 Melt the butter in a pan. Add the flour and cook, stirring constantly, for 1 minute. Remove from the heat, then stir in the stock and milk and return to the heat. Bring to a boil, stirring, and add ½ cup of the cheese. Season to taste with salt and pepper.

5 Spoon the cauliflower, broccoli, and onion into the pastry case. Pour over the sauce and sprinkle with the cheese. Return to the oven for 10 minutes, until the cheese is bubbling. Dust with paprika, then garnish and serve.

Cheese & Potato Braid

This bread has a delicious cheese and garlic flavor, and is best eaten straight from the oven, as soon as it is the right temperature.

NUTRITIONAL INFORMATION

Calories 387   Sugars 1g
Protein ....13g   Fat 8g
Carbohydrate ...70g   Saturates 4g

2½ HOURS   55 MINS

SERVES 8

INGREDIENTS

1 cup diced mealy potatoes

½ oz/15 g envelopes active dry yeast

4½ cups white bread flour

2 cups vegetable stock

2 garlic cloves, crushed

2 tbsp chopped rosemary

1 cup grated Gruyère cheese

1 tbsp vegetable oil

1 Lightly grease and flour a cookie sheet. Cook the potatoes in a pan of boiling water for 10 minutes, or until soft. Drain and mash.

2 Transfer the mashed potatoes to a large mixing bowl, then stir in the yeast, flour, and stock and mix to form a smooth dough. Add the garlic, rosemary, and ¾ cup of the cheese and knead the dough for 5 minutes. Make a hollow in the dough, then pour in the oil and knead again.

3 Cover the dough and leave it to rise in a warm place for 1½ hours, until doubled in size.

4 Knead the dough again and divide it into 3 equal portions. Roll each portion into a sausage shape about 14 inch/35 cm long.

5 Press one end of each of the sausage shapes firmly together, then carefully braid the dough, without breaking it, and fold the remaining ends under, sealing them firmly.

6 Place the braid on the cookie sheet, then cover and leave to rise for 30 minutes.

7 Sprinkle the remaining cheese over the top of the braid and cook in a preheated oven, 375°F/190°C, for 40 minutes, until the base of the loaf sounds hollow when tapped. Serve warm.

Garlic & Sage Bread

This freshly made bread is an ideal accompaniment to salads and soups and is suitable for vegans.

NUTRITIONAL INFORMATION

Calories	141	Sugars	.........2g
Protein	.........6g	Fat	..........0.8g
Carbohydrate	...30g	Saturates	.....0.1g

2¼ HOURS   30 MINS

SERVES 6

INGREDIENTS

1¼ cups strong brown bread flour

1 x ¼ oz/10 g envelope active dry yeast

3 tbsp chopped sage

2 tsp sea salt

3 garlic cloves, finely chopped

1 tsp honey

⅔ cup tepid water

1 Grease a cookie sheet. Sift the flour into a large mixing bowl and stir in the bran remaining in the strainer.

2 Stir in the yeast, sage, and half of the sea salt. Reserve 1 teaspoon of the chopped garlic for sprinkling and stir the rest into the bowl. Add the honey, together with the tepid water and mix to form a dough.

3 Turn the dough out onto a lightly floured surface and knead it for about 5 minutes.

4 Place the dough in a greased bowl, then cover and leave to rise in a warm place for 1½ hours, until doubled in size.

5 Knead the dough again for a few minutes, shape it into a circle (see Cook's Tip) and place on the cookie sheet.

6 Cover and leave to rise for an additional 30 minutes, until springy to the touch. Sprinkle with the rest of the sea salt and garlic.

7 Bake in a preheated oven, 400°F/200°C, for 25–30 minutes. Transfer to a wire rack to cool completely before serving.

COOK'S TIP

Roll the dough into a long sausage and then curve it into a circular shape.

Sweet Potato Bread

This is a great tasting loaf, colored light orange by the sweet potato. Added sweetness from the honey is offset by the tangy orange rind.

NUTRITIONAL INFORMATION

Calories 267   Sugars 7g
Protein . . . . .4g   Fat 9g
Carbohydrate . . .45g   Saturates 4g

1½ HOURS   1¼ HOURS

SERVES 8

INGREDIENTS

1¾ cups diced sweet potatoes

⅔ cup tepid water

2 tbsp clear honey

2 tbsp vegetable oil

3 tbsp orange juice

generous ⅓ cup semolina

1½ cups white bread flour

1 x ¼ oz/10 g envelope active dry yeast

1 tsp ground cinnamon

grated rind of 1 orange

¼ cup butter

1 Lightly grease a 1 lb 8 oz/675 g loaf pan. Cook the sweet potatoes in a pan of boiling water for 10 minutes, until soft. Drain well and mash until smooth.

2 Meanwhile, mix the water, honey, oil, and orange juice together in a large mixing bowl.

3 Add the mashed sweet potatoes, semolina, three-fourths of the flour, the yeast, ground cinnamon, and grated orange rind and mix thoroughly to form a dough. Leave to stand for 10 minutes.

4 Cut the butter into small pieces and knead it into the dough with the remaining flour. Knead for 5 minutes, until the dough is smooth.

5 Place the dough in the prepared loaf pan. Cover and leave in a warm place to rise for 1 hour, until it has doubled in size.

6 Cook the loaf in a preheated oven, 375°F/190°C, for 45–60 minutes, until the base sounds hollow when tapped. Serve the bread warm, cut into slices.

Grills

Grills don't have to be meat feasts, there are lots of vegetarian options, too. Throughout this chapter you will find imaginative and delicious recipes that will really spice up your barbecue. The recipes provide plenty of protein—either from cheese, beans, or tofu. And because they contain lots of vegetables, they supply important vitamins,

minerals, and carbohydrates. Some preparation is needed before the grill starts. For instance, some foods need marinating, or threading onto skewers, but with a little forward planning you'll find plenty of time to relax with your guests and enjoy your grill.

Tasty Barbecue Sauce

Just the thing for brushing onto vegetable kabobs and burgers, this sauce is easy and quick to make.

NUTRITIONAL INFORMATION

Calories 100   Sugars 9g
Protein . . . . .1g   Fat 6g
Carbohydrate . . .10g   Saturates 1g

5 MINS   40 MINS

SERVES 4

INGREDIENTS

2 tbsp butter or margarine

1 garlic clove, crushed

1 onion, finely chopped

14 oz/400 g canned chopped tomatoes

1 tbsp dark muscovado sugar

1 tsp hot chili sauce

1–2 gherkins

1 tbsp capers, drained

salt and pepper

1 Melt the butter in a pan and cook the garlic and onion for 8–10 minutes, until well browned.

2 Add the chopped tomatoes, sugar, and chili sauce. Bring to a boil, then reduce the heat and simmer gently for 20–25 minutes, until thick and pulpy.

COOK'S TIP

To make sure that the sauce has a good color, it is important to brown the onions really well to begin with. When fresh tomatoes are cheap and plentiful, they can be used instead of canned ones. Peel and chop 1 cup.

3 Chop the gherkins and capers finely. Add to the sauce, stirring to mix. Cook the sauce over low heat for 2 minutes.

4 Taste the sauce and season with a little salt and pepper to taste. Use as a baste for vegetarian kabobs and burgers, or as an accompaniment to other grilled food.

Citrus & Herb Marinades

Choose one of these marinades to give a marvelous flavor to barbecued food. The nutritional information is for Orange & Marjoram only.

NUTRITIONAL INFORMATION

Calories ....269 Sugars 3g
Protein ....0.4g Fat 6g
Carbohydrate ....3g Saturates 1g

🥕 20 MINS   🕙 0 MINS

SERVES 4

INGREDIENTS

ORANGE & MARJORAM

1 orange

½ cup olive oil

4 tbsp dry white wine

4 tbsp white wine vinegar

1 tbsp snipped chives

1 tbsp chopped marjoram

salt and pepper

THAI-SPICED LIME

1 lemon grass stalk

finely grated rind and juice of 1 lime

4 tbsp sesame oil

2 tbsp light soy sauce

pinch of ground ginger

1 tbsp chopped cilantro

salt and pepper

BASIL & LEMON

finely grated rind of 1 lemon

4 tbsp lemon juice

1 tbsp balsamic vinegar

2 tbsp red wine vinegar

2 tbsp virgin olive oil

1 tbsp chopped oregano

1 tbsp chopped basil

salt and pepper

1 To make the Orange & Marjoram marinade, remove the rind from the orange with a zester, or grate it finely, then squeeze the juice.

2 Mix the orange rind and juice with all the remaining ingredients in a small bowl, whisking together to combine. Season with salt and pepper.

3 To make the Thai-spiced Lime marinade, bruise the lemon grass by crushing it with a rolling pin. Mix the remaining ingredients together in a small bowl and add the lemon grass.

4 To make the Basil & Lemon marinade, whisk all the ingredients together in a small bowl. Season to taste with salt and pepper.

5 Keep the marinades covered with clear plastic wrap or store them in screw-top jars, ready for using as marinades or bastes.

Three Favorite Dressings

You can rely on any of these dressings to bring out the best in your salads.
The nutritional information is for the Mustard and Vinegar dressing only.

NUTRITIONAL INFORMATION

Calories ....245 Sugars 0.5g
Protein ....0g Fat 27g
Carbohydrate ...0.5g Saturates 4g

45 MINS   0 MINS

SERVES 4

INGREDIENTS

WHOLE-GRAIN MUSTARD & CIDER VINEGAR

½ cup olive oil

4 tbsp cider vinegar

2 tsp whole-grain mustard

½ tsp superfine sugar

salt and pepper

GARLIC & PARSLEY

1 small garlic clove

1 tbsp parsley

⅔ cup light cream

4 tbsp plain yogurt

1 tsp lemon juice

pinch of superfine sugar

salt and pepper

RASPBERRY & HAZELNUT

4 tbsp raspberry vinegar

4 tbsp light olive oil

4 tbsp hazelnut oil

½ tsp superfine sugar

2 tsp chopped chives

salt and pepper

1 To make the Whole-grain Mustard & Cider Vinegar Dressing, whisk all the ingredients together in a small bowl.

2 To make the Garlic & Parsley Dressing, crush the garlic clove and finely chop the parsley.

3 Mix the garlic and parsley with the remaining ingredients. Whisk together

until combined, then cover and chill for 30 minutes.

4 To make the Raspberry & Hazelnut Vinaigrette, whisk all the ingredients together until combined.

5 Keep the dressings covered with plastic wrap or sealed in screw-top jars. Chill until ready for use.

Mixed Vegetables

The wonderful aroma of vegetables as they are chargrilled over hot coals will set the taste buds tingling.

NUTRITIONAL INFORMATION

Calories ....155 Sugars 6g
Protein ....2g Fat 12g
Carbohydrate ....7g Saturates 7g

10 MINS   25 MINS

SERVES 6

INGREDIENTS

8 baby eggplants

4 zucchini

2 red onions

4 tomatoes

salt and pepper

1 tsp balsamic vinegar, to serve

BASTE

6 tbsp butter

2 tsp walnut oil

2 garlic cloves, chopped

4 tbsp dry white wine or cider

1 To prepare the vegetables, cut the eggplants in half. Trim and cut the zucchini in half lengthwise. Thickly slice the onion and halve the tomatoes.

2 Season all of the vegetables with salt and pepper to taste.

3 To make the baste, melt the butter with the oil in a pan. Add the garlic and cook gently for 1–2 minutes. Remove the pan from the heat and stir in the wine.

4 Add the vegetables to the pan and toss them in the baste mixture. You may need to do this in several batches to ensure that all of the vegetables are coated evenly.

5 Remove the vegetables from the baste mixture, reserving any excess baste. Place the vegetables on an oiled rack over medium hot coals. Grill the vegetables for 15–20 minutes, basting with the reserved baste mixture, turning once or twice during cooking.

6 Transfer the vegetables to warm serving plates and serve immediately, sprinkled with balsamic vinegar.

Roasted Vegetables

Rosemary branches can be used as brushes for basting and as skewers.
Soak the rosemary skewers well in advance to cut down preparation time.

NUTRITIONAL INFORMATION

Calories ....16 Sugars 3g
Protein ....1g Fat 0.3g
Carbohydrate ....3g Saturates 0g

8½ HOURS   10 MINS

SERVES 6

INGREDIENTS

1 small red cabbage

1 head fennel

1 orange bell pepper, cut into
    1½-inch/3.5-cm dice

1 eggplant, halved and sliced
    into ½-inch/1-cm pieces

2 zucchini, sliced thickly diagonally

olive oil, for brushing

6 rosemary twigs, about 6 inches/15 cm
    long, soaked in water for 8 hours

salt and pepper

1 Put the red cabbage on its side on a chopping board and cut through the middle of its stem and heart. Divide each piece into four, each time including a bit of the stem in the slice to hold it together.

VARIATION

Fruit skewers are a deliciously quick and easy dessert. Thread pieces of banana, mango, peach, strawberry, apple, and pear onto soaked wooden skewers and cook over the dying embers. Brush with sugar syrup toward the end of cooking.

2 Prepare the fennel in the same way as the red cabbage.

3 Blanch the red cabbage and fennel in boiling water for 3 minutes, then drain well.

4 With a wooden skewer, pierce a hole through the middle of each piece of vegetable.

5 On to each rosemary twig, thread a piece of orange bell pepper, fennel, red cabbage, eggplant, and zucchini, pushing the rosemary through the holes.

6 Brush liberally with olive oil and season with plenty of salt and pepper.

7 Cook over a hot grill for 8–10 minutes, turning occasionally. Serve.

Corn Cobs & Parsley Butter

There are a number of ways of cooking corn-on-the-cob on the barbecue. Leaving on the husks protects the tender corn niblets.

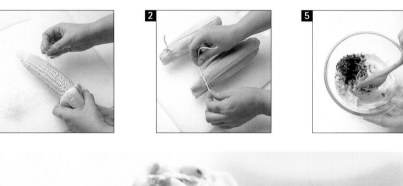

NUTRITIONAL INFORMATION	
Calories 178	Sugars 7g
Protein 2g	Fat 11g
Carbohydrate ...19g	Saturates 7g

10 MINS   30 MINS

SERVES 4

INGREDIENTS

4 corn cobs, with husks

scant ½ cup butter

1 tbsp chopped parsley

1 tsp chopped chives

1 tsp chopped thyme

grated rind of 1 lemon

salt and pepper

1 To prepare the corn cobs, peel back the husks and remove the silken hairs.

2 Fold back the husks and secure them in place with string, if necessary.

3 Blanch the corn cobs in a large pan of boiling water for 5 minutes. Remove the cobs with a slotted spoon and drain thoroughly.

4 Grill the cobs over medium hot coals for 20–30 minutes, turning frequently.

5 Meanwhile, soften the butter and beat in the parsley, chives, thyme, and lemon rind and season with salt and pepper to taste.

6 Transfer the corn cobs to serving plates, remove the string, if used, and pull back the husks. Serve with a generous

portion of herb butter. Eat with two forks or corn cob holders and provide plenty of paper napkins.

COOK'S TIP

If you are unable to get fresh cobs, cook frozen corn cobs on the grill. Spread some of the herb butter onto a double thickness of aluminum foil. Wrap the cobs in the foil and grill among the coals for 20–30 minutes.

Nutty Rice Burgers

Serve these burgers in toasted sesame seed burger rolls. If you wish, add a slice of cheese to top the burger at the end of cooking.

NUTRITIONAL INFORMATION

Calories 517   Sugars 5g
Protein . . . . .16g   Fat 26g
Carbohydrate . . .59g   Saturates 6g

1¼ HOURS   30 MINS

SERVES 6

INGREDIENTS

1 tbsp corn oil

1 small onion, finely chopped

scant 2 cups finely chopped mushrooms

scant 5 cups cooked brown rice

2 cups fresh bread crumbs

½ cup chopped walnuts

1 egg

2 tbsp brown fruity sauce

dash of Tabasco sauce

salt and pepper

oil, to baste

6 individual cheese slices (optional)

TO SERVE

6 sesame seed baps

slices of onion

slices of tomato

1 Heat the oil in a large pan and cook the onion for 3–4 minutes, until just beginning to soften. Add the mushrooms and cook for an additional 2 minutes.

2 Remove the pan from the heat and mix the cooked rice, bread crumbs, walnuts, egg, and both the sauces into the vegetables. Season to taste with salt and pepper and mix well.

3 Shape the mixture into 6 burgers, pressing the mixture together with your fingers. Set aside to chill in the refrigerator for at least 30 minutes.

4 Grill the burgers on an oiled rack over medium coals for 5–6 minutes on each side, turning once and frequently basting with oil.

5 If liked, top the burgers with a slice of cheese 2 minutes before the end of the cooking time. Grill the onion and tomato slices for 3–4 minutes until they are just beginning to color.

6 Toast the sesame seed burger rolls at the side of the grill. Serve the burgers in the rolls, together with the grilled onions and tomatoes.

COOK'S TIP

It is quicker and more economical to use leftover rice to make these burgers. However, if you are cooking the rice for this dish you will need to use scant 1 cup uncooked rice.

Curried Kabobs

Warmed Indian bread is served with grilled vegetable kabobs, which are brushed with a curry-spiced yogurt baste.

NUTRITIONAL INFORMATION

Calories	396	Sugars	........11g
Protein	........13g	Fat	..........13g
Carbohydrate	...60g	Saturates	.....0.3g

🐘 🐘

🍲 30 MINS   🕐 25–30 MINS

SERVES 4

INGREDIENTS

naan bread, to serve

mint sprigs, to garnish

YOGURT BASTE

⅔ cup plain yogurt

1 tbsp chopped mint or
   1 tsp dried mint

1 tsp ground cumin

1 tsp ground coriander

½ tsp chili powder

pinch of turmeric

pinch of ground ginger

salt and pepper

KABOBS

8 small new potatoes

1 small eggplant

1 zucchini, cut into chunks

8 chestnut or closed-cup mushrooms

8 small tomatoes

1 To make the spiced yogurt baste, mix together the yogurt, mint, cumin, coriander, chili powder, turmeric, and ginger. Season to taste with salt and pepper. Cover and chill.

2 Cook the potatoes in boiling water until just tender.

3 Meanwhile, chop the eggplant into chunks and sprinkle them liberally with salt. Set aside for 10–15 minutes to extract the bitter juices. Rinse thoroughly and drain them well. Drain the potatoes.

4 Thread the potatoes, eggplant, zucchini, mushrooms, and tomatoes alternately onto 4 skewers.

5 Place the skewers in a shallow dish and brush with the yogurt baste, coating them evenly. Cover and chill until ready to cook.

6 Wrap the naan bread in foil and place toward one side of the grill to warm through.

7 Cook the kabobs over the grill, basting with any remaining spiced yogurt, until they begin to char slightly. Serve with the warmed naan bread, garnished with mint sprigs.

Spicy Sweet Potato Slices

Serve these as an accompaniment to other grill dishes or with a spicy dip as nibbles while the main dishes are being cooked.

NUTRITIONAL INFORMATION

Calories	178	Sugars	.......0.8g
Protein	.........2g	Fat	...........6g
Carbohydrate	...32g	Saturates	.....0.7g

10 MINS   25 MINS

SERVES 4

INGREDIENTS

1 lb/450 g sweet potatoes

2 tbsp corn oil

1 tsp chili sauce

salt and pepper

1 Bring a large pan of water to a boil, add the sweet potatoes and parboil them for 10 minutes. Drain thoroughly and transfer to a cutting board.

2 Peel the potatoes and cut them into thick slices.

3 Mix together the corn oil, chili sauce, and salt and pepper to taste in a small bowl.

COOK'S TIP

For a simple spicy dip combine ²/₃ cup sour cream with ¹/₂ teaspoon sugar, ¹/₂ teaspoon Dijon mustard, and salt and pepper to taste. Leave to chill until required.

4 Brush the spicy mixture liberally over one side of the potatoes. Place the potatoes, oil side down, over medium hot coals and grill for 5–6 minutes.

5 Lightly brush the tops of the potatoes with the oil, then turn them over and grill for an additional 5 minutes, until crisp and golden.

6 Transfer the potatoes to a warm serving dish and serve at once.

Barbecue Bean Burgers

These tasty patties are ideal for a grill in the summer, but they are equally delicious cooked indoors at any time of year.

NUTRITIONAL INFORMATION

Calories 443   Sugars 12g
Protein . . . . .17g   Fat 14g
Carbohydrate . . .68g   Saturates 2g

15 MINS   1 HR 5 MINS

SERVES 6

I N G R E D I E N T S

½ cup dried adzuki beans

½ cup dried black-eye pea

6 tbsp vegetable oil

1 large onion, finely chopped

1 tsp yeast extract

¾ cup grated carrot

1½ cups fresh whole-wheat bread crumbs

2 tbsp whole-wheat flour

salt and pepper

B A R B E C U E   S A U C E

½ tsp chili powder

1 tsp celery salt

2 tbsp light muscovado sugar

2 tbsp red wine vinegar

2 tbsp vegetarian Worcestershire sauce

3 tbsp tomato paste

dash of Tabasco sauce

T O   S E R V E

6 whole-wheat burger rolls, toasted

mixed salad

baked potato fries

1 Place the beans in separate pans, then cover with water and bring to a boil. Cover and simmer the adzuki beans for 40 minutes and the black-eye peas for 50 minutes, until tender. Drain and rinse well.

2 Transfer to a mixing bowl and lightly mash together with a potato masher or fork. Set aside.

3 Heat 1 tablespoon of the oil in a skillet and gently cook the onion for 3–4 minutes, until softened. Mix into the beans with the yeast extract, grated carrot, bread crumbs, and seasoning. Bind together well.

4 With wet hands, divide the mixture into 6 and form into burgers 3½ inches/8 cm in diameter. Put the flour on a plate and use to coat the burgers.

5 To make the sauce, mix all the ingredients together until well blended.

6 Cook the burgers on a medium hot grill for 3–4 minutes on each side, brushing with the remaining oil from time to time. Put the burgers in the toasted rolls and serve with a mixed salad, baked potato fries, and a spoonful of the barbecue sauce.

Turkish Kabobs

A spicy chickpea sauce is served with grilled colorful vegetable kabobs.

NUTRITIONAL INFORMATION

Calories	303	Sugars	........13g
Protein	........13g	Fat	..........15g
Carbohydrate	...30g	Saturates	.......2g

20 MINS   20 MINS

SERVES 4

I N G R E D I E N T S

SAUCE

4 tbsp olive oil

3 garlic cloves, crushed

1 small onion, finely chopped

1½ cups canned chickpeas,
   rinsed and drained

1¼ cups plain yogurt

1 tsp ground cumin

½ tsp chili powder

lemon juice

salt and pepper

KABOBS

1 eggplant

1 red bell pepper, seeded

1 green bell pepper, seeded

4 plum tomatoes

1 lemon, cut into wedges

8 small fresh bay leaves

olive oil, for brushing

1 To make the sauce, heat the olive oil in a small skillet. Add the garlic and onion and fry over medium heat, stirring occasionally, for 5 minutes, until the onion is softened and golden brown.

2 Put the chickpeas and yogurt into a blender or food processor and add the cumin, chili powder, and onion mixture. Process for 15 seconds, until smooth. Alternatively, mash the chickpeas with a potato masher and stir in the yogurt, ground cumin, chili powder, and onion.

3 Place the puréed mixture in a bowl and season to taste with lemon juice and salt and pepper. Cover and chill until ready to serve.

4 To prepare the kabobs, cut the vegetables into large chunks and thread them onto 4 skewers, placing a bay leaf and lemon wedge at both ends of each kabob.

5 Brush the kabobs with olive oil and cook them over the grill, turning frequently, for 5–8 minutes. Heat the chickpea sauce and serve with the kabobs.

Roast Leeks

Use a good-quality French or Italian olive oil for this deliciously simple yet sophisticated vegetable accompaniment.

NUTRITIONAL INFORMATION

Calories 71   Sugars 2g
Protein . . . . .2g   Fat 6g
Carbohydrate . . . .3g   Saturates 1g

5 MINS   7 MINS

SERVES 6

INGREDIENTS

4 leeks

3 tbsp olive oil

2 tsp balsamic vinegar

sea salt and pepper

1 Cut the leeks in half lengthwise, making sure that you hold the knife straight, so that the leek is held together by the root. Brush each leek liberally with the olive oil.

2 Cook over a hot grill for 6–7 minutes, turning once.

3 Remove the leeks from the grill and brush lightly with the balsamic vinegar.

4 Season to taste with salt and pepper and serve hot or warm.

Cheese & Onion Baguettes

Part-baked baguettes are split and filled with a tasty cheese and onion mixture, then wrapped in foil and cooked over the grill.

NUTRITIONAL INFORMATION

Calories	715	Sugars	.........5g
Protein	........21g	Fat	..........41g
Carbohydrate	...70g	Saturates	......25g

15 MINS   20 MINS

SERVES 4

I N G R E D I E N T S

4 part-baked baguettes

2 tbsp tomato relish

¼ cup butter

8 scallions, finely chopped

½ cup cream cheese

generous 1 cup grated Cheddar cheese

1 tsp snipped chives

pepper

TO SERVE

mixed salad greens

herbs

1 Split the part-baked baguettes in half lengthwise, without cutting right through. Spread a little tomato relish on each split baguette.

2 Melt the butter in a skillet and add the scallions. Cook them over medium heat, stirring frequently, for 5 minutes, until softened and golden. Remove from the heat and set aside to cool slightly.

3 Beat the cream cheese in a mixing bowl to soften it. Mix in the scallions, with any remaining butter. Add the grated cheese and snipped chives and mix well. Season to taste with pepper.

4 Divide the cheese mixture between the baguettes, then spread it over the cut surfaces and sandwich the baguettes together again. Wrap each baguette tightly in kitchen foil.

5 Heat the baguettes over the grill for about 10–15 minutes, turning them occasionally. Peel back the foil to check that they are cooked and if the cheese mixture has melted. Serve with salad greens and garnished with fresh herbs.

COOK'S TIP

If there's no room on the grill, and you want to eat these at the same time as the rest of the food, bake them in a preheated oven, at 400°F/200°C, for 15 minutes.

Vegetarian Sausages

The delicious cheese flavor will make these sausages a hit with vegetarians who need not feel left out when it comes to a grill.

NUTRITIONAL INFORMATION

Calories 213   Sugars 4g
Protein . . . . .8g   Fat 12g
Carbohydrate . . .19g   Saturates 4g

🍴 50 MINS   🕑 25 MINS

MAKES 8

I N G R E D I E N T S

1 tbsp corn oil

1 small onion, finely chopped

1 cup finely chopped mushrooms

½ red bell pepper,
    seeded and finely chopped

14 oz/400 g canned cannellini beans,
    rinsed and drained

2 cups fresh bread crumbs

scant 1 cup grated Cheddar cheese

1 tsp dried mixed herbs

1 egg yolk

seasoned all-purpose flour

oil, to baste

TO SERVE

bread rolls

slices of fried onion

1 Heat the oil in a pan. Add the onion, mushrooms, and bell peppers and cook over low heat, stirring frequently, for 5 minutes, until softened.

2 Mash the cannellini beans in a large mixing bowl with a potato masher. Add the onion, mushroom, and bell pepper mixture, the bread crumbs, grated Cheddar, herbs, and egg yolk, and mix together well.

3 Press the mixture together with your fingers and shape into 8 sausages. Roll each sausage in the seasoned flour to coat evenly. Set aside to chill in the refrigerator for at least 30 minutes.

4 Grill the sausages on a sheet of oiled foil set over medium coals for 15–20 minutes, turning and basting frequently with oil, until golden.

5 Split a bread roll down the middle and insert a layer of fried onions. Place the sausage in the roll and serve.

Sidekick Vegetables

Colorful vegetables are grilled over hot coals to make this unusual hot salad, which is served with a spicy chile sauce on the side.

NUTRITIONAL INFORMATION

Calories 224   Sugars 14g
Protein . . . . .4g   Fat 15g
Carbohydrate . . .21g   Saturates 2g

15 MINS   30 MINS

SERVES 4

INGREDIENTS

1 red bell pepper, seeded

1 orange or yellow bell pepper, seeded

2 zucchini

2 corn cobs

1 eggplant

olive oil, for brushing

chopped thyme, rosemary, and parsley

salt and pepper

lime or lemon wedges, to serve

DRESSING

2 tbsp olive oil

1 tbsp sesame oil

1 garlic clove, crushed

1 small onion, finely chopped

1 celery stalk, finely chopped

1 small green chile, seeded and chopped

4 tomatoes, chopped

2-inch/5-cm piece of cucumber, chopped

1 tbsp tomato paste

1 tbsp lime or lemon juice

1 To make the dressing, heat the olive and sesame oils together in a pan or skillet. Add the garlic and onion, and cook over low heat for 3 minutes, until softened.

2 Add the celery, chile, and tomatoes to the pan and cook, stirring frequently, for 5 minutes.

3 Stir in the cucumber, tomato paste, and lime juice, and simmer over low heat for 8–10 minutes, until thick and pulpy. Season to taste with salt and pepper.

4 Cut the vegetables into thick slices and brush with a little olive oil.

5 Cook the vegetables over the hot coals of the grill for 5–8 minutes, sprinkling them with salt and pepper and fresh herbs as they cook, and turning once.

6 Divide the vegetables between 4 serving plates and spoon some of the dressing onto the side. Serve at once, sprinkled with a few more chopped herbs and accompanied by the lime wedges.

Garlic Potato Wedges

Serve this tasty potato dish with grilled kabobs, bean burgers, or vegetarian sausages.

NUTRITIONAL INFORMATION

Calories 257   Sugars 1g
Protein ....3g   Fat 16g
Carbohydrate ...26g   Saturates 5g

10 MINS   30-35 MINS

SERVES 4

INGREDIENTS

3 large baking potatoes, scrubbed

4 tbsp olive oil

2 tbsp butter

2 garlic cloves, chopped

1 tbsp chopped rosemary

1 tbsp chopped parsley

1 tbsp chopped thyme

salt and pepper

1 Bring a large pan of water to a boil, add the potatoes and parboil them for 10 minutes. Drain the potatoes, refresh under cold water and then drain them again thoroughly.

2 Transfer the potatoes to a cutting board. When the potatoes are cold enough to handle, cut them into thick wedges, but do not peel.

3 Heat the oil and butter in a small pan together with the garlic. Cook gently until the garlic begins to brown, then remove the pan from the heat.

4 Stir the herbs and salt and pepper to taste into the mixture in the pan.

5 Brush the herb mixture all over the potato wedges.

6 Grill the potatoes over hot coals for 10–15 minutes, brushing liberally with any of the remaining herb and butter mixture, until the potato wedges are just tender.

7 Transfer the garlic potato wedges to a warm serving plate and serve as an appetizer or as a side dish.

COOK'S TIP

You may find it easier to grill these potatoes in a hinged rack or in a specially designed grill roasting pan.

Marinated Brochettes

These tofu and mushroom brochettes are marinated in a lemon, garlic, and herb mixture so that they soak up a delicious flavor.

NUTRITIONAL INFORMATION

Calories ....192 Sugars 0.5g
Protein ....11g Fat 16g
Carbohydrate ....1g Saturates 2g

2¼ HOURS   6 MINS

SERVES 4

INGREDIENTS

1 lemon

1 garlic clove, crushed

4 tbsp olive oil

4 tbsp white wine vinegar

1 tbsp chopped herbs, such as rosemary,
   parsley, and thyme

10½ oz/300 g smoked bean curd

3 cups mushrooms

salt and pepper

herbs, to garnish

TO SERVE

mixed salad greens

cherry tomatoes, halved

1 Finely grate the rind from the lemon and squeeze out the juice.

2 Add the garlic, olive oil, vinegar and chopped herbs to the lemon rind and juice, mixing well. Season to taste with salt and pepper.

3 Slice the bean curd into large chunks with a sharp knife. Thread the pieces onto metal or wooden skewers, alternating them with the mushrooms.

4 Place the kabobs in a shallow dish and pour over the marinade. Cover and chill in the refrigerator for 1–2 hours, turning the brochettes in the marinade from time to time.

5 Cook the brochettes on a medium hot grill, frequently brushing them with the marinade and turning often, for 6 minutes until cooked through and golden brown.

6 Transfer to warm serving plates, garnish with fresh herbs and serve with mixed salad greens and cherry tomatoes.

Chunky Italian Slices

The flavor of chargrilled eggplants is hard to beat. The nutritional information includes the pesto dressing.

NUTRITIONAL INFORMATION

Calories	318	Sugars	. . . . .1g
Protein	. . . . .4g	Fat	. . . . .33g
Carbohydrate	. . . .1g	Saturates	. . . . . . .6g

20 MINS   10 MINS

SERVES 4

I N G R E D I E N T S

1 large eggplant

3 tbsp olive oil

1 tsp sesame oil

salt and pepper

P E S T O

1 garlic clove

scant ¼ cup pine nuts

½ cup fresh basil leaves

2 tbsp freshly grated Parmesan cheese

6 tbsp olive oil

salt and pepper

C U C U M B E R   S A U C E

⅔ cup plain yogurt

2-inch/5-cm piece of cucumber

½ tsp mint sauce

1 Remove the stalk from the eggplant, then cut it lengthwise into 8 thin slices.

2 Lay the slices on a plate or board and sprinkle them liberally with salt to remove the bitter juices. Leave to stand.

3 Meanwhile, prepare the baste. Combine the olive and sesame oils, season with pepper and set aside.

4 To make the pesto, process the garlic, pine nuts, basil, and cheese in a food processor until finely chopped. With the machine running, gradually add the oil in a thin stream. Season to taste.

5 To make the minty cucumber sauce, place the yogurt in a mixing bowl. Remove the seeds from the cucumber and finely dice the flesh. Stir into the yogurt with the mint sauce.

6 Rinse the eggplant slices and pat them dry with absorbent paper towels. Baste with the oil mixture and grill over hot coals for 10 minutes, turning once. The eggplant should be golden and tender.

7 Transfer the eggplant slices to serving plates and serve with either the cucumber sauce or the pesto.

Grape Leaf Pockets

A wonderful combination of soft cheese, chopped dates, ground almonds, and lightly fried nuts is encased in grape leaves.

NUTRITIONAL INFORMATION

Calories	459	Sugars	.........8g
Protein	........12g	Fat	..........42g
Carbohydrate	....9g	Saturates	......20g

25 MINS   15 MINS

SERVES 4

INGREDIENTS

1¼ cups full-fat soft cheese

⅔ cup ground almonds

2 tbsp dates, pitted and chopped

2 tbsp butter

¼ cup slivered almonds

12–16 grape leaves

salt and pepper

grilled baby corn, to serve

TO GARNISH

rosemary sprigs

tomato wedges

1 Beat the soft cheese in a large bowl until smooth. Add the ground almonds and chopped dates, and mix together thoroughly. Season to taste with salt and pepper.

2 Melt the butter in a small skillet. Add the slivered almonds and cook over very low heat, stirring constantly, for 2–3 minutes, until golden brown. Remove from the heat and set aside to cool for a few minutes.

3 Mix the fried almonds into the soft cheese mixture, stirring well to combine thoroughly.

4 Soak the grape leaves in water to remove some of the saltiness, if specified on the package. Drain them, then lay them out on a counter and spoon an equal amount of the soft cheese mixture on to each one. Fold over the leaves to enclose the filling.

5 Wrap the grape leaf pockets in foil, 1 or 2 per foil package. Place over the grill to heat through for 8–10 minutes, turning once. Serve with grilled baby corn and garnish with sprigs of rosemary and tomato wedges.

Filled Pita Breads

Pita breads are warmed over the hot coals, then split and filled with a Greek salad tossed in a fragrant rosemary dressing.

NUTRITIONAL INFORMATION

Calories 456	Sugars 4g
Protein 13g	Fat 25g
Carbohydrate . . .49g	Saturates 7g

🍲 15 MINS   🕙 10 MINS

SERVES 4

INGREDIENTS

½ iceberg lettuce, roughly chopped

2 large tomatoes, cut into wedges

3-inch/7.5-cm piece of cucumber,
   cut into chunks

scant ¼ cup pitted black olives

4½ oz/125 g feta cheese

4 pita breads

DRESSING

6 tbsp olive oil

3 tbsp red wine vinegar

1 tbsp crushed rosemary

½ tsp superfine sugar

salt and pepper

1 To make the salad, combine the lettuce, tomatoes, cucumber, and black olives.

2 Cut the feta cheese into chunks and add to the salad. Toss gently.

3 To make the dressing, whisk together the olive oil, red wine vinegar, rosemary, and sugar. Season to taste with salt and pepper. Place in a small pan or heatproof bowl and heat gently or place over the grill to just warm through.

4 Wrap the pita breads tightly in foil and place over the hot grill for 2–3 minutes, turning once, to warm through.

5 Unwrap the breads and split them open. Fill with the Greek salad mixture and drizzle over the warm dressing. Serve at once.

COOK'S TIP

Substitute different herbs for the rosemary—either oregano or basil would make a delicious alternative. Pack plenty of the salad into the pita breads—they taste much better when they are full to bursting!

Salads

A salad makes a refreshing accompaniment or side dish, but can also make a substantial main course meal. Salads are also a very good source of vitamins and minerals; always use the freshest possible ingredients for maximum flavor, texture, and goodness. Salads are quick to "rustle up" and good for times when you need to prepare a meal-in-a-moment and have to use pantry ingredients. A splash of culinary inspiration and you will find that you have prepared a fantastic salad that you had no idea was lurking in your kitchen! Experiment with new ingredients in order to add taste and interest to ordinary salad leaves. The only limit is your imagination!

Mexican Salad

This is a colorful salad with a Mexican theme, using beans, tomatoes, and avocado. The chili dressing adds a little kick.

NUTRITIONAL INFORMATION

Calories	307	Sugars	.........7g
Protein	.........5g	Fat	..........26g
Carbohydrate	...13g	Saturates	.......5g

10-15 MINS   0 MINS

SERVES 4

INGREDIENTS

lollo rosso lettuce

2 ripe avocados

2 tsp lemon juice

4 medium tomatoes

1 onion

6 oz/175 g mixed canned beans, drained

DRESSING

4 tbsp olive oil

drop of chili oil

2 tbsp garlic wine vinegar

pinch of superfine sugar

pinch of chili powder

1 tbsp chopped parsley

COOK'S TIP

The lemon juice is sprinkled on to the avocados to prevent discoloration when in contact with the air. For this reason the salad should be prepared, assembled, and served quite quickly.

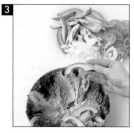

1 Line a large serving bowl with the lettuce leaves.

2 Using a sharp knife, cut the avocados in half and remove the pits. Thinly slice the flesh and sprinkle with the lemon juice.

3 Thinly slice the tomatoes and onion and push the onion out into rings. Arrange the avocado, tomatoes, and onion around the salad bowl, leaving a space in the center.

4 Spoon the beans into the center of the salad and whisk the dressing ingredients together. Pour the dressing over the salad and serve.

Goat Cheese Salad

A delicious hot salad of melting goat cheese over sliced tomato and basil on a base of hot ciabatta bread.

NUTRITIONAL INFORMATION

Calories 379   Sugars 3g
Protein . . . . .15g   Fat 23g
Carbohydrate . . .30g   Saturates 10g

10 MINS   6 MINS

SERVES 4

I N G R E D I E N T S

3 tbsp olive oil

1 tbsp white wine vinegar

1 tsp black olive paste

1 garlic clove, crushed

1 tsp chopped fresh thyme

1 ciabatta loaf

4 small tomatoes

12 fresh basil leaves

2 x 4½ oz/125 g logs goat cheese

TO SERVE

mixed salad greens, including
   arugula and radicchio

1 Mix the oil, vinegar, olive paste, garlic, and thyme together in a screw-top jar and shake vigorously.

2 Cut the ciabatta in half horizontally, then in half vertically to make 4 pieces.

3 Drizzle some of the dressing over the bread, then arrange the tomatoes and basil leaves on the top.

4 Cut each roll of goat cheese into 6 slices and place 3 slices on each piece of ciabatta.

5 Brush with some of the dressing and bake in a preheated oven, 450°F/230°C, for 5–6 minutes until turning brown at the edges.

6 Pour the remaining dressing over the salad greens and serve with the baked bread.

COOK'S TIP

Many French goat cheeses are widely available. Those labeled *chèvre* or *pur chèvre* must be made purely from goat's milk. The goat's milk in *mi-chèvre* cheeses is mixed with up to 75 percent cow's milk.

Green & White Salad

This potato, arugula, and apple salad is flavored with creamy, salty goat cheese—perfect with salad greens.

NUTRITIONAL INFORMATION

Calories 282   Sugars 10g
Protein . . . . .8g   Fat 17g
Carbohydrate . . .26g   Saturates 5g

🍞

🥔 15 MINS   🕐 20 MINS

SERVES 4

INGREDIENTS

2 large potatoes, unpeeled and sliced

2 green eating apples, diced

1 tsp lemon juice

¼ cup walnut pieces

4½ oz/125 g goat cheese, cubed

2–3 bunches arugula leaves

salt and pepper

DRESSING

2 tbsp olive oil

1 tbsp red wine vinegar

1 tsp clear honey

1 tsp fennel seeds

COOK'S TIP

Serve this salad immediately to prevent the apple from discoloring. Alternatively, prepare all of the other ingredients in advance and add the apple at the last minute.

1 Cook the potatoes in a pan of boiling water for 15 minutes, until tender. Drain and set aside to cool. Transfer the cooled potatoes to a serving bowl.

2 Toss the diced apples in the lemon juice, then drain and stir them into the cold potatoes.

3 Add the walnut pieces, cheese cubes, and arugula leaves, then toss the salad to mix.

4 In a small bowl, whisk the dressing ingredients together until well combined and pour the dressing over the salad. Serve immediately.

Moroccan Salad

Couscous is a type of semolina made from durum wheat. It is wonderful in salads, as it readily takes up the flavor of the dressing.

NUTRITIONAL INFORMATION

Calories 195   Sugars 15g
Protein . . . . .8g   Fat 2g
Carbohydrate . . .40g   Saturates 0.3g

30-35 MINS   0 MINS

SERVES 6

INGREDIENTS

2 cups couscous

1 bunch scallions, finely chopped

1 small green bell pepper, seeded
    and chopped

4-inch/10-cm piece of cucumber, chopped

6 oz/175 g canned chickpeas,
    rinsed and drained

generous ⅓ cup golden raisins or raisins

2 oranges

salt and pepper

mint sprigs, to garnish

lettuce leaves, to serve

DRESSING

finely grated rind of 1 orange

1 tbsp chopped fresh mint

⅔ cup natural yogurt

1 Put the couscous into a bowl and cover with boiling water. Leave it to soak for 15 minutes to swell the grains, then stir gently with a fork to separate them.

2 Add the scallions, green bell pepper, cucumber, chickpeas, and golden raisins to the couscous, stirring to combine. Season well with salt and pepper.

3 To make the dressing, place the orange rind, mint, and yogurt in a bowl and mix together until well combined. Pour over the couscous mixture and stir to mix well.

4 Using a sharp serrated knife, remove the peel and pith from the oranges. Cut the flesh into segments, removing all the membrane.

5 Arrange the lettuce leaves on 4 serving plates. Divide the couscous mixture between the plates and arrange the orange segments on top. Garnish with sprigs of fresh mint and serve.

Green Vegetable Salad

This salad uses lots of green-colored ingredients, which look and taste wonderful with the minty yogurt dressing.

NUTRITIONAL INFORMATION

Calories ....50 Sugars 6g
Protein ....4g Fat 1g
Carbohydrate ....6g Saturates 0.4g

10–15 MINS   10 MINS

SERVES 4

INGREDIENTS

2 zucchini, cut into sticks

¾ cup green beans, cut into three

1 green bell pepper, seeded and cut into strips

2 celery stalks, sliced

1 bunch watercress or arugula

DRESSING

¾ cup plain yogurt

1 garlic clove, crushed

2 tbsp chopped mint

pepper

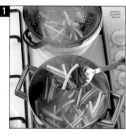

1 Cook the zucchini and green beans in a pan of salted boiling water for 7–8 minutes. Drain and set aside to cool completely.

2 Mix the zucchini and green beans with the bell pepper, celery, and watercress in a large serving bowl.

3 To make the dressing, mix together the plain yogurt, garlic, and chopped mint in a bowl. Season with pepper to taste.

4 Spoon the dressing onto the salad and serve immediately.

COOK'S TIP

The salad must be served as soon as the yogurt dressing has been added—the dressing will start to separate if kept for any length of time.

Middle Eastern Salad

This attractive-looking salad can be served with a couple of vegetable kabobs for a delicious light lunch or an informal supper.

NUTRITIONAL INFORMATION

Calories 163	Sugars 12g
Protein 8g	Fat 3g
Carbohydrate ...27g	Saturates 0.4g

🍲 15 MINS   🕐 0 MINS

SERVES 4

I N G R E D I E N T S

14 oz/400 g canned chickpeas

4 carrots

1 bunch scallions

1 medium cucumber

½ tsp salt

½ tsp pepper

3 tbsp lemon juice

1 red bell pepper, sliced

1 Drain the chickpeas and place them in a large salad bowl.

2 Using a sharp knife, thinly slice the carrots. Cut the scallions into small pieces. Thickly slice the cucumber and then cut the slices into fourths.

3 Add the carrot slices, scallions, and cucumber to the chickpeas and mix.

4 Season to taste with the salt and pepper and sprinkle with the lemon juice. Toss the salad ingredients together gently, using 2 serving spoons.

5 Using a sharp knife, thinly slice the red bell pepper. Arrange the slices of red bell pepper decoratively on top of the chickpea salad. Serve the salad immediately or chill in the refrigerator and serve when required.

VARIATION

This salad would also be delicious made with *ful medames*. If they are not available canned, use 1 cup dried, soaked for 5 hours and then simmered for 2½ hours. Another alternative would be canned gunga beans.

Warm Goat Cheese Salad

This delicious salad combines soft goat cheese with walnut halves, served on a bed of mixed salad greens.

NUTRITIONAL INFORMATION

Calories .... .408   Sugars 8g
Protein .... .9g   Fat .... .38g
Carbohydrate ....8g   Saturates 8g

5 MINS   5 MINS

SERVES 4

INGREDIENTS

scant ⅔ cup walnut halves

mixed salad greens

4½ oz/125 g soft goat cheese

snipped chives, to garnish

DRESSING

6 tbsp walnut oil

3 tbsp white wine vinegar

1 tbsp clear honey

1 tsp Dijon mustard

pinch of ground ginger

salt and pepper

1 To make the dressing, whisk together the walnut oil, wine vinegar, honey, mustard, and ginger in a small pan. Season to taste with salt and pepper.

2 Heat the dressing gently, stirring occasionally, until warm. Add the walnut halves and continue to heat for 3–4 minutes.

3 Arrange the salad greens on 4 serving plates and place spoonfuls of goat cheese on top. Lift the walnut halves from the dressing with a slotted spoon, and scatter them over the salads.

4 Transfer the warm dressing to a small pitcher. Sprinkle chives over the salads and serve with the dressing.

VARIATION

You could also use a ewe's milk cheese, such as feta, in this recipe for a sharper flavor.

Gado Gado

This is a well-known and very popular Indonesian salad of mixed vegetables with a peanut dressing.

NUTRITIONAL INFORMATION

Calories ....392 Sugars 8g
Protein ....9g Fat 35g
Carbohydrate ....11g Saturates 5g

10 MINS   25 MINS

SERVES 4

I N G R E D I E N T S

1½ cups shredded white cabbage

¾ cup green beans, cut into three

¾ cup carrots, cut into short, thin sticks

1 cup cauliflower florets

1 cup bean sprouts

D R E S S I N G

scant ½ cup vegetable oil

⅔ cup unsalted peanuts

2 garlic cloves, crushed

1 small onion, finely chopped

½ tsp chili powder

½ tsp light brown sugar

2 cups water

juice of ½ lemon

salt

sliced scallions, to garnish

1 Cook the vegetables separately in a pan of salted boiling water for 4–5 minutes, then drain well and chill.

2 To make the dressing, heat the oil in a skillet and cook the peanuts, tossing frequently, for 3–4 minutes.

3 Remove from the skillet with a slotted spoon and drain on absorbent paper towels. Process the peanuts in a food processor or crush with a rolling pin until a fine mixture is formed.

4 Pour all but 1 tablespoon of the oil from the skillet and cook the garlic and onion for 1 minute. Add the chili powder, sugar, a pinch of salt, and the water and bring to a boil.

5 Stir in the peanuts. Reduce the heat and simmer for 4–5 minutes, until the sauce thickens. Add the lemon juice and set aside to cool.

6 Arrange the vegetables in a serving dish and spoon the peanut dressing into the center. Garnish and serve.

Three-Bean Salad

Fresh young green beans are combined with soy beans and red kidney beans in a chive and tomato dressing to make a tasty salad.

NUTRITIONAL INFORMATION

Calories 276   Sugars 7g
Protein ....18g   Fat 15g
Carbohydrate ...18g   Saturates 4g

15 MINS   10 MINS

SERVES 6

INGREDIENTS

3 tbsp olive oil

1 tbsp lemon juice

1 tbsp tomato paste

1 tbsp light malt vinegar

1 tbsp chopped chives

6 oz/175 g young green beans

14 oz/400 g canned soy beans,
    rinsed and drained

14 oz/400 g canned red kidney beans,
    rinsed and drained

2 tomatoes, chopped

4 scallions, chopped

4½ oz/125 g feta cheese, cut into cubes

salt and pepper

mixed salad greens, to serve

chopped chives, to garnish

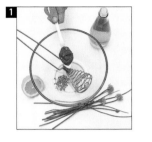

1 Put the olive oil, lemon juice, tomato paste, light malt vinegar, and chopped chives into a large bowl and whisk together well until thoroughly combined. Set aside.

2 Cook the green beans in boiling, lightly salted water for 4–5 minutes, until just cooked. Drain, then refresh under cold running water and drain again. Pat dry with paper towels.

3 Add the green beans, soy beans, and red kidney beans to the dressing, stirring to mix.

4 Add the tomatoes, scallions, and feta cheese to the bean mixture, tossing gently to coat in the dressing. Season well with salt and pepper.

5 Arrange the mixed salad greens on 6 serving plates. Pile the bean salad onto the plates and garnish with chopped chives.

Potato & Radish Salad

The radishes and the herb and mustard dressing give this colorful salad a mild mustard flavor, which complements the potatoes perfectly.

NUTRITIONAL INFORMATION

Calories	140	Sugars	.........3g
Protein	.........3g	Fat	...........6g
Carbohydrate	...20g	Saturates	.......1g

🛆 50 MINS   🕐 20 MINS

SERVES 4

INGREDIENTS

1 lb 2 oz/500 g new potatoes, scrubbed
  and halved

½ cucumber, thinly sliced

2 tsp salt

1 bunch radishes, thinly sliced

DRESSING

1 tbsp Dijon mustard

2 tbsp olive oil

1 tbsp white wine vinegar

2 tbsp mixed chopped herbs

1 Cook the potatoes in a pan of boiling water for 10–15 minutes, until tender. Drain and set aside to cool.

2 Meanwhile, spread out the cucumber slices on a plate and sprinkle with the salt. Leave to stand for 30 minutes, then rinse under cold running water and pat dry with paper towels.

3 Arrange the cucumber and radish slices on a serving plate in a decorative pattern and pile the cooked potatoes in the center of the slices.

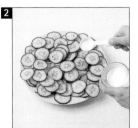

4 In a small bowl, mix all the dressing ingredients together, whisking until thoroughly combined. Pour the dressing over the salad, tossing well to coat all of the ingredients. Chill in the refrigerator before serving.

COOK'S TIP

The cucumber adds not only color, but also a real freshness to the salad. It is salted and left to stand to remove the excess water, which would make the salad soggy. Wash the cucumber well to remove all of the salt, before adding to the salad.

Three-Way Potato Salad

Small new potatoes, served warm in a delicious dressing. The nutritional information is for the potato salad with the curry dressing only.

NUTRITIONAL INFORMATION

Calories	310	Sugars	........12g
Protein	.........6g	Fat	..........19g
Carbohydrate	...31g	Saturates	.......4g

15-20 MINS | 20 MINS

SERVES 4

I N G R E D I E N T S

1 lb 2 oz/500 g new potatoes (for each
　　dressing)

herbs, to garnish

LIGHT CURRY DRESSING

1 tbsp vegetable oil

1 tbsp medium curry paste

1 small onion, chopped

1 tbsp mango chutney, chopped

6 tbsp plain yogurt

3 tbsp light cream

2 tbsp mayonnaise

salt and pepper

1 tbsp light cream, to garnish

VINAIGRETTE DRESSING

6 tbsp hazelnut oil

3 tbsp cider vinegar

1 tsp whole-grain mustard

1 tsp superfine sugar

few basil leaves, torn

PARSLEY CREAM

⅔ cup sour cream

3 tbsp light mayonnaise

4 scallions, finely chopped

1 tbsp chopped fresh parsley

1 To make the Light Curry Dressing, heat the vegetable oil in a pan, then add the curry paste and onion and cook, stirring frequently, until the onion is soft. Remove from the heat and set aside to cool slightly.

2 Mix together the mango chutney, yogurt, cream, and mayonnaise. Add the curry mixture and blend together. Season with salt and pepper.

3 To make the Vinaigrette Dressing, whisk the oil, vinegar, mustard, sugar, and basil together in a small pitcher or bowl. Season with salt and pepper.

4 To make the Parsley Cream, combine the mayonnaise, sour cream, scallions, and parsley, mixing well. Season with salt and pepper.

5 Cook the potatoes in lightly salted boiling water until just tender. Drain well and set aside to cool for 5 minutes, then add the chosen dressing, tossing to coat. Serve, garnished with fresh herbs, spooning a little light cream onto the potatoes if you have used the curry dressing.

Marinated Vegetable Salad

Lightly steamed vegetables taste superb served slightly warm in a marinade of olive oil, white wine, vinegar, and fresh herbs.

NUTRITIONAL INFORMATION

Calories 114   Sugars 4g
Protein . . . . .3g   Fat 9g
Carbohydrate . . . .5g   Saturates 1g

10 MINS   10 MINS

SERVES 6

I N G R E D I E N T S

6 oz/175 g baby carrots

2 celery hearts, cut into 4 pieces

1½ cups sugar snap peas or snow peas

1 fennel bulb, sliced

6 oz/175 g small asparagus spears

1½ tbsp sunflower seeds

dill sprigs, to garnish

D R E S S I N G

4 tbsp olive oil

4 tbsp dry white wine

2 tbsp white wine vinegar

1 tbsp chopped dill

1 tbsp chopped parsley

salt and pepper

1 Put the carrots, celery, sugar snap peas, fennel, and asparagus into a steamer and cook over gently boiling water until just tender. It is important that they retain a little "bite."

2 Meanwhile, make the dressing. Mix together the olive oil, wine, vinegar, and chopped herbs, whisking until thoroughly combined. Season to taste with salt and pepper.

3 When the vegetables are cooked, transfer them to a serving dish and pour over the dressing at once. The hot vegetables will absorb the flavor of the dressing as they cool.

4 Spread out the sunflower seeds on a cookie sheet and toast them under a preheated broiler for 3–4 minutes, until lightly browned. Sprinkle the toasted sunflower seeds over the vegetables.

5 Serve the salad while the vegetables are still slightly warm, garnished with sprigs of fresh dill.

Melon & Strawberry Salad

This refreshing fruit-based salad is perfect for a hot summer's day and would go well with grilled food.

NUTRITIONAL INFORMATION

Calories 112	Sugars 22g	
Protein 5g	Fat 1g	
Carbohydrate . . .22g	Saturates 0.3g	

15 MINS   0 MINS

SERVES 4

INGREDIENTS

½ iceberg lettuce, shredded

1 small honeydew melon

1½ cups sliced strawberries

2-inch/5-cm piece of cucumber,
 thinly sliced

mint sprigs to garnish

DRESSING

scant 1 cup plain yogurt

2-inch/5-cm piece of cucumber, peeled

a few mint leaves

½ tsp finely grated lime or lemon rind

pinch of superfine sugar

3–4 ice cubes

1 Arrange the shredded lettuce on 4 serving plates.

VARIATION

Omit the ice cubes in the dressing if you prefer, but make sure that the ingredients are well-chilled. This will ensure that the finished dressing is really cool.

2 Cut the melon lengthwise into quarters. Scoop out the seeds and cut through the flesh down to the skin at 1-inch/2.5-cm intervals. Cut the melon close to the skin and detach the flesh.

3 Place the chunks of melon on the beds of lettuce with the strawberries and cucumber slices.

4 To make the dressing, put the yogurt, cucumber, mint leaves, lime rind,

superfine sugar, and ice cubes into a blender or food processor. Blend together for 15 seconds, until smooth. Alternatively, chop the cucumber and mint finely, then crush the ice cubes and combine with the other ingredients.

5 Serve the salad with a little dressing poured over it. Garnish with sprigs of fresh mint.

Multicolored Salad

The beet adds a rich color to this dish, tinting the potato an appealing pink. Mixed with cucumber, it makes a really vibrant salad.

NUTRITIONAL INFORMATION

Calories 174   Sugars 8g
Protein ....4g   Fat 6g
Carbohydrate ...27g   Saturates 1g

15-20 MINS   20 MINS

SERVES 4

INGREDIENTS

1 lb 2 oz/500 g waxy potatoes, diced

4 small cooked beets, sliced

½ small cucumber, thinly sliced

2 large dill pickles, sliced

1 red onion, halved and sliced

dill sprigs, to garnish

DRESSING

1 garlic clove, crushed

2 tbsp olive oil

2 tbsp red wine vinegar

2 tbsp chopped fresh dill

salt and pepper

1 Cook the diced potatoes in a pan of boiling water for 15 minutes, until just tender. Drain and set aside to cool.

2 When cool, mix the potato and beets together in a bowl and set aside.

3 To make the dressing, whisk together the garlic, olive oil, vinegar, and dill and season to taste with salt and pepper.

4 When ready to serve, line a large serving platter with the slices of cucumber, dill pickles, and red onion.

Spoon the potato and beet mixture into the center of the platter.

5 Pour the dressing over the salad and serve immediately, garnished with fresh dill sprigs.

VARIATION

Line the salad platter with 2 heads of chicory, separated into leaves, and arrange the cucumber, dill pickle, and red onion slices on top of the leaves.

Carrot & Nut Coleslaw

This simple salad has a dressing made from poppy seeds pan-fried in sesame oil to bring out their flavor and aroma.

NUTRITIONAL INFORMATION

Calories	220	Sugars	.........7g
Protein	.........4g	Fat	..........19g
Carbohydrate	...10g	Saturates	.......3g

15 MINS   5–10 MINS

SERVES 4

I N G R E D I E N T S

1 large carrot, grated

1 small onion, finely chopped

2 celery stalks, chopped

¼ small hard white cabbage, shredded

1 tbsp chopped parsley

4 tbsp sesame oil

½ tsp poppy seeds

generous ⅓ cup cashew nuts

2 tbsp white wine vinegar or cider vinegar

salt and pepper

parsley sprigs, to garnish

1 In a large salad bowl, mix together the carrot, onion, celery, and cabbage. Stir in the chopped parsley and season to taste with salt and pepper.

2 Heat the sesame oil in a pan with a lid. Add the poppy seeds and cover the pan. Cook over medium-high heat until the seeds start to make a popping sound. Remove from the heat and set aside to cool.

3 Spread out the cashew nuts on a cookie sheet. Place them under a medium-hot broiler and toast until lightly browned, being careful not to burn them. Leave to cool.

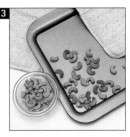

4 Add the vinegar to the oil and poppy seeds, then pour the dressing over the carrot mixture. Add the cooled cashew nuts. Toss together to coat well.

5 Garnish the salad with sprigs of fresh parsley and serve immediately.

Broiled Salad

The vegetables for this dish are best prepared well in advance and chilled in the refrigerator before serving.

NUTRITIONAL INFORMATION

Calories	230	Sugars	........10g
Protein	.........2g	Fat	..........20g
Carbohydrate	....11g	Saturates	.......3g

1¼ HOURS   10 MINS

SERVES 4

INGREDIENTS

1 zucchini, sliced

1 yellow bell pepper, seeded and sliced

1 eggplant, sliced

1 fennel bulb, cut into eight

1 red onion, cut into eight

16 cherry tomatoes

3 tbsp olive oil

1 garlic clove, crushed

rosemary sprigs, to garnish

DRESSING

4 tbsp olive oil

2 tbsp balsamic vinegar

2 tsp chopped rosemary

1 tsp Dijon mustard

1 tsp clear honey

2 tsp lemon juice

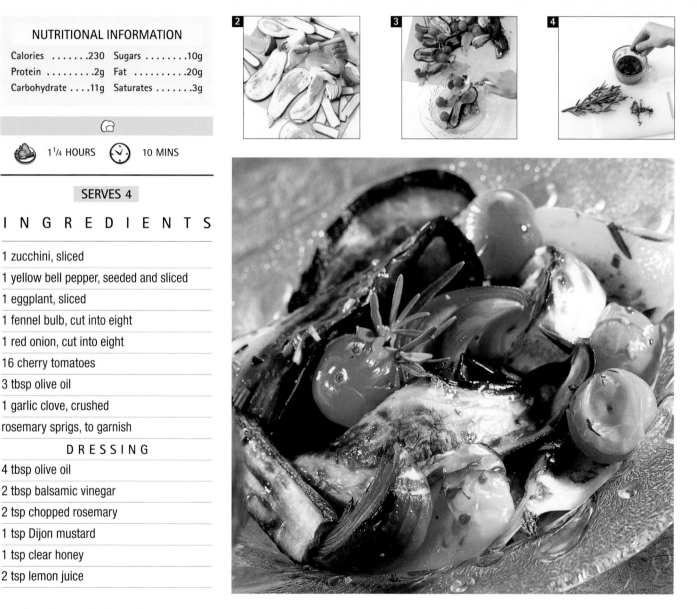

1 Spread out the slices of zucchini, bell pepper, eggplant, fennel, onion, and the tomatoes on a large cookie sheet.

2 Mix together the oil and garlic and brush all over the vegetables. Cook under a medium-hot broiler for 10 minutes, until tender and just beginning to char. Remove from the heat and set aside to cool.

3 When cool, spoon the vegetables into a serving bowl and mix together gently.

4 Whisk together the dressing ingredients until thoroughly combined and pour over the vegetables. Cover and chill in the refrigerator for 1 hour.

5 Garnish the salad with rosemary sprigs and serve.

COOK'S TIP

This dish could also be served warm—heat the dressing in a pan over low heat and then pour over the vegetables.

Melon & Mango Salad

A little freshly grated gingerroot mixed with creamy yogurt and clear honey makes a perfect dressing for this refreshing melon salad.

NUTRITIONAL INFORMATION

Calories 189	Sugars 30g
Protein 5g	Fat 7g
Carbohydrate ...30g	Saturates 1g

15-20 MINS   0 MINS

SERVES 4

INGREDIENTS

1 cantaloupe melon

½ cup black grapes, halved and seeded

½ cup seedless green grapes

1 large mango

1 bunch of watercress or arugula

iceberg lettuce leaves, shredded

2 tbsp olive oil

1 tbsp cider vinegar

1 passion fruit

salt and pepper

DRESSING

¾ cup plain thick yogurt

1 tbsp clear honey

1 tsp grated gingerroot

1 First, make the dressing for the melon. Mix together the yogurt, honey, and ginger in a small bowl, stirring to combine.

2 Halve the melon and scoop out the seeds. Slice, peel, and cut into chunks. Mix with the grapes.

3 Slice the mango on each side of its large flat pit. On each mango half, slash the flesh into a criss-cross pattern down to, but not through the skin. Push the skin from underneath to turn the mango halves inside out. Now remove the flesh and add to the melon mixture.

4 Arrange the watercress and lettuce on 4 serving plates. Make the dressing for the salad greens. Whisk together the olive oil and cider vinegar and season to taste with salt and pepper. Drizzle the dressing over the watercress and lettuce.

5 Divide the melon mixture equally between the 4 plates and spoon over the yogurt dressing. Scoop the seeds out of the passion fruit and sprinkle them over the salads. Serve immediately.

COOK'S TIP

Grated gingerroot gives a marvelous flavor to this recipe, but if you can't get fresh ginger, substitute ¹/₂ teaspoon of ground ginger instead.

Alfalfa & Spinach Salad

This is a really refreshing salad that must be assembled just before serving to prevent everything being colored by the beet.

NUTRITIONAL INFORMATION

Calories 139	Sugars 7g	
Protein 2g	Fat 11g	
Carbohydrate 8g	Saturates 2g	

🍲 10 MINS 🕐 0 MINS

SERVES 4

I N G R E D I E N T S

3½ oz/100 g baby spinach

1⅛ cups alfalfa sprouts

2 celery stalks, sliced

4 cooked beets, cut into eight

D R E S S I N G

4 tbsp olive oil

4½ tsp garlic wine vinegar

1 garlic clove, crushed

2 tsp clear honey

1 tbsp chopped chives

1 Place the spinach and alfalfa sprouts in a large bowl and mix together.

2 Add the celery to the bowl and mix together well.

3 Toss in the beet and mix until well combined.

4 To make the dressing, mix the oil, wine vinegar, garlic, honey, and chopped chives.

5 Pour the dressing over the salad, toss well and serve immediately.

VARIATION

Add the segments of 1 large orange to the salad to make it even more colorful and refreshing. Replace the garlic wine vinegar with a different flavored oil such as chili or herb, if you prefer.

Potato, Bean & Apple Salad

Use any mixture of beans you have to hand in this recipe, but the wider the variety, the more colorful the salad.

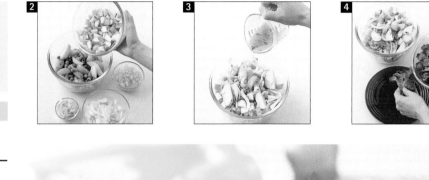

NUTRITIONAL INFORMATION

Calories ....183 Sugars 8g
Protein ....6g Fat 7g
Carbohydrate ...26g Saturates 1g

20 MINS   20 MINS

SERVES 4

INGREDIENTS

8 oz/225 g new potatoes, scrubbed
    and cut into fourths

8 oz/225 g mixed canned beans, such as
    red kidney beans, flageolet, and borlotti
    beans, drained and rinsed

1 red eating apple, diced and tossed
    in 1 tbsp lemon juice

1 yellow bell pepper, seeded and diced

1 shallot, sliced

½ fennel bulb, sliced

oak leaf lettuce leaves

DRESSING

1 tbsp red wine vinegar

2 tbsp olive oil

½ tbsp American mustard

1 garlic clove, crushed

2 tsp chopped fresh thyme

VARIATION

Use Dijon or whole-grain
mustard in place of American
mustard for a different flavor.

1 Cook the potatoes in a pan of boiling water for 15 minutes, until tender. Drain and transfer to a mixing bowl.

2 Add the mixed beans to the potatoes, together with the apple, bell pepper, shallots, and fennel. Mix well, taking care not to break up the cooked potatoes.

3 To make the dressing, whisk all the dressing ingredients together until thoroughly combined, then pour it over the potato salad.

4 Line a serving plate or salad bowl with the oak leaf lettuce leaves and spoon the potato mixture into the center. Serve immediately.

Garden Salad

This chunky salad includes tiny new potatoes tossed in a minty dressing, and has a mustard dip for dunking.

NUTRITIONAL INFORMATION

Calories	227	Sugars	.........6g
Protein	.........4g	Fat	..........17g
Carbohydrate	...16g	Saturates	.......4g

15-20 MINS ⏱ 20 MINS

SERVES 8

I N G R E D I E N T S

1 lb 2 oz/500 g tiny new or salad potatoes

3 cups broccoli florets

1½ cups sugar snap peas

2 large carrots

4 celery stalks

1 yellow or orange bell pepper, seeded

1 bunch scallions

1 head chicory

D R E S S I N G

3 tbsp olive oil

1 tbsp white wine vinegar

1 tsp Dijon mustard

2 tbsp chopped mint

M U S T A R D   D I P

6 tbsp sour cream

3 tbsp thick mayonnaise

2 tsp balsamic vinegar

1½ tsp coarse-grain mustard

½ tsp creamed horseradish

pinch of brown sugar

salt and pepper

1 Cook the potatoes in boiling salted water for 10 minutes, until just tender. While they cook, combine the dressing ingredients.

2 Drain the potatoes thoroughly and add to the dressing while hot, then toss well and set aside until cold, giving them an occasional stir.

3 To make the dip, combine the sour cream, mayonnaise, vinegar, mustard, horseradish, and sugar and season to taste with salt and pepper. Transfer to a small serving bowl, then cover and refrigerate until ready to serve.

4 Cut the broccoli into bite-size florets and blanch for 2 minutes in boiling water. Drain and toss immediately in cold water; when cold, drain thoroughly.

5 Blanch the sugar snap peas in boiling water for 1 minute. Drain, then rinse in cold water and drain again.

6 Cut the carrots and celery into short, thin sticks 2½ x ½ inches/6 x 1 cm. Slice the bell pepper or cut it into small cubes. Cut off some of the green parts of the scallions and separate the chicory leaves.

7 Arrange the vegetables attractively in a fairly shallow bowl with the potatoes piled up in the center. Serve accompanied with the mustard dip.

Side Dishes

The main aim of the recipes in this chapter is to complement the main course recipes found throughout the rest of this book. The side dishes include a range of different vegetable dishes—you will be amazed at the variety! Try potatoes flavored with exotic saffron and mustard, or green beans full of the sun-drenched flavors

of Greece. Whatever the entrée, you're sure to find a suitable side dish among the wealth of recipes in this chapter. They're all perfect for elaborate dinner parties, or for simple family meals. You could even use some of them for a snack or a light meal on its own. The choice is yours!

Spicy Potatoes & Onions

Masala aloo are potatoes cooked in spices and onions. Semi-dry when cooked, they make an excellent accompaniment to almost any curry.

NUTRITIONAL INFORMATION

Calories 313	Sugars 5g
Protein 2g	Fat 25g
Carbohydrate . . .21g	Saturates 3g

🍲

🧊 10–15 MINS   🕐 10 MINS

SERVES 4

I N G R E D I E N T S

6 tbsp vegetable oil

2 medium-size onions, finely chopped

1 tsp finely chopped fresh gingerroot

1 tsp crushed garlic

1 tsp chili powder

1½ tsp ground cumin

1½ tsp ground coriander

1 tsp salt

14 oz/400 g canned new potatoes

1 tbsp lemon juice

B A G H A R

3 tbsp oil

3 dried red chiles

½ tsp onion seeds

½ tsp mustard seeds

½ tsp fenugreek seeds

TO GARNISH

fresh cilantro leaves

1 green chile, finely chopped

1 Heat the oil in a large, heavy-bottomed pan. Add the onions and fry, stirring, until golden brown. Reduce the heat, then add the ginger, garlic, chili powder, ground cumin, ground coriander, and salt and stir-fry for 1 minute. Remove the pan from the heat and set aside until required.

2 Drain the water from the potatoes. Add the potatoes to the onion mixture and spice mixture and heat through. Sprinkle over the lemon juice and mix well.

3 To make the baghar, heat the oil in a separate pan. Add the red chiles, onion seeds, mustard seeds, and fenugreek seeds and cook until the seeds turn a shade darker. Remove the pan from the heat and pour the baghar over the potatoes.

4 Garnish with cilantro leaves and chiles, then serve.

Seasonal Vegetables

These vegetables are ideal for a special occasion, such as Christmas Day. Do not start cooking them too early, as they take little time to cook.

NUTRITIONAL INFORMATION

Calories	434	Sugars	........20g
Protein	.........7g	Fat	..........19g
Carbohydrate	...62g	Saturates	.......5g

🍲 20 MINS   🕐 1 HR 40 MINS

SERVES 8

INGREDIENTS

CRISPY ROAST POTATOES

4 lb 8 oz/2 kg potatoes

½ tsp salt

vegetable oil, for roasting

HONEY-GLAZED CARROTS

2 lb 4 oz/1 kg carrots

1 tbsp clear honey

2 tbsp butter

2 tsp sesame seeds, toasted

SPICED WINTER CABBAGE

1 hard white cabbage

2 eating apples, peeled, cored, and chopped

few drops of lemon juice

2 tbsp butter

freshly grated nutmeg

salt

1 To make Crispy Roast Potatoes, peel the potatoes and cut them into large, even-size chunks. Put them into a large pan of cold water with the salt. Bring to a boil, and then reduce the heat.

Cover and simmer for 8–10 minutes to parboil them. Drain thoroughly.

2 Heat about ⅔ cup vegetable oil in a large roasting pan until very hot. Add the potatoes, basting thoroughly. Roast in a preheated oven, 400°F/200°C, for 1 hour, basting occasionally, until crisp and golden brown.

3 To make Honey-Glazed Carrots, cut the carrots into a pan and barely cover with water. Add the honey and butter. Cook, uncovered, for 15 minutes, until the liquid has just evaporated and the carrots are glazed. Serve in a warmed dish, sprinkled with toasted sesame seeds.

4 To make Spiced Winter Cabbage, shred the cabbage just before cooking it to retain the vitamins. Add the chopped apples and lemon juice, and cook in a small amount of water in a covered pan over a medium heat for 6 minutes. Drain thoroughly. Season to taste with salt and add the butter, tossing to melt. Transfer to a warmed serving dish, then sprinkle with freshly grated nutmeg and serve immediately.

Pommes Anna

This is a classic potato dish, which may be left to cook unattended while the remainder of the meal is being prepared, so it is ideal with stews.

NUTRITIONAL INFORMATION

Calories 237	Sugars 1g	
Protein 4g	Fat 13g	
Carbohydrate . . .29g	Saturates 8g	

15 MINS   2 HOURS

SERVES 4

INGREDIENTS

¼ cup butter, melted

1 lb 8 oz/675 g waxy potatoes

4 tbsp chopped mixed herbs

chopped fresh herbs, to garnish

salt and pepper

1 Brush a shallow 4-cup ovenproof dish with a little of the melted butter.

2 Slice the potatoes thinly and pat dry with paper towels.

3 Arrange a layer of potato slices in the prepared dish until the base is covered. Brush with a little butter and sprinkle with one-fourth of the chopped mixed herbs. Season to taste.

4 Continue layering the potato slices, brushing each layer with melted butter and sprinkling with herbs, until they are all used up.

5 Brush the top layer of potato slices with butter, cover the dish and cook in a preheated oven, 375°F/190°C, for 1½ hours.

6 Turn out onto a warm ovenproof platter and return to the oven for an additional 25–30 minutes, until golden brown. Serve at once, garnished with fresh herbs.

COOK'S TIP

Make sure that the potatoes are sliced very thinly so that they are almost transparent. This will ensure that they cook thoroughly.

Kashmiri Spinach

This is an imaginative way to serve spinach, which adds a little zip to it. It is a very simple dish, which will complement almost any curry.

NUTRITIONAL INFORMATION

Calories . . . . .81 Sugars 2g
Protein . . . . .4g Fat 7g
Carbohydrate . . . .2g Saturates 1g

5 MINS   25 MINS

SERVES 4

INGREDIENTS

1 lb 2 oz/500 g spinach or Swiss chard or
    baby leaf spinach

2 tbsp mustard oil

¼ tsp garam masala

1 tsp yellow mustard seeds

2 scallions, sliced

1 Remove the tough stems from the spinach.

2 Heat the mustard oil in a preheated wok or large heavy-bottomed skillet until it smokes. Add the garam masala and mustard seeds. Cover the pan quickly—you will hear the mustard seeds popping inside.

3 When the popping has ceased, remove the cover, then add the scallions and spinach. Cook, stirring constantly, until the spinach has wilted.

4 Continue cooking the spinach, uncovered, over medium heat for 10–15 minutes, until most of the water has evaporated. If using frozen spinach, it will not need to cook for so long—cook it until most of the water has evaporated.

5 Remove the spinach and scallions with a slotted spoon, draining off any remaining liquid. (This dish is nicer to eat when it is served as dry as possible.)

6 Transfer to a warmed serving dish and serve immediately, while it is still piping hot.

COOK'S TIP

Mustard oil is made from mustard seeds and is very fiery when raw. However, when it is heated to this smoking stage, it loses a lot of the fire and takes on a delightful sweet quality.

Sweet & Sour Vegetables

This is a dish of Persian origin, not Chinese as it sounds. Eggplants are fried and mixed with tomatoes, mint, sugar, and vinegar.

NUTRITIONAL INFORMATION

Calories	218	Sugars	........12g
Protein	.........3g	Fat	..........17g
Carbohydrate	...14g	Saturates	.......3g

45 MINS   30 MINS

SERVES 4

INGREDIENTS

2 large eggplants

6 tbsp olive oil

4 garlic cloves, crushed

1 onion, cut into eight

4 large tomatoes, seeded and chopped

3 tbsp chopped mint

⅔ cup vegetable stock

4 tsp brown sugar

2 tbsp red wine vinegar

1 tsp chili flakes

salt and pepper

1 Using a sharp knife, cut the eggplants into cubes. Put them in a colander, then sprinkle with plenty of salt and leave to stand for 30 minutes. Rinse thoroughly under cold running water to remove all traces of the salt and drain thoroughly. This process removes all the bitter juices from the eggplants. Pat dry with absorbent paper towels.

2 Heat the oil in a large, heavy-bottomed skillet.

3 Add the eggplants and sauté over medium heat, stirring, for 1–2 minutes, until beginning to color.

4 Stir in the garlic and onion wedges and cook, stirring constantly, for an additional 2–3 minutes.

5 Stir in the tomatoes, mint, and vegetable stock. Lower the heat, then cover with a lid and simmer for 15–20 minutes, until the eggplants are tender.

6 Add the brown sugar, red wine vinegar, and chili flakes, then season with salt and pepper according to taste and cook for an additional 2–3 minutes, stirring constantly.

7 Transfer to a warmed serving dish, then garnish the eggplants with fresh mint sprigs and serve immediately.

Zucchini Curry

This delicious curry is spiced with fenugreek seeds, which have a beautiful aroma and a distinctive taste.

NUTRITIONAL INFORMATION

Calories ....188 Sugars 5g
Protein ....3g Fat 17g
Carbohydrate ....6g Saturates 2g

20 MINS   15 MINS

SERVES 4

INGREDIENTS

6 tbsp vegetable oil

1 medium onion, finely chopped

3 fresh green chiles, finely chopped

1 tsp finely chopped fresh gingerroot

1 tsp crushed garlic

1 tsp chili powder

1 lb 2 oz/500 g zucchini, thinly sliced

2 tomatoes, sliced

fresh cilantro leaves, plus extra to garnish

2 tsp fenugreek seeds

chapatis, to serve

1 Heat the oil in a large, heavy-bottomed skillet.

2 Add the onion, fresh green chiles, ginger, garlic, and chili powder to the skillet, stirring well to combine.

3 Add the sliced zucchini and the sliced tomatoes to the skillet and stir-fry over medium heat, for 5–7 minutes.

4 Add the cilantro leaves and fenugreek seeds to the zucchini mixture in the skillet and stir-fry over medium heat for 5 minutes, until the vegetables are tender.

5 Remove the skillet from the heat and transfer the zucchini and fenugreek seed mixture to serving dishes. Garnish and serve hot with chapatis

VARIATION

You could use coriander seeds instead of the fenugreek seeds, if you prefer.

Chili Roast Potatoes

Small new potatoes are scrubbed and boiled in their skins, before being coated in a chili mixture and roasted to perfection in the oven.

NUTRITIONAL INFORMATION

Calories 178   Sugars 2g
Protein ....2g   Fat 11g
Carbohydrate ...18g   Saturates 1g

5–10 MINS   30 MINS

SERVES 4

INGREDIENTS

1 lb 2 oz/500 g small new potatoes,
    scrubbed

⅔ cup vegetable oil

1 tsp chili powder

½ tsp caraway seeds

1 tsp salt

1 tbsp chopped basil

1 Cook the potatoes in a pan of boiling water for 10 minutes, then drain thoroughly.

2 Pour a little of the oil into a shallow roasting pan to coat the base. Heat the oil in a preheated oven, 400°F/200°C, for 10 minutes. Add the potatoes to the pans and brush them with the hot oil.

3 In a small bowl, mix together the chili powder, caraway seeds, and salt. Sprinkle the mixture over the potatoes, turning to coat them all over.

4 Add the remaining oil to the pan and roast in the oven for 15 minutes, until the potatoes are cooked through.

5 Using a slotted spoon, remove the potatoes from the the oil, draining them well, and transfer them to a warmed serving dish. Sprinkle the chopped basil over the top and serve immediately.

VARIATION

Use any other spice of your choice, such as curry powder or paprika, for a variation in flavor.

Potatoes Dauphinois

This is a classic potato dish of layered potatoes, cream, garlic, onion, and cheese. Serve with pies, bakes, and casseroles.

NUTRITIONAL INFORMATION

Calories 580   Sugars 5g
Protein . . . . .10g   Fat 46g
Carbohydrate . . .34g   Saturates 28g

25 MINS   1½ HOURS

SERVES 4

INGREDIENTS

1 tbsp butter

1 lb 8 oz/675 g waxy potatoes, sliced

2 garlic cloves, crushed

1 red onion, sliced

¾ cup grated Gruyère cheese

1¼ cups heavy cream

salt and pepper

1 Lightly grease a 4-cup shallow ovenproof dish with the butter.

2 Arrange a single layer of potato slices in the base of the prepared dish.

3 Top the potato slices with half the garlic, half the sliced red onion, and one-third of the grated Gruyère cheese. Season to taste with a little salt and pepper.

4 Repeat the layers in exactly the same order, finishing with a layer of potatoes topped with grated cheese.

5 Pour the cream over the top of the potatoes and cook in a preheated oven, 350°F/180°C, for 1½ hours, until the potatoes are cooked through and the top is browned and crispy. Serve at once, straight from the dish.

COOK'S TIP

There are many versions of this classic potato dish, but the different recipes always contain heavy cream, making it a rich and very filling side dish or accompaniment. This recipe must be cooked in a shallow dish to ensure there is plenty of crispy topping.

Spicy Lentils & Spinach

This is quite a filling accompaniment and so should be served with a fairly light main course.

NUTRITIONAL INFORMATION

Calories	340	Sugars	.........6g
Protein	........21g	Fat	..........14g
Carbohydrate	...34g	Saturates	.......2g

2 HRS 5 MINS   25 MINS

SERVES 4

I N G R E D I E N T S

1¼ cups green split peas

2 lb/900 g spinach

4 tbsp vegetable oil

1 onion, halved and sliced

1 tsp grated fresh gingerroot

1 tsp ground cumin

½ tsp chili powder

½ tsp ground coriander

2 garlic cloves, crushed

1¼ cups vegetable stock

salt and pepper

fresh cilantro sprigs and
    lime wedges, to garnish

COOK'S TIP

Once the split peas have been added, stir occasionally to prevent them from sticking to the base of the pan.

1 Rinse the peas under cold running water. Transfer to a mixing bowl, then cover with cold water and set aside to soak for 2 hours. Drain well.

2 Meanwhile, cook the spinach in a large pan, in just the water clinging to its leaves after washing, for 5 minutes, until wilted. Drain well and coarsely chop.

3 Heat the oil in a large pan and add the onion, spices, and garlic. Sauté, stirring constantly, for 2–3 minutes.

4 Add the peas and spinach and stir in the stock. Cover and simmer for 10–15 minutes, until the peas are cooked and the liquid has been absorbed. Season with salt and pepper to taste, then garnish and serve.

Brindil Bhaji

This is one of the most delicious of the Indian bhaji dishes, and has a wonderful sweet spicy flavor.

NUTRITIONAL INFORMATION

Calories . . . . 117 Sugars 8g
Protein . . . . .3g Fat 8g
Carbohydrate . . . .9g Saturates 5g

20 MINS   20 MINS

SERVES 4

INGREDIENTS

1 lb 2 oz/500 g eggplants, sliced

2 tbsp vegetable ghee

1 onion, thinly sliced

2 garlic cloves, sliced

1-inch/2.5-cm piece of fresh gingerroot, grated

½ tsp ground turmeric

1 dried red chile

½ tsp salt

14 oz/400 g canned tomatoes

1 tsp garam masala

cilantro sprigs, to garnish

1 Cut the eggplant slices into finger-width strips.

2 Heat the ghee in a pan. Add the onion and cook over medium heat, stirring constantly, for 7–8 minutes, until very soft.

3 Add the garlic and eggplant strips, then increase the heat and cook for 2 minutes.

4 Stir in the ginger, turmeric, chile, salt, and tomatoes, together with their can juices. Use the back of a wooden spoon to break up the tomatoes. Simmer, uncovered, for 15–20 minutes, until the eggplant is very soft.

5 Stir in the garam masala. Simmer for an additional 4–5 minutes.

6 Transfer the brindil bhaji to a warmed serving plate. Garnish with fresh cilantro sprigs and serve immediately.

VARIATION

Other vegetables can be used instead of the eggplants. Try zucchini, potatoes, or bell peppers, or any combination of these vegetables, using the same sauce.

Greek Green Beans

This dish contains many Greek flavors, including lemon, garlic, oregano, and olives, for a really flavorful recipe.

NUTRITIONAL INFORMATION

Calories 115   Sugars 4g
Protein . . . . .6g   Fat 4g
Carbohydrate . . .15g   Saturates 0.6g

🕔 5 MINS   🕐 1 HR 5 MINS

SERVES 4

I N G R E D I E N T S

14 oz/400 g canned navy beans, drained

1 tbsp olive oil

3 garlic cloves, crushed

1¾ cups vegetable stock

1 bay leaf

2 sprigs oregano

1 tbsp tomato paste

juice of 1 lemon

1 small red onion, chopped

10 pitted black olives, halved

salt and pepper

COOK'S TIP

This dish may be made in advance and served cold, but not chilled, with crusty bread, if preferred.

1 Put the navy beans in a large flameproof casserole.

2 Add the olive oil and crushed garlic and cook over moderate heat, stirring occasionally, for 4–5 minutes, until the garlic is beginning to color.

3 Add the stock, bay leaf, oregano, tomato paste, lemon juice, and red onion, then cover and simmer for 1 hour, until the sauce has thickened.

4 Stir in the olives, then season with salt and pepper to taste and serve.

Gingered Potatoes

This is a simple spicy dish, which is ideal with a plain entrée. The cashew nuts and celery add extra crunch.

NUTRITIONAL INFORMATION

Calories	325	Sugars	.........1g
Protein	.........5g	Fat	..........21g
Carbohydrate	...30g	Saturates	.......9g

20 MINS

30 MINS

SERVES 4

INGREDIENTS

1 lb 8 oz/675 g waxy potatoes, cubed

2 tbsp vegetable oil

2-inch/5-cm piece of fresh gingerroot, grated

1 fresh green chile, chopped

1 celery stalk, chopped

scant ¼ cup cashew nuts

few strands of saffron

3 tbsp boiling water

¼ cup butter

celery leaves, to garnish

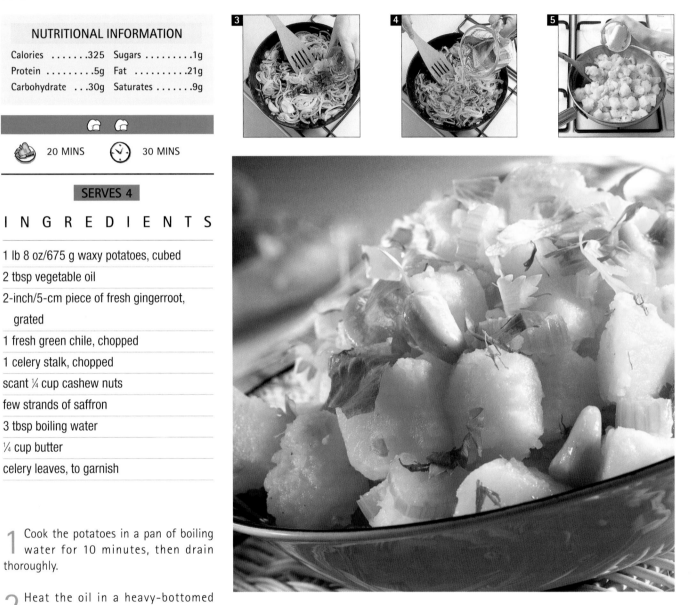

1 Cook the potatoes in a pan of boiling water for 10 minutes, then drain thoroughly.

2 Heat the oil in a heavy-bottomed skillet and add the potatoes. Cook over medium heat, stirring constantly, for 3-4 minutes.

3 Add the grated ginger, chile, celery, and cashew nuts and cook for 1 minute.

4 Meanwhile, place the saffron strands in a small bowl. Add the boiling water and set aside to soak for 5 minutes.

5 Add the butter to the skillet, then lower the heat and stir in the saffron mixture. Cook over low heat for 10 minutes, until the potatoes are tender.

6 Transfer to a warm serving dish, then garnish the gingered potatoes with the celery leaves and serve at once.

COOK'S TIP

Use a nonstick, heavy-bottomed skillet as the potato mixture is fairly dry and may stick to an ordinary pan.

Potato Crumble

This is a delicious way to liven up mashed potato by topping it with a crumble mixture flavored with herbs, mustard, and onion.

NUTRITIONAL INFORMATION

Calories	.451	Sugars	.5g
Protein	.13g	Fat	.19g
Carbohydrate	.60g	Saturates	.12g

25 MINS

30 MINS

SERVES 4

INGREDIENTS

2 lb/900 g mealy potatoes, diced

2 tbsp butter

2 tbsp milk

½ cup grated sharp cheese or blue cheese

CRUMBLE TOPPING

3 tbsp butter

1 onion, cut into chunks

1 garlic clove, crushed

1 tbsp whole-grain mustard

3 cups fresh whole-wheat bread crumbs

2 tbsp chopped parsley

salt and pepper

1 Cook the potatoes in a pan of lightly salted boiling water for 10 minutes, until cooked through.

2 Meanwhile, make the crumble topping. Melt the butter in a skillet. Add the onion, garlic, and mustard and cook over medium heat, stirring constantly, for 5 minutes, until the onion has softened.

3 Put the bread crumbs in a mixing bowl and stir in the fried onion and chopped parsley. Season to taste with salt and pepper.

4 Drain the potatoes thoroughly and place them in another mixing bowl. Add the butter and milk, then mash until smooth. Stir in the grated cheese while the potato is still hot.

5 Spoon the mashed potato into a shallow ovenproof dish and sprinkle with the crumble topping.

6 Cook in a preheated oven, 400°F/200°C, for 10–15 minutes, until the crumble topping is golden brown and crunchy. Serve immediately.

COOK'S TIP

For extra crunch, add freshly cooked vegetables, such as celery and bell peppers, to the mashed potato in step 4.

Curried Okra

Okra, also known as bhindi and ladies' fingers, is a favorite Indian vegetable. It is sold in many of the larger supermarkets.

NUTRITIONAL INFORMATION

Calories	156	Sugars	.........5g
Protein	.........5g	Fat	..........12g
Carbohydrate	....6g	Saturates	.......2g

10 MINS   20 MINS

SERVES 4

I N G R E D I E N T S

1 lb 2 oz/500 g fresh okra

4 tbsp vegetable ghee or oil

1 bunch scallions, sliced

2 garlic cloves, crushed

2-inch/5-cm piece of fresh gingerroot, chopped

1 tsp minced chile

1½ tsp ground cumin

1 tsp ground coriander

1 tsp ground turmeric

8 oz/225 g canned chopped tomatoes

⅔ cup vegetable stock

salt and pepper

1 tsp garam masala

chopped cilantro, to garnish

1 Wash the okra, trim off the stems and pat dry. Heat the ghee in a large pan, then add the scallions, garlic, ginger, and chile and cook over low heat, stirring frequently, for 1 minute.

2 Stir in the spices and cook gently for 30 seconds, then add the tomatoes, stock, and okra. Season with salt and pepper to taste and simmer, stirring and turning the mixture occasionally, for

15 minutes, until the okra is cooked, but still a little crisp.

3 Sprinkle with the garam masala, then taste and adjust the seasoning, if necessary. Transfer to a warm serving dish, then garnish with the chopped cilantro and serve hot.

COOK'S TIP

If preferred, slice the okra into rings, then add to the mixture (step 2), and cook, covered, until tender-crisp, stirring occasionally. When you buy fresh okra, make sure that the pods are not shriveled or do not have any brown spots.

Easy Cauliflower & Broccoli

Whole baby cauliflowers are used in this recipe. Try to find them if you can, if not use large bunches of florets.

NUTRITIONAL INFORMATION

Calories 433   Sugars 2g
Protein . . . . .8g   Fat 44g
Carbohydrate . . . .3g   Saturates 9g

🧊 10 MINS   🕐 20 MINS

SERVES 4

I N G R E D I E N T S

2 baby cauliflowers

8 oz/225 g broccoli

salt and pepper

S A U C E

8 tbsp olive oil

4 tbsp butter or margarine

2 tsp grated fresh gingerroot

juice and rind of 2 lemons

5 tbsp chopped cilantro

5 tbsp grated Cheddar cheese

1 Using a sharp knife, cut the cauliflowers in half and the broccoli into very large florets.

2 Cook the cauliflower and broccoli in a pan of boiling salted water for 10 minutes. Drain well, then transfer to a shallow ovenproof dish and keep warm until required.

3 To make the sauce, put the oil and butter in a pan and heat gently until the butter melts. Add the grated gingerroot, lemon juice, lemon rind, and cilantro and simmer for 2–3 minutes, stirring occasionally.

4 Season the sauce with salt and pepper to taste, then pour over the vegetables in the dish and sprinkle the cheese on top.

5 Cook under a preheated hot broiler for 2–3 minutes, until the cheese is bubbling and golden. Leave to cool for 1–2 minutes and then serve.

COOK'S TIP

Lime or orange could be used instead of the lemon for a fruity and refreshing sauce.

Spanish Potatoes

This type of dish is usually served as part of a Spanish *tapas*, and is delicious with salad or a simply cooked main course dish.

NUTRITIONAL INFORMATION

Calories	176	Sugars	........9g
Protein	.........5g	Fat	..........6g
Carbohydrate	...27g	Saturates	.......1g

20 MINS   35 MINS

SERVES 4

INGREDIENTS

2 tbsp olive oil

1 lb 2 oz/500 g small new potatoes, halved

1 onion, halved and sliced

1 green bell pepper, seeded and
    cut into strips

1 tsp chili powder

1 tsp prepared mustard

1¼ cups crushed tomatoes

1¼ cups vegetable stock

salt and pepper

chopped parsley, to garnish

1 Heat the olive oil in a large heavy-bottomed skillet. Add the halved new potatoes and the sliced onion and cook, stirring frequently, for 4–5 minutes, until the onion slices are soft and translucent.

2 Add the green bell pepper strips, chili powder, and mustard to the skillet and cook for an additional 2–3 minutes.

3 Stir the crushed tomatoes and the vegetable stock into the skillet and bring to a boil. Reduce the heat and simmer for 25 minutes, until the potatoes are tender.

4 Transfer the potatoes to a warmed serving dish. Sprinkle the parsley over the top and serve immediately. Alternatively, leave the Spanish potatoes to cool completely and serve cold, at room temperature.

COOK'S TIP

In Spain, tapas are traditionally served with a glass of chilled sherry or some other aperitif.

Palak Panir

Panir, curd cheese, figures widely on Indian menus. It is combined with all sorts of ingredients, but most popularly with spinach and vegetables.

NUTRITIONAL INFORMATION

Calories	287	Sugars	.........7g
Protein	........12g	Fat	..........18g
Carbohydrate	...22g	Saturates	......11g

20 MINS   40 MINS

SERVES 6

INGREDIENTS

2 tbsp vegetable ghee

1 onion, sliced

1 garlic clove, crushed

1 dried red chile

1 tsp ground turmeric

1 lb 2 oz/500 g waxy potatoes, cut into
    1-inch/2.5-cm cubes

14 oz/400 g canned tomatoes, drained

⅔ cup water

8 oz/225 g fresh spinach

1 lb 2 oz/500 g curd cheese, cut into
    1-inch/2.5-cm cubes

1 tsp garam masala

1 tbsp chopped cilantro

1 tbsp chopped parsley

salt and pepper

naan bread, to serve

VARIATION

Fresh Italian Romano
cheese can be used as a
substitute for Indian panir.

1 Heat the ghee in a pan. Add the onion and cook over low heat, stirring frequently, for 10 minutes, until very soft. Add the garlic and chile and cook for an additional 5 minutes.

2 Add the turmeric, salt, potatoes, canned tomatoes, and water and bring to a boil.

3 Simmer for 10–15 minutes, until the potatoes are cooked.

4 Stir in the spinach, cheese cubes, garam masala, cilantro, and parsley to taste.

5 Simmer for an additional 5 minutes and season well. Serve with naan bread.

Carrot & Orange Bake

Poppy seeds add texture and flavor to this recipe and counteract the slightly sweet flavor of the carrots.

NUTRITIONAL INFORMATION

Calories	138	Sugars 31g
Protein	.........2g	Fat 1g
Carbohydrate	...32g	Saturates 0.2g

20 MINS 40 MINS

SERVES 4

INGREDIENTS

1 lb 8 oz/675 g carrots, cut into thin strips

1 leek, sliced

1¼ cups fresh orange juice

2 tbsp clear honey

1 garlic clove, crushed

1 tsp mixed spice

2 tsp chopped thyme

1 tbsp poppy seeds

salt and pepper

thyme sprigs and orange rind,
  to garnish

1 Cook the carrots and leek in a pan of boiling lightly salted water for 5–6 minutes. Drain well and transfer to a shallow ovenproof dish until required.

2 Mix together the orange juice, honey, garlic, mixed spice, and thyme and pour the mixture over the vegetables. Season with salt and pepper to taste.

3 Cover the dish and cook in a preheated oven, 350°F/180°C, for 30 minutes, until the vegetables are tender.

4 Remove the lid and sprinkle with poppy seeds. Transfer to a warmed serving dish, then garnish with fresh thyme sprigs and orange rind and serve.

COOK'S TIP

Lemon or lime juice could be used instead of the orange juice, if you prefer. Garnish with lemon or lime rind.

Cheese & Potato Layer Bake

This really is a great side dish, perfect for serving with main meals cooked in the oven.

NUTRITIONAL INFORMATION

Calories	295	Sugars	.........5g
Protein	........13g	Fat	..........17g
Carbohydrate	...24g	Saturates	......11g

20 MINS   1½ HOURS

SERVES 4

INGREDIENTS

1 lb 2 oz/500 g potatoes

1 leek, sliced

3 garlic cloves, crushed

½ cup grated Cheddar cheese

½ cup grated mozzarella cheese

¼ cup grated Parmesan cheese

2 tbsp chopped parsley

⅔ cup light cream

⅔ cup milk

salt and pepper

chopped flat-leaf parsley, to garnish

1 Cook the potatoes in a pan of boiling salted water for 10 minutes. Drain well.

COOK'S TIP

Potatoes make a very good basis for a vegetable accompaniment. They are a good source of complex carbohydrate and contain a number of vitamins. From the point of view of flavor, they combine well with a vast range of other ingredients.

2 Cut the potatoes into thin slices. Arrange a layer of potatoes in the base of an ovenproof dish. Layer with a little of the leek, garlic, cheeses, and parsley. Season to taste.

3 Repeat the layers until all of the ingredients have been used, finishing with a layer of cheese. Mix the cream and milk together, then season to taste and pour over the potato layers.

4 Cook in a preheated oven, 325°F/160°C, for 1–1¼ hours, until the cheese is golden brown and bubbling and the potatoes are cooked through and tender.

5 Garnish with chopped fresh flat-leaf parsley and serve immediately.

Spinach & Cauliflower Bhaji

This excellent vegetable dish goes well with most Indian food—and it is simple and quick-cooking, too.

NUTRITIONAL INFORMATION

Calories	212	Sugars	........12g
Protein	........10g	Fat	.........13g
Carbohydrate	...14g	Saturates	.......2g

10 MINS   25 MINS

SERVES 4

INGREDIENTS

1 cauliflower

1 lb 2 oz/500 g fresh spinach, washed, or 8 oz/225 g frozen spinach, thawed

4 tbsp vegetable ghee or oil

2 large onions, coarsely chopped

2 garlic cloves, crushed

1-inch/2.5-cm piece of fresh gingerroot, chopped

1¼ tsp cayenne pepper, or to taste

1 tsp ground cumin

1 tsp ground turmeric

2 tsp ground coriander

14 oz/400 g canned chopped tomatoes

1¼ cups vegetable stock

salt and pepper

1 Divide the cauliflower into small florets, discarding the hard central stalk. Trim the stems from the spinach leaves. Heat the ghee in a large pan, then add the onions and cauliflower florets and cook over low heat, stirring frequently, for 3 minutes.

2 Add the garlic, ginger, and spices and cook gently, stirring occasionally, for 1 minute. Stir in the tomatoes and the vegetable stock and season to taste with salt and pepper. Bring to a boil. Cover, then reduce the heat and simmer gently for 8 minutes.

3 Add the spinach to the pan, stirring and turning to wilt the leaves. Cover and simmer gently, stirring frequently, for 8-10 minutes, until the spinach and the cauliflower is tender. Transfer to a warmed serving dish and serve hot.

COOK'S TIP

When buying cauliflower, look for firm, white curds with no discoloration or signs of wilting.

Long Beans with Tomatoes

Indian meals often need some green vegetables to complement the spicy dishes and to set off the rich sauces.

NUTRITIONAL INFORMATION

Calories 76   Sugars 3g
Protein ....2g   Fat 6g
Carbohydrate ....4g   Saturates 3g

15 MINS   25 MINS

SERVES 6

I N G R E D I E N T S

1 lb 2 oz/500 g green beans, cut into
2-inch/5-cm lengths

2 tbsp vegetable ghee

1-inch/2.5-cm piece of fresh gingerroot,
grated

1 garlic clove, crushed

1 tsp turmeric

½ tsp cayenne

1 tsp ground coriander

4 tomatoes, peeled, seeded, and diced

⅔ cup vegetable stock

1 Blanch the beans briefly in boiling water. Drain, then refresh under cold running water and drain again.

2 Melt the ghee in a large pan over moderate heat. Add the grated ginger

and crushed garlic, then stir and add the turmeric, cayenne, and ground coriander. Stir over low heat for 1 minute.

3 Add the diced tomatoes, tossing them until they are thoroughly coated in the spice mix.

4 Add the vegetable stock to the pan, then bring to a boil and cook over

medium-high heat, stirring occasionally, for 10 minutes, until the sauce has thickened.

5 Add the beans, then reduce the heat to moderate and heat through, stirring constantly, for 5 minutes.

6 Transfer to a warmed serving dish and serve immediately.

COOK'S TIP

Ginger graters are an invaluable piece of equipment to have when cooking Indian food. These small flat graters, made of either bamboo or china, can be held directly over the pan while you grate.

Fried Cauliflower

A dry dish flavored with a few herbs, this is a very versatile accompaniment to curries and rice dishes.

NUTRITIONAL INFORMATION

Calories 135   Sugars 3g
Protein ....4g   Fat 12g
Carbohydrate ....4g   Saturates 1g

5 MINS   20 MINS

SERVES 4

I N G R E D I E N T S

4 tbsp vegetable oil

½ tsp onion seeds

½ tsp mustard seeds

½ tsp fenugreek seeds

4 dried red chiles

1 small cauliflower, cut into small florets

1 tsp salt

1 green bell pepper, seeded and diced

1 Heat the oil in a large, heavy-bottomed pan over a moderate heat.

2 Add the onion seeds, mustard seeds, fenugreek seeds, and the dried red chiles to the pan, stirring to mix.

3 Reduce the heat and gradually add all of the cauliflower and the salt to the pan. Stir-fry the mixture for 7–10 minutes, thoroughly coating the cauliflower in the spices.

4 Add the diced green bell pepper to the pan and stir-fry over low heat for 3–5 minutes.

5 Transfer the spicy fried cauliflower to a warmed serving dish and serve hot.

Vegetable Galette

This is a dish of eggplant and zucchini layered with a quick tomato sauce and melted cheese.

NUTRITIONAL INFORMATION

Calories 412	Sugars 12g
Protein 13g	Fat 34g
Carbohydrate . . .13g	Saturates 11g

40 MINS   1¼ HOURS

SERVES 4

INGREDIENTS

2 large eggplants, sliced

4 zucchini, sliced

1 lb 12 oz/800 g canned chopped
   tomatoes, drained

2 tbsp tomato paste

2 garlic cloves, crushed

4 tbsp olive oil

1 tsp superfine sugar

2 tbsp chopped basil

olive oil, for frying

8 oz/225 g mozzarella cheese, sliced

salt and pepper

basil leaves, to garnish

1 Put the eggplant slices in a colander and sprinkle with salt. Leave to stand for 30 minutes, then rinse well under cold water and drain. Thinly slice the zucchini.

2 Meanwhile, put the tomatoes, tomato paste, garlic, olive oil, sugar, and chopped basil into a pan and simmer for 20 minutes, until reduced by half. Season to taste with salt and pepper.

3 Heat 2 tablespoons of olive oil in a large skillet and cook the eggplant slices for 2–3 minutes, until just beginning to brown. Remove from the skillet.

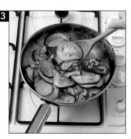

4 Add an additional 2 tablespoons of oil to the skillet and cook the zucchini slices until browned.

5 Lay half of the eggplant slices in the base of an ovenproof dish. Top with half of the tomato sauce and the zucchini and then half of the mozzarella.

6 Repeat the layers and bake in a preheated oven, 350°F/180°C, for 45–50 minutes, until the vegetables are tender. Garnish with basil leaves and serve.

Candied Sweet Potatoes

A taste of the Caribbean is introduced in this recipe, where sweet potatoes are cooked with sugar and lime with a dash of brandy.

NUTRITIONAL INFORMATION

Calories 348   Sugars 21g
Protein . . . . .3g   Fat 9g
Carbohydrate . . .67g   Saturates 6g

15 MINS   25 MINS

SERVES 4

I N G R E D I E N T S

1 lb 8 oz/675 g sweet potatoes, sliced

3 tbsp butter

1 tbsp lime juice

generous ⅓ cup soft dark brown sugar

1 tbsp brandy

grated rind of 1 lime

lime wedges, to garnish

1 Cook the sweet potatoes in a pan of boiling water for 5 minutes. Test the potatoes have softened by pricking with a fork. Remove the sweet potatoes with a perforated spoon and drain thoroughly.

2 Melt the butter in a large skillet. Add the lime juice and brown sugar and heat gently, stirring, to dissolve the sugar.

3 Stir the sweet potatoes and the brandy into the sugar and lime juice mixture. Cook over low heat for 10 minutes, until the potato slices are cooked through.

4 Sprinkle the lime rind over the top of the sweet potatoes and mix well.

5 Transfer the candied sweet potatoes to a serving plate. Garnish with lime wedges and serve at once.

COOK'S TIP

Sweet potatoes have a pinkish skin and either white, yellow, or orange flesh. It doesn't matter which type is used for this dish.

Spicy Corn

This dish is an ideal accompaniment to a wide range of Indian dishes and would also go well with a Western-style casserole.

NUTRITIONAL INFORMATION

Calories	162	Sugars	.........6g
Protein	.........2g	Fat	...........11g
Carbohydrate	...15g	Saturates	.......7g

10 MINS   10 MINS

SERVES 4

INGREDIENTS

scant 2 cups canned or frozen corn

1 tsp ground cumin

1 tsp crushed garlic

1 tsp ground coriander

1 tsp salt

2 fresh green chiles

1 medium onion, finely chopped

3 tbsp unsalted butter

4 red chiles, crushed

½ tsp lemon juice

fresh cilantro leaves

1 Thaw or drain the corn, if using canned corn, and set aside.

2 Place the ground cumin, garlic, ground coriander, salt, 1 fresh green chile, and the onion in a mortar or a food processor and grind to form a smooth paste.

3 Heat the butter in a large skillet. Add the onion and spice mixture to the skillet and cook over medium heat, stirring occasionally, for 5–7 minutes.

4 Add the crushed red chiles to the mixture in the skillet and stir to combine.

5 Add the corn to the skillet and stir-fry for an additional 2 minutes.

6 Add the remaining green chile, lemon juice, and the fresh cilantro leaves to the skillet, stirring occasionally to combine.

7 Transfer the spicy corn mixture to a warm serving dish. Garnish with fresh cilantro and serve hot.

COOK'S TIP

Coriander is available ground or as seeds and is one of the essential ingredients in Indian cooking. Coriander seeds are often dry roasted before use to develop their flavor.

Spiced Potatoes & Spinach

This is a classic Indian accompaniment for many different curries or plainer main vegetable dishes. It is very quick to cook.

NUTRITIONAL INFORMATION

Calories 176   Sugars 4g
Protein ....6g   Fat 9g
Carbohydrate ...18g   Saturates 1g

10 MINS   20-25 MINS

SERVES 4

INGREDIENTS

3 tbsp vegetable oil

1 red onion, sliced

2 garlic cloves, crushed

½ tsp chili powder

2 tsp ground coriander

1 tsp ground cumin

⅔ cup vegetable stock

2 cups diced potatoes

1 lb 2 oz/500 g baby spinach

1 red chile, sliced

salt and pepper

1 Heat the oil in a heavy-bottomed skillet. Add the onion and garlic and sauté over medium heat, stirring occasionally, for 2–3 minutes.

2 Stir in the chili powder, ground coriander, and cumin and cook, stirring constantly, for an additional 30 seconds.

3 Add the vegetable stock, diced potatoes, and spinach and bring to a boil. Reduce the heat, then cover the skillet and simmer for 10 minutes, until the potatoes are cooked through and tender.

4 Uncover, then season to taste with salt and pepper and add the chile. Cook for an additional 2–3 minutes. Transfer to a warmed serving dish and serve immediately.

COOK'S TIP

Besides adding extra color to a dish, red onions have a sweeter, less pungent flavor than other varieties.

Tamarind Chutney

A mouthwatering chutney, which is extremely popular all over India and served with various vegetarian snacks, particularly with samosas.

NUTRITIONAL INFORMATION

Calories	8	Sugars	.........1g
Protein	........0.3g	Fat	..........0.3g
Carbohydrate	....1g	Saturates	.......0g

🥗 10 MINS   🕐 0 MINS

SERVES 6

INGREDIENTS

2 tbsp tamarind paste

5 tbsp water

1 tsp chili powder

½ tsp ground ginger

½ tsp salt

1 tsp sugar

finely chopped cilantro leaves,
   to garnish

COOK'S TIP

Vegetable dishes are often given a sharp, sour flavor with the addition of tamarind. This is made from the semidried, compressed pulp of the tamarind tree. You can buy bars of the pungent-smelling pulp in Indian and oriental grocery stores.

1 Place the tamarind paste in a medium-size mixing bowl.

2 Gradually add the water to the tamarind paste, gently whisking with a fork to form a smooth, runny paste.

3 Add the chili powder and the ginger to the mixture and blend well.

4 Add the salt and the sugar and mix well.

5 Transfer the chutney to a serving dish and garnish with the cilantro.

Curried Roast Potatoes

This is the kind of Indian-inspired dish that would fit easily into any Western menu, or how about serving with a curry in place of rice?

NUTRITIONAL INFORMATION

Calories	297	Sugars	.........2g
Protein	.........3g	Fat	..........19g
Carbohydrate	...30g	Saturates	......12g

5 MINS   30-35 MINS

SERVES 4

INGREDIENTS

2 tsp cumin seeds

2 tsp coriander seeds

scant ½ cup butter

1 tsp ground turmeric

1 tsp black mustard seeds

2 garlic cloves, crushed

2 dried red chiles

1 lb 10 oz/750 g baby new potatoes

1 Grind the cumin and coriander seeds together in a mortar with a pestle or spice grinder. Grinding them fresh like this captures all of the flavor before it has a chance to dry out.

2 Melt the butter gently in a roasting pan and add the turmeric, mustard seeds, garlic, and chiles and the ground cumin and coriander seeds. Stir well to combine evenly. Place in a preheated oven at 400°F/200°C for 5 minutes.

3 Remove the pan from the oven—the spices should be very fragrant at this stage—and add the potatoes. Stir well so that the butter and spice mix coats the potatoes completely.

4 Return to the oven and bake for 20–25 minutes. Stir occasionally to ensure that the potatoes are coated evenly. Test the potatoes with a skewer—if they drop off the end of the skewer when lifted, they are done. Transfer to a serving dish and serve immediately.

COOK'S TIP

Baby new potatoes are now available all year round from supermarkets. However, they are not essential for this recipe. Red or white old potatoes can be substituted, cut into 1-inch/2.5-cm cubes. You can also try substituting parsnips, carrots, or turnips, cut into 1-inch/2.5-cm cubes.

Colcannon

This is an old Irish recipe, usually served with a piece of bacon, but it is equally delicious with a vegetarian main course dish.

NUTRITIONAL INFORMATION

Calories 102	Sugars 4g
Protein 4g	Fat 4g
Carbohydrate . . .14g	Saturates 2g

20 MINS   20 MINS

SERVES 4

I N G R E D I E N T S

2 cups shredded green cabbage

5 tbsp milk

8 oz/225 g mealy potatoes, diced

1 large leek, chopped

pinch of grated nutmeg

1 tbsp butter, melted

salt and pepper

1 Cook the shredded cabbage in a pan of boiling salted water for 7–10 minutes. Drain thoroughly and set aside.

2 Meanwhile, in a separate pan, bring the milk to a boil and add the potatoes and leek. Reduce the heat and simmer for 15–20 minutes, until they are cooked through.

3 Stir in the grated nutmeg and thoroughly mash the potatoes and leek together.

4 Add the drained cabbage to the mashed potato and leek mixture and mix well.

5 Spoon the mixture into a warmed serving dish, making a hollow in the center with the back of a spoon.

6 Pour the melted butter into the hollow and serve the colcannon immediately.

COOK'S TIP

There are many different varieties of cabbage, which produce hearts at varying times of year, so you can be sure of being able to make this delicious cabbage dish all year round.

Saffron-Flavored Potatoes

Saffron is made from the dried stigma of the crocus and is native to Greece. It is very expensive, but only a very small amount is needed.

NUTRITIONAL INFORMATION

Calories 197   Sugars 4g
Protein ....4g   Fat 6g
Carbohydrate ...30g   Saturates 1g

25 MINS   40 MINS

SERVES 4

I N G R E D I E N T S

1 tsp saffron strands

6 tbsp boiling water

1 lb 8 oz/675 g waxy potatoes,
    unpeeled and cut into wedges

1 red onion, cut into 8 wedges

2 garlic cloves, crushed

1 tbsp white wine vinegar

2 tbsp olive oil

1 tbsp whole-grain mustard

5 tbsp vegetable stock

5 tbsp dry white wine

2 tsp chopped rosemary

salt and pepper

1 Place the saffron strands in a small bowl and pour over the boiling water. Set aside to soak for about 10 minutes.

2 Place the potatoes in a roasting pan, together with the red onion wedges and crushed garlic.

3 Add the vinegar, oil, mustard, vegetable stock, white wine, rosemary, and saffron water to the potatoes and onion in the pans. Season to taste with salt and pepper.

4 Cover the roasting pan with kitchen foil and bake in a preheated oven, 400°F/200°C, for 30 minutes.

5 Remove the foil and cook the potatoes for an additional 10 minutes, until crisp, browned, and cooked through. Serve hot.

COOK'S TIP

Turmeric may be used instead of saffron to provide the yellow color in this recipe. However, it is worth using saffron, if possible, for the lovely nutty flavor it gives a dish.

Bombay Potatoes

Although virtually unknown in India, this dish is a very popular item on Indian restaurant menus in other parts of the world.

NUTRITIONAL INFORMATION

Calories 307	Sugars 9g	
Protein 9g	Fat 9g	
Carbohydrate . . .51g	Saturates 5g	

5 MINS   1 HR 10 MINS

SERVES 4

I N G R E D I E N T S

2 lb 4 oz/1 kg waxy potatoes

2 tbsp vegetable ghee

1 tsp panch poran spice mix

3 tsp ground turmeric

2 tbsp tomato paste

1¼ cups plain yogurt

salt

chopped cilantro, to garnish

1 Put the whole potatoes into a large pan of salted cold water and bring to a boil, then simmer until the potatoes are just cooked, but not tender; the time depends on the size of the potato, but an average-size one should take about 15 minutes.

COOK'S TIP

Panch poran spice mix can be bought from Asian or Indian grocery stores, or make your own from equal quantities of cumin seeds, fennel seeds, mustard seeds, nigella seeds, and fenugreek seeds.

2 Heat the ghee in a pan over medium heat and add the panch poran, turmeric, tomato paste, yogurt, and salt. Bring to a boil, and simmer, uncovered, for 5 minutes.

3 Drain the potatoes and cut each one into 4 pieces. Add the potatoes to the pan, cover and cook briefly. Transfer to an ovenproof casserole, then cover and cook in a preheated oven, 350°F/180°C, for 40 minutes, until the potatoes are tender and the sauce has thickened a little.

4 Sprinkle with chopped cilantro and serve immediately.

Eggplant Bake

This is an unusual dish, in that the eggplant is first baked in the oven, then cooked in a pan.

NUTRITIONAL INFORMATION

Calories ....140 Sugars 5g
Protein ....3g Fat 12g
Carbohydrate ....6g Saturates 1g

10 MINS   55 MINS

SERVES 4

INGREDIENTS

2 medium eggplants

4 tbsp vegetable oil

1 medium onion, sliced

1 tsp white cumin seeds

1 tsp chili powder

1 tsp salt

3 tbsp plain yogurt

½ tsp mint sauce

mint leaves, to garnish

1 Rinse the eggplants under cold running water and pat thoroughly dry with absorbent paper towels.

2 Place the eggplants side by side in an ovenproof dish or roasting pan. Bake in a preheated oven, 325°F/160°C, for 45 minutes. Remove the baked eggplants from the oven and set aside to cool.

3 Using a teaspoon, scoop out the eggplant flesh and set aside.

4 Heat the oil in a heavy-bottomed pan over low heat. Add the onion and cumin seeds and cook, stirring constantly, for 1-2 minutes.

5 Add the chili powder, salt, plain yogurt, and mint sauce to the pan and stir well to mix.

6 Add the eggplant flesh to the onion and yogurt mixture and cook over medium heat, stirring constantly, for 5–7 minutes, until all of the liquid has been absorbed and the mixture is quite dry.

7 Transfer the eggplant and yogurt mixture to a warmed serving dish and garnish with fresh mint leaves. Serve immediately.

Potatoes Lyonnaise

In this classic French recipe, sliced potatoes are cooked with onions to make a delicious accompaniment to an entrée.

NUTRITIONAL INFORMATION

Calories	277	Sugars	.........4g
Protein	.........5g	Fat	..........12g
Carbohydrate	...40g	Saturates	.......4g

10 MINS   25 MINS

SERVES 6

INGREDIENTS

2 lb 12 oz/1.25 kg potatoes

4 tbsp olive oil

2 tbsp butter

2 onions, sliced

2–3 garlic cloves, crushed (optional)

salt and pepper

chopped parsley, to garnish

1 Slice the potatoes into ¼-inch/5 mm slices. Put in a large pan of lightly salted water and bring to a boil. Cover and simmer gently for 10–12 minutes, until just tender. Avoid boiling too rapidly or the potatoes will break up and lose their shape. When cooked, drain well.

2 While the potatoes are cooking, heat the oil and butter in a very large skillet. Add the onions and garlic, if using, and cook over medium heat, stirring frequently, until the onions are softened.

3 Add the cooked potato slices to the skillet and cook with the onions, carefully stirring occasionally, for 5–8 minutes, until the potatoes are well browned.

4 Season to taste with salt and pepper. Sprinkle over the chopped parsley to serve. If wished, transfer the potatoes and onions to a large ovenproof dish and keep warm in a low oven until ready to serve.

COOK'S TIP

If the potatoes blacken slightly as they are boiling, add a spoonful of lemon juice to the cooking water.

Cauliflower & Spinach Curry

The contrast in color in this recipe makes it very appealing to the eye, especially as the cauliflower is lightly colored with yellow turmeric.

NUTRITIONAL INFORMATION

Calories	228	Sugars	.........6g
Protein	.........8g	Fat	..........18g
Carbohydrate	....8g	Saturates	.......2g

🍲

🧈 10 MINS   🕐 25 MINS

SERVES 4

I N G R E D I E N T S

1 medium cauliflower

6 tbsp vegetable oil

1 tsp mustard seeds

1 tsp ground cumin

1 tsp garam masala

1 tsp turmeric

2 garlic cloves, crushed

1 onion, halved and sliced

1 green chile, sliced

1 lb 2 oz/500 g spinach

5 tbsp vegetable stock

1 tbsp chopped cilantro

salt and pepper

cilantro sprigs, to garnish

1 Break the cauliflower into small florets.

2 Heat the oil in a deep flameproof casserole dish. Add the mustard seeds and cook until they begin to pop.

3 Stir in the remaining spices, the garlic, onion, and chile and cook, stirring constantly, for 2–3 minutes.

4 Add the cauliflower, spinach, vegetable stock, chopped cilantro, and

seasoning and cook over gentle heat for 15 minutes, until the cauliflower is tender. Uncover the dish and boil for 1 minute to thicken the juices.

5 Transfer to a warmed serving dish. Garnish with cilantro sprigs and serve.

COOK'S TIP

Mustard seeds are used throughout India and are particularly popular in southern vegetarian cooking. They are fried in oil first to bring out their flavor before the other ingredients are added.

Fried Spiced Potatoes

Deliciously good and a super accompaniment to almost any main course dish, although rather high in calories!

NUTRITIONAL INFORMATION

Calories	430	Sugars	.........7g
Protein	.........4g	Fat	..........35g
Carbohydrate	...26g	Saturates	......11g

15 MINS   30 MINS

SERVES 6

INGREDIENTS

2 onions, cut into fourths

2-inch/5-cm piece of gingerroot,
   finely chopped

2 garlic cloves

2–3 tbsp mild or medium curry paste

4 tbsp water

1 lb 10 oz/750 g new potatoes

vegetable oil, for deep frying

3 tbsp vegetable ghee or oil

⅔ cup strained plain yogurt

⅔ cup heavy cream

3 tbsp chopped mint

salt and pepper

½ bunch scallions, chopped,
   to garnish

1 Place the onions, ginger, garlic, curry paste, and water in a blender or food processor and process until smooth, scraping down the sides of the machine and processing again, if necessary.

2 Cut the potatoes into fourths—the pieces need to be about 1-inch/2.5-cm in size—and pat dry with absorbent paper towels. Heat the oil in a deep fryer to 350°F/180°C, or until a cube of bread browns in 30 seconds and cook the potatoes, in batches, for 5 minutes, until golden brown, turning frequently. Remove from the pan and drain on paper towels.

3 Heat the ghee in a large skillet, then add the curry and onion mixture and cook gently, stirring constantly, for 2 minutes. Add the yogurt, cream and 2 tablespoons of mint and mix well.

4 Add the fried potatoes and stir until coated in the sauce. Cook, stirring frequently, for an additional 5–7 minutes, until heated through and sauce has thickened. Season with salt and pepper to taste and sprinkle with the remaining mint and sliced scallions. Serve immediately.

COOK'S TIP

When buying new potatoes, look for the freshest you can find. The skin should be beginning to rub off. Cook them as soon after purchase as possible, but if you have to store them, keep them in a cool, dark well-ventilated place.

Mango Chutney

Everyone's favorite chutney, this has a sweet and sour taste. It is best made well in advance and stored for at least 2 weeks before use.

NUTRITIONAL INFORMATION

Calories 2819   Sugars 731g
Protein . . . . .12g   Fat 2g
Carbohydrate ..734g   Saturates 1g

10–15 MINS   1 HR 5 MINS

MAKES 1 QUANTITY

INGREDIENTS

2 lb 4 oz/1 kg mangoes

4 tbsp salt

2½ cups water

2½ cups sugar

1¾ cups vinegar

2 tsp finely chopped fresh gingerroot

2 tsp crushed garlic

2 tsp chili powder

2 cinnamon sticks

½ cup raisins

½ cup dates,pitted

1 Using a sharp knife, peel and halve, then pit the mangoes. Cut the mango flesh into cubes. Place the mango flesh in a large bowl. Add the salt and water and leave overnight. Drain the liquid from the mangoes and set aside.

2 Bring the sugar and vinegar to a boil in a large pan over low heat, stirring constantly.

3 Gradually add the mango cubes, stirring to coat them in the mixture.

4 Add the ginger, garlic, chili powder, cinnamon sticks, raisins, and dates, and bring to a boil again, stirring occasionally. Reduce the heat and cook for 1 hour, until the mixture thickens. Remove from the heat and set aside to cool.

5 Remove the cinnamon sticks from the chutney and discard.

6 Spoon the chutney into clean dry jars and cover tightly with lids. Leave in a cool place for the flavors to develop fully.

COOK'S TIP

When choosing mangoes, select ones that are shiny with unblemished skins. To test if they are ripe, gently cup the mango in your hand and squeeze—it should give slightly to the touch if it is ready for eating.

Herby Potatoes & Onion

Fried potatoes are a classic favorite; here they are given extra flavor by frying them in butter with onion, garlic, and herbs.

NUTRITIONAL INFORMATION

Calories 413	Sugars 4g	
Protein 5g	Fat 26g	
Carbohydrate . . .42g	Saturates 17g	

10 MINS   50 MINS

SERVES 4

INGREDIENTS

2 lb/900 g waxy potatoes, cut into cubes

½ cup butter

1 red onion, cut into 8

2 garlic cloves, crushed

1 tsp lemon juice

2 tbsp chopped thyme

salt and pepper

1 Cook the cubed potatoes in a pan of boiling water for 10 minutes. Drain thoroughly.

2 Melt the butter in a large, heavy-bottomed skillet and add the red onion wedges, garlic, and lemon juice. Cook, stirring constantly for 2–3 minutes.

3 Add the potatoes to the pan and mix well to coat in the butter mixture.

COOK'S TIP

Keep checking the potatoes and stirring throughout the cooking time to ensure that they do not burn or stick to the base of the skillet.

4 Reduce the heat, cover and cook for 25–30 minutes, until the potatoes are golden brown and tender.

5 Sprinkle the chopped thyme over the top of the potatoes and season.

6 Transfer to a warm serving dish and serve immediately.

Naan Bread

There are many ways of making naan bread, but this recipe is very easy to follow. Naan bread should be served immediately after cooking.

NUTRITIONAL INFORMATION

Calories 152	Sugars 1g	
Protein 3g	Fat 7g	
Carbohydrate ...20g	Saturates 4g	

2¼ HOURS   10 MINS

SERVES 8

INGREDIENTS

1 tsp sugar

1 tsp fresh yeast

⅔ cup warm water

1⅓ cups all-purpose flour

1 tbsp ghee

1 tsp salt

4 tbsp unsalted butter

1 tsp poppy seeds

1 Put the sugar and yeast in a small bowl or jug together with the warm water and mix thoroughly until the yeast has completely dissolved. Set aside for 10 minutes, until the mixture is frothy.

2 Place the flour in a large mixing bowl. Make a well in the center of the flour, then add the ghee and salt and pour in the yeast mixture. Mix thoroughly to form a dough, using your hands and adding more water if required.

3 Turn the dough out on to a floured counter and knead for 5 minutes, until smooth.

4 Return the dough to the bowl, then cover and set aside to rise in a warm place for 1½ hours, until doubled in size.

5 Turn the dough out on to a floured counter and knead for an additional 2 minutes. Break off small balls with your hand and pat them into rounds about 5 inches/12 cm in diameter and ½ inch/ 1 cm thick.

6 Place the dough rounds on a greased sheet of foil and broil under a very hot preheated broiler for 7–10 minutes, turning twice and brushing with the butter and sprinkling with the poppy seeds.

7 Serve warm immediately, or keep wrapped in foil until required.

Poori

Although pooris are deep-fried, they are very light. The nutritional information supplied is for each poori.

NUTRITIONAL INFORMATION

Calories 165	Sugars 0.7g
Protein 3g	Fat 10g
Carbohydrate ...17g	Saturates 1g

🌮 🌮 🌮

🍲 35 MINS   🕐 15–20 MINS

MAKES 10

I N G R E D I E N T S

1½ cups whole-wheat ata, or chapati, flour

½ tsp salt

⅔ cup water

2½ cups vegetable oil

1 Place the flour and salt in a large mixing bowl and stir to combine.

2 Make a well in the center of the flour. Gradually pour in the water and mix together to form a dough, adding more water if necessary.

3 Knead the dough until it is smooth and elastic and set aside in a warm place to rise for 15 minutes.

COOK'S TIP

You can serve pooris either piled one on top of the other or spread out in a layer on a large serving platter so that they remain puffed up.

4 Divide the dough into about 10 equal portions and with lightly oiled or floured hands pat each into a smooth ball.

5 On a lightly oiled or floured work counter, roll out each ball to form a thin round.

6 Heat the oil in a deep skillet. Deep-fry the rounds, in batches, turning once, until golden brown in color.

7 Remove the pooris from the skillet and drain. Serve hot.

Parathas

These triangular-shaped breads are so easy to make and are the perfect addition to most Indian meals. Serve hot, spread with a little butter.

NUTRITIONAL INFORMATION

Calories 127   Sugars 0.5g
Protein . . . . .3g   Fat 4g
Carbohydrate . . .22g   Saturates 0.4g

50 MINS   10 MINS

SERVES 6

INGREDIENTS

⅔ cup whole-wheat flour

scant ⅔ cup all-purpose flour

pinch of salt

1 tbsp vegetable oil, plus extra for greasing

generous ¼ cup tepid water

1 Place the flours and the salt in a bowl. Drizzle 1 tablespoon of oil over the flour, then add the tepid water and mix to form a soft dough, adding a little more water, if necessary. Knead on a lightly floured surface until smooth, then cover and leave for 30 minutes.

2 Knead the dough on a floured surface and divide into 6 equal pieces. Shape each one into a ball. Roll out on a floured surface to a 6-inch/15-cm round and brush very lightly with oil.

3 Fold in half, and then in half again to form a triangle. Roll out to form an 7-inch/18-cm triangle (when measured from point to center top), dusting with extra flour as necessary.

4 Brush a large, heavy-bottomed skillet with a little oil and heat until hot, then add one or two parathas and cook for about 1–1½ minutes. Brush the surfaces

very lightly with oil, then turn and cook the other sides for 1½ minutes, until completely cooked through.

5 Place the cooked parathas on a plate and cover with foil, or place between the folds of a clean dish cloth to keep warm, while you are cooking the remainder in the same way, greasing the skillet between cooking each batch.

VARIATION

For added flavor, try brushing the parathas with a garlic- or chili-flavored oil as they are cooking.

Peshwari Naan

A tandoor oven throws out a ferocious heat; this bread is traditionally cooked on its side wall, where the heat is slightly less intense.

NUTRITIONAL INFORMATION

Calories	420	Sugars	........13g
Protein	........11g	Fat	...........9g
Carbohydrate	...77g	Saturates	.......3g

3¾ HOURS   30 MINS

SERVES 6

INGREDIENTS

scant ¼ cup warm water

pinch of sugar

½ tsp easy blend active dry yeast

1 lb 2 oz/500 g strong bread flour

½ tsp salt

scant ¼ cup plain yogurt

2 tart eating apples, peeled, cored, and diced

scant ⅓ cup golden raisins

½ cup slivered almonds

1 tbsp cilantro leaves

2 tbsp grated coconut

1 Combine the water and sugar in a bowl and sprinkle over the yeast. Leave for 5–10 minutes, until the yeast has dissolved and the mixture is foamy.

2 Put the flour and salt into a bowl and make a well in the center. Add the yeast mixture and yogurt. Draw in the flour until it is all absorbed. Mix together, adding enough tepid water to form a soft dough. Turn out onto a floured board and knead for 10 minutes, until smooth. Put into an oiled bowl, then cover and leave for 3 hours in a warm place.

3 Line the broiler pan with foil, shiny side up.

4 Put the apples into a pan with a little water. Bring to a boil, then mash them down. Reduce the heat and simmer for 20 minutes, mashing occasionally.

5 Divide the dough into 4 pieces and roll each piece out to a 8-inch/20-cm oval. Pull one end out into a teardrop shape, about ¼ inch/5 mm thick. Lay on a floured surface and prick the dough all over with a fork.

6 Brush both sides of the bread with oil. Place under a preheated broiler at the highest setting. Cook for 3 minutes, then turn the bread over and cook for an additional 3 minutes. It should have dark brown spots all over.

7 Spread a teaspoonful of the apple purée all over the bread, then sprinkle over a quarter of the golden raisins, the slivered almonds, the cilantro leaves, and the coconut. Repeat with the remaining 3 ovals of dough.

Mixed Bell Pepper Pooris

These pooris are easy to make and so good to eat served with a scrumptious topping of spicy mixed bell peppers and yogurt.

NUTRITIONAL INFORMATION

Calories 386   Sugars 6g
Protein ....5g   Fat 32g
Carbohydrate ...21g   Saturates 4g

55 MINS   15 MINS

SERVES 6

INGREDIENTS

POORIS

generous ⅔ cup whole-wheat flour

1 tbsp vegetable ghee or oil

pinch of salt

5 tbsp hot water

vegetable oil, for shallow frying

cilantro sprigs, to garnish

plain yogurt, to serve

TOPPING

4 tbsp vegetable ghee or oil

1 large onion, cut into fourths and
   thinly sliced

½ red bell pepper, seeded and thinly
   sliced

½ green bell pepper, seeded and
   thinly sliced

¼ eggplant, cut lengthwise into 6 wedges
   and thinly sliced

1 garlic clove, crushed

1-inch/2.5-cm piece of fresh gingerroot,
   chopped

½–1 tsp ground chili

2 tsp mild or medium curry paste

8 oz/225 g canned chopped tomatoes

salt

1 To make the pooris, put the flour in a bowl with the ghee and salt. Add hot water and mix to form a fairly soft dough. Knead gently, then cover with a damp towel and leave for 30 minutes.

2 Meanwhile, prepare the topping. Heat the ghee in a large pan. Add the onion, bell peppers, eggplant, garlic, ginger, chili, and curry paste and fry gently for 5 minutes. Stir in the tomatoes and salt to taste and simmer gently, uncovered, for 5 minutes, stirring occasionally until the sauce thickens. Remove from the heat.

3 Knead the dough on a floured counter and divide into 6. Roll each piece to a round about 6 inches/15 cm in diameter. Cover each one as you finish rolling to prevent drying out.

4 Heat about ½ inch/1 cm oil in a large skillet. Add the pooris, one at a time, and cook for 15 seconds on each side, until puffed and golden, turning frequently. Drain on paper towels and keep warm while you are cooking the remainder in the same way.

5 Reheat the vegetable mixture. Place a poori on each serving plate and top with the vegetable mixture. Add a spoonful of yogurt to each, then garnish with the cilantro sprigs and serve.

Lightly Fried Bread

This is perfect with egg dishes and vegetable curries. Allow 2 portions of bread per person. The nutritional information is for each portion.

NUTRITIONAL INFORMATION	
Calories 133	Sugars 1g
Protein 3g	Fat 7g
Carbohydrate ...17g	Saturates 4g

35 MINS   20–25 MINS

MAKES 10

INGREDIENTS

scant 1½ cups whole-wheat ata,
    or chapati, flour

½ tsp salt

1 tbsp ghee

1¼ cups water

1 Place the flour and the salt in a large mixing bowl and mix to combine.

2 Make a well in the center of the flour. Add the ghee and rub in well. Gradually pour in the water and work to form a soft dough. Set the dough aside to rise for 10–15 minutes.

3 Carefully knead the dough for 5–7 minutes. Divide the dough into about 10 equal portions.

4 On a lightly floured counter, roll out each dough portion to form a flat crêpe shape.

5 Using a sharp knife, lightly draw lines in a crisscross pattern on each rolled-out dough portion.

6 Heat a heavy-bottomed skillet. Gently place the dough portions, one by one, into the skillet.

7 Cook the bread for 1 minute, then turn over and spread with 1 teaspoon of ghee. Turn the bread over again and fry gently, moving it around the skillet with a spatula, until golden. Turn the bread over once again, then remove from the skillet and keep warm while you cook the remaining batches.

COOK'S TIP

In India, breads are cooked on a tava, a traditional flat griddle. A large skillet makes an adequate substitute.

Spicy Oven Bread

This is a Western-style bread with an Indian touch. It is very quick once the dough is made and is quite a rich mix and very tasty.

NUTRITIONAL INFORMATION

Calories ....445 Sugars 1g
Protein ....6g Fat 26g
Carbohydrate ...49g Saturates 17g

1½ HOURS   10 MINS

SERVES 8

INGREDIENTS

½ tsp active dry yeast

1¼ cups warm water

1 lb 2 oz/500 g strong white flour

1 tsp salt

1 cup butter, melted and cooled

½ tsp garam masala

½ tsp coriander seeds, ground

1 tsp cumin seeds, ground

1 Mix the yeast with a little of the warm water until it starts to foam and is completely dissolved.

2 Put the flour and salt into a large bowl, then make a well in the center and add the yeast mixture, and ½ cup of the melted butter. Blend the yeast and butter together before drawing in the flour and kneading lightly. Add the water gradually until a firm dough is obtained; you may not need it all.

3 Turn the dough out on to a floured counter and knead for 10 minutes, until smooth and elastic. Put it into an oiled bowl and turn it over so that it is coated. Cover and leave in a warm place to rise for 30 minutes, until doubled in size. Alternatively, leave in the refrigerator overnight.

4 Knead the dough again and divide into 8 balls. Roll each one out to a 6-inch/15-cm round. Place on a floured cookie sheet. Sprinkle with flour and leave for 20 minutes.

5 Mix the spices together with the remaining melted butter.

6 Brush each bread with the spice and butter mixture and cover with foil.

Place on the middle shelf of a preheated oven, 425°F/220°C, for 5 minutes. Remove the foil, then brush with the butter once again and cook for an additional 5 minutes.

7 Remove from the oven and wrap in a clean dish towel until ready to eat.

Desserts

Vegetarian or not, confirmed dessert lovers feel a meal is lacking if there isn't a tempting dessert to finish off with. Desserts are often loaded with fat and sugar, but this chapter contains recipes that are light but still full of flavor so that you can enjoy a sweet treat without piling on the calories. A lot of the recipes contain fruit, which is

 the perfect ingredient for healthy desserts that are still deliciously tempting. A few rich chocolate recipes are also included—they are particularly decadent, so that you can treat yourself

now and again! Whatever the occasion, you're sure to find the perfect recipe in this chapter to satisfy every craving! Enjoy!

Chocolate Fudge Pudding

This pudding has a hidden surprise when cooked, as it separates to give a rich chocolate sauce at the bottom of the dish.

NUTRITIONAL INFORMATION

Calories 397	Sugars 27g
Protein 10g	Fat 25g
Carbohydrate . . .36g	Saturates 5g

10 MINS   40 MINS

SERVES 4

I N G R E D I E N T S

4 tbsp margarine, plus extra
   for greasing

6 tbsp light brown sugar

2 eggs, beaten

1¼ cups milk

⅓ cup chopped walnuts

generous ¼ cup all-purpose flour

2 tbsp unsweetened cocoa

confectioners' sugar and
   unsweetened cocoa, to dust

1 Lightly grease a 4-cup ovenproof dish.

2 Cream together the margarine and sugar in a large mixing bowl until fluffy. Beat in the eggs.

VARIATION

Add 1–2 tbsp brandy
or rum to the mixture for a
slightly alcoholic pudding, or
1–2 tbsp orange juice for a
child-friendly version.

3 Gradually stir in the milk and add the walnuts, stirring to mix.

4 Sift the flour and unsweetened cocoa into the mixture and fold in gently, with a metal spoon, until well mixed.

5 Spoon the mixture into the dish and cook in a preheated oven, 350°F/180°C, for 35–40 minutes, until the sponge is cooked.

6 Dust with confectioners' sugar and unsweetened cocoa and serve.

Raspberry Fool

This dish is very easy to make and can be prepared in advance and stored in the refrigerator until required.

NUTRITIONAL INFORMATION

Calories	288	Sugars	........19g
Protein	.........4g	Fat	..........22g
Carbohydrate	...19g	Saturates	......14g

1¼ HOURS   0 MINS

SERVES 4

INGREDIENTS

10½ oz/300 g fresh raspberries

½ cup confectioners' sugar

1¼ cups sour cream, plus extra to decorate

½ tsp vanilla extract

2 egg whites

raspberries and lemon balm leaves,
   to decorate

1 Put the raspberries and confectioners' sugar in a food processor or blender and process until smooth. Alternatively, press through a strainer with the back of a spoon.

2 Reserve 1 tablespoon per portion of sour cream for decorating.

3 Put the vanilla extract and remaining sour cream in a bowl and stir in the raspberry mixture.

4 Whisk the egg whites in a separate mixing bowl until stiff peaks form. Gently fold the egg whites into the raspberry mixture using a metal spoon, until fully incorporated.

5 Spoon the raspberry fool into individual serving dishes and chill for at least 1 hour. Decorate with the reserved sour cream, raspberries, and lemon balm leaves and serve.

COOK'S TIP

Although this dessert is best made with fresh raspberries in season, an acceptable result can be achieved with frozen raspberries, which are available from most supermarkets.

Coconut Cream Molds

Smooth, creamy, and refreshing—these tempting little custards are made with an unusual combination of coconut milk, cream, and eggs.

NUTRITIONAL INFORMATION

Calories 288   Sugar 24g
Protein ....4g   Fat 20g
Carbohydrate ...25g   Saturates 14g

10 MINS   45 MINS

SERVES 8

INGREDIENTS

CARAMEL

generous ½ cup granulated sugar

⅔ cup water

CUSTARD

1¼ cups water

3 oz/85 g creamed coconut, chopped

2 eggs

2 egg yolks

1½ tbsp superfine sugar

1¼ cups light cream

sliced banana or slivers of fresh pineapple

1–2 tbsp freshly grated or
     dry unsweetened coconut

1 Have ready 8 small ovenproof dishes about ⅔-cup capacity. To make the caramel, place the granulated sugar and water in a pan and heat gently to dissolve the sugar, then boil rapidly, without stirring, until the mixture turns a rich golden brown.

2 Immediately remove the pan from the heat and dip the bottom into a bowl of cold water in order to stop it cooking further. Quickly, but carefully, pour the caramel into the ovenproof dishes to coat the bottoms.

3 To make the custard, place the water in the same pan, then add the coconut and heat, stirring constantly, until the coconut dissolves. Place the eggs, egg yolks, and superfine sugar in a bowl and beat well with a fork. Add the hot coconut milk and stir well to dissolve the sugar. Stir in the cream and strain the mixture into a pitcher.

4 Arrange the dishes in a roasting pan and fill with enough cold water to come halfway up the sides of the dishes.

Pour the custard mixture into the caramel-lined dishes, then cover with waxed paper or foil and cook in a preheated oven, 300°F/150°C for 40 minutes, until set.

5 Remove the dishes and set aside to cool, then chill overnight. To serve, run a knife around the edge of each dish and turn out onto a serving plate. Serve with slices of banana and sprinkled with freshly grated coconut.

Almond Slices

A mouthwatering dessert that is sure to impress your guests, especially if it is served with whipped cream.

NUTRITIONAL INFORMATION

Calories 416   Sugars 37g
Protein . . . . .11g   Fat 26g
Carbohydrate . . .38g   Saturates 12g

5 MINS   5 MINS

SERVES 8

I N G R E D I E N T S

3 eggs

generous ⅔ cup ground almonds

scant 1¾ cups milk powder

1 cup sugar

½ tsp saffron strands

scant ½ cup unsalted butter

1 tbsp slivered almonds

1 Beat the eggs together in a bowl and set aside.

2 Place the ground almonds, milk powder, sugar, and saffron in a large mixing bowl and stir to mix well.

3 Melt the butter in a small pan. Pour the melted butter over the dry ingredients and mix well until thoroughly combined.

4 Add the reserved beaten eggs to the mixture and stir to blend well.

5 Spread the mixture in a shallow 7–9 inch/15–20 cm ovenproof dish and bake in a preheated oven, 325°F/160°C, for 45 minutes. Test whether the cake is cooked through by piercing with the tip of a sharp knife or a skewer—it will come out clean if it is cooked thoroughly.

6 Cut the almond cake into slices. Decorate the almond slices with slivered almonds and transfer to serving plates. Serve hot or cold.

COOK'S TIP

These almond slices are best eaten hot, but they may also be served cold. They can be made a day or even a week in advance and re-heated. They also freeze beautifully.

Steamed Coffee Sponge

This sponge pudding is very light and is quite delicious served with a sweet chocolate sauce.

NUTRITIONAL INFORMATION

Calories	300	Sugars	21g
Protein	8g	Fat	13g
Carbohydrate	40g	Saturates	4g

🥧 10 MINS 🕐 1¼ HOURS

SERVES 4

INGREDIENTS

2 tbsp margarine

2 tbsp soft brown sugar

2 eggs

⅓ cup all-purpose flour

¾ tsp baking powder

6 tbsp milk

1 tsp coffee extract

SAUCE

1¼ cups milk

1 tbsp soft brown sugar

1 tsp unsweetened cocoa

2 tbsp cornstarch

1 Lightly grease a 2½-cup ovenproof bowl. Cream the margarine and sugar until light and fluffy and beat in the eggs.

2 Gradually stir in the flour and baking powder and then the milk and coffee extract to make a smooth batter.

3 Spoon the mixture into the prepared ovenproof bowl and cover with a pleated piece of baking parchment and then a pleated piece of foil, securing around the bowl with string. Place in a steamer or large pan and half fill with boiling water. Cover and steam for 1–1¼ hours, until cooked through. Top up with boiling water from the kettle when necessary.

4 To make the sauce, put the milk, soft brown sugar, and unsweetened cocoa in a pan and heat, stirring constantly, until the sugar dissolves. Blend the cornstarch with 4 tablespoons of cold water to make a smooth paste and stir into the pan. Bring to a boil, stirring constantly until thickened. Cook over gentle heat for 1 minute.

5 Turn the pudding out onto a warmed serving plate and spoon the sauce over the top. Serve immediately.

COOK'S TIP

The pudding is covered with pleated paper and foil to let it rise. The foil will react with the steam and must therefore not be placed directly against the pudding.

Chocolate Chip Ice Cream

This marvellous frozen dessert offers the best of both worlds, delicious chocolate chip cookies and a rich dairy-flavored ice.

NUTRITIONAL INFORMATION

Calories 238   Sugars 23g
Protein . . . . .9g   Fat 10g
Carbohydrate . . .30g   Saturates 4g

6 HOURS   5 MINS

SERVES 6

INGREDIENTS

1¼ cups milk

1 vanilla bean

2 eggs

2 egg yolks

generous ¼ cup superfine sugar

1¼ cups plain yogurt

4½ oz/125 g chocolate chip cookies,
   broken into small pieces

1 Pour the milk into a small pan, then add the vanilla bean and bring to a boil over low heat. Remove from the heat, then cover the pan and set aside to cool.

2 Beat the eggs and egg yolks in a double boiler or in a bowl set over a pan of simmering water. Add the sugar and continue beating until the mixture is pale and creamy.

3 Reheat the milk to simmering point and strain it over the egg mixture. Stir continuously until the custard is thick enough to coat the back of a spoon. Remove the custard from the heat and stand the pan or bowl in cold water to prevent any further cooking. Wash and dry the vanilla bean for future use.

4 Stir the yogurt into the cooled custard and beat until it is well blended. When the mixture is thoroughly cold, stir in the broken cookies.

5 Transfer the mixture to a chilled metal cake pan or plastic container, then cover and freeze for 4 hours. Remove from the freezer every hour, then transfer to a chilled bowl and beat vigorously to prevent ice crystals from forming then return to the freezer. Alternatively, freeze the mixture in an ice-cream maker, following the manufacturer's directions.

6 To serve the ice cream, transfer it to the main part of the refrigerator for 1 hour. Serve in scoops.

Banana & Mango Tart

Bananas and mangoes are a great combination of colors and flavors, especially when topped with toasted coconut chips.

NUTRITIONAL INFORMATION

Calories . . . . . . .235 Sugars 17g
Protein . . . . .4g Fat 10g
Carbohydrate . . .35g Saturates 5g

1¼ HOURS   5 MINS

SERVES 8

INGREDIENTS

PASTRY

8-inch/20-cm baked pastry shell

FILLING

2 small ripe bananas

1 mango, sliced

3½ tbsp cornstarch

6 tbsp raw brown sugar

1¼ cups soy milk

⅔ cup coconut milk

1 tsp vanilla extract

toasted coconut chips, to decorate

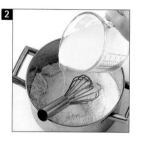

COOK'S TIP

Coconut chips are available in some supermarkets and most health food shops. It is worth using them as they look much more attractive and are not so sweet as dry coconut.

1 Slice the bananas and arrange half in the baked pastry shell with half of the mango pieces.

2 Put the cornstarch and sugar in a pan and mix together. Gradually, stir in the soy and coconut milks until combined and cook over low heat, beating until the mixture thickens.

3 Stir in the vanilla extract, then pour the mixture over the fruit.

4 Top with the remaining fruit and toasted coconut chips. Chill in the refrigerator for 1 hour before serving.

Rice & Banana Brûlée

Take a can of rice pudding and flavor it with orange rind, preserved ginger, raisins, and sliced bananas, then top with a brown sugar glaze.

NUTRITIONAL INFORMATION

Calories	509	Sugars	........98g
Protein	.........9g	Fat	..........6g
Carbohydrate	...112g	Saturates	.......4g

5 MINS   5 MINS

SERVES 2

INGREDIENTS

14 oz/400 g canned creamed rice pudding

grated rind of ½ orange

2 pieces preserved ginger,
   finely chopped

2 tsp ginger syrup from the jar

generous ¼ cup raisins

1–2 bananas

1–2 tsp lemon juice

4–5 tbsp raw brown sugar

1 Empty the can of rice pudding into a bowl and mix in the grated orange rind, ginger, ginger syrup, and raisins.

2 Cut the bananas diagonally into slices and toss in the lemon juice to prevent them from discoloring, then drain and divide between 2 individual flameproof dishes.

3 Spoon the rice mixture in an even layer over the bananas so the dishes are almost full.

4 Sprinkle an even layer of sugar over the rice in each dish.

5 Place the dishes under a preheated moderate broiler and heat until the sugar melts, taking care the sugar does not burn.

6 Set aside to cool until the caramel sets, then chill in the refrigerator until ready to serve. Tap the caramel with the back of a spoon to break it.

COOK'S TIP

Canned rice pudding is very versatile and is delicious heated with orange segments and grated apples added. Try it served cold with grated chocolate and mixed chopped nuts stirred through it.

Indian Bread Pudding

This, the Indian equivalent of the English bread and butter pudding, is rather a special dessert, usually cooked for special occasions.

NUTRITIONAL INFORMATION

Calories 445   Sugars 43g
Protein ....10g   Fat 20g
Carbohydrate ...60g   Saturates 11g

20 MINS   25 MINS

SERVES 6

INGREDIENTS

6 medium slices bread

5 tbsp ghee (preferably pure)

¾ cup sugar

1¼ cups water

3 green cardamoms, without husks

2½ cups milk

¾ cup evaporated milk or khoya
    (see Cook's Tip)

½ tsp saffron strands

heavy cream, to serve (optional)

TO DECORATE

8 pistachio nuts, soaked,
    peeled, and chopped

chopped almonds

2 leaves varq (silver leaf) (optional)

1 Cut the bread slices into fourths. Heat the ghee in a large, heavy-bottom skillet. Add the bread slices and cook, turning once, until a crisp golden brown color. Place the fried bread in the base of a heatproof dish and set aside.

2 To make a syrup, place the sugar, water and cardamom seeds in a pan and bring to a boil over medium heat, stirring constantly, until the sugar has dissolved. Boil until the syrup thickens. Pour the syrup over the fried bread.

3 Put the milk, evaporated milk or khoya (see Cook's Tip), and the saffron in a separate pan and bring to a boil over low heat. Simmer until it has halved in volume. Pour the mixture over the syrup-coated bread.

4 Decorate with the pistachios, chopped almonds, and varq (if using). Serve the bread pudding with cream, if liked.

COOK'S TIP

To make khoya, bring 3¾ cups milk to a boil in a large, heavy pan. Reduce the heat and boil, stirring occasionally, for 35-40 minutes, until reduced to one quarter of its volume and resembling a sticky dough.

Almond Sherbet

It is best to use whole almonds rather than ready-ground almonds for this dish because they give it a better texture.

NUTRITIONAL INFORMATION

Calories 836   Sugars 33g
Protein ....29g   Fat 65g
Carbohydrate ...36g   Saturates 7g

3¾ HOURS   0 MINS

SERVES 2

INGREDIENTS

1¼ cups whole almonds

2 tbsp sugar

1¼ cups milk

1¼ cups water

1 Put the almonds in a bowl, then cover with water and set aside to soak for at least 3 hours or preferably overnight.

2 Using a sharp knife, chop the almonds into small pieces. Grind to a fine paste in a food processor or in a mortar with a pestle.

3 Add the sugar to the almond paste and grind once again to form a very fine paste.

4 Add the milk and water and mix thoroughly, preferably in a blender or food processor.

5 Transfer the almond sherbet to a large serving dish.

6 Chill the almond sherbet in the refrigerator for about 30 minutes. Stir it well just before serving.

Warm Currants in Cassis

Crème de cassis is a black currant–based liqueur that comes from France and it is an excellent flavoring for fruit dishes.

NUTRITIONAL INFORMATION

Calories 202   Sugars 35g
Protein . . . . .2g   Fat 6g
Carbohydrate . . .35g   Saturates 4g

10 MINS   10 MINS

SERVES 4

INGREDIENTS

3 cups black currants

2 cups red currants

4 tbsp superfine sugar

grated rind and juice of 1 orange

2 tsp arrowroot

2 tbsp crème de cassis

whipped cream, to serve

1 Using a fork, strip the currants from their stems and put in a pan.

2 Add the sugar and orange rind and juice, and heat gently until the sugar has dissolved. Bring to a boil, then simmer gently for 5 minutes.

3 Strain the currants and place in a bowl. Return the juice to the pan. Blend the arrowroot with a little water to a smooth paste and mix into the juice. Bring to a boil over medium heat and cook until thickened.

4 Set aside to cool slightly, then stir in the crème de cassis.

5 Serve in individual dishes with whipped cream.

Lime Cheesecakes

These cheesecakes are flavored with lime and mint, and set on a base of crushed graham crackers mixed with chocolate.

NUTRITIONAL INFORMATION

Calories	696	Sugars	. . . . .44g
Protein	. . . . .18g	Fat	. . . . .40g
Carbohydrate	. . .70g	Saturates	. . . . . .22g

3 HOURS   5 MINS

SERVES 2

INGREDIENTS

BASE

2 tbsp butter

1 square dark chocolate

1½ cups crushed graham crackers

FILLING

finely grated rind of 1 lime

generous ⅓ cup creamed cottage cheese

⅓ cup lowfat soft cheese

1 mint sprig, very finely chopped (optional)

1 tsp gelozone

1 tbsp lime juice

1 egg yolk

3 tbsp superfine sugar

TO DECORATE

whipped cream

kiwifruit slices

mint sprigs

1 Grease 2 fluted, preferably loose-based 4½-inch/11-cm flan pans thoroughly. To make the base, melt the butter and chocolate in a heatproof bowl over a pan of gently simmering water, or melt in a microwave set on HIGH power for 1 minute. Stir until smooth.

2 Stir the crushed crackers evenly through the melted chocolate and then press into the bases of the flan pans, leveling the surface. Chill until set.

3 To make the filling, put the grated lime rind and cheeses into a bowl and beat until smooth and evenly blended, then beat in the mint, if using.

4 Dissolve the gelozone in the lime juice in a heatproof bowl over a pan of simmering water or in a microwave oven set on High power for about 30 seconds.

5 Beat the egg yolk and sugar together until creamy and fold into the cheese mixture, followed by the dissolved gelozone. Pour over the base and chill until set.

6 To serve, remove the cheesecakes carefully from the flan pans. Decorate with whipped cream, slices of kiwifruit, and mint sprigs.

Chocolate Mousse

This is a light and fluffy mousse with a subtle hint of orange. It is wickedly delicious served with a fresh fruit sauce.

NUTRITIONAL INFORMATION

Calories	164	Sugars	........24g
Protein	.........5g	Fat	...........5g
Carbohydrate	...25g	Saturates	.......3g

2¼ HOURS   5 MINS

SERVES 8

INGREDIENTS

4 squares dark chocolate, melted

1¼ cups plain yogurt

⅔ cup quark

4 tbsp superfine sugar

1 tbsp orange juice

1 tbsp brandy

1½ tsp gelozone

9 tbsp cold water

2 large egg whites

coarsely grated dark and white chocolate
 and orange rind, to decorate

1 Put the melted chocolate, yogurt, quark, sugar, orange juice, and brandy in a food processor and process for 30 seconds. Transfer the mixture to a large bowl.

COOK'S TIP

For a quick fruit sauce, process a can of mandarin segments in natural juice in a food processor and press through a strainer. Stir in 1 tablespoon clear honey and serve with the mousse.

2 Sprinkle the gelozone over the water and stir until dissolved.

3 In a pan, bring the gelozone and water to a boil for 2 minutes. Cool slightly, then stir into the chocolate.

4 Whisk the egg whites until stiff peaks form and fold into the chocolate mixture using a metal spoon.

5 Line a 1 lb 2 oz/500 g loaf pan with plastic wrap. Spoon the mousse into the pan. Chill in the refrigerator for 2 hours, until set. Turn the mousse out onto a serving plate, then decorate and serve.

Quick Syrup Sponge

You won't believe your eyes when you see just how quickly this light-as-air sponge pudding cooks in the microwave oven!

NUTRITIONAL INFORMATION

Calories	650	Sugars	........60g
Protein	........10g	Fat	..........31g
Carbohydrate	...89g	Saturates	.......7g

15 MINS   5 MINS

SERVES 4

I N G R E D I E N T S

½ cup butter or margarine

4 tbsp light corn syrup

scant ½ cup superfine sugar

2 eggs

scant 1 cup self-rising flour

1 tsp baking powder

about 2 tbsp warm water

custard, to serve

1 Grease a 1½-quart microwave bowl with a small amount of the butter. Spoon the syrup into the bowl.

2 Cream the remaining butter with the sugar until light and fluffy. Gradually add the eggs, beating well between each addition.

3 Sift the flour and baking powder together, then fold into the creamed mixture using a large metal spoon. Add enough water to give a soft, dropping consistency. Spoon into the bowl and level the surface.

4 Cover with microwave-safe plastic wrap to allow the air to escape. Microwave on High power for 4 minutes, then remove from the microwave and

allow the pudding to stand for 5 minutes, while it continues to cook.

5 Turn the pudding out onto a serving plate. Serve with custard.

COOK'S TIP

If you don't have a microwave, this pudding can be steamed. See step 3 on page 332.

Mixed Fruit Crumble

In this crumble, tropical fruits are flavored with ginger and coconut, for something a little different and very tasty.

NUTRITIONAL INFORMATION

Calories 602   Sugars 51g
Protein . . . . .6g   Fat 29g
Carbohydrate . . .84g   Saturates 11g

10 MINS   50 MINS

SERVES 4

INGREDIENTS

2 mangoes, sliced

1 papaya, seeded and sliced

8 oz/225 g fresh pineapple, cubed

1½ tsp ground ginger

scant ½ cup margarine

scant ½ cup light brown sugar

1½ cups all-purpose flour

generous ½ cup dry unsweetened
   coconut, plus extra to decorate

1 Place the fruit in a pan with ½ teaspoon of the ginger, 2 tablespoons of the margarine and ¼ cup of the sugar. Cook over low heat for 10 minutes, until the fruit softens. Spoon the fruit into the base of a shallow ovenproof dish.

VARIATION

Use other fruits, such as plums, apples, or blackberries, as a fruit base and add chopped nuts to the topping instead of the coconut.

2 Mix the flour and remaining ginger together. Rub in the remaining margarine until the mixture resembles fine bread crumbs. Stir in the remaining sugar and the coconut and spoon over the fruit to cover completely.

3 Cook the crumble in a preheated oven, 350°F/180°C, for 40 minutes, until the top is crisp. Decorate and serve.

Saffron-Spiced Rice Pudding

This rich pudding is cooked in milk delicately flavored with saffron, then mixed with dried fruit, almonds, and cream before baking.

NUTRITIONAL INFORMATION

Calories	339	Sugars	........28g
Protein	.........9g	Fat	..........16g
Carbohydrate	...41g	Saturates	.......9g

5 MINS   1 HOUR

SERVES 4

I N G R E D I E N T S

2½ cups whole milk

several pinches of saffron strands, finely crushed (see Cook's Tip)

¼ cup short-grain rice

1 cinnamon stick or piece of cassia bark

scant ¼ cup sugar

scant ¼ cup seedless raisins or golden raisins

scant ¼ cup ready-to-eat dried apricots, chopped

1 egg, beaten

5 tbsp light cream

1 tbsp butter, diced

2 tbsp flaked almonds

freshly grated nutmeg, for sprinkling

cream, for serving (optional)

1 Place the milk and crushed saffron in a nonstick pan and bring to a boil. Stir in the rice and cinnamon stick, then reduce the heat and simmer very gently, uncovered, stirring frequently, for 25 minutes, until tender.

2 Remove the pan from the heat. Remove and discard the cinnamon stick from the rice mixture. Stir in the sugar, raisins, and dried apricots, then beat in the egg, cream, and diced butter.

3 Transfer the mixture to a greased ovenproof pie or flan dish, sprinkle with the almonds and freshly grated nutmeg to taste. Cook in a preheated oven, 350°F/180°C, for 25–30 minutes, until mixture is set and lightly golden. Serve hot with extra cream, if wished.

COOK'S TIP

For a slightly stronger flavor, place the saffron strands on a small piece of kitchen foil and toast them lightly under a hot broiler for a few moments and then crush between your fingers and thumb.

Christmas Shortbread

Make this wonderful shortbread and then give it the Christmas touch by cutting it into shapes with seasonal cookie cutters.

NUTRITIONAL INFORMATION

Calories	162	Sugars	........10g
Protein	.........1g	Fat	...........9g
Carbohydrate	...21g	Saturates	.......6g

45 MINS   15 MINS

MAKES 24

I N G R E D I E N T S

generous ½ cup superfine sugar

1 cup butter

3 cups all-purpose flour, sifted

pinch of salt

TO DECORATE

generous ½ cup confectioners' sugar

silver balls

candied cherries

angelica

1 Beat the sugar and butter together in a large bowl until combined (thorough creaming is not necessary).

2 Sift in the flour and salt and work together to form a stiff dough. Turn out onto a lightly floured counter. Knead lightly for a few moments until smooth, but avoid overhandling. Chill in the refrigerator for 10–15 minutes.

3 Roll out the dough on a lightly floured work surface and cut into shapes with small Christmas cutters, such as bells, stars, and trees. Place on greased cookie sheets.

4 Bake the cookies in a preheated oven, 350°F/180°C for 10–15 minutes, until pale golden brown. Leave on the cookie sheets for 10 minutes, then transfer to wire racks to cool completely.

5 Mix the confectioners' sugar with a little water to make a glacé frosting, and use to frost the cookies. Decorate with silver balls, tiny pieces of candied cherries, and angelica. Store in an airtight container or wrap the cookies individually in cellophane, then tie with colored ribbon or string and then hang them on the Christmas tree as edible decorations.

Passion Cake

Decorating this moist, rich carrot cake with sugared flowers lifts it into the celebration class. It is a perfect choice for Easter.

NUTRITIONAL INFORMATION

Calories	506	Sugars	........40g
Protein	.........10g	Fat	..........27g
Carbohydrate	...60g	Saturates	.......4g

🥄 15 MINS   🕐 1½ HOURS

SERVES 10

INGREDIENTS

⅔ cup corn oil

¾ cup golden superfine sugar

4 tbsp plain yogurt

3 eggs, plus 1 extra yolk

1 tsp vanilla extract

scant 1 cup walnut pieces, chopped

1 cup grated carrots

1 banana, mashed

generous 1 cup all-purpose flour

½ cup fine oatmeal

1 tsp baking soda

1 tsp baking powder

1 tsp ground cinnamon

½ tsp salt

FROSTING

⅔ cup soft cheese

4 tbsp plain yogurt

scant 1 cup confectioners' sugar

1 tsp grated lemon rind

2 tsp lemon juice

DECORATION

primroses and violets

1 egg white, lightly beaten

3 tbsp superfine sugar

1 Grease and line a 9-inch/23-cm round cake pan. Beat together the oil, sugar, yogurt, eggs, egg yolk, and vanilla extract. Beat in the chopped walnuts, grated carrot, and banana.

2 Sift together the remaining ingredients and gradually beat into the mixture.

3 Pour the mixture into the pan and level the surface. Bake in a preheated oven, 350°F/180°C, for 1½ hours, until firm. To test, insert a fine skewer into the center: it should come out clean. Leave to cool in the pan for 15 minutes, then turn out on to a wire rack.

4 To make the frosting, beat together the cheese and yogurt. Sift in the confectioners' sugar and stir in the lemon rind and juice. Spread over the top and sides of the cake.

5 To prepare the decoration, dip the flowers quickly in the beaten egg white, then sprinkle with superfine sugar to cover the surface completely. Place well apart on baking parchment. Leave in a warm, dry place for several hours until they are dry and crisp. Arrange the flowers in a pattern on top of the cake.

Cherry Clafoutis

This is a hot dessert that is simple and quick to put together. Try the batter with other fruits. Apricots and plums are particularly delicious.

10 MINS   40 MINS

SERVES 6

INGREDIENTS

scant 1 cup all-purpose flour

4 eggs, lightly beaten

2 tbsp superfine sugar

pinch of salt

2½ cups milk

butter, for greasing

1 lb 2 oz/500 g black cherries,
   fresh or canned, pitted

3 tbsp brandy

1 tbsp sugar, to decorate

5 Bake in a preheated oven, 350°F/ 180°C, for 40 minutes, until risen and golden.

6 Remove from the oven and sprinkle over the sugar just before serving. Serve warm.

1 Sift the flour into a large mixing bowl. Make a well in the center and add the eggs, sugar, and salt. Gradually, draw in the flour from around the edges and whisk.

2 Pour in the milk and whisk the batter thoroughly until very smooth.

3 Thoroughly grease a 7½-cup ovenproof serving dish with butter and pour in about half of the batter.

4 Spoon over the cherries and pour the remaining batter over the top. Sprinkle the brandy over the batter.

Bread & Butter Pudding

Everyone has their own favorite recipe for this dish. This one has added marmalade and grated apples for a really rich and unique taste.

NUTRITIONAL INFORMATION

Calories 427   Sugars 63g
Protein . . . . .9g   Fat 13g
Carbohydrate . . .74g   Saturates 7g

45 MINS   1 HOUR

SERVES 6

INGREDIENTS

about ¼ cup butter, softened

4–5 slices white or brown bread

4 tbsp chunky orange marmalade

grated rind of 1 lemon

½–¾ cup raisins or golden raisins

¼ cup chopped candied peel

1 tsp ground cinnamon or allspice

1 cooking apple, peeled,
   cored, and coarsely grated

scant ½ cup light brown sugar

3 eggs

2 cups milk

2 tbsp raw brown sugar

1 Use the butter to grease an ovenproof dish and to spread on the slices of bread, then spread the bread with the marmalade.

2 Place a layer of bread in the base of the dish and sprinkle with the lemon rind, half the raisins, half the candied peel, half the spice, all of the apple, and half the light brown sugar.

3 Add another layer of bread, cutting so it fits the dish.

4 Sprinkle over most of the remaining raisins and the remaining peel, spice, and light brown sugar, sprinkling it evenly over the bread. Top with a final layer of bread, again cutting to fit the dish.

5 Lightly beat together the eggs and milk and then carefully strain the mixture over the bread in the dish. If time allows, set aside to stand for 20–30 minutes.

6 Sprinkle the top of the pudding with the raw brown sugar and scatter over the remaining raisins and cook in a preheated oven, 400°F/200°C, for 50–60 minutes, until risen and golden brown. Serve immediately or leave to cool and then serve cold.

Fruit & Nut Loaf

This loaf is like a fruit bread and may be served warm or cold, perhaps spread with a little margarine or butter or topped with jelly.

NUTRITIONAL INFORMATION

Calories	354	Sugars	........36g
Protein	.........8g	Fat	..........9g
Carbohydrate	...64g	Saturates	.....1.2g

35 MINS   40 MINS

SERVES 6

INGREDIENTS

scant 1¾ cups white bread flour,
  plus extra for dusting

½ tsp salt

1 tbsp margarine, plus extra for greasing

2 tbsp light brown sugar

scant ⅔ cup sultanas (golden raisins)

¼ cup ready-to-eat dried apricots, chopped

⅓ cup chopped hazelnuts

2 tsp active dry yeast

6 tbsp orange juice

6 tbsp plain yogurt

2 tbsp strained apricot jelly

VARIATION

You can vary the nuts according to whatever you have at hand—try chopped walnuts or almonds.

1 Sift the flour and salt into a mixing bowl. Add the margarine and rub in with the fingertips. Stir in the sugar, sultanas, apricots, nuts, and yeast.

2 Warm the orange juice in a pan, but do not let boil.

3 Stir the warm orange juice into the flour mixture, together with the plain yogurt and bring the mixture together to form a dough.

4 Knead the dough on a lightly floured counter for 5 minutes, until smooth and elastic. Shape into a round and place on a lightly greased cookie sheet. Cover with a clean dish cloth and leave to rise in a warm place until doubled in size.

5 Cook the loaf in a preheated oven, 425°F/220°C, for 35–40 minutes, until cooked through. Transfer to a wire rack and brush with the apricot jelly. Leave to cool before serving.

Apricot Brûlée

Serve this melt-in-the-mouth dessert with crisp-baked meringues for an extra-special occasion.

NUTRITIONAL INFORMATION

Calories 307	Sugars 38g	
Protein 5g	Fat 16g	
Carbohydrate . . .38g	Saturates 9g	

2¼ HOURS   35 MINS

SERVES 6

I N G R E D I E N T S

generous ⅔ cup unsulfured
   dried apricots

⅔ cup orange juice

4 egg yolks

2 tbsp superfine sugar

⅔ cup plain yogurt

⅔ cup heavy cream

1 tsp vanilla extract

½ cup raw brown sugar

meringues, to serve (optional)

1 Place the apricots and orange juice in a bowl and set aside to soak for at least 1 hour. Pour into a small pan, then bring slowly to a boil and simmer for 20 minutes. Process in a blender or food processor or chop very finely and push through a strainer.

2 Beat together the egg yolks and sugar until the mixture is light and fluffy. Place the yogurt in a small pan, then add the cream and vanilla and bring to a boil over low heat.

3 Pour the yogurt mixture over the eggs, beating all the time, then transfer to the top of a double boiler or place the bowl over a pan of simmering water. Stir until the custard thickens. Divide the apricot mixture between 6 ramekins and carefully pour on the custard. Cool, then chill in the refrigerator at least 1 hour.

4 Sprinkle the raw brown sugar evenly over the custard and place under a preheated broiler until the sugar caramelizes. Set aside to cool. To serve the brûlée, crack the hard caramel topping with the back of a tablespoon.

Spiced Steamed Pudding

Steamed puddings are irresistible on a winter's day, but the texture of this pudding is so light it can be served throughout the year.

NUTRITIONAL INFORMATION

Calories	488	Sugars	........56g
Protein	.........5g	Fat	..........19g
Carbohydrate	...78g	Saturates	.......4g

15 MINS   1½ HOURS

SERVES 6

INGREDIENTS

2 tbsp light corn syrup, plus extra
   to serve

generous ½ cup butter or margarine

generous ½ cup superfine or
   light brown sugar

2 eggs

generous 1 cup self-rising flour

¾ tsp ground cinnamon or allspice

grated rind of 1 orange

1 tbsp orange juice

½ cup golden raisins

5 tbsp finely chopped preserved ginger

1 eating apple, peeled, cored, and
   coarsely grated

1 Thoroughly grease a 3³/₄-cup ovenproof bowl. Put the light corn syrup into the bowl.

2 Cream the butter and sugar together until very light and fluffy and pale in color. Beat in the eggs, one at a time, following each with a spoonful of the flour.

3 Sift the remaining flour with the cinnamon or allspice and fold into the mixture, followed by the orange rind and juice. Fold in the golden raisins, then the ginger and apple.

4 Turn the mixture into the bowl and level the top. Cover with a piece of pleated greased baking parchment, tucking the edges under the rim of the bowl.

5 Cover with a sheet of pleated foil. Tie securely in place with string, with a piece of string tied over the top of the bowl for a handle to make it easy to lift out of the pan.

6 Put the bowl into a pan half-filled with boiling water, then cover and steam for 1½ hours, adding more boiling water to the pan as necessary during cooking.

7 To serve the pudding, remove the foil and baking parchment, turn the pudding onto a warmed serving plate and serve immediately.

Pistachio Dessert

Rather an attractive-looking dessert, especially when decorated with varq (silver leaf), this is another dish that can be prepared in advance.

NUTRITIONAL INFORMATION

Calories	676	Sugars	. . . . .98g
Protein	. . . . .15g	Fat	. . . . .27g
Carbohydrate	. . .98g	Saturates	. . . . . . .9g

15 MINS   10 MINS

SERVES 6

I N G R E D I E N T S

3¾ cups water

1½ cups pistachio nuts

¾ cups whole dried milk

2⅓ cups sugar

2 cardamoms, with seeds crushed

2 tbsp rosewater

a few strands of saffron

TO DECORATE

¼ cup slivered almonds

mint leaves

1 Put about 2½ cups water in a pan and bring to a boil. Remove the pan from the heat and soak the pistachios in this water for 5 minutes. Drain the pistachios thoroughly and remove the skins.

2 Process the pistachios in a food processor or grind in a mortar with a pestle.

3 Add the dried milk powder to the ground pistachios and mix well.

4 To make the syrup, place the remaining water and the sugar in a pan and heat gently. When the liquid begins to thicken, add the cardamom seeds, rosewater, and saffron.

5 Add the syrup to the pistachio mixture and cook, stirring constantly, for about 5 minutes, until the mixture thickens. Set the mixture aside and to cool slightly.

6 Once cool enough to handle, roll the mixture into balls in the palms of your hands. Decorate with the slivered almonds and fresh mint leaves and leave to set before serving.

COOK'S TIP

It is best to buy whole pistachio nuts and grind them yourself, rather than using packets of ready-ground nuts. Freshly ground nuts have the best flavor, as grinding releases their natural oils.

Upside-Down Cake

This recipe shows how a classic favorite can be adapted for vegans by using vegetarian margarine and oil instead of butter and eggs.

NUTRITIONAL INFORMATION

Calories	354	Sugars	........31g
Protein	.........3g	Fat	..........15g
Carbohydrate	...56g	Saturates	.......2g

15 MINS   50 MINS

SERVES 6

INGREDIENTS

¼ cup vegan margarine, cut into small
    pieces, plus extra for greasing

15 oz/425 g canned unsweetened
    pineapple pieces, drained and juice
    reserved

4 tsp cornstarch

¼ cup soft brown sugar

½ cup water

rind of 1 lemon

SPONGE

¼ cup corn oil

scant ⅓ cup soft brown sugar

⅔ cup water

1 cup all-purpose flour

2 tsp baking powder

1 tsp ground cinnamon

1 Grease a deep 7-inch/18-cm cake pan. Mix the reserved juice from the pineapple with the cornstarch until it forms a smooth paste. Put the paste in a pan with the sugar, margarine, and water and stir over low heat until the sugar has dissolved. Bring to a boil and simmer for 2–3 minutes, until thickened. Set aside to cool slightly.

2 To make the sponge, place the oil, sugar, and water in a pan. Heat gently until the sugar has dissolved; do not let it boil. Remove from the heat and leave to cool. Sift the flour, baking powder, and ground cinnamon into a mixing bowl. Pour over the cooled sugar syrup and beat well to form a batter.

3 Place the pineapple pieces and lemon rind on the base of the prepared pan

and pour over 4 tablespoons of the pineapple syrup. Spoon the sponge batter on top.

4 Bake in a preheated oven, 350°F/ 180°C, for 35–40 minutes, until set and a fine metal skewer inserted into the center comes out clean. Invert onto a plate, leave to stand for 5 minutes, then remove the pan. Serve with the remaining syrup.

Baked Semolina Pudding

Succulent plums simmered in orange juice and allspice complement this rich and creamy semolina pudding perfectly.

NUTRITIONAL INFORMATION

Calories	304	Sugars	........32g
Protein	.........9g	Fat	..........12g
Carbohydrate	...43g	Saturates	.......4g

5 MINS   45 MINS

SERVES 4

I N G R E D I E N T S

2 tbsp butter or margarine

2½ cups milk

finely pared rind and juice of 1 orange

⅓ cup semolina

pinch of grated nutmeg

2 tbsp superfine sugar

1 egg, beaten

TO SERVE

knob of butter

grated nutmeg

SPICED PLUMS

8 oz/225 g plums, halved and pitted

⅔ cup orange juice

2 tbsp superfine sugar

½ tsp ground allspice

1 Grease a 4-cup ovenproof dish with a little of the butter. Put the milk, the remaining butter, and the orange rind in a pan. Sprinkle in the semolina and heat until boiling, stirring constantly. Simmer gently for 2–3 minutes. Remove from the heat.

2 Add the nutmeg, orange juice, and sugar to the semolina mixture, stirring well. Add the egg and stir to mix.

3 Transfer the mixture to the prepared dish and bake in a preheated oven, 375°F/190°C, for 30 minutes, until lightly browned.

4 To make the spiced plums, put the plums, orange juice, sugar, and spice into a pan and simmer gently for 10 minutes, until just tender. Set aside to cool slightly.

5 Top the semolina pudding with a knob of butter and grated nutmeg and serve with the spiced plums.

Traditional Apple Pie

This apple pie has a double crust and can be served either hot or cold.
The apples can be flavored with other spices or grated citrus rind.

NUTRITIONAL INFORMATION

Calories 577	Sugars 36g	
Protein 6g	Fat 28g	
Carbohydrate ...80g	Saturates 9g	

55 MINS   50 MINS

SERVES 6

I N G R E D I E N T S

1 lb 10 oz–2 lb 4 oz/750 g–1 kg cooking
   apples, peeled, cored, and sliced

about generous ½ cup brown or white
   sugar, plus extra for sprinkling

½–1 tsp ground cinnamon, allspice,
   or ground ginger

1–2 tbsp water

S H O R T C R U S T   P I E
D O U G H

3 cups all-purpose flour

pinch of salt

6 tbsp butter or margarine

⅓ cup shortening

about 6 tbsp cold water

beaten egg or milk, for glazing

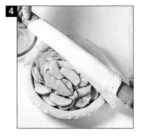

1 To make the pie dough, sift the flour and salt into a mixing bowl. Add the butter and shortening and rub in with the fingertips until the mixture resembles fine bread crumbs. Add the water and gather the mixture together into a dough. Wrap the dough and chill for 30 minutes.

2 Roll out almost two-thirds of the pie dough thinly and use to line a 8–9-inch/20–23-cm deep pie plate or shallow pie pan.

3 Mix the apples with the sugar and spice and pack into the pie shell; the filling can come up above the rim. Add the water if liked, particularly if the apples are a dry variety.

4 Roll out the remaining pie dough to form a lid. Dampen the edges of the pie rim with water and position the lid, pressing the edges firmly together. Trim and crimp the edges.

5 Use the trimmings to cut out leaves or other shapes to decorate the top of the pie, dampen and attach. Glaze the top of the pie with beaten egg or milk, then make 1–2 slits in the top and put the pie on a cookie sheet.

6 Bake in a preheated oven, 425°F/ 220°C, for 20 minutes, then reduce the temperature to 350°F/180°C and cook for 30 minutes, until the pastry is a light golden brown. Serve hot or cold, sprinkled with sugar.

Lemon & Lime Syllabub

This dessert is rich but absolutely delicious. It is not, however, for the calorie conscious as it contains a high proportion of cream.

NUTRITIONAL INFORMATION

Calories 403   Sugars 16g
Protein . . . . .2g   Fat 36g
Carbohydrate . . .16g   Saturates 22g

4¼ HOURS   0 MINS

SERVES 4

INGREDIENTS

¼ cup superfine sugar

grated rind and juice of 1 small lemon

grated rind and juice of 1 small lime

scant ¼ cup Marsala or medium sherry

1¼ cups heavy cream

lime and lemon rind, to decorate

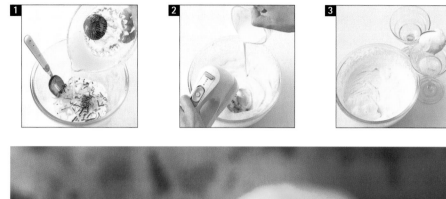

1 Put the sugar, lemon juice, and rind, lime juice and rind and sherry in a bowl, then mix well and set aside to infuse for 2 hours.

2 Add the cream to the fruit juice mixture and whisk until it just holds its shape.

3 Spoon the mixture into 4 tall serving glasses and chill in the refrigerator for 2 hours.

4 Decorate with lime and lemon rind and serve.

Potato & Nutmeg Biscuits

These baking powder biscuits made with mashed potato have a slightly different texture from traditional biscuits, but they are just as delicious.

NUTRITIONAL INFORMATION

Calories	178	Sugars	. . . . .8g
Protein	. . . . .4g	Fat	. . . . .5g
Carbohydrate	. . .30g	Saturates	. . . . . . .3g

15 MINS   30 MINS

MAKES 6

INGREDIENTS

1½ cups diced potatoes

scant 1 cup all-purpose flour

1½ tsp baking powder

½ tsp grated nutmeg

⅓ cup golden raisins

1 egg, beaten

scant ¼ cup heavy cream

2 tsp light brown sugar

1 Line and lightly grease a cookie sheet.

2 Cook the diced potatoes in a pan of boiling water for 10 minutes, until soft. Drain thoroughly and mash the potatoes.

3 Transfer the mashed potatoes to a large mixing bowl and stir in the flour, baking powder, and grated nutmeg, mixing well to combine.

4 Stir in the golden raisins, beaten egg and cream and then beat the mixture thoroughly with a spoon until completely smooth.

5 Shape the mixture into 8 rounds, ¾ inch/2 cm thick, and put on the cookie sheet.

6 Cook in a preheated oven, 400°F/ 200°C, for 15 minutes, until the biscuits have risen and are golden. Sprinkle with sugar and serve warm and spread with butter.

COOK'S TIP

For extra convenience, make a batch of scones in advance and open-freeze them. Thaw thoroughly and warm in a moderate oven when ready to serve.

Rice Pudding

Indian rice pudding is cooked in a pan over low heat, rather than in the oven like the British version—which is also far less sweet.

NUTRITIONAL INFORMATION

Calories 152   Sugars 23g
Protein ....5g   Fat 3g
Carbohydrate ...29g   Saturates 1g

10 MINS   30 MINS

SERVES 10

INGREDIENTS

scant ⅓ cup basmati rice

5 cups milk

8 tbsp sugar

varq (silver leaf) or chopped pistachio nuts,
   to decorate

1 Rinse the rice and place in a large pan. Add 2½ cups of the milk and bring to a boil over very low heat. Cook, stirring occasionally, until the milk has been completely absorbed by the rice.

2 Remove the pan from the heat. Mash the rice, making swift, round movements in the pan, for at least 5 minutes, until all of the lumps have been removed.

3 Gradually add the remaining 2½ cups milk. Bring to a boil over low heat, stirring occasionally.

4 Add the sugar and continue to cook, stirring constantly, for 7–10 minutes, until the mixture is quite thick in consistency.

5 Transfer the rice pudding to a heatproof serving bowl. Decorate with varq (silver leaf) or chopped pistachio nuts and serve on its own or with pooris.

COOK'S TIP

Varq is edible silver that is used to decorate elaborate dishes prepared for special occasions and celebrations in India. It is pure silver that has been beaten until it is wafer thin. It comes with a backing paper that is peeled off as the varq is laid on the cooked food.

Chocolate Cheesecake

This cheesecake takes a little time to prepare and cook but is well worth the effort. It is quite rich and is good served with a little fresh fruit.

NUTRITIONAL INFORMATION

Calories	.471	Sugars	.20g
Protein	.10g	Fat	.33g
Carbohydrate	.28g	Saturates	.5g

15 MINS   1¼ HOURS

SERVES 12

I N G R E D I E N T S

⅔ cup all-purpose flour

1 cup ground almonds

1 cup raw brown sugar

scant 1¼ cup margarine

1 lb 8 oz/675 g firm tofu

¾ cup vegetable oil

½ cup orange juice

¾ cup brandy

scant ½ cup unsweetened cocoa,
   plus extra to decorate

2 tsp almond extract

confectioners' sugar and
   cape gooseberries, to decorate

1 Put the flour, ground almonds, and 1 tablespoon of the sugar in a bowl and mix well. Rub the margarine into the mixture to form a dough.

2 Lightly grease and line the base of a 9-inch/23-cm springform pan. Press the dough into the base of the pan to cover, pushing the dough right up to the edge of the pan.

3 Roughly chop the tofu and put in a food processor with the vegetable oil, orange juice, brandy, unsweetened cocoa, almond extract, and remaining sugar and process until smooth and creamy. Pour over the base in the pan and cook in a preheated oven, 325°F/160°C, for 1–1¼ hours, until set.

4 Leave to cool in the pan for 5 minutes, then remove from the pan and chill in the refrigerator. Dust with confectioners' sugar and unsweetened cocoa. Decorate with cape gooseberries and serve.

COOK'S TIP

Cape gooseberries make an attractive decoration for many desserts. Peel open the papery husks to expose the bright orange fruits.

Chocolate Bread Pudding

This chocolate pudding is served with hot fudge sauce, making it the most delicious way to use up bread that is slightly stale.

NUTRITIONAL INFORMATION

Calories	633	Sugars	........50g
Protein	........18g	Fat	.........29g
Carbohydrate	...79g	Saturates	......11g

2¼ HOURS   45 MINS

SERVES 4

I N G R E D I E N T S

6 thick slices white bread, crusts removed

1¾ cups milk

6 oz/175 g canned evaporated milk

2 tbsp unsweetened cocoa

2 eggs

dark muscovado sugar

1 tsp vanilla extract

confectioners' sugar, for dusting

HOT FUDGE SAUCE

2 squares dark chocolate,
   broken into pieces

1 tbsp unsweetened cocoa

2 tbsp light corn syrup

¼ cup butter or margarine

2 tbsp dark muscovado sugar

⅔ cup milk

1 tbsp cornstarch

1 Grease a shallow ovenproof dish. Cut the bread into squares and layer them in the dish.

2 Put the milk, evaporated milk, and unsweetened cocoa in a pan and heat gently, stirring occasionally, until lukewarm.

3 Whisk together the eggs, sugar, and vanilla extract. Add the warm milk mixture and beat well.

4 Pour into the prepared dish, making sure that all the bread is completely covered. Cover the dish with plastic wrap and chill in the refrigerator for 1–2 hours.

5 Bake the pudding in a preheated oven, 350°F/180°C, for 35–40 minutes, until set. Leave to stand for 5 minutes.

6 To make the sauce, put the chocolate, unsweetened cocoa, syrup, butter, sugar, milk, and cornstarch into a pan. Heat gently, stirring until smooth.

7 Dust the pudding with confectioners' sugar and serve with the hot fudge sauce.

Ground Almonds in Milk

Traditionally served at breakfast in India, this almond-based dish is said to sharpen the mind! However, it can be served as a delicious dessert.

NUTRITIONAL INFORMATION

Calories 314	Sugars 18g
Protein 8g	Fat 21g
Carbohydrate . . .23g	Saturates 3g

5 MINS   10 MINS

SERVES 4

I N G R E D I E N T S

2 tbsp vegetable or pure ghee

scant ¼ cup all-purpose flour

1 cup ground almonds

1¼ cups milk

¼ cup sugar

mint leaves, to decorate

1 Place the ghee in a small, heavy-bottom pan. Melt the ghee over a gentle heat, stirring constantly so that it doesn't burn.

2 Reduce the heat and add the flour, stirring vigorously all the time to remove any lumps.

COOK'S TIP

Ghee comes in two forms and can be bought from Asian grocers. It is worth noting that pure ghee, made from melted butter, is not suitable for vegans, although there is a vegetable ghee available from Indian grocers and some health-food stores.

3 Add the almonds to the ghee and flour mixture, stirring continuously.

4 Gradually add the milk and sugar to the mixture in the pan and bring to a boil. Continue cooking for 3–5 minutes,

until the liquid is smooth and reaches the consistency of a creamy soup.

5 Transfer to a serving dish and decorate, then serve hot.

Summer Puddings

A wonderful mixture of summer fruits encased in slices of white bread that soak up all the deep red, flavorsome juices.

NUTRITIONAL INFORMATION

Calories 250	Sugars 41g
Protein 4g	Fat 4g
Carbohydrate ...53g	Saturates 2g

10 MINS   10 MINS

SERVES 6

I N G R E D I E N T S

vegetable oil or butter, for greasing

6–8 thin slices white bread, crusts removed

generous ¾ cup superfine sugar

1¼ cups water

8 oz/225 g strawberries

1 lb 2 oz/500 g raspberries

1½ cups black and/or red currants

6 oz/175 g blackberries or loganberries

mint sprigs, to decorate

pouring cream, to serve

1 Grease six ⅔-cup molds with butter or oil.

2 Line the molds with the bread, cutting it so it fits snugly.

3 Place the sugar in a pan with the water and heat gently, stirring frequently until dissolved, then bring to a boil and boil for 2 minutes.

4 Reserve 6 large strawberries for decoration. Add half the raspberries and the rest of the fruits to the syrup, cutting the strawberries in half if large, and simmer gently for a few minutes, until beginning to soften but still retaining their shape.

5 Spoon the fruits and some of the liquid into molds. Cover with more slices of bread. Spoon a little juice around the sides of the molds so the bread is well soaked. Cover with a saucer and a heavy weight and leave to cool, then chill thoroughly, preferably overnight.

6 Process the remaining raspberries in a food processor or blender, or press through a nonmetallic strainer. Add enough of the liquid from the fruits to give a coating consistency.

7 Turn on to serving plates and spoon the raspberry sauce over. Decorate with the mint sprigs and reserved strawberries and serve with cream.

Fruit Brûlée

This is a cheat's brûlée, in that yogurt is used to cover a base of fruit, before being sprinkled with sugar and broiled.

NUTRITIONAL INFORMATION

Calories 311   Sugars 48g
Protein . . . . .7g   Fat 11g
Carbohydrate . . .48g   Saturates 7g

1¼ HOURS   15 MINS

SERVES 4

INGREDIENTS

4 plums, pitted and sliced

2 cooking apples, peeled and sliced

1 tsp ground ginger

2½ cups strained plain yogurt

2 tbsp confectioners' sugar, sifted

1 tsp almond extract

scant ⅓ cup raw brown sugar

1 Put the plums and apples in a pan with 2 tablespoons of water and cook for 7–10 minutes, until tender, but not mushy. Set aside to cool, then stir in the ginger.

2 Using a slotted spoon, spoon the mixture into the base of a shallow serving dish.

COOK'S TIP

Use any variety of fruit, such as mixed berries or mango pieces, for this dessert, but in that case, do not poach them.

3 Mix the yogurt, confectioners' sugar, and almond extract and spoon on to the fruit to cover.

4 Sprinkle the raw brown sugar over the top of the yogurt and cook under a hot broiler for 3–4 minutes, until the sugar has dissolved and formed a crust.

5 Leave to chill in the refrigerator for 1 hour and serve.

Toasted Tropical Fruit

Spear some chunks of exotic tropical fruits on to kabob sticks and sear them over the grill, then serve with this amazing chocolate dip.

NUTRITIONAL INFORMATION

Calories	435	Sugars	........60g
Protein	.........6g	Fat	............11g
Carbohydrate	...68g	Saturates	.......6g

45 MINS   5 MINS

SERVES 4

I N G R E D I E N T S

D I P

4 squares dark chocolate,
  broken into pieces

2 tbsp light corn syrup

1 tbsp unsweetened cocoa

1 tbsp cornstarch

generous ¾ cup milk

K A B O B S

1 mango

1 papaya

2 kiwifruit

½ small pineapple

1 large banana

2 tbsp lemon juice

⅔ cup white rum

1 Put all the ingredients for the chocolate dip into a heavy-bottom pan. Heat over the grill or low heat, stirring constantly, until thickened and smooth. Keep warm at the edge of the grill.

2 Slice the mango on each side of its large, flat pit. Cut the flesh into chunks, removing the peel. Halve and seed, then peel the papaya and cut it into chunks. Peel the kiwifruit and slice. Peel and cut the pineapple into chunks. Peel and slice the banana and dip the pieces in the lemon juice to prevent it from discoloring.

3 Thread the pieces of fruit alternately onto 4 wooden skewers. Place them in a shallow dish and pour over the rum.

Leave to soak up the flavor of the rum for at least 30 minutes, until ready to barbecue.

4 Cook the kabobs over the hot coals, turning frequently, for 2 minutes, until seared. Serve, accompanied by the hot chocolate dip.

Rhubarb & Orange Crumble

A mixture of rhubarb and apples flavored with orange rind, brown sugar, and spices and topped with a crunchy crumble topping.

NUTRITIONAL INFORMATION

Calories	516	Sugars	........45g
Protein	.........6g	Fat	..........22g
Carbohydrate	...77g	Saturates	.......4g

15 MINS   45 MINS

SERVES 6

INGREDIENTS

1 lb 2 oz/500 g rhubarb

1 lb 2 oz/500 g cooking apples

grated rind and juice of 1 orange

½–1 tsp ground cinnamon

about ½ cup light soft brown sugar

CRUMBLE

1½ cups all-purpose flour

generous ½ cup butter or margarine

generous ½ cup light soft brown sugar

¼–⅓ cup toasted chopped hazelnuts

2 tbsp raw brown sugar (optional)

1 Cut the rhubarb into 1-inch/2.5-cm lengths and place in a large pan.

2 Peel, core, and slice the apples and add to the rhubarb, together with the grated orange rind and juice. Bring to a boil, then lower the heat and simmer for 2–3 minutes, until the fruit begins to soften.

3 Add the cinnamon and sugar to taste and turn the mixture into an ovenproof dish, so it is not more than two-thirds full.

4 Sift the flour into a bowl and rub in the butter until the mixture resembles fine bread crumbs (this can be done by hand or in a food processor). Stir in the sugar, followed by the nuts.

5 Spoon the crumble mixture evenly over the fruit in the dish and level the top. Sprinkle with raw brown sugar, if liked.

6 Cook in a preheated oven, 400°F/200°C, for 30–40 minutes, until the topping is browned. Serve hot or cold.

VARIATION

Other flavorings, such as generous ¼ cup chopped preserved ginger, can be added either to the fruit or the crumb mixture. Any fruit, or mixtures of fruit, can be topped with crumble.

Potato Muffins

These light-textured muffins rise like little soufflés in the oven and are best eaten warm. The dried fruits can be varied according to taste.

NUTRITIONAL INFORMATION

Calories 98	Sugars 11g
Protein 3g	Fat 2g
Carbohydrate ...18g	Saturates 0.5g

20 MINS   35 MINS

MAKES 12

INGREDIENTS

1¼ cups diced mealy potatoes

¾ cup self-rising flour

2 tbsp soft light brown sugar

1 tsp baking powder

¾ cup raisins

4 eggs, separated

1 Lightly grease and flour 12 muffin pans.

2 Cook the diced potatoes in a pan of boiling water for 10 minutes, until tender. Drain well and mash until completely smooth.

3 Transfer the mashed potatoes to a mixing bowl and add the flour, sugar, baking powder, raisins, and egg yolks. Stir well to mix thoroughly.

4 In a clean bowl, whisk the egg whites until standing in peaks. Using a metal spoon, gently fold them into the potato mixture until fully incorporated.

5 Divide the mixture between the prepared pans.

6 Cook in a preheated oven, 400°F/ 200°C, for 10 minutes. Reduce the oven temperature to 325°F/160°C and cook the muffins for an additional 7-10 minutes, or until risen.

7 Remove the muffins from the pans and serve warm.

COOK'S TIP

Instead of spreading the muffins with plain butter, serve them with cinnamon butter made by blending ¼ cup butter with a large pinch of ground cinnamon.

Butterscotch Melts

This delicious dessert will go down a treat with children of all ages. Bananas and marshmallows taste fantastic with butterscotch sauce.

NUTRITIONAL INFORMATION

Calories	385	Sugar	.......67g
Protein	........2g	Fat	..........13g
Carbohydrate	...70g	Saturates	.......8g

5 MINS   5 MINS

SERVES 4

I N G R E D I E N T S

4 bananas

4 tbsp lemon juice

8 oz/225 g marshmallows

S A U C E

generous ½ cup butter

⅔ cup light muscovado sugar

⅓ cup light corn syrup

4 tbsp hot water

1 Slice the bananas into large chunks and dip them into the lemon juice to prevent them from going brown.

2 Thread the marshmallows and pieces of banana alternately on to kabob sticks or bamboo skewers, placing 2 marshmallows and 1 piece of banana on to each one.

COOK'S TIP

The warm butterscotch sauce tastes wonderful with vanilla ice cream. Make double the quantity of sauce if you plan to serve ice cream at a grill. Ideally, prepare the kabobs just before they are cooked to prevent the bananas from turning brown.

3 To make the sauce, melt the butter, sugar, and syrup together in a small pan. Add the hot water, stirring until blended and smooth. Do not boil or else the mixture will become toffee-like. Keep the sauce warm at the edge of the grill, stirring from time to time.

4 Sear the kabobs over the grill coals for 30–40 seconds, turning constantly, so that the marshmallows are just beginning to brown and melt.

5 Serve the kabobs with a little of the butterscotch sauce spooned over them. (Use half of the sauce to serve 4; the remainder can be used later.)

Traditional Tiramisu

A favorite Italian dessert flavored with coffee and Amaretto. You could substitute the Amaretto with brandy or Marsala.

NUTRITIONAL INFORMATION

Calories	569	Sugars 28g
Protein	........12g	Fat 43g
Carbohydrate	...34g	Saturates 22g

2¼ HOURS   5 MINS

SERVES 6

INGREDIENTS

20–24 lady-fingers

2 tbsp cold black coffee

2 tbsp coffee extract

2 tbsp Amaretto

4 egg yolks

scant ½ cup superfine sugar

few drops of vanilla extract

grated rind of ½ lemon

1½ cups mascarpone cheese

2 tsp lemon juice

1 cup heavy cream

1 tbsp milk

¼ cup slivered almonds, lightly toasted

2 tbsp unsweetened cocoa

1 tbsp confectioners' sugar

1 Arrange almost half of the lady-fingers in the base of a glass bowl or serving dish.

2 Combine the black coffee, coffee extract, and Amaretto together and sprinkle just over half of the mixture over the lady-fingers.

3 Put the egg yolks into a heatproof bowl with the sugar, vanilla extract, and lemon rind. Stand over a pan of gently simmering water and whisk until very thick and creamy and the whisk leaves a very heavy trail when lifted from the bowl.

4 Put the mascarpone in a bowl with the lemon juice and beat until smooth.

5 Combine the egg and mascarpone cheese mixtures and when evenly blended pour half over the lady-fingers and spread out evenly.

6 Add another layer of fingers and sprinkle with the remaining coffee, then cover with the rest of the cheese mixture. Chill for at least 2 hours and preferably longer, or overnight.

7 To serve, whip the cream and milk together until fairly stiff and spread or pipe over the dessert. Sprinkle with the slivered almonds and then sift an even layer of cocoa powder so the top is completely covered. Finally sift a light layer of confectioners' sugar over the cocoa.

Pink Syllabubs

The pretty pink color of this dessert is achieved by adding black currant liqueur to the wine and cream before whipping.

NUTRITIONAL INFORMATION

Calories	536	Sugars	........17g
Protein	.........2g	Fat	..........48g
Carbohydrate	...17g	Saturates	......30g

45 MINS   0 MINS

SERVES 2

INGREDIENTS

5 tbsp white wine

2–3 tsp black currant liqueur

finely grated rind of ½ lemon or orange

1 tbsp superfine sugar

scant 1 cup heavy cream

4 lady-fingers (optional)

TO DECORATE

fresh fruit, such as strawberries,
  raspberries, or red currants, or pecan
  or walnut halves

mint sprigs

1 Mix together the white wine, black currant liqueur, grated lemon rind, and superfine sugar in a bowl and set aside for at least 30 minutes.

COOK'S TIP

These syllabubs will keep in the refrigerator for 48 hours, so it is worth making more than you need, and keeping the extra for another day.

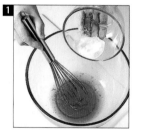  

2 Add the cream to the wine mixture and whip until the mixture has thickened enough to stand in soft peaks.

3 If you are using the lady-fingers, break them up roughly and divide them between 2 glasses.

4 Put the mixture into a pastry bag fitted with a large star or plain tip and pipe it over the lady-fingers. Alternatively, simply pour the syllabub over the lady-fingers. Chill until ready to serve.

5 Before serving, decorate each syllabub with slices or small pieces of fresh soft fruit or nuts, and sprigs of mint.

Berry Cheesecake

Use a mixture of berries, such as blueberries, blackberries, raspberries, and strawberries, for a really fruity cheesecake.

NUTRITIONAL INFORMATION

Calories 478   Sugars 28g
Protein . . . . .10g   Fat 32g
Carbohydrate . . .40g   Saturates 15g

2¼ HOURS   5 MINS

SERVES 8

INGREDIENTS

BASE

6 tbsp margarine

6 oz/175 g oatmeal cookies

generous ½ cup dry unsweetened coconut

TOPPING

1½ tsp vegetarian gelozone

½ cup cold water

½ cup evaporated milk

1 egg

6 tbsp light brown sugar

2 cups soft cream cheese

12 oz/350 g mixed berries

2 tbsp clear honey

1 Put the margarine in a pan and heat until melted. Put the cookies in a food processor and process until thoroughly crushed or crush finely with a rolling pin. Stir the crumbs into the margarine, together with the coconut.

2 Press the mixture evenly into a base-lined 8-inch/20-cm springform pan and set aside to chill in the refrigerator while you are preparing the filling.

3 To make the topping, sprinkle the gelozone over the water and stir to dissolve. Bring to a boil and boil for 2 minutes. Let cool slightly.

4 Put the milk, egg, sugar, and soft cream cheese in a bowl and beat until smooth. Stir in ¼ cup of the berries. Add the gelozone in a stream, stirring constantly.

5 Spoon the mixture onto the cookie base and return to the refrigerator to chill for 2 hours, until set.

6 Remove the cheesecake from the pan and transfer to a serving plate. Arrange the remaining berries on top of the cheesecake and drizzle the honey over the top. Serve.

Mango Ice Cream

This delicious ice cream with its refreshing tang of mango and lime makes the perfect ending to a hot and spicy meal.

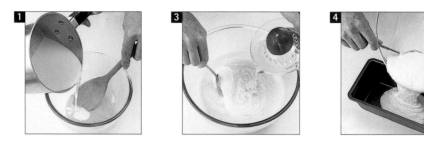

NUTRITIONAL INFORMATION

Calories 275   Sugars 25g
Protein ....2g   Fat 19g
Carbohydrate ...26g   Saturates 11g

5¾ HOURS   5 MINS

SERVES 6

INGREDIENTS

⅔ cup light cream

2 egg yolks

½ tsp cornstarch

1 tsp water

1 lb 12 oz/800 g canned mango slices
    in syrup, drained

1 tbsp lime or lemon juice

⅔ cup heavy cream

mint sprigs, to decorate

1 Heat the light cream in a pan until hot (but do not let it boil). Place the egg yolks in a bowl with the cornstarch and water and mix together until smooth. Pour the hot cream onto the egg yolk mixture, stirring all the time.

COOK'S TIP

Use the drained mango syrup for adding to fruit salads or for mixing into drinks.

2 Return the mixture to the pan and place over very low heat, whisking or stirring all the time until the mixture thickens and coats the back of a wooden spoon. (Do not try and hurry this process or the mixture will overcook and spoil.) Pour into a bowl.

3 Process the mango slices in a blender or food processor until smooth. Mix with the custard and stir in the lime juice. Whip the heavy cream until softly peaking and fold into the mango mixture until thoroughly combined.

4 Transfer the mixture to a loaf pan or shallow freezerproof container. Cover and freeze for 2–3 hours, until half-frozen and still mushy in the center. Turn the mixture into a bowl and mash well with a fork until smooth. Return to the container, then cover and freeze until firm.

5 Transfer the container of ice cream to the main compartment of the refrigerator for 30 minutes before serving to let it soften slightly. Scoop or spoon the ice cream into serving dishes and decorate with mint sprigs.

Ginger & Apricot Alaskas

No ice cream in this Alaska, but a mixture of apples and apricots poached in orange juice enclosed in meringue.

NUTRITIONAL INFORMATION

Calories . . . . . . .442 Sugars 77g
Protein . . . . .7g Fat 9g
Carbohydrate . . .83g Saturates 3g

15 MINS   10 MINS

SERVES 2

I N G R E D I E N T S

2 slices rich, dark ginger cake,
   about ¾ inch/2 cm thick

1–2 tbsp ginger wine or rum

1 eating apple

6 ready-to-eat dried apricots, chopped

4 tbsp orange juice or water

1 tbsp slivered almonds

2 small egg whites

½ cup superfine sugar

1 Place each slice of ginger cake on an ovenproof plate and sprinkle with the ginger wine.

2 Cut the apple into four, then core and slice. Put into a small pan, then add the chopped apricots and orange juice, and simmer over low heat for 5 minutes, until tender.

3 Stir the almonds into the fruit and spoon the mixture equally over the slices of soaked cake, piling it up in the center.

4 Whisk the egg whites until very stiff and dry, then whisk in the sugar, a little at a time, making sure the meringue has become stiff again before adding any more sugar.

5 Either pipe or spread the meringue over the fruit and cake, making sure that both are completely covered.

6 Place in a preheated oven, 400°F/ 200°C, for 4–5 minutes, until golden brown. Serve hot.

VARIATION

A slice of vanilla, coffee, or chocolate ice cream can be placed on the fruit before adding the meringue, but this must be done at the last minute and the dessert must be eaten immediately after it is removed from the oven.

Apricot Slices

These vegan slices are ideal for children's lunches. They are full of flavor and made with healthy ingredients.

NUTRITIONAL INFORMATION

Calories	198	Sugars	........13g
Protein	.........4g	Fat	...........9g
Carbohydrate	...25g	Saturates	.......2g

🐑 🐑 🐑

🍠 50 MINS   🕐 1 HOUR

MAKES 12

I N G R E D I E N T S

PIE DOUGH

1⅓ cups whole-wheat flour

⅓ cup finely ground mixed nuts

scant ½ cup margarine,
    cut into small pieces

4 tbsp water

soy milk, to glaze

FILLING

1⅓ cup dried apricots

grated rind of 1 orange

1½ cups apple juice

1 tsp ground cinnamon

scant ⅓ cup raisins

1 Lightly grease a 9-inch/23-cm square cake pan. To make the pie dough, place the flour and nuts in a mixing bowl and rub in the margarine with your fingers until the mixture resembles bread crumbs. Stir in the water and bring together to form a dough. Wrap and set aside to chill in the refrigerator for 30 minutes.

2 To make the filling, place the apricots, orange rind, and apple juice in a pan and bring to a boil. Simmer for 30 minutes, until the apricots are mushy. Cool slightly, then process in a food processor or blender to a purée. Alternatively, press the mixture through a fine strainer. Stir in the cinnamon and raisins.

3 Divide the pie dough in half, then roll out one half and use to line the base of the pan. Spread the apricot purée over the top and brush the edges of the pastry with water. Roll out the rest of the dough to fit over the top of the apricot purée. Press down and seal the edges.

4 Prick the top of the pie dough with a fork and brush with soy milk. Bake in a preheated oven, 400°F/200°C, for 20–25 minutes, until the pastry is golden. Leave to cool slightly before cutting into 12 bars. Serve either warm or cold.

COOK'S TIP

These slices will keep in an airtight container for 3-4 days.

Boston Chocolate Pie

This lighter version of the popular chocolate cream pie is made with yogurt and sour cream.

NUTRITIONAL INFORMATION

Calories ....795 Sugars 73g
Protein ....13g Fat 40g
Carbohydrate ...99g Saturates 21g

25 MINS   35 MINS

SERVES 6

INGREDIENTS

8 oz/225 g Shortcrust Pie Dough (see
   page 354)

CHOCOLATE CARAQUE

8 oz/225 g dark chocolate

FILLING

3 eggs

generous ½ cup superfine sugar

scant ⅓ cup flour, plus extra for dusting

1 tbsp confectioners' sugar

pinch of salt

1 tsp vanilla extract

1¾ cups milk

⅔ cup plain yogurt

5½ oz/150 g dark chocolate, broken
   into pieces

2 tbsp kirsch

TOPPING

⅔ cup sour cream

1 Roll out the pastry and use to line a 9-inch/23-cm loose-based flan pan. Prick the base with a fork, then line with baking parchment and fill with dried beans. Bake blind for 20 minutes. Remove the beans and paper and return to the oven for 5 minutes. Remove from the oven and place on a wire rack to cool.

2 To make the chocolate caraque, put pieces of chocolate on a plate over a pan of simmering water until melted. Spread on a cool surface with a spatula. When cool, scrape it into curls with a sharp knife.

3 To make the filling, beat the eggs and sugar until fluffy. Sift in the flour, confectioners' sugar, and salt. Stir in the vanilla extract.

4 Bring the milk and yogurt to a boil in a small pan and strain onto the egg mixture. Pour into a double boiler or set over a pan of simmering water. Stir until it coats the back of a spoon.

5 Gently heat the chocolate and kirsch in a small pan until melted. Stir into the custard. Remove from the heat and stand the double boiler or bowl in cold water. Leave it to cool .

6 Pour the chocolate mixture into the pastry case. Spread the sour cream over the chocolate, and arrange the caraque rolls on top.

Coconut Candy

Quick and easy to make, this candy is very similar to coconut ice. Pink food coloring may be added toward the end if desired.

NUTRITIONAL INFORMATION

Calories	338	Sugars	.........5g
Protein	.........4g	Fat	..........34g
Carbohydrate	....5g	Saturates	......26g

1¼ HOURS   15 MINS

SERVES 6

I N G R E D I E N T S

6 tbsp butter

2 cups dry unsweetened coconut

¾ cup condensed milk

a few drops of pink food coloring (optional)

1 Place the butter in a heavy-bottom pan and melt over low heat, stirring constantly so that the butter doesn't burn on the base of the pan.

2 Add the dry unsweetened coconut to the melted butter, stirring to mix.

3 Stir in the condensed milk and the pink food coloring (if using) and mix continuously for 7–10 minutes.

VARIATION

If you prefer, you could divide the coconut mixture in step 2, and add the pink food coloring to only one half of the mixture. This way, you will have an attractive combination of pink and white coconut sweets.

4 Remove the pan from the heat, then set aside and leave the coconut mixture to cool slightly.

5 Once cool enough to handle, shape the coconut mixture into long blocks and cut into equal-size rectangles. Leave to set for about 1 hour, then serve.

Fresh Fruit Compôte

Elderflower cordial is used in the syrup for this refreshing fruit compôte, giving it a delightfully summery flavor.

NUTRITIONAL INFORMATION

Calories	255	Sugars 61g
Protein	. . . . .4g	Fat 1g
Carbohydrate	. . .61g	Saturates 0.2g

20 MINS   15 MINS

SERVES 4

I N G R E D I E N T S

1 lemon

generous ¼ cup superfine sugar

4 tbsp elderflower cordial

1¼ cups water

4 eating apples

8 oz/225 g blackberries

2 fresh figs

T O P P I N G

⅔ cup thick plain yogurt

2 tbsp clear honey

1 Thinly pare the rind from the lemon using a swivel vegetable peeler. Squeeze the juice. Put the lemon rind and juice into a pan, together with the sugar, elderflower cordial, and water. Set over low heat and simmer, uncovered, for 10 minutes.

2 Peel and core, then slice the apples. Add the apples to the pan. Simmer gently for 4–5 minutes, until just tender. Remove the pan from the heat and set aside to cool.

3 When cold, transfer the apples and syrup to a serving bowl and add the blackberries. Slice and add the figs. Stir gently to mix. Cover and chill in the refrigerator until ready to serve.

4 Spoon the yogurt into a small serving bowl and drizzle the honey over the top. Cover and chill before serving.

COOK'S TIP

Strained plain yogurt may be made from cow's or ewe's milk. The former is strained to make it more concentrated and has a high fat content, which perfectly counterbalances the sharpness and acidity of fruit.

Autumn Fruit Bread Pudding

This is like a summer pudding, but it uses fruits which appear later in the year. This dessert requires chilling overnight so prepare in advance.

NUTRITIONAL INFORMATION

Calories 177   Sugars 29g
Protein ....3g   Fat 1g
Carbohydrate ...42g   Saturates 0.1g

10 MINS   15 MINS

SERVES 8

INGREDIENTS

2 lb/900 g mixed blackberries,
   chopped apples, chopped pears

¾ cup soft light brown sugar

1 tsp cinnamon

8 oz/225 g white bread, thinly sliced,
   crusts removed (about 12 slices)

1 Place the fruit in a large pan with the soft light brown sugar, cinnamon, and scant ½ cup of water, then stir and bring to a boil. Reduce the heat and simmer for 5–10 minutes so that the fruits soften but still hold their shape.

2 Meanwhile, line the base and sides of a 3¾-cup pudding bowl with the bread slices, ensuring that there are no gaps between the pieces of bread.

3 Spoon the fruit into the center of the bread-lined bowl and cover the fruit with the remaining bread.

4 Place a saucer on top of the bread and weigh it down. Chill the pudding in the refrigerator overnight.

5 Turn the pudding out onto a serving plate and serve immediately.

COOK'S TIP

This pudding would be delicious served with vanilla ice cream to counteract the tartness of the blackberries. Stand the pudding on a plate when chilling to catch any juices that run down the sides of the bowl.

Satsuma & Pecan Pavlova

Make this spectacular dessert for the perfect way to round off a special occasion. You can make the meringue base well in advance.

NUTRITIONAL INFORMATION

Calories	339	Sugars	.......36g
Protein	.........3g	Fat	..........21g
Carbohydrate	...37g	Saturates	......10g

2½ HOURS   3 HOURS

SERVES 8

I N G R E D I E N T S

4 egg whites

generous 1 cup light muscovado sugar

1¼ cups heavy or whipping cream

generous ⅓ cup pecan nuts

4 satsumas, peeled

1 passion fruit or pomegranate

1 Line 2 cookie sheets with non-stick baking parchment or waxed paper. Draw a 9-inch/23-cm round on one of them.

2 Whip the egg whites in a large grease-free bowl until stiff. Add the sugar gradually, continuing to beat until the mixture is very glossy.

3 Pipe or spoon a layer of meringue mixture onto the round marked on the baking parchment; then pipe large rosettes or place spoonfuls on top of the meringue's outer edge. Pipe any remaining meringue mixture in tiny rosettes on the second cookie sheet.

4 Bake in a preheated oven, 275°F/140°C, for 2–3 hours, making sure that the oven is well-ventilated by using a folded dish cloth to keep the door slightly open. Remove from the oven and leave to

cool completely. When cold, peel off the baking parchment carefully.

5 Whip the heavy or whipping cream in a large chilled bowl until thick. Spoon about one-third of the cream into a pastry bag, fitted with a star tip. Reserve a few pecan nuts and 1 satsuma for decoration. Chop the remaining nuts

and fruit, and fold into the remaining cream.

6 Pile on top of the meringue base and decorate with the tiny meringue rosettes, piped cream, segments of satsuma, and pecan nuts. Scoop the seeds from the passion fruit with a teaspoon and sprinkle them on top.

Baked Cheesecake

This cheesecake has a rich creamy texture, but contains no dairy produce, as it is made with tofu.

NUTRITIONAL INFORMATION

Calories	282	Sugars	........17g
Protein	.........9g	Fat	..........15g
Carbohydrate	...29g	Saturates	.......4g

2¼ HOURS   45 MINS

SERVES 6

INGREDIENTS

4½ oz/125 g graham crackers, crushed

4 tbsp margarine, melted

⅓ cup chopped pitted dates

4 tbsp lemon juice

rind of 1 lemon

3 tbsp water

12 oz/350 g firm tofu

⅔ cup apple juice

1 banana, mashed

1 tsp vanilla extract

1 mango, peeled and chopped

1 Lightly grease a 7-inch/18-cm round loose-bottomed cake pan.

2 Mix together the graham cracker crumbs and melted margarine in a bowl. Press the mixture into the base of the prepared pan.

3 Put the chopped dates, lemon juice, lemon rind, and water into a pan and bring to a boil. Simmer for 5 minutes until the dates are soft, then mash them roughly with a fork.

4 Place the mixture in a blender or food processor with the tofu, apple juice, mashed banana, and vanilla extract and process until the mixture is a thick, smooth purée.

5 Pour the tofu purée into the prepared cracker crumb base.

6 Bake in a preheated oven, 350°F/180°C, for 30–40 minutes, until lightly golden. Leave to cool in the pan, then chill thoroughly before serving.

7 Place the chopped mango in a blender and process until smooth. Serve it as a sauce with the cheesecake.

VARIATION

Silken tofu may be substituted for the firm tofu to give a softer texture; it will take 40–50 minutes to set.

Cherry Crêpes

This dish can be made with either fresh pitted cherries or, if time is short, with canned cherries for extra speed.

NUTRITIONAL INFORMATION

Calories	345	Sugars 25g
Protein	. . . . .8g	Fat 11g
Carbohydrate	. . .56g	Saturates 2g

10 MINS   15 MINS

SERVES 4

INGREDIENTS

FILLING

14 oz/400 g canned pitted cherries

½ tsp almond extract

½ tsp allspice

2 tbsp cornstarch

CRÊPES

⅔ cup all-purpose flour

pinch of salt

2 tbsp chopped mint

1 egg

1¼ cups milk

vegetable oil, for frying

confectioners' sugar and
   toasted slivered almonds, to decorate

1 Put the cherries and 1¼ cups of the can juice in a pan with the almond extract and allspice. Stir in the cornstarch and bring to a boil, stirring until thickened and clear. Set aside.

2 To make the crêpes, sift the flour into a bowl with the salt. Add the chopped mint and make a well in the center. Gradually beat in the egg and milk to make a smooth batter.

3 Heat 1 tablespoon of oil in a 7-inch/18-cm skillet; pour off the oil when hot. Add just enough batter to coat the base of the skillet and cook for 1–2 minutes, until the underside is cooked. Flip the crêpe over and cook for 1 minute. Remove from the pan and keep warm. Heat 1 tablespoon of the oil in the pan again and repeat to use up all the batter.

4 Spoon one-fourth of the cherry filling onto one-fourth of each crêpe and fold the crêpe into a cone shape. Dust with confectioners' sugar and sprinkle the slivered almonds over the top. Serve immediately.

Index

A

alfalfa & spinach salad, 277
almond
    ground almonds in milk, 360
    sherbet, 337
    slices, 331
appetizers, 62–87
apple
    & cider vinegar dressing, 32
    potato, bean & apple salad, 278
    relish, 164
    traditional apple pie, 354
apricot
    brûlée, 349
    ginger & apricot alaskas, 371
    slices, 372
artichokes, 16
    & cheese tart, 216
asparagus, 15
autumn fruit bread pudding, 376
avocado, 19
    & mint soup, 37
    & vegetable soup, 57

B

baghar, 73, 168, 282
baguettes, cheese & onion, 250
baked potatoes with beans, 222
bakes, 119, 214, 224, 298, 300, 313
banana
    & mango tart, 334
    potato & banana salad, 271
    rice & banana brûlée, 335
basil & lemon marinade, 239
beans, 24
    baked potatoes with beans, 222
    barbecue bean burgers, 247
    Deep South rice &, 146
    Indian bean soup, 38
    kidney bean kiev, 183
    mixed bean pan-fry, 93
    mixed bean pâté, 71
    mixed bean soup, 42
    potato, bean & apple salad, 278
    red bean stew & dumplings, 163
    refried beans with tortillas, 111
    soup, 50
    three-bean salad, 268
bean sprout salad, 112
bean sprouts, 25
béchamel sauce, 30
beet
    soup, 51
bell peppers, 19
    bell pepper & chile soup, 36
    mixed bell pepper pooris, 323

roast bell pepper tart, 230
berry cheesecake, 369
bhajis, 64, 291, 301
biryani, 167
biscuits, 45, 356
boiling, 20
Bombay potatoes, 312
Boston chocolate pie, 372
braising, 22
bread
    filled pita, 257
    garlic, 53
    garlic & sage, 234
    lightly fried, 324
    minted garlic, 37
    naan, 319, 322
    parathas, 321
    spicy oven, 325
    sweet potato, 235
bread & butter pudding, 347
bread pudding, 336, 359, 376
brochettes, marinated, 254
broccoli, 15
    broccoli & potato soup, 54
    cauliflower & broccoli flan, 232
    cauliflower & broccoli soup, 52
    easy cauliflower & broccoli, 296
broiled salad, 275
broiled potatoes, 95
brown rice gratin, 114
brûlée, 335, 349, 362
Brussels sprouts, 15
bubble & squeak, 184
buck rarebit, 104
burgers, 122, 244, 247
butterscotch melts, 366

C

cabbage, 15
    colcannon, 310
    spiced winter cabbage, 283
cakes
    cheese potato, 186
    passion, 345
    potato mushroom, 108
    upside-down, 352
cannelloni, 130
caraque, 373
carrots, 16
    & orange bake, 299
    & potato soufflé, 105
    honey-glazed, 283
    spicy dhal & carrot soup, 55
cashew nuts
    cashew nut paella, 189
    red curry with cashews, 181

casseroled potatoes, 115
casseroles, 200, 203, 218
cauliflower, 15
    & broccoli flan, 232
    & broccoli soup, 52
    cauliflower & spinach curry, 315
    bake, 224
    easy cauliflower & broccoli, 296
    fried, 303
    roulade, 78
    spinach & cauliflower bhaji, 301
celery, 16
celery root, 16
cereals, 28
chana, 161, 170, 171, 174
cheese
    & onion baguettes, 250
    & onion rosti, 116
    & potato layer bake, 300
    & potato plait, 233
    & potato slices, 125
    artichoke & cheese tart, 216
    biscuits, 45
    cream cheese & herb soup, 59
    cress & cheese tartlets, 97
    feta cheese patties, 195
    feta cheese tartlets, 63
    garlic & herb pâté, 83
    goat cheese salad, 261
    macaroni cheese & tomato, 133
    potato & cheese soufflé, 204
    potato cakes, 186
    sauce, 131
    spinach & cheese curry, 193
    three-cheese fondue, 124
    walnut, egg & cheese pâté, 68
    warm goat cheese salad, 266
cheesecake, 339, 358, 369, 378
cherry
    clafoutis, 346
    pancakes, 379
chicory, 18
chile
    bell pepper & chile soup, 36
        spicy chile dressing, 252
    tofu, 217
chili
    dressing, 260
    Mexican chili corn pie, 228
    roast potatoes, 288
chocolate
    Boston chocolate pie, 373
    bread pudding, 359
    caraque, 373
    cheesecake, 358
    chip ice cream, 333

fudge pudding, 328
mousse, 340
chow mein, 138
Christmas shortbread, 344
chutney, 308, 317
ciabatta rolls, 113
clafoutis, 346
cobbler, winter vegetable, 205
coconut
    cream molds, 330
    sweet, 374
    vegetable curry, 215
colcannon, 310
compôte, 375
cooking techniques, 20–22
corn
    corn cobs & parsley butter, 243
    Mexican chili corn pie, 228
    patties, 103
    spicy corn, 306
    vegetable & corn chowder, 46
couscous, 143, 148
crêpes, 94, 202, 379
cress & cheese tartlets, 97
croquettes, lentil, 107
croûtons, 50
crumble, 294, 342, 364
cucumber, 18
    dip, 166
    dressing, 32
    sauce, 255
currants in cassis, warm, 338
curly kale, 15
curried kabobs, 245
curried okra, 295
curried parsnip soup, 49
curried roast potatoes, 309
curry
    cauliflower & spinach curry, 315
    coconut vegetable, 215
    creamy vegetable, 156
    egg, 190
    fragrant, 165
    green bean & potato, 194
    green curry with tempeh, 187
    light curry dressing, 270
    midweek curry special, 166
    okra, 188
    pasties, 206
    potato, 182
    red curry with cashews, 181
    spicy mixed vegetable, 191
    spinach & cheese curry, 193
    zucchini, 287

D
dhal
    chana, 175
    chana dhal & rice, 161
    dry moong, 168

oil-dressed, 176
onion, 174
soup, 39
spicy dhal & carrot soup, 55
spinach & chana dhal, 170
tarka, 177
dauphinois, 289
Deep South rice & beans, 146
desserts, 328–79
dips
    buttered nut & lentil, 86
    chocolate, 363
    cucumber, 166
    heavenly garlic, 70
    mustard, 279
    tzatziki & black olive, 84
dressing
    apple & cider vinegar, 32
    chili, 260
    cucumber, 32
    garlic & parsley, 240
    green herb, 32
    herb & mustard, 269
    light curry, 270
    minty dressing, 279
    peanut, 267
    raspberry & hazelnut, 240
    sesame, 30
    spicy chile, 252
    tomato, 32
    vinaigrette, 270
    warm walnut, 32
    whole-grain mustard & cider vinegar, 240
    yogurt, 264, 272, 276
    see also 262, 263, 266, 275, 277–8
dry moong dhal, 168
dumplings, 65, 85, 163

E
egg
    curry, 190
    walnut, egg & cheese pâté, 68
eggplant, 19
    eggplant bake, 313
enchiladas, 121
escarole, 18

F
falafel, 91
fava beans,15
fats & oils, 29
fennel, 16
    creamy baked, 207
feta cheese
    patties, 195
    tartlets, 63
flan, 162, 232
fondue, three-cheese, 124
fries, 122
fritters, 92, 119, 164

fruit
    & nut loaf, 348
    autumn fruit bread pudding, 376
    brûlée, 362
    fresh fruit compôte, 375
    mixed fruit crumble, 342
    toasted tropical 363

G
gado gado, 267
galette, 304
garden salad, 279
garlic
    & parsley dressing, 240
    & sage bread, 234
    bread, 53
    cheese, garlic & herb pâté, 83
    garlicky mushroom pakoras, 82
    heavenly garlic dip, 70
    hummus & garlic toasts, 74
    minted garlic bread, 37
    mushrooms on on toast, 102
    potato wedges, 253
gazpacho, 47
ginger & apricot alaskas, 371
gingered potatoes, 293
globe artichokes 16
goat cheese salad, 261
gougère, green vegetable, 221
grains & cereals, 28
grape leaf pockets, 256
gratins, 114, 212
Greek green beans, 292
green & white salad, 262
green bean & potato curry, 194
green beans, 15
    Greek green beans, 292
    green bean & potato curry, 194
    long beans with tomatoes, 302
green curry with tempeh, 187
green vegetable gougère, 221
green vegetable salad, 264
green herb
    dressing, 32
    rice, 158
grilling, 22

H
harvest loaf, nutty, 229
hash 127, 192
heavenly garlic dip, 70
herbs
    & mustard dressing, 269
    cheese, garlic & herb pâté, 83
    cream cheese & herb soup, 59
    green herb dressing, 32
    green herb rice, 158
    herby potatoes & onion, 318
    leek & herb soufflé, 211
    sauce, 90

honey-glazed carrots, 283
hummus & garlic toasts, 74
Hyderabad pickles, 73

I
ice cream, 333, 370
Indian bean soup, 38
Indian bread pudding, 336
Indian potato & pea soup, 58
Indian-style omelet, 100
Italian
    chunky Italian slices, 255
    vegetable tart, 213

J
jalousie, 209
jambalaya, 126
Japanese noodles
    spicy, 139
    stir-fried, 136
Jerusalem artichokes, 16

K
kabobs
    curried, 245
    kofta, 147
    mini, 117
    toasted tropical fruit, 363
    Turkish, 248
    vegetable, 106
kabli chana sag, 171
kale, 15
Kashmiri spinach, 285
kidney bean kiev, 183
kitchouri, 155
kofta, 147, 169

L
lasagna, 131
layered pies, 220
leeks, 16
    leek & herb soufflé, 211
    roast, 249
lemon & lime syllabub, 355
lentils, 24; see also dhal
    & vegetable biryani, 167
    & vegetable shells, 210
    & mixed vegetables, 98
    & rice casserole, 200
    buttered nut & lentil dip, 86
    croquettes, 107
    potato-topped lentil bake, 214
    spiced rice & lentils, 160
    spiced spinach & lentils, 172
    spicy lentils & spinach, 290
    white, 173
lettuce, 18
lime
    cheesecakes, 339
    lemon & lime syllabub, 355

mayonnaise, 95
long beans with tomatoes, 302

M
macaroni cheese & tomato, 133
mango
    banana & mango tart, 334
    chutney, 317
    ice cream, 370
marinades, 239
mayonnaise
    lime, 95
melon & strawberry salad, 272
Mexican chili corn pie, 228
Mexican salad, 260
Middle Eastern salad, 265
midweek curry special, 166
mint
    avocado & mint soup, 37
minted garlic bread, 37
minted pea & yogurt soup, 44
minty dressing, 279
mooli, 18
Moroccan salad, 263
mousse, chocolate, 340
muffins, potato, 365
multicolored salad, 273
mushrooms, 26
    & pine nut tarts 219
    & spinach puffs, 208
    creamy mushroom & potato, 99
    garlic mushrooms on on toast, 102
    mushroom & garlic soufflés, 62
    potato & mushroom bake, 120
    potato mushroom cakes, 108
    stuffed, 118
mustard dip, 279
muttar panir, 185

N
naan, 319–320
Napa cabbage, 15
nibbles, toasted, 77
noodles, 135-9
nuts & seeds, 25
    buttered nut & lentil dip, 86
    cashew nut paella, 189
    nutty harvest loaf, 229
    nutty rice burgers, 244
    raspberry & hazelnut dressing, 240
    spicy potato & nut terrine, 227
    spinach & nut pasta, 132
    spinach & nut pilaf, 151
    vegetable & nut samosas, 80
    white nut phyllo pockets, 225

O
okra
    curried, 295
    curry, 188
omelet
    Indian-style, 100
    potato, 123
onion
    & tomato relish, 92
    cheese & onion baguettes, 250
    cheese & onion rosti, 116
    dhal, 174
    herby potatoes & onion, 318
    thick onion soup, 45
onions, 16
    à la Grecque, 81
    spicy potatoes &, 282
orange
    & marjoram marinade, 239
    carrot & orange bake, 299
    rhubarb & orange crumble, 364

P
paella, cashew nut, 189
pakoras, 82, 87
palak panir, 298
paprika chips, 96
parathas, 321
parsley
    cream, 270
    garlic & parsley dressing, 240
parsnips, 16
    curried parsnip soup, 49
passion cake, 345
pasta, 29, 130–134, 197
pasties, 206
pâté
    cheese, garlic & herb, 83
    mixed bean, 71
    walnut, egg & cheese, 68
patties, 103, 183, 195
pavlova, satsuma & pecan, 377
peas, 15
    minted pea & yogurt, 44
Peshwari naan, 322
pesto, 226, 255
phyllo baskets, spinach, 66
phyllo pockets, white nut, 225
pilaf, 144, 151
pine nuts
    mushroom & pine nut tart, 219
pink syllabubs, 368
pistachio dessert, 351
pommes anna, 284
poori, 320, 323
potato
    & cheese soufflé, 204
    & nutmeg biscuits, 356
    & mushroom bake, 120
    & radish salad, 269

& split pea, 56
& vegetable gratin, 212
bean & apple salad, 278
broccoli & potato soup, 54
carrot & potato soufflé, 105
cheese & potato layer bake, 300
cheese & potato plait, 233
cheese & potato slices, 125
cheese potato cakes, 186
creamy mushroom &, 99
crumble, 294
curry, 182
fritters, 119
fritters with relish, 92
garlic potato wedges, 253
green bean & potato curry, 194
hash, 192
Indian potato & pea soup, 58
muffins, 365
mushroom cakes, 108
omelet, 123
pommes anna, 284
spicy potato & nut terrine, 227
spicy potato casserole, 218
spicy potato fries, 110
three-way potato salad, 270
-topped lentil bake, 214
potatoes, 16
baked potatoes with beans, 222
baked potatoes with pesto, 226
Bombay, 312
broiled, 95
casseroled, 115
chili roast, 288
crispy roast, 283
curried roast, 309
dauphinois, 289
fried spiced potatoes, 316
gingered, 293
herby potatoes & onion, 318
Lyonnaise, 314
saffron-flavored, 311
Spanish, 297
spiced potatoes & spinach, 307
spicy potatoes & onions, 282
puddings
autumn fruit bread, 376
baked semolina, 353
bread & butter, 347
chocolate bread, 359
chocolate fudge, 328
Indian bread, 336
rice, 357
saffron-spiced rice, 343
spiced steamed, 350
summer, 361
see also desserts
puffs, 79, 208
pilaf, 152, 159
pulses, dried, 24

pumpkin, 19
pumpkin soup, 43

R
radishes, 18
potato & radish salad, 269
radicchio, 18
rarebit, 104
raspberry
& hazelnut dressing, 240
fool 319
refried beans with tortillas, 111
relish, 92, 164
rhubarb & orange crumble, 364
rice, 28
& banana brûlée, 335
brown rice gratin, 114
chana dhal &, 161
Deep South rice & beans, 146
fried spicy, 157
green herb, 158
lentil & rice casserole, 200
nutty rice burgers, 244
pudding, 357
pilaf, 152
saffron-spiced rice pudding, 343
special fried, 150
spiced rice & lentils, 160
Thai Jasmine, 154
tomato, 153
risotto
in shells, 149
verde, 142
roast bell pepper tart, 230
roast leeks, 249
roasted vegetables, 90, 242
rocket, 18
rosti, cheese & onion, 116
roulade, 78, 231

S
saffron
-flavored potatoes, 311
-spiced rice pudding, 343
salad, 260–79
bean-sprout salad, 112
tabbouleh, 145
vegetables, 18
salsa, fiery, 75
samosas, 69, 80, 101
satsuma & pecan pavlova, 377
sauces
butterscotch, 366
cheese, 131
chocolate, 332
cucumber, 255
herb, 90
hot fudge, 359
sweet & sour, 67

tasty barbecue, 238
tomato, 130, 133
yogurt, 64, 65
see also 296
sausages, 251
sauté of summer vegetables, 180
sautéing, 22
savory flan, 162
scallions, 18
seasonal vegetables, 283
semolina
baked semolina pudding, 353
fritters, 164
sesame dressing, 30
shallots, 16
shallow frying, 22
sherbet, 337
shortbread, 344
sidekick vegetables, 252
slices, 125, 246, 255, 331, 372
snow peas, 15
soufflés
carrot & potato, 105
leek & herb, 211
mushroom & garlic, 62
potato & cheese, 204
soups, 36–59
avocado & mint, 37
avocado & vegetable, 57
bean, 50
beet, 51
bell pepper & chile, 36
broccoli & potato, 54
cauliflower & broccoli, 52
cream cheese & herb, 59
curried parsnip, 49
dhal, 39
gazpacho, 47
Indian bean, 38
Indian potato & pea soup, 58
minted pea & yogurt, 44
mixed bean, 42
plum tomato, 41
potato & split pea, 56
pumpkin, 43
Spanish tomato, 53
spicy dhal & carrot, 55
thick onion soup, 45
vegetable & corn chowder, 46
Vichyssoise, 48
winter, 40
soy, 24
Spanish potatoes, 297
Spanish tomato soup, 53
Spanish tortilla, 72
spicy fried noodles, 137
spinach, 15
alfalfa & spinach salad, 277
& cauliflower bhaji, 301
& chana dhal, 170

& cheese curry, 193
& nut pasta, 132
& nut pilaf 151
cauliflower & spinach curry, 315
crêpe layer, 202
crêpes, 94
Kashmiri, 285
mushroom & spinach puffs, 208
phyllo baskets, 66
roulade, 231
spiced potatoes & spinach, 307
spiced spinach & lentils, 172
spicy lentils & spinach, 290
split peas, 24
sponges, 332, 341
spring rolls, 76
sprouting beans, peas & seeds, 25
steamed coffee sponge, 332
steaming, 20
stewing, 22
stir-fries, 20
  Japanese noodles, 136
  Thai-style noodles, 135
  vegetable pasta, 197
stock, fresh vegetable, 30
strawberry
  melon & strawberry salad, 272
string beans, 15
sugar snap peas, 15
summer puddings, 361
summer squashes, 19
summertime tagliatelle, 134
sweating, 22
swedes, 18
sweet & sour
  sauce, 67
  vegetables, 196, 286
sweet potatoes, 18
  candied sweet potatoes, 305
  spicy sweet potato slices, 246
  bread, 234
syallabub, 355, 368
syrup sponge, quick, 341

T
taboulleh, 145, 147
tagliatelle, summertime, 134
tahini cream, 30
tamarind chutney, 308
tarka dhal, 177
tartlets
  cress & cheese, 97
  feta cheese, 63
tarts
  artichoke & cheese, 216
  banana & mango, 334
  Italian vegetable, 213
  mushroom & pine nut, 219
  roast bell pepper tart, 230
tempeh, green curry with, 187

terrine, spicy nut & potato, 227
Thai Jasmine rice, 154
Thai-spiced lime marinade, 239
Thai-style stir-fried noodles, 135
three-bean salad, 268
three-cheese salad, 124
three-way potato salad, 270
tiramisu, traditional, 367
tofu, 25
  chile tofu, 217
  vegetable & tofu strudels, 223
tomato
  dressing, 32
  macaroni cheese &, 133
  onion & tomato relish, 92
  plum tomato soup, 41
  rice, 153
  sauce, 130, 133
  Spanish tomato soup, 53
tomatoes, 19
  long beans with, 302
tortillas
  Spanish tortilla, 72
Turkish kabobs, 248
turnips, 18
tzatziki & black olive dip, 84

U
upside-down cake, 352

V
vegetable, 14
  & corn chowder, 46
  & lentil koftas, 169
  & nut samosas, 80
  avocado & vegetable soup, 57
  burgers, 122
  cannelloni, 130
  coconut vegetable curry, 215
  couscous, 148
  creamy vegetable curry, 156
  crispy batter 201
  enchiladas, 121
  fritters, 67
  galette, 304
  green vegetable gougère, 221
  green vegetable salad, 264
  hash, 127
  Italian vegetable tart, 213
  jalousie, 209
  jambalaya, 126
  kabobs, 106
  lasagna, 131
  lentil & vegetable biryani, 167
  lentil & vegetable shells, 210
  marinated vegetable salad, 271
  pasta stir-fry, 197
  pilaf, 159
  potato & vegetable gratin, 212
  samosas 101

spicy mixed vegetable curry, 191
stock, fresh, 30
stuffed vegetable snacks, 109
winter vegetable casserole, 203
winter vegetable cobbler, 205
vegetables
  buying, 14
  lentils & mixed, 98
  mixed, 241
  preparing, 14
  roasted, 90, 242
  salad, 18
  seasonal, 283
  sidekick, 252
  sauté of summer vegetables, 180
  sweet & sour, 196, 286
vegetarian sausages, 251
Vichyssoise, 48
vinaigrette, 270

W
walnut
  egg & cheese pâté, 68
  warm walnut dressing, 32
watercress, 18
white lentils, 173
white nut phyllo pockets, 225

Y
yogurt
  dressing, 264, 272, 276
  dumplings in yogurt sauce, 65
  minted pea & yogurt soup, 44
  sauce, 64, 65, 169
  soft dumplings in yogurt, 85

Z
zucchini, 19
  curry, 287